RIGGED

The Incredible True Story of the Whistleblowers Jailed after Exposing the Rotten Heart of the Financial System

ANDY VERITY

FL🔷NT

For Izzy, Lucy, Cecily – and a better future.
And for my beloved stepfather, Will, who taught me the powerful
role of the irrational in politics.

First published 2023

FLINT is an imprint of The History Press
97 St George's Place, Cheltenham,
Gloucestershire, GL50 3QB
www.flintbooks.co.uk

British Library Cataloguing in Publication Data.
A catalogue record for this book is available from the British Library.

ISBN 978 0 7509 9885 7

Typesetting and origination by The History Press
Printed and bound in Great Britain by TJ Books Limited, Padstow, Cornwall.

Trees for LYfe

CONTENTS

ACKNOWLEDGEMENTS

Thanks to the whistleblowers who took a stand for honesty, only to find themselves punished, their lives ruined. To the traders and brokers, vilified in the media and wrongly prosecuted for doing their jobs, who overcame their understandable distrust and spoke to me. To those lawyers who fought for logic and sanity. To all the people, some of whom I have never met, who took risks to leak documents and audio recordings in the hope that the truth would come out so that justice might prevail.

Thanks to Sarah Tighe for not letting the bullies get away with it, whoever they might be. To Jonathan Russell for putting me on to the most ghastly, astonishing story I have ever come across. To the source who made 'Project Righteous' happen (you know who you are). To the journalists of BBC *Panorama* and *The Times* for seeing that something lay beneath and upholding our country's great tradition of investigative journalism as a democratic force. To Sarah Bowen for her brilliant work on *The Lowball Tapes*.

Thanks to my dearest mum Mary Rosalind, sister Tara and Canadian siblings Pete and Sarah. And to my wonderful and gifted wife Natasha for her steadfast love, humour and support.

AUTHOR'S NOTE

The conversations and exchanges of messages recounted in this book tell a story that the authorities on both sides of the Atlantic have known about for more than a decade but have chosen to keep quiet. Quotes are not recreated but taken directly from audio recordings and transcripts of the actual words spoken at the time in phone calls, recorded as a matter of routine on banks' trading floors, and from contemporaneous emails and messages. They have been shared with more than a dozen regulators and investigative agencies around the world as well as with banks' legal departments – but not with the public. Much of this is exclusive material and most of the information contained in it had never been reported.

These audio recordings and documents not only cast serious doubt on the prosecutions of traders and brokers for 'rigging' interest rates, they also contain evidence of illegal activity at the top of the financial system that has never been called to account – a secret history to which the public would otherwise have had no access. The true story they reveal would have been left untold had I not obtained crucial material on a flash drive, sent to me anonymously after I began writing and broadcasting about the scandal. Some of the audio recordings were broadcast in the 2022 BBC Radio 4 investigative podcast series *The Lowball Tapes*. The material has been thoroughly authenticated by cross-referencing it with public sources, including regulators' notices and court materials.

Editorial note:
The dialogue has been edited for relevance, clarity and for the purposes of storytelling. Where the dialogue is unclear, the spelling or grammar has in some cases been edited or tidied up. Where material has been omitted, this has been indicated through the use of bracketed ellipses.

PREFACE

As a BBC reporter, I've spent the last twenty years reporting financial scandals and investigating financial crimes. I've confronted Ukrainian gangsters over their secret investments (google my name and you'll soon come across video footage of a corrupt politician's goon kicking me in the balls for my trouble) and investigated money laundering on an industrial scale in the Middle East. But in terms of sheer jaw-dropping, mind-boggling corruption, greed and injustice, nothing comes close to what's revealed in these pages.

This investigation has been a rollercoaster ride like no other I've ever been on. Just when I thought I knew all its twists and turns, I was presented with a cache of thousands of hours of recordings of bankers' phone calls, made during the financial crisis, and I was whipped upside down at 100mph through a hall of distorted mirrors until I didn't know what was true, or who the good and bad guys were anymore.

Rigged starts by unveiling one extraordinary story: the big banks illegally rigging interest rates during the financial crisis that began in 2007, in the full knowledge – and sometimes with the encouragement – of Bank of England and Federal Reserve Bank of New York officials, along with several other financial institutions. Enough material for any book, you would think, but then comes the twist (which everyone, me included, missed at the time), morphing the story into something far more disturbing.

When the UK's Serious Fraud Office (SFO) and the USA's Department of Justice (DOJ) opened their criminal investigations into interest rate-rigging, the press reported that, at last, some of those bankers at the rotten heart of the financial crisis were going to jail. I imagine that people would have paid to sit on the juries that got the chance to find these junior bankers guilty on all counts. Indeed, the rate-rigging trials took place in a political context of justified public anger towards the banks, for all the lasting damage that their mismanagement had done to economies around the world, and therefore to the prosperity of millions upon millions of families.

As this book will show, those bankers were always innocent of the crimes with which they were charged. Even more astonishingly, when they committed the alleged foul deeds, they weren't crimes at all.

Yes, you read that right.

The thirty-seven bankers whom the USA or UK have prosecuted since the financial crisis are innocent.

Nineteen of them were convicted, with one trader receiving a fourteen-year sentence (reduced to eleven years on appeal).

But why, you ask, should we care about some high-paid bankers going to jail? They're all crooks, aren't they? It's a great question with an unsettling answer. The bankers who went to jail were the ones who put their faith in the justice system and told the truth. Even more incredibly, some were the very people who had brought the authorities' attention to the crimes in the first place. They were whistleblowers.

Suppose you witnessed something criminal at work. If you worked in medicine, for example, and you saw a doctor abusing patients. Or in construction, and you knew your boss was using illegal materials that were cheap but highly inflammable. Or for the police, and you saw a senior officer planting evidence on an innocent person. Or for the media, and your editor ordered reporters to hack a phone illegally to get a story. You'd want to speak up, wouldn't you? You wouldn't want to carry that knowledge around with you for the rest of your life, knowing you did nothing. You'd like to think that if you reported any of these crimes, you would be protected.

Imagine instead that you found yourself under investigation, then arrested and your family's future threatened. Then you were put on trial for something you didn't do, for a crime that didn't even exist and, several years later, were sentenced to years in prison, just for doing the right thing.

That is what happened to the traders who spoke up. Thousands of people in the banking world knew there was something rotten about the rate-rigging trials but did nothing. Because they knew if they did, then their livelihoods – and perhaps their freedom – would be in danger. This also means that they're unlikely to speak out the next time. And there will be a next time.

Shattered by the experience of injustice, the prosecuted traders, including those who stayed out of jail, have suffered nervous breakdowns. The real perpetrators – not just of the real rate-rigging scandal but of the whole financial crisis – escaped with their multi-million-pound bonuses and giant pension funds intact.

The trials of junior bankers accused of rate-rigging were about sending out a message: bankers were being locked up. There is justice. Nothing more to see here, move along folks, it's OK to start borrowing again. Of course, there is much, much more to see. *Rigged* uncovers the shocking truth behind the rate-rigging scandal, thanks to years of investigation, thousands of hours of recorded phone calls, emails between traders, bank executives and politicians, interviews and trial transcripts. It's a chilling tale, jaw-dropping in its immensity. Because as it turns out, it's not just interest rates that can be rigged – it's the entire system.

1

LOWBALL

'Peter Johnson?'
'Hey Peter, it's Ryan.'
'Hello, Ryan.'
'Hey man, uh—'
'This is so fucking sick. It's so, so fucking wrong.'
'Should be higher?'
'Much, much higher.'
'Really.'
'Much, much higher. Believe me, you've got no idea how much higher.'
'Wow.'

(Barclays traders Ryan Reich, 25, in New York
and Peter Johnson, 52, in London
29 November 2007)

Barclays cash trader Peter Johnson returned from a three-week family holiday at the end of August 2007 to find the world's financial system on the verge of meltdown. The 5,000 workers streaming towards the gleaming thirty-three-storey, million-square-foot Barclays headquarters in Canary Wharf that morning had plenty to worry about. French bank BNP Paribas (the eighth largest in the world) had announced that it had frozen three of its hedge funds because they'd put billions of dollars in investments linked to defaulting mortgages in the USA that might never be repaid. There were rumours that British banks – Northern Rock in particular – were similarly exposed and fast running out of cash. No bank was willing to lend to any other bank for fear that they might go bust. The global credit crunch, the biggest financial disaster since the Great Depression of the 1930s, was officially under way.

Johnson, a greying 52-year-old smoker with a gravelly voice, had been with Barclays since 1981. Known to everyone at work as PJ, he had an unusually strong sense of right and wrong, and liked to speak his mind in forceful language, no matter who was listening. It was his job to borrow billions at a time and lend it on to departments within Barclays that needed cash, making sure the money flowing out of the bank in loans and investments was matched by money coming in. He'd seen his fair share of financial crises over the course of his career, so, putting rumours to one side, he got on with the business at hand.

Checking the ever-changing streams of data on the computer screens gathered in a crescent around his desk, PJ spotted something amiss: Barclays' Libor rate was far too low.

What the Dow Jones or the FTSE 100 is to share prices, Libor (London Interbank Offered Rate, pronounced Lie-bor) is to interest rates: an index, updated every day, that tracks what banks are paying to borrow cash from each other. For the past thirty-five years, the repayments on millions of consumer loans and mortgages have depended not on the official interest rates you hear about on the news, set by central banks like the Federal Reserve or the Bank of England. Instead, they go up or down with the real cost to banks of getting hold of cash on the international money markets. Libor keeps track of that cost by showing the average interest rate banks are paying to borrow funds.

Every morning, PJ had a chore to do – a chore he'd been carrying out for two decades. He was the bank's 'Libor submitter' for US dollars. That meant he had to submit an estimate, to at least two decimal places, of what interest rate he thought Barclays would have to pay to borrow a large lump of cash – in dollars – from the other banks just before 11 a.m. that day. He might put in, say, 3.43%. His counterparts at the fifteen other Libor-setting banks would each do the same thing; for example, Citigroup might estimate 3.41%, Lloyds 3.42%, and so on. Their estimates, known as 'submissions', would be ranked, high to low, and made public. The top four and bottom four submissions were struck out and an average taken of the middle eight to get the official London Interbank Offered Rate. Banks like Barclays had billions of dollars in loans, investments and trades linked to the Libor average, so they could make or lose money if Libor rose or fell. A tiny movement might sometimes make or lose the bank a million dollars.

Of course, PJ couldn't just submit any old rate. It had to be realistic, based on the interest rates his bank was really paying, or could pay, to borrow funds that morning. If there was more than one offer to lend in the market that Barclays might take up, those offers wouldn't be at exactly the same rate. Chase London might offer 3.41%, HSBC Hong Kong slightly higher at 3.43%, Bank of China Beijing 3.42% and so on. PJ could realistically borrow at the highest interest rate, or the lowest, or somewhere in the middle. That gave him a narrow range of accurate rates to choose from as his Libor estimate: up or down by no more than a hundredth of a percentage point or two.

Libors were calculated in ten currencies from US dollars to sterling to yen, and PJ could see that the Libor submissions in all currencies that morning were way out. There was no way anyone was offering cash at the cheap rates the banks were posting. He prided himself on setting an honest rate and, after studying the latest market data, corrected Barclays' dollar number upwards by 0.15%.

This simple action – an attempt at honesty – set off a chain of events that would end up exposing the financial and judicial systems' rotten heart, wrecking PJ's life (among many others) in the process.

That morning, however, PJ had no idea of the consequences of his actions. After setting Barclays' dollar Libor, he checked and rechecked the data for every other bank. He could hardly believe what he was seeing. All the banks were 'lowballing' – pretending it was much cheaper to borrow cash than it really was. The banks, almost devoid of cash and with no one prepared to lend to them, were lying through gritted teeth to prevent anyone realising how desperate they were. They were pretending they could get cash at the same cheap interest rate that other banks were putting in as their Libor estimate. But then they were going into the market to borrow funds at a much higher rate.

It proved the rates were false. If the cheap rates they were saying they could borrow at were accurate, why would they pay more? PJ called a colleague to vent: 'I think these Libors are all fucked.' He then emailed his boss, Mark Dearlove, head of liquidity management, a more polite assessment, finishing with: 'Draw your own conclusions about why people are going for unrealistically low Libors.'

Dearlove came from a wealthy establishment family. His uncle was Sir Richard Dearlove, the former head of MI6. PJ had known Mark since the 1990s, when he'd been introduced as the new managing director of the cash desk where PJ worked. Dearlove was thirteen years PJ's junior and on a gilded career path to the top of the bank, but PJ was pleasantly surprised to discover that didn't mean he'd be pulling rank. He'd always taken time to listen, and they'd struck up a close working relationship over the years. When it had been a stressful day on the trading floor, they'd frequently blow off steam together after work as the alcohol flowed freely, and the younger boss relied heavily upon the benefit of PJ's experience, especially during the financial crisis.

A concerned Dearlove forwarded PJ's email to the Federal Reserve Bank of New York[1] (the New York Fed, the USA's equivalent of the Bank of England). He received no reply. PJ then received a call from Thomson Reuters. This was the financial information service to which he sent his Libor number. Reuters gathered all the numbers into a tidy report and sent it on to the Bank of England, the British Bankers' Association (BBA, at the time the administrators of Libor and a trade organisation that represented 200 banks), along with other financial institutions. Reuters wanted to know why Barclays' Libor was so much higher than everyone else's. Was PJ sure it should be that high? He told Reuters he was absolutely sure. The other banks were putting in their Libor estimates way too low. His was the most honest rate.

PJ then copied several colleagues into an email: 'Have a look at the range of Libors set by contributor banks. Needless to say I think I am correct and UBS at 5.10 is obviously smoking something fairly powerful.' He told another colleague on the phone: 'Some of the Libors that people have been putting in have been an absolute disgrace [...] I'm leading the campaign to get Libors more realistic [...] I think they're doing it to try to persuade themselves that if they keep on putting in low Libors they might get some money, but it doesn't work that way.' On the phone to another trader: 'It's just such bollocks [...] it's absolute rubbish [...] I mean you cannot get money there.' Followed by another email: 'Fun and games in Libor land where the popular premise seems to be that Barclays must be in trouble because it is setting its Libors so high. But other Libor contributors will almost certainly be setting their Libors lower than where they are paying [...] As you can see there is something wrong in the State of Denmark and it certainly is not my Libors.'

What was wrong, of course, was that most banks, like Northern Rock, were fast running out of cash. No one was prepared to lend them money for more than a few days, for fear that they might have lost so much money on bad US mortgages that they wouldn't even exist in a month. The only way they could get money was if they paid significantly higher interest rates. But they weren't ready to admit what they would really have to pay to get the funds they needed. PJ's campaign soon got the attention of the media. Bloomberg journalist Mark Gilbert called Barclays to ask if its higher Libor meant it was in trouble. Bob Diamond, at this time Barclays' president and chief executive of its investment bank division, Barclays Capital,[2] was unnerved enough by Gilbert's call to email his concerns to his fellow directors.

Diamond, labelled the 'unacceptable face of banking' by an MP appalled by a Barclays Capital tax dodge, was widely regarded within the financial world as 'the future of banking' (indeed, he would go on to take the top job at Barclays, group chief executive, in 2011). The Bostonian, one of nine siblings and the son of a headmaster, had, true to the American stereotype, rubbed the Brits up the wrong way as he brought the immense profits of global investment banking to a Barclays that had, until his arrival, been struggling to make traditional banking pay.

'Tucker [Paul Tucker, then Bank of England's executive director for markets] said we were above the market on Libor,' Diamond wrote in an email to senior executives, 'and Bloomberg are looking at this story [...] this could be the next leg in silly/bad press, can we get on it? AAAAAAARRRRRRGGGGHHHH!!!'

Barclays had already been receiving unwanted press attention for its recent reliance on the Bank of England's 'discount window': a lending facility which provided funds to banks so tied up in the ebb and flow of myriad financial products that they had 'liquidity issues' – meaning a shortage of cash that day.

One of the people copied in on Diamond's email was Jerry del Missier, then president of Barclays Capital. A clever, dark-haired French Canadian described by one colleague as 'boringly competent', del Missier had spent ten years working in Barclays' investment banking division, making the bank more money than anyone else in the early 2000s, becoming one of the highest-paid bankers in London.[3] He replied: 'The whole Libor curve is rubbish. The real story is that these are all fantasy rates. Nobody is lending anything at the rates they are posting.'

The next day, del Missier received a call from Paul Tucker. In recent days, Tucker's attention had been brought to Barclays' share price: it was tanking. He was already engaged in the battle to save Northern Rock, having arrived at Threadneedle Street early that morning, marching quickly through the ornate, high-ceilinged lobbies and corridors of the Bank of England's headquarters.

The rumour-mongers had been right. Northern Rock had been caught with its trousers down right in the middle of the US mortgage mess. The debt-ridden bank's business model had relied upon it being able to borrow money from other banks and investors on a daily basis, but no one was lending, so it was down to the Bank of England to save it. Tucker, who had joined his beloved Bank of England immediately after graduating from Cambridge in 1980, needed to find £3 billion in emergency funding just to keep the Rock afloat for a few days or so.

Staring at the front page of the *Financial Times* as he drank his coffee, 'Anxious Market Catches Barclays Short of £1.6 billion', Tucker's alarm was growing. It was the worst headline about a bank in living memory. He knew that Barclays had borrowed huge sums and that it had sacked a senior banker who'd tried to raise the alert over the vast amount of US mortgage investments it had accumulated, investments that no one now wanted to buy. And now, with these above-the-market Libor rates, it looked like Barclays was 'bidding up' the market – paying more than other banks because it was desperate for cash. Tucker feared that the true weak state of Barclays' finances was now being exposed. No one would want to keep lending to a bank that was in some kind of distress and which might then struggle to borrow the funds it needed to keep going; and that could mean another Northern Rock on his hands – but much bigger. If it continued … The failure of one of the UK's biggest banks was unimaginable, a total catastrophe; millions of customers panicking, a run on the bank, with no access to their money, even for a few hours could lead to a loss of confidence in the entire banking system – and that could lead to a depression. It didn't bear thinking about.

Tucker knew that Libor was still way too low to reflect what banks were really paying to borrow cash. It had been set at 5.20% the previous morning, but the market data suggested that it should have been about 5.55%. A difference of 0.35% might not seem like much, but if you were a bank that had made loans of $50 billion, it could cost you $17.5 million

(£13 million) every month. Lowballing was dishonest – and arguably downright criminal. Because smaller US and European banks lent trillions of dollars in loans linked to the Libor rate, the interest they collected was now lower than it should have been – much less than what they would have to pay to get hold of dollars on international money markets. With less money coming in than going out, they were losing millions of dollars every day.

Tucker also knew that the Libor rates that banks put in normally moved by just one or two hundredths of a percentage point per day (0.01–0.02%, known in the City as 1 or 2 'basis points'). A leap of 35 basis points would have caused total panic.

As it was, PJ, in an effort to ease Barclays' dollar Libor up to where it should be, had gone as far as to correct it to 5.35%. It made no impact on the published Libor rate because it was among the top four excluded from the average. Other traders on the market, however, could see that Barclays' Libor estimate was way higher than any other bank. An increase of 0.15 percentage points in Barclays' dollar Libor appeared to signal that it was in trouble – Northern Rock kind of trouble. On Friday 31 August, they were even talking about it on national radio news programmes: was Barclays struggling to get hold of the funds it needed to keep going?

Barclays executives kept telling the Bank of England that PJ's higher Libor rates were the accurate ones; it was the rest of the market that was wrong. True as that might be, it didn't help Tucker to manage the situation. Speculation was growing that Barclays would imminently run out of cash. Early the next day, Saturday 1 September, Tucker emailed Jerry del Missier asking him to call him over the weekend. Del Missier forwarded it to Bob Diamond, who bounced it back: he guessed it was about Libor and decided Jerry was the best person to handle it. Later that day, del Missier picked up the phone to Tucker, who told him he was concerned about Barclays' Libor submissions; they didn't always need to be that high. It was the first of many such conversations, not only with del Missier but with Mark Dearlove and Bob Diamond, where Paul Tucker would ask why Barclays' Libor rates were higher than other banks. Del Missier at first responded by defending the rates they'd put in. Barclays' cash traders (PJ and others) were calling it where they saw it; it was costing more to borrow cash, so they were putting in higher Libor rates to reflect that. But for Tucker, that still wasn't good enough.

Years later, in 2011, when del Missier was interviewed by the US Department of Justice, he was asked what Paul Tucker had told him that day. His reply was unequivocal: 'That we should get our Libor rates down.' That evidence, revealing that the Bank of England began instructing Barclays to post inaccurately low Libor rates in September 2007, was kept out of the subsequent UK trials of traders for rigging rates.[4] Yet it revealed a much bigger manipulation of Libor by the Bank of England than any that the prosecution alleged against the traders.

After the weekend phone call with Tucker, del Missier called Miles Storey. A Barclays career man from the north of England, Storey already knew that the bank's Libor rates were way off. He was the bank's head of group balance sheet management, which in August 2007 was a bit like being head of tidal management for King Canute. Cash was flowing out of Barclays with alarming speed, threatening to leave a multi-billion-pound hole in the bank's finances. Aged 43 and slim with straight dark hair, Storey was always immaculately dressed and carefully calculated what he said, to the point where he'd developed an awkward conversational habit of asking himself a question out loud and then answering it. Discussing PJ's correction with a colleague he said, 'Any Libor is, I shouldn't really say this, but almost fiction [...] Why are credit departments saying don't lend to any bank [...] over one month? Because we don't know whether that bank will be there in one month. That could be the only reason.'

Immediately after del Missier hung up, passing on the fact that the Bank of England wanted them to lowball, Storey called Mark Dearlove. Both of them knew PJ was planning to set a higher Libor again to make it more accurate. He wanted to raise his estimate of the cost of borrowing cash by 10 basis points to get closer to the real interest rates on the markets where dollars were changing hands. After the instructions from above, that was looking awkward. 'What I would like us to do is set exactly the same today as we did Friday,' Storey told Dearlove. 'That's what we've agreed to do.'

Twenty minutes later, PJ was finishing a phone call with a colleague, telling him, 'It pisses me off that we're the only people being honest about this, and we are getting pilloried for it,' before someone yelled at him that Storey was on the other line.

Storey trod carefully. 'I [...] will [...] in no way try to get you to change your Libors. However, if you were comfortable in not raising them, again [...] from a purely presentational point of view that would be good.'

PJ sounded uncertain as he replied. 'Riiight, oookay.'

'It would help if we sort of took the market with us rather than leading the market,' Storey continued, 'just from the external presentational point of view and all the hassle that the bigwigs get. And, to be blunt with you, the press that we've had [...] So that, i-if you can still ... in good conscience, not raise them or not raise them as much as you're saying.'

The next day PJ kept his Libor at the top of the pack but refrained from raising it any higher. 'I'd like to set it higher,' he said in a phone call to a colleague, 'but at the moment there's a little bit of political pressure on me not to go any higher than I am at the moment. Like internal political, like big – big boys like Jerry. Jerry wanted me to set them lower today. I refused.'

PJ wasn't the only Libor setter worried about the rates being set. Peter Spence, his equivalent for sterling Libor, said in a call to PJ: 'I just want to adhere to the rules and every other bank is breaking 'em. I might be wrong, I mean, you know, don't get me wrong: the higher Libor goes, I'm losing money like everybody else. But, I mean, sod it if you don't tell the truth. The worst I find is we're getting slated for everything that's going on [...] but I think in the end we'll be vindicated.'

PJ agreed. 'This Libor is an absolute fucking farce, you know,' he told another colleague. 'I mean it should be so much higher, but you've got all these arseholes like Citibank, sort of pushing out charts saying that Barclays' Libors are too high – they must be in trouble. But I know I'm going too low. It's ridiculous!'

Frustrated at being forced to lie, PJ kept trying to post higher, more accurate rates as his estimate of the cost of borrowing dollars. But the pressure from above to post false, low ones kept coming. At just after 8 a.m. on 19 November, PJ told Pete Spence what he'd just heard from Mark Dearlove. 'Mark had a talk with Jon Stone [Barclays' then group treasurer] on the phone, saying, "Oh what are you doing with Libors? You know, you're going above the market again." And he said, "Well that's where they are, in fact they're probably not high enough." [Stone said:] "Ah, but you know every time [...] that happens, if there's any risk to our reputation, I've got to go to the board and explain it." Mark said, "Well, I'll go to the board and explain it if you want ..."'

Later that day, PJ emailed Dearlove: 'Just had a call from Miles [Storey] asking me to keep my Libors within the group (pressure from above).' He gave in to the pressure, setting it within the middle of the pack. Two days later a jubilant Jonathan Stone called Mark Dearlove. Stone had been keeping a close eye on Libor because it was his responsibility to make sure the bank could raise funds as cheaply as possible.

'Credit Suisse is now the outlier,' Dearlove said.

'Good ... Isn't it nice not to be the person, Mark?' said Stone. 'We've begged him for it [...] Miles did say you were at the top end of the range. But provided you're not the highest, I don't mind.'

'Yeah, they're tempering it exactly right.'

'Y'know, you've heard Bob [Diamond] as well,' said Stone. 'We don't want to be in the press, it just ain't worth it.'

PJ's bosses were all too aware of the views of Diamond and other executives on the Barclays board. If PJ told the truth about the interest rates he was really paying to borrow dollars, Barclays would stand out too much from the 'pack' of lowballing banks. And that might attract press speculation just like it did in September that they were paying more because they were desperate to get hold of funds. Dearlove and Storey weren't the ones ultimately telling PJ to lie. They were only the messengers carrying out an edict from senior management: stay out of the press. The pressure on PJ to lie was coming from the top of the bank.

By 29 November, PJ was posting Libors so far out from reality he was embarrassed. That morning the cheapest offer in the market to lend dollars over one month was at 5.60%. The other banks were clearly lowballing, telling brokers they were putting in submissions claiming that they could borrow dollars at anything from 5.15% (Royal Bank of Scotland) to 5.30% (Bank of Scotland) – 30 to 45 points below reality. They were already paying more than that to borrow cash – proving they were lying. Just in case that wasn't bad enough, the Financial Services Authority (FSA, the UK's financial regulator, since renamed the Financial Conduct Authority) had started to take an interest, warning one of the money brokers that arranged borrowing and lending between the banks, Tullett Prebon, of their obligation to show 'fair and reflective prices' about Libor on their screens. This was becoming impossible; how could they do the right thing? Dearlove set up an emergency conference call with Jonathan Stone and Miles Storey. PJ and his colleague on the cash desk, Colin Bermingham, joined the call.

'Okay, so the dilemma we have,' Dearlove told Stone, 'is that we think 1-month Libor should be 5.50 [...] Now if you put 5.50, we're going to be 20 basis [points above every other bank] ... It's going to cause a shitstorm.'

Stone got it. If you put your head too far above the parapet, it might get shot off.

'So, what I propose as a halfway house is, er – PJ you can shout me down; he's already pulling faces at me – if you go with [...] Bank of Scotland's levels. But we kinda need to have a meeting to figure out what we're going to publish [...] tomorrow and I think we need to get a bigger audience involved in this. Jon, I understand the sensitivities and I think we need to take it upstairs.'

'I'm with Chris [Lucas] and meeting Patrick [Clackson] at 12 anyway so [...] if I can, off the back of that, maybe find five minutes to catch him.'

They discussed why other banks were lowballing. Their fear, Storey said, was, 'If we let the Libors go up and up and up, we'll all appear like we're in a problematic situation.'

'We are,' interjected PJ.

'No, I know – I know. I agree it's kidding themselves,' Storey came back. 'And I appreciate that you, PJ, have been pragmatic in your approach throughout this. I think if we can stick – as Jon and Mark have said – stick with "at the high end along the lines of HBOS" [Halifax Bank of Scotland] ... for today.'

'OK, Miles.' PJ had no choice. He had made it clear he wanted to put in a rate for borrowing dollars over one month at 5.50%. His bosses had over-ruled him and instructed him to go 20 points lower.

Dearlove, Stone and Storey knew that, in effect, they had just instructed PJ to post false Libor rates that morning – to lowball. But Dearlove was most worried about the next day's Libor fix. The last day of November was impor-tant because it was when some banks and investment funds worked out the value of their assets and liabilities, including investments and loans that were linked to Libor. That meant their assets would be revalued – making or losing money based on that day's Libor average, also known as the 'fix'. If it were false, that would mean a false market, based on a false, lowballed Libor. Stone said he was already about to meet the Barclays group finance director Chris Lucas, who sat on the board of directors of Barclays, in the office of Patrick Clackson, then chief financial officer of Barclays Capital. Before the conference call finished, Storey agreed to contact the BBA to try and get them to do something (see page 57). Later that day, Stone spoke to Chris Lucas and asked him what he wanted him to tell the cash traders about Libor. Lucas told him he would prefer that they stay where they were the next day (rather than go higher as PJ thought they should). Stone passed the message down to Dearlove.

As PJ sat down at his desk the next morning, he glanced at the window on his screen listing yesterday's false Libor submissions, including his. He asked the money brokers who were on the end of permanent, open phone lines to his desk: what were the other banks going to put in as their Libors? Once again, he learned, they were all going to lowball, pretending they'd pay far less than they'd really pay. Enough of this game.

'Hello Miles, it's Johnson here.'

'Hello Johnson, it's Miles.'

PJ was proposing to post a more accurate Libor: 5.40. Storey cleared his throat. 'Have you had a chance to talk to Mark? [...] Just one sec, Pete, hold on one sec mate.'

PJ could barely make out Storey's voice speaking to someone on another phone, explaining that banks were still paying far more to borrow dollars than they were admitting in their publicly stated Libor rates. He was trying to find out what Barclays' top bosses wanted to do. 'So the guidance is stick within the bounds? [...] So no head above the parapet, no partial bleeding, etcetera? Okay.'

Storey returned to PJ's line. 'Did you overhear any of that?'

'Er, not really ...' PJ's tone was wary.

'Right. Mr Lucas doesn't want us to be outside the top end.'

'Jesus Christ,' PJ said, exhaling. Then, sounding slightly incredulous, reluctantly agreeing: 'Alright, so ... OK.'

'And apparently they chatted [about this] on the whole of the thirty-first floor, by the way,' Storey added. PJ knew what that meant: the thirty-first floor of Barclays group headquarters at 1 Churchill Place, Canary Wharf, where Bob Diamond, Chris Lucas and group chief executive John Varley had their offices.

Soon after the renewed instruction from the top of his bank, PJ, still filled with frustration, picked up a call from a young derivatives trader named Ryan Reich at the US headquarters of Barclays in New York. Aged 25, shaven-headed and physically fit from a youth spent playing sports, Ryan came from a wealthy East Coast family and had been hired just over a year before to trade financial products that went up or down in value depending on movements in the dollar Libor rate. Energetic and eager to succeed, it was part of Ryan's job to call PJ in London at least once a week and ask if he could tweak his Libor settings up or down by a hundredth of a percentage point or two to help the trading positions of the New York desk he worked for. Neither of them saw anything wrong with that. So long as PJ put in interest rates at which the bank could realistically borrow, he was simply choosing a rate from the narrow range of offers to lend in the market which Barclays could take up. But this lowballing they'd been seeing for the last three months was something else altogether.

'Hey Peter, it's Ryan.'

'Hello Ryan … This is so fucking sick,' PJ told him.

'Why?' Ryan suppressed a laugh.

'It's so, so fucking wrong.'

Ryan knew he was talking about Libor. 'Should be higher?'

'Much, much higher.'

'Really.'

'Much, much higher. Believe me, you've got no idea how much higher.'

'Wow.'

'I mean the only reason I went 30 in one month [5.30%[5] – PJ's Libor estimate of the interest rate he'd pay to borrow dollars for a month] was because that's the highest that anyone else was gonna go and I didn't want to be seen to be an outsider. I wanted to go 50 [5.50%] … It's just ridiculous […] The best offer of cash is at 60 [5.60%] […] If you pay [to borrow euros] and swap them back into dollars, you're paying 5.70.'

'Wow.'

'You sort of get the drift. People are setting these so ridiculously low, it's just getting to be a laugh. And I'm actually quite worried that there's some kind of reputational risk here for any bank which sets them this low,' PJ said. 'You look at some of the people – these arseholes. Right, you've got Deutsche – set at 5.18. Well, we all know he's in the shit […] WestLB set at 5.22: he's in the shit. Royal Bank of Scotland 5.18. Well, if Royal Bank of Scotland are setting at 5.18, why is ABN [Amro], who I believe they took over, paying 5.40? So that's one to think about. Citibank – he's in the shit – he set at 5.18 […] and UBS, in the shit, 5.16. So you tell me whether those Libors are right? They're wrong. They are so fucking wrong. And unfortunately, unless I'm given the green light to go ahead and put rates where I think they are, I don't think I can have any influence.'

A week later, feeling very emotional, PJ again vented to Ryan. Since the crisis began, he'd been writing short pieces circulated within Barclays to anyone who wanted to read them, explaining why he was right to be setting higher Libor rates and other banks were wrong to be lowballing. He'd openly said he was leading a campaign to make Libors more honest. But now he kept getting instructions from the top, via Storey or Dearlove, forbidding him from being any more truthful than the other banks. That day, Barclays had borrowed $600 million from Citibank at an interest rate of 5.40%. Yet because of the pressure from above, PJ couldn't post his Libor rate where he was paying. 'I actually feel embarrassed that I set my 1-month Libor at 5.30 and I was paying 5.40 in the market,' he told Ryan. 'I'm 4 over the next highest contributor and nearly 5 over the average.'

'You get shit for that, don't you?' asked Ryan.

'Well; people just think I look like an absolute prat.' PJ's indignation was growing. 'What worries me is it's getting – I think it's getting down to a sort of ethical and legal thing now.'

'Yeah, you mentioned that to me last time.'

'I'm patently giving a false rate!'

Unable to stand much more, PJ again told his boss that banks were posting rates far lower than they were really paying in the market – including Barclays. 'I've set 1-month at 30 [5.30%]. It's a load of bollocks [...] I'm paying 40 [5.40%]. WestLB Dusseldorf, in fact, is paying 50 and [...] will probably set at 25, so that'll be an interesting one.'

'It's outrageous, isn't it,' Dearlove said.

'Yeah, I mean it really is just sick [...] I tried to get in touch with Jon Stone but he wasn't there – cos I really do feel people must think we're bloody stupid [...] I think we should take a stand.'

'You know I agree with you. I – I've represented your views very strongly.'

'I'm going to write you an email, and then you can do with it what you want,' said PJ.

'Okay, fair enough! You're right because I want to get, um, something written from the guys upstairs.'

'So I'll just write a thing – I'll just say I think it's bringing the Libor market into disrepute, Barclays into disrepute, me into disrepute. That's what I really object to.'

Dearlove knew how forceful PJ's language could be. 'Make sure you do it in a way I can forward it.'

'Don't worry, I'll be as sweet as I possibly can.'

In his email PJ wrote: 'I am feeling increasingly uncomfortable about the way in which USD libors are being set by the contributor banks, Barclays included [...] Barclays set at 5.30% (4 bps over the next highest contributor and nearly 5 bps over the actual Libor). At the same time that we were setting at 5.30%, I was paying 5.40% in the market [...] My worry is that we are being seen to be contributing patently false rates. We are therefore being dishonest by definition and are at risk of damaging our reputation in the market and with the regulators. Can we discuss urgently please?'

Aware that pressure to lowball came from the very top of the bank, from Barclays' board of directors, Dearlove called Stone the next day at 7.49 a.m.

'I've actually had an official email now from Peter Johnson, who's basically saying, look, I want something in writing now because I think, um, you know, that this is all wrong.'

'Well, have you talked to Jerry del Missier about it?' Stone asked.

'Well, he's – he's in Nepal.'

'Oh, for fuck's sake.'

'So I don't, I don't quite know who to escalate it within BarCap [Barclays Capital, the bank's investment bank division] [...] I guess the best person I can think of is Rich Ricci and Bob.'

'I think Bob understands it,' said Stone. 'And the answer is up until now ... it's like guys this is just ... continue to push further.'

Dearlove wanted Barclays to be setting a good example, rather than just following the low standards of every other lowballing bank. 'The fact of the matter is, that we're not setting Libors where we should be,' he told Stone. 'We're at the top of the range so we're not affecting the Libor settings because we're, we are being excluded anyway because we're too high [...] But on the other side I can understand the board's perspective, but what frustrates me a-above all, uh, is that the board seems very concerned, and I think that these guys should be on the front foot rather than the back foot.'

'Listen, they haven't had a conversation about it for the last, you know, the last two weeks,' said Stone.

Dearlove knew the board was already familiar with the Libor problem. But he was concerned it might become a bigger issue and urged Stone to raise it again with them. Stone suggested he should speak to Rich Ricci, Bob Diamond's aptly named lieutenant from Nebraska who loved to spend the tens of millions of pounds of share awards he collected on racehorses, flamboyant suits and showy hats. A friend and ally of Diamond's since the mid-1990s, Ricci was chief operating officer of Barclays Capital, running it alongside Jerry del Missier.

Stone said he'd speak to Chris Lucas, the finance director who sat on the Barclays group board. Just under an hour later, Stone called Dearlove back. 'I caught up with Chris and at the moment he's still much in the same camp as well,' said Stone, 'I know what you say about being on the front foot and I don't think he sees the benefit we achieve from that. I think he too, like myself, said, "Well, what does Bob think on the issue?" [...] I just don't want to find out, you know, that you and I make a decision, and everyone says, "You've gone barking mad, guys."'

There Dearlove was, trying to get the board of Barclays to do the right thing. Yet the board didn't 'see the benefit'. As his own frustration grew, he circulated PJ's email to Barclays' top bosses and called the compliance director, Stephen Morse: 'I've been liaising with Jon Stone every day about our settings. We've been telling him we want to be putting high rates in. He has been told by the thirty-first floor that we can be the highest, but we must not be a standout person because they're worried we're at the stress point,' Dearlove told Morse. 'I've just had a conversation with the Stone man [Jonathan Stone] this morning and I have asked him to go back to the thirty-first floor, so he went back to Chris Lucas this morning and said, look, you know this is wrong. And I was at a meeting yesterday with the ECB [European Central Bank] with a whole lot of other banks and all the banks were saying – this is just bullshit – but people said, "Your settings are the most realistic because they're the highest."

'I'm actually going to see Rich Ricci about it because Jerry is away at the moment,' Dearlove said. 'I need to try and get some advice from somebody as to what I'm supposed to do. Cos I don't think – I can no longer make that decision. I don't think it's fair on PJ to be setting something which he knows is wrong.'

'I agree,' said Morse.

'I actually got an email from PJ, which I will forward to you. Because he wants something in writing – cover your arse, whatever you want to call it. And I agree with him.'

Dearlove had a meeting with Morse and Rich Ricci at lunchtime, where Ricci said he'd call Lucas but believed they needed to go to the FSA and talk to them explicitly about their problem.

The next morning, Morse phoned the FSA, located in Canary Wharf in London's Docklands area, a stone's throw from Barclays' headquarters. He spoke to Mark Wharton, who led the team at the regulator that supervised

Barclays and knew Ricci, Lucas and Diamond. Barclays had kept the FSA informed in September when PJ tried to submit a higher, more accurate rate, the media misreported the reasons and the share price tumbled. Since then, Morse explained, they'd been justifiably reluctant to go higher, too far above the rest of the pack. The FSA was familiar with this as an issue. Morse gave some examples of banks submitting one low rate, and then paying another higher one in the market. Could that be regarded as manipulation or market abuse?

Wharton had been involved in drawing up the regulator's Code of Market Conduct years before, when they'd looked at the issue and concluded Libor couldn't be manipulated by one bank alone. You'd need at least four banks colluding together to shift the average artificially. The FSA didn't regulate Libor, he told Morse. If rates were inaccurate, Barclays should go to the BBA.

Later that day, Morse sent an email reporting the phone call to senior managers including Chris Lucas, Jerry del Missier, Rich Ricci, Jonathan Stone and Barclays' top lawyer and general counsel, Mark Harding. 'Mark [Wharton] seemed grateful for the "heads up",' Morse wrote. 'He informed me that he would escalate this to an appropriate level within the FSA and will get back to me ASAP with any planned response. In the meantime, Mark agreed that the approach we've been adopting seems sensible in the circumstances, so I suggest we maintain status quo for now.' The email was forwarded to Dearlove, who sent it on to PJ. To him, the 'status quo' meant he was allowed to put his head above the parapet, so he was the highest of the 'pack' of banks submitting their estimates of the cost of borrowing cash, but not too far away from the next one down. Now the FSA knew all about it and they weren't complaining. The FSA seemed to be OK with the approach Barclays had been taking.

Morse hadn't quite told the FSA that PJ's view of where Libor should be had been overruled by the bank's top bosses. But from that point on, as far as senior Barclays executives were concerned, they'd told the regulator about Libor rates being too low and the FSA didn't think it broke their rules. After Wharton escalated the issue within the FSA, no one raised the alert or reported it to the police. To Barclays executives and lawyers, the FSA had been told about the understated, inaccurate Libor submissions that had been going on for months now, later to become known as 'lowballing'. And the regulator wasn't troubled by it. When, years later, the FSA and the US regulators began to fine banks hundreds of millions of pounds for rigging interest rates, that awkward fact wouldn't feature in their press releases.

In his one-man campaign for honesty, PJ sometimes felt quite alone. He seemed to be the only one in the City of London or Wall Street who cared about this industry-wide fraud, ordered from the top, that he'd been pressured, against his protests, to take part in. As the crisis intensified in the months to come, he would resolutely keep up his campaign, undeterred by any premonition of the high price he, personally, would come to pay. Neither he nor Ryan Reich could have guessed how closely their fates would be intertwined, or how the fraud now visible to them on a screen of false figures would morph into a financial and political firestorm that would leave them, and dozens like them, badly burned.

2

INSTRUCTIONS TO LIE

Week after week, month after month, as the banks muddled their way through the credit crunch, PJ was pressured to keep his Libor low, and week after week, month after month, PJ resisted as much as he dared and set Barclays' dollar Libor at the top of the pack. Then, in the autumn of 2008, the crisis reached a new pitch of intensity. When Lehman Brothers collapsed on 15 September, it became impossible for any bank to pretend it was business as usual.

From his corner of the trading floor on the second floor of Barclays Capital's headquarters at 5 North Colonnade, Canary Wharf, PJ watched in mounting alarm as news about the worsening crisis streamed in to the eight large computer monitors above his desk. Every day, there was a shock headline of the sort you'd normally see only once a year. On 16 September, a once-mighty investment bank sunk by losses on US mortgages, Merrill Lynch, announced it was selling itself to Bank of America. Then one of the biggest insurers in the world, AIG, which had underwritten vast amounts of insurance against US mortgages defaulting and couldn't afford to pay the huge claims that were now being made, was bailed out by the US government at a cost of $80 billion. Then on the morning of 17 September, the biggest mortgage bank in the UK, Halifax Bank of Scotland (HBOS), stricken by bad loans it had made, which prompted a relentless battering of its share price, was taken over by a rival bank, Lloyds TSB.

To PJ, it was a perfect storm. Getting funds to borrow for more than a day or two was harder than he could ever remember in his twenty-six years at the bank. But Libor rates still weren't reflecting that. On the phone to the Bank of England, he warned an official that Barclays' Libor rate was lower than the real cost of borrowing cash – even though it was higher than everyone else's. 'We set at 3.20 in 3 months [PJ's estimated interest rate to borrow dollars over three months], which actually I thought was too low. But I didn't want to be too high because the story would get out that Barclays is in trouble. If I set at 4%, everyone's going to say that I'm in deep shit, but I'm not in deep shit, I'm just trying to be honest about where the market is.'

Not for the first time, PJ was telling the Bank of England that all banks' Libor rates were false and far too low. A week later, an official on Paul Tucker's team sent a memo, reporting that there were recriminations among Libor-setting banks over who was pushing the fixings higher, with some pointing at Barclays. But PJ gave the Bank of England evidence to justify its higher rates. He was posting 5% as Barclays' Libor submission, the same interest rate he was bidding in the market to borrow dollars. Yet he wasn't getting any offers from other banks to lend cash at that rate – proving it was still unrealistically low.

With banks desperate to borrow and almost no one willing to lend in case they never got their money back, the real cost of borrowing cash rocketed. As officially measured by Libor, however, the cost of borrowing dollars over three months merely doubled. It still wasn't enough to reflect the much higher interest rates that banks were really paying to get funds. On 18 September, central banks around the world including the Federal Reserve, European Central Bank (ECB), Bank of Japan and Bank of England were forced to flood the money markets with cash to try and ensure banks had enough funds to start lending again. If they didn't, super-high interest rates threatened to turn the banking crisis into a depression. On the phone to Ryan Reich the next day, PJ was even more blunt.

'Well basically I came in at 5 this morning and it was Armageddon,' PJ said. 'Morgan Stanley had paid the equivalent of 27% for overnight dollars. He paid 12% for 1-month dollars. UBS had paid 11% for 2-week dollars [...] It's really fucking serious. Yesterday I had the Bank of England talking to me at 7.30 saying, "What's going on?" And I said, "You've got a real problem." Because it really felt this morning as if someone was going to go under today. It really felt bad.'

The central banks' emergency measures were extreme and unprecedented – but they still weren't enough to get the cost of cash as low as Libor said it was.

'I've got to say, Ryan, that Libors are still fucked, mate,' PJ said.

'They're still flat?' Ryan asked.

'Fucked. Fucked and flat [...] It's just such bollocks [...] people will start talking about me, though, because I'm gonna be so far above everyone else. But I'm right. They're wrong. It's as simple as that [...] there are no offers out there.'

On Wednesday 8 October 2008, the UK prime minister, Gordon Brown, announced £50 billion in emergency funding to recapitalise UK banks along with two emergency lending schemes designed to ensure banks could borrow funds cheaply. The same day, six central banks including the Federal Reserve, the ECB, the Bank of England and the banks of Canada, Sweden and Switzerland launched a co-ordinated cut in official interest rates. Brown had become prime minister just before the credit crunch hit in 2007 and was desperate to see that the Treasury's £50 billion had had an effect, reducing the cost of borrowing for millions of consumers. But to Brown's dismay, the real cost of borrowing, shown by the Libor average, wasn't coming down any time soon. The £50 billion seemed to have achieved nothing. On 9 October, far from celebrating an unprecedented government injection of cash, share prices tanked and Libor rose. The scale of the intervention had spooked the markets, forcing traders in company shares to recognise how bad the crisis had become.

At the Bank of England, Paul Tucker and another senior director, Mike Cross, were sent a round-up of market intelligence.[1] Other banks were angry that Barclays hadn't cut the interest rate it was bidding to borrow dollars – 6.25%. With Barclays paying that much, it was going to snap up any money on offer, making it hard for any other bank to get the funds at the lower rates they were putting in. Having seen little sign yet that it was getting any cheaper to borrow money, PJ was still trying to reflect the true cost of borrowing dollars. That meant the interest rate he submitted was anything from 40 to 70 basis points (0.4%–0.7%) higher than any other banks – a huge and noticeable difference.

On Friday 10 October, the BBC reported on an early morning radio programme that Gordon Brown regularly tuned into, Radio 5 Live's *Wake*

Up to Money, that the markets had reacted badly to his unprecedented intervention. With Libor higher, it looked like the medicine wasn't working – at least, not yet. A listener texted the programme suggesting the solution could be to put central banks in charge of setting Libor interest rates.[2] Later that day, finance ministers from the G7 group of advanced industrialised nations flew to Washington alongside Treasury officials and bankers.[3] Even as they travelled, markets around the world were in a full-blown panic, with share prices plummeting, wiping $2.7 trillion off the market value of the world's listed companies. The following day, Gordon Brown travelled to Paris for a hastily convened meeting with European leaders. Brown was now on a mission to get governments and central banks across the globe to take co-ordinated action to tackle the crisis.

The central banks had already co-ordinated cuts in their official rates. Now they'd act together to get real borrowing rates down. At a brainstorming event at the Peterson Institute in Washington, the ECB told an audience of bankers and regulators that it would be doing everything in its power to get rates down in Euribor, the equivalent of Libor for euros. Yet even as the powerbrokers discussed how to get real interest rates lower, PJ was telling an official at the Federal Reserve that Libor was already too low. 'I can tell you that I'm putting levels in that I'm not sure I could trade or not, but I know they're more realistic than anyone else's,' he warned the official.[4] Once again, PJ was telling a central bank that Libor rates were false and once again, no one did anything about it.

On Sunday 12 October, after talks between Gordon Brown, the German chancellor Angela Merkel, the French president Nicolas Sarkozy, the European Union (EU) president José Manuel Barroso and the ECB president Jean-Claude Trichet, Brown urged the EU to adopt a plan like his to recapitalise their banks and pull the world back from the brink of a financial meltdown that might turn into something even worse. Calling for a more co-ordinated response to the credit crisis, he said, 'We are seeing, in addition to the national action we are taking, that these global problems need global solutions.' German Chancellor Angela Merkel called for a 'co-ordinated common procedure for the eurozone that enables us in the next few days to take national steps to stabilise the financial market'. Barroso said, 'It is very important that this response is co-ordinated and coherent,' while the French president Nicholas Sarkozy called for 'an ambitious and co-ordinated plan'.

On Monday 13 October, after an intense working weekend in Whitehall where top officials ordered takeaway balti curries as they worked around the clock, it was announced that both Lloyds TSB (which had just bought its rival HBOS a month before) and Royal Bank of Scotland (RBS) were accepting £37 billion of taxpayers' cash. In exchange, the government would take a large, controlling stake in each of them, effectively nationalising two of the UK's biggest banks. It was meant to have been three. But Barclays' chief executive John Varley had stayed away from what was later called the 'balti weekend', announcing early on 13 October that his bank would raise funds privately to recapitalise itself. Senior government officials were furious at Barclays, not at all convinced that it didn't also need to be nationalised, like the other banks, to dig it out of a hole of its own senior managers' making.

Still Libor wouldn't fall. At the top of the UK government, senior civil servants wrestled with the issue. They included Gordon Brown's principal private secretary, Jeremy Heywood, who'd also recently been appointed chief of staff at 10 Downing Street, and the second permanent secretary to the Treasury, Tom Scholar. The emergency measures were experimental and vastly expensive. No one could be sure they would work. The best sign that their £50 billion medicine was healing the real economy would be if Libor, the best measure they had of the real cost of borrowing cash, fell. So why, after all they'd done, were Libor rates staying so high? How could they get Libor to come down?

There were two possibilities. One: make money cheaper to borrow by flooding the market with cheap offers to lend from central banks at lower interest rates. They'd tried that but there was a problem. Banks had to have assets for the Bank of England to lend against – collateral, in other words, which they lacked. So far, the schemes on offer weren't working to get real interest rates to come down, as measured by Libor. The other way was simpler, if a little less legitimate: simply order the banks to put in lower rates.

PJ's boss Mark Dearlove was already coming under pressure. Soon after Brown's £50 billion emergency package, he was called by the top treasurer at RBS, John Cummins, who told him Barclays was 'spoiling it for everyone' by keeping Libor so high. He was then called to a meeting at the Bank of England with Paul Tucker, who told him Libor was causing concern and that it should be 'put down' as it was receiving attention from 'the West'.[5] That was City of London code for the UK government in Westminster, about 2 miles west of the Bank of England's City of London headquarters. Knowing everything that PJ, Pete Spence and Colin Bermingham had told him, that Libor and Euribor were already far too low to reflect the real cost of borrowing cash, he defied the Bank of England's instruction to push the rates down further and didn't pass on Tucker's instruction. But Tucker and others wouldn't stop with Dearlove. They would soon go 'over his head'.

In Downing Street and Whitehall, Heywood and Scholar turned their sights on Barclays. They had noticed that after the Bank of England cut its official rate, Barclays kept bidding for funds at 6% or more.

'Sterling 3m Libor is high because Barclays are bidding it. They are bidding 2 basis points ABOVE Libor,' Heywood wrote to Tucker on 22 October. 'This has been going on for three weeks. The day BoE [Bank of England] cut 50, Barclays continued to bid the old level (as tho rates had not been cut). A lot of speculation about what they are up to.'

'I know. But I don't think that can be all of it [...] But we are trying to monitor what's going on,' Tucker replied.

'Thanks,' wrote Heywood. 'Obviously we are v concerned that US rates are tumbling but we remain stuck!' By 'we', of course, he meant Downing Street.

The same day, Paul Tucker emailed Bob Diamond and John Varley, the group chief executive of Barclays. 'Could I talk to one or other of you about Libor pl. Sorry to bother you but I think Mark D is away. It's a slightly sensitive point.' Diamond emailed him back at 4.27 p.m. to say he was 'calling right now'.[6] When they spoke, Tucker told Diamond he'd received calls from a number of senior figures in Whitehall to question why Barclays was always towards the top end of the Libor pricing[7] (i.e. at the top end of the sixteen banks who'd submitted their rates). Diamond explained, as he had before, that Barclays had a policy to submit rates based on the interest rates being offered in the markets. That was why their submissions to the Libor average were towards the top.

Downing Street's question – why was Barclays' Libor rate so high? – filtered down to PJ and Pete Spence, who traded cash in sterling and set Libors for borrowing pounds. Spence was indignant, writing an email to Bob Diamond, Jerry del Missier, Mark Dearlove and others on 23 October: 'I have consistently set Libor rates as to where we could possible [sic] obtain cash. We have not deviated from that stance for the last 18 months [...] RBS and HBOS and ourselves have been paying above the Libor rate in the 3 months. Political arguments are one thing, reality will not enable me to reach the ratios[8] set by group Treasury, the Bank of England and the FSA [...] All banks are setting their rates at one level but paying another.'[9]

On Friday 24 October, PJ took a call from an official named Tania at the Federal Reserve Bank of New York, designed to gather market intelligence. He seized the opportunity to lay out the evidence of lowballing. 'Three-month [dollar] Libor is going to come in at 3.53 [...] It's a touch lower than yesterday's but please don't believe it. It's absolute rubbish [...] I'm putting my Libor at 4% and I can tell you I've just gone through three money brokers in London: Prebon, Icap and Tradition. Prebon have no offers at all in the market [...] Icap have no offers. When I said, "Where can I get money if I wanted it?" they said "4.5" [...] I think the problem is that the market so desperately wants Libors down it's actually putting wrong rates in.'

'Uh-huh.'

PJ told the official there'd been a new development. At a time when no other banks were lending dollars, the dollar cash trader at Chase New York had come into the market the previous day, telling the money brokers PJ spoke to all day that he was prepared to lend at 4% – far lower than the 4.53% he might have collected if he'd lent dollars via the foreign exchange markets. 'But basically what I'm saying is, ah, maybe this market shouldn't be setting Libor at 3.5 but at 4.5.'

Unsure if his point was getting through, PJ decided to be even clearer. 'I have to say, dollar Libors are incorrect and they're too low ... Much too low.'

'Why?' asked the puzzled official.

'I'd love to know. I really would love to know [...] Recently you've had certain banks who I know have been paying 25 basis points over where they've set their Libors [...] I think people are afraid to be seen as ... if they put a high Libor, the market automatically assumes they're paying too much. But in a perverse kind of way, if you put a low Libor, it's almost as if the market knows that you're scared to put it where you really think it is. I mean, I know that I'm consistently high, but I think I'm consistently correct.'

Sounding as if she couldn't wait to get off the phone, the official ended the call abruptly. 'Alright. Well thank you very much for your time. I appreciate it. Take care.' Clearly PJ's attempt to blow the whistle on false Libor rates to the US authorities wasn't getting through.

Three days later, on Monday 27 October at 12.17 p.m., PJ took another call from the New York Fed, where he explained to another official (identified only as 'Peggy')[10] that there were no offers. 'There is no money out there,' he told her.

'I mean in terms of the Libor settings, I mean, what are your general thoughts on them?' asked Peggy.

'Um. I can see why people are trying to push them down but don't think it's justified,' said PJ, recalling how he'd told her colleague on Friday that if he'd raised dollars through the foreign exchange markets, the only place where they were available, it would have cost him 4.5%.

'I don't know. Do you have Bloomberg up on your desk?' asked PJ.

'Yes, I do,' said Peggy.

PJ told her what to type into Bloomberg, the financial news and information service that most traders used to stay across market movements. 'Put up "FXIA" [...] If you put "Swap Period 3", "Go".'

'Okay,' said Peggy, tapping away as they spoke.

'It shows you that if you want to get money, at, er, 3-month Euro Libor, you can afford to pay up to 4.94%.'

'Oooh, wow! Okay. Oh Peter, this is great. Thank you!!'

'This is what we look at all the time and at the beginning of the year when people were saying, "Why are you setting your Libors so high?" I was saying, "Well, I know the money funds are in, but you can't take away from the fact that other currencies are prepared to pay way over Libor to get money in." [...] Because they look at all this and say, "Right, okay. Well if I go and give 3-month Euros, I'll have myself a dollar asset at 4.94." And so, this is what we look at all the time. So you can see that ...'

'That's great,' said Peggy. 'Okay. Thank you so much.'

PJ had shown the New York Fed the exact page on Bloomberg that proved that banks were lowballing; but preoccupied with managing the wider crisis, it took no action. No reports of suspicious activity were filed. On 26 October and again on 28 October, Heywood emailed Paul Tucker and Tom Scholar, wanting to find a way to speed up the fall in Libor.

On Wednesday 29 October, the weather was unseasonably cold. London was quilted with snow from the previous day, the first to settle on the ground in the month of October since 1934. Looking out from the offices of Bob Diamond, Chris Lucas and John Varley on the thirty-first floor of Barclays' headquarters, the neighbouring skyscrapers of Canary Wharf were obscured by renewed snowfall. At around 3 p.m., Bob Diamond took a call from Tucker, who repeated the same point he'd made a week before: that he'd been called by a number of senior figures in Whitehall[11] asking why Barclays' Libor rates were always towards the top. Tucker explained that he'd told them, 'You have to pay what you have to pay.' But that didn't satisfy them.

Diamond felt frustrated. He'd been talking to Tucker about this for more than a year now, repeatedly explaining why Barclays' Libor rates were high relative to the other banks. It wasn't paying more because it was desperate to borrow funds. It was because other banks were submitting rates that were artificially low – lower than where they could really borrow cash. Now Tucker was telling him that top government officials were making the same mistaken assumption that the Bloomberg journalist had made more than a year before: that it was being forced to pay higher interest rates because it was running out of money.

Diamond asked Tucker if he could tell the senior figures in Whitehall what was really going on. Not all banks were submitting Libors at the interest rates where cash was changing hands. 'Oh, that would be worse,' said Tucker. It seemed he didn't want to tell Whitehall that other banks' interest rate estimates were already too low.

Diamond tried one more time to explain that Barclays had a policy of putting in Libor submissions as close as possible to interest rates where cash was on offer in the money markets. Other banks were posting rates that were not representative of where they were doing business – lowballing. That was why Barclays' Libor rates looked high compared to those other banks. It wasn't at all because the bank was having to 'pay up' – paying higher interest rates because it was desperate for cash. But Tucker didn't back down. Shortly after putting the phone down, Diamond dictated a file note to his chief of staff, recording that 'Mr Tucker said the levels of calls he was receiving from Whitehall were "senior" and that while he was certain we did not need advice, that it did not always need to be the case that we appeared as high as we have recently.'

This was serious. Diamond and other senior executives were already under extreme pressure. They had gone to great lengths to secure the agreement of the Sheikh of Qatar to invest £6.7 billion in Barclays so it wouldn't have to take the government's money and lose its independence (and with it, the outsized bonuses). After months of preparation, Diamond had flown to the Middle East to set up the deal and it was now on the verge of being completed. But that plan could be wrecked if the government officials were misreading the situation and thought Barclays was struggling to raise funds on the money markets. The big risk was that the senior government officials Tucker had spoken to might say, 'They can't fund themselves. We need to nationalise them.'

Diamond was now worried that might happen before he could clinch the deal with the Sheikh. He had to act. His first reaction was to cross the thirty-first floor from his office to John Varley's. 'John, you have to get to Whitehall,' said Diamond. 'You have to make sure they know that we are funding fine.'[12] Next, Diamond called Jerry del Missier to tell him about the call from Tucker. Because of its Libor rates above the pack, Diamond told his old friend and colleague, the Bank of England was getting pressure from Whitehall around the bank's financial health. We should get our Libor rates down, Diamond said. 'We shouldn't be outliers.'[13]

Jerry del Missier wasn't altogether surprised. For the last two months, governments on both sides of the Atlantic had been making unprecedented interventions. The US Treasury had rescued two giant mortgage companies known as Fannie Mae and Freddie Mac, and bailed out AIG from its huge losses on defaulting US mortgages. The UK government had nationalised both RBS and a newly merged Lloyds Bank and Halifax Bank of Scotland[14] to try and stop the banking crisis turning into a depression. In normal times, the dividing line between the public and private sectors was in sharp focus. But in this crisis, it was blurry. As the government tried to cope with an emergency, Downing Street was calling the shots. Far from sensing anything inappropriate, del Missier could see this was clearly an instruction from the top of the British state that he couldn't ignore. He picked up his phone to speak to the head of the money markets desk where Libor was set, Mark Dearlove, who was on a business trip in Singapore. Jerry del Missier relayed to Dearlove what Diamond had told him, fully expecting the cash desk to take the views of the UK government and the Bank of England into account and lower its Libor rates.

After his earlier meeting with Tucker, Dearlove didn't doubt what del Missier told him. To meet the wishes of the UK government, Paul Tucker had clearly gone 'over his head' to get Barclays' Libor rates down. Dearlove made two phone calls immediately. First, he spoke to Pete Spence who set Libors in pounds sterling.[15] Then he called PJ.

This is one of many key pieces of evidence that authorities on both sides of the Atlantic have covered up (many more are yet to come), a phone call in which the UK government, the Bank of England and the Barclays directors are implicated in what is now regarded as a criminal act.

'Mate, I've been on fire tonight,' Dearlove said, clearly stressed and dreading what he was about to order PJ to do. 'The bottom line is you're going to absolutely hate this, and I've spoken to Spence about it as well, but we've had some very serious pressure from the UK government and the Bank of England about pushing our Libors lower.'

'Can I have the pricing from them?'

'Ah, well it's on record and I think what you need to do is to put an email out to me or whatever saying that, "I hear what you say and I will, ah, you know, as requested I'll push my Libors down lower [...] blah, blah, blah." Okay.'

'So I'll push them below a realistic level of where I think I can get money?'

'Absolutely. I think – you know, PJ, I'm completely 100 per cent on your side on this. But the fact of the matter is we've got the Bank of England, all sorts of people involved in the whole thing.'

'Why don't they fix the problem?'

'PJ, I'm on your side, 100 per cent. These guys don't see it. They're bent out of shape. They're calling everybody from Diamond to Varley [John Varley, Barclays' chief executive] to Jerry [del Missier].'

'Well, Colin's just told us he's going to be getting a call from the ECB telling him to put his Libors lower as well,' said PJ.

'Well forget the ECB, I'm not worried about what the ECB says. But if they call our senior management, you know, we understand that. You and I and Pete Spence and everyone agree that it's the wrong thing to do [...] but I think the thing to do is to go into the pack, to see if we can help the money markets improve by creating a virtuous circle by keeping our Libors lower, or within the pack [...] Please, please send me the email Pete, because it's important that I pass on to these guys. I am as reluctant as you are. I've had several of these conversations already and these guys have just turned around and said, "Just do it".'

'Okay, so when all the sales force, who've been reading all my comments [...] about where money really is coming and where I'm happy to set my Libors because I'm confident I'm right – when they say, "So PJ, why have you suddenly set your Libor 50 basis points lower?" What am I meant to say?'

'I think that you're supposed to say things like – and this is all bullshit – like, you know, "the CPFF[16] has provided liquidity in the market"; that it's helped out. I think that, "the dollar TAFFs have come into ..." You know. It's all of that sort of crap.'

'I think I'll just say, "No comment."'

'Okay. Fair enough.'

'I'm not going to lie.'

'Okay, that's fine. I'm just telling you what the "out" can be. You and I are on the same page. I've had the argument as well, as you've said, and the bottom line is I'm being told to do something different.'

At this point, PJ couldn't help expressing his feelings: 'Unbelievable!'

'And what I would say, Pete, is the following: let's hope and let's try to create a virtuous circle where Libors go lower. But if they don't, in three [or] four days or [a] week's time, let's go back and challenge Jerry, Bob Diamond, all of those guys and say, go back to the Bank of England and say, "You guys are full of shit."'

'Well, you know, it's not a question of getting Libors lower [...] It's a question of making money come lower.'

'Yeah, I know, I know.'

'Because I can set Libors at 1% if you want me to.'

Dearlove sighed. 'No, no, no. You don't need to do that. Just come in within the pack.' He told PJ he'd spoken to Pete Spence about five minutes before he'd called PJ and Spence had agreed to get 'within the pack' over the following three or four days.

'I'm gonna get to the top of the pack. I'm not going any lower than that. How about that? Is that fair enough?'

'Yeah, yeah, yeah, yeah, okay. That's fair enough. Absolutely. Okay mate, I'm sorry. You know this is ... No I'm pissed already I'm going back to my hotel. As the Americans say, "I'm pissed off". Okay?'

'I'm pissed!' said PJ in a mock American accent.

Both PJ and Pete Spence, who was at a colleague's retirement do at a restaurant in Islington, started writing emails, copying in their immediate bosses and vehemently protesting that they disagreed with the instruction; that it was out of line with the BBA's definition and that they wouldn't be submitting honest Libor rates. When PJ got a call five minutes later from a colleague he spoke to every day in New York, Rick Frisbee, he was still reeling from the shock. 'I just had a call from Mark. I think Diamond's had a call from the Bank of England. We are to put our Libors lower.'

'Oh, really?'

'Yeah. The ECB apparently is going to phone Colin to tell him – put his Libors lower. I'm sending a note to Mark saying how unhappy I am that I'm contributing unrealistic and dishonest Libors. It's going on record.'

'Okay. As you should, why not?'

'Fucking ridiculous. Erm [...] So that's that.'

'Wow ... I mean. Did they tell you – to put them where? Or just "lower"?'

'Get within the pack. So, within four days I'll be at the top of the pack. I'm not going any fucking lower than that.'

Frisbee didn't know what to say. 'Okay ... interesting ...'

'And I said, "Wouldn't it be better for them to solve the problem rather than just pretend it's solved?" You know, it's all very well putting Libors lower but if money ain't fucking coming there ... It's ridiculous.'

'Yeah, it's artificial. Perpetuating the scam, yeah. What does that solve, you know?'

'I'll copy you in. But no one's really meant to know that we are being asked.'

'Okay.'

'But I'm going to find it very difficult when people say, "Why have you brought your Libors down?" Mark said, well just talk about how the CPFF is working and everything else. I said, "No. I can't lie, Mark. I'm just going to say, 'No comment'".'

PJ finished his email to Dearlove, copying in Spence, and hit 'send' at 3.57 p.m.: 'Following on from my conversation with you, I will reluctantly, gradually and artificially get my libors in line with the rest of the contributors as requested. I disagree with this approach as you are well aware. I will be contributing rates which are nowhere near the clearing rates for unsecured cash and therefore will not be posting honest prices. I am not sure that the BBA definition of libor would accept this approach. Today for instance the only cash offer in 3 months has been Chase Nyk who is offering at 4%. Please do not tell me that 3.42% was the correct rate as we both patently know that it was not.'

Spence wrote that he would comply with the request and that it would take him a week to comply. 'But it should be noted that this will be breaking the BBA rules with regard to the setting of Sterling Libor rates (i.e. a reasonable amount offered in the market in the period concerned) and as such the breaking of such rules will happen until the instruction demanded by senior management will be rescinded or the BBA rules are changed.'

The next morning, PJ dropped his Libor estimate of the cost of borrowing dollars by no less than 60 basis points.[17] Sure enough, Barclays' Libor came in lower, but at the top of the pack, as PJ had promised. Prime Minister Gordon Brown finally got the response he wanted in return for his cash injection. Whether or not he knew it, it was taking an already fraudulent Libor to new lows.

On 6 November, the Bank of England slashed its official interest rate by 1.5 percentage points to 3%. Mark Dearlove and PJ's colleagues on the cash desk, Pete Spence and Colin Bermingham, were called to a meeting with Jerry del Missier where he reiterated the instruction that he'd passed down a week before: due to pressure from the Bank of England, they were to lower their Libor submissions. Later that day, Dearlove received a phone call from John Varley, the tall, bespectacled group chief executive who shared the thirty-first floor of Barclays' group headquarters with Chris Lucas and Bob Diamond.

'I've been summoned [...] for one of my lovely breakfasts with the Chancellor tomorrow and the other bank CEOs [...] I just wanted to get a few thoughts from you.'

Dearlove told him there was still huge illiquidity in the markets. No one, in other words, was prepared to lend cash.

'There's been a lot of criticism around where Barclays is setting its sterling Libor fixings,' Dearlove told Varley. 'We have now come very much into the pack so we're in line with all of the other banks.'

'Yeah, I mean, I had heard it from Tucker,' Varley responded.

'And I understand that that's been coming from, sort of, Downing Street?'

'Well, so he said, yeah,' said Varley.

After the meeting with the Chancellor, Alistair Darling, and Paul Myners, a leading City investor who'd been brought in as a junior Treasury minister to help tackle the crisis, Varley wrote up a note. The government urgently wanted to see Libor falling so that they could know the Bank of England's official rate cut had been passed on. They wanted to know: why hadn't the official rate cut shown up in lower Libor rates?

Varley had tried to explain. The fear stalking the markets hadn't yet gone away. Until it did, it wouldn't get much cheaper to borrow cash, regardless of what the central banks did. They could only pass on some of the official rate cut, not all of it. 'The incomprehension of ministers at the absence [of] complete flow-through into Libor of yesterday's easing was very visible,' he wrote.

On 11 November, PJ took a phone call from Miles Storey, who was sunning himself on the Greek island of Rhodes after tendering his resignation from

Barclays a few weeks before. He'd heard about the instructions to push rates down. What was going on?

'We sort of got an edict that we had to get our Libors low,' PJ told him.

'Do you know where that came from? And I'm not trying to put you on the spot, but I'm just curious because it's a bit of an invidious—'

'Well, Mark told me—'

'Right, okay.'

'And I think he'd heard from Diamond who I think had talked to Paul Tucker,' PJ said with a laugh.

It wasn't just the Bank of England, PJ told him. 'The ECB's been pushing the French banks to get their Libors lower. Just "set your Libors lower!" and they have been to a man [...] The Fed's been trying to get Libors lower by getting Chase [JPMorgan Chase] to come in [to offer to lend cash on the money markets] [...] you know, in current market conditions, without Chase there, I think I'd struggle to get anything better than 3.75, so I don't feel I'm setting a particularly truthful Libor.'

'Okay. I'm just trying to get the background on what the authorities are endeavouring to do,' said Storey. 'And whether the BBA happened to know of it. Because in a way you could say, "Well, it's all manipulation". But then again, the whole market is a managed market, isn't it?'

'I think it's a sort of virtuous circle thing,' PJ replied, 'It's sort of, "Get Libors down. That'll make the market think that things are better, so they'll start lending money." So we're getting Libors down. But the clearing levels [the level where you could actually borrow cash] don't justify the Libors.'

Storey shrugged. 'If the bigwigs right at the very top of the whole financial system want this to happen then, quote, "so be it". But—'

'If it helps you, when I was asked to do so by Mark, I sent him an email back saying I disagreed fundamentally with doing what I did because I didn't think it was being honest or depicted the truth.'

'Yeah, I saw the Spence one of that.'

'Yeah, I thought it said the same thing. I mean, I didn't send mine to Compliance. But it's filed away, mate.'

A few weeks later, soon after Paul Tucker was promoted to be the Bank of England's deputy governor, he received an email from Bob Diamond. 'Congratulations. Well done, man. I am really, really proud of you.'

'Thanks so much Bob,' Tucker replied. 'You've been an absolute brick through this.'

PJ could only sit and fume. No one seemed interested in whether Libor was honest or fraudulent. The banks were holding on, still lying through gritted teeth, hoping for a miracle, fingers crossed for bonus time. PJ thought no one had been listening to him but he was wrong. The 'shitstorm' that Dearlove had feared was coming at the end of 2007 was at last going to break. The form it would eventually take, however, would take everyone by surprise, PJ more than anyone else.

3

THE SECRET ORCHESTRA

16 April 2008. *The Wall Street Journal*'s (*WSJ*) front-page lead story read: 'Bankers Cast Doubt On Key Rate Amid Crisis'. 'One of the most important barometers of the world's financial health could be sending false signals [...] [which] suggests that banks' troubles could be worse than they're willing to admit.'

When the newspaper landed on the desk of Angela Knight, the chief executive of the British Bankers' Association (the UK banks' trade association, which ran Libor and owned the Libor brand), she knew she had to do something.[1] It was the first time anyone in the media had come so close to exposing something she had been growing ever more painfully aware of.

Libor had become a lie.

Or, as the *WSJ* more delicately put it, some banks may be 'fibbing'. They 'don't want to report the high rates they're paying for short-term loans because they don't want to tip off the market that they're desperate for cash'. The article quoted a mortgage banker saying it was 'actually kind of frightening if you really sit and think about it'.[2] If Libor was inaccurate, borrowers all around the world could be paying billions of dollars too much or too little in interest.

For Angela Knight, this spelled danger. If widespread distortions in the Libor rates were reported, she feared it could very easily and very rapidly wreck the reputation of the rates and damage the reputation of the BBA and its member banks. Especially in a credit crunch when everyone's eyes were on them. Libor was used everywhere to track the real cost of borrowing money – in dollars, in pounds, in yen. It was used as a benchmark to set interest rates on millions of mortgages and commercial loans amounting to trillions of dollars (the small print of US and UK commercial mortgages or large loans most commonly quotes an interest rate such as 'Libor + 1%', 'Libor +2%' or similar). It was also a big stream of income for the BBA, which was paid a fee by each organisation that used the Libor benchmark to price the loans, investments and other financial products they bought and sold by the billion. Knight was all too aware of the risks.[3] If its reliability kept taking a battering in the press, someone else would simply produce a rival index and rob the BBA of all that income. Yet now even the journalists were waking up to the fact that Libor was no longer anywhere near accurate.

The system depended on banks telling the truth. What counted was whether the interest rate published as Libor truly reflected the real cost of borrowing cash. The process of setting (or 'fixing') Libor went like this: each morning cash traders (like PJ) at sixteen banks answered a simple question: at what interest rate do you think you could borrow cash at 11 a.m.? They submitted their answers to two decimal points (e.g. 3.55%, 3.57%, etc.). The same process would come up with a Libor average to track the cost of borrowing cash in each currency and over different lengths of time (e.g. one month, three months, twelve months). The BBA struck off the outliers, averaged the middle eight and the resulting interest rate was 'fixed' for the day as Libor.

Going back to the 1990s, this averaging method implicitly acknowledged an in-built conflict of interest. Knowing the banks had big trading bets linked to Libor, it was obvious they would seek to influence it in their favour. But striking off the outliers meant no single bank could do much to shift the Libor average. If they tried to nudge it up or down by submitting interest rates that were too high or too low, out of line with what it would really cost them to borrow cash, it wouldn't work. They would be 'kicked out', excluded from the fix as outliers. Only if enough banks colluded together could it be effectively manipulated.

Knight, aged 56, a tall, well-spoken, privately educated politician who liked to come straight to the point, had served as a junior minister in the Conservative government in the 1990s before losing her seat in 1997 and starting a new career running trade associations. With short dark hair, several strands of pearls and an emphatic, uninterruptible way of speaking that reminded some of her listeners of Margaret Thatcher, she had taken up the job of chief executive of the BBA a year before, in April 2007. It wasn't quite what she expected. Being the public face of British banking was a job that highly paid bankers were happy to leave to a lower-paid outsider with no banking experience, especially in the crisis. When the banks were bailed out by taxpayers at vast expense, no senior banker appeared on radio or TV to apologise. Instead, it was left to her.

Angela Knight didn't have the background in banking or trading that might have made her wary of a fateful risk she was about to take. One of the dangers that traders feared most was the risk of being seen to collude to manipulate the markets. If two, three or more banks agreed to try and nudge an index like Libor up or down, it could be seen as illegal price fixing that violated basic principles of competition law. Colluders who were caught could bring fines down on their banks and might well lose their licences to trade. They could even be prosecuted for running a secret cartel.

As she read the *WSJ* article, Knight was focused on the opposite risk: that the banks wouldn't act together when they needed to. It was to lead some of the most powerful bank bosses in the world into a bigger manipulation of Libor than anything any trader has been prosecuted for. But it's been kept secret. The full story of how bank bosses collectively, repeatedly and unlaw-fully manipulated Libor has never been told before.

Knight knew on 16 April 2008 that because all the banks were lowballing, Libor was way off the mark – far lower than it needed to be to reflect the real cost of borrowing cash – especially in dollars. Ever since Barclays saw its share price plummet after PJ posted an honest Libor rate, no single bank would put its head above the parapet and tell the truth. The market would think they were being forced to 'pay up' – paying higher interest rates than others because they were desperate for funds. Their bank's share price would tank and the trader who'd posted an honest rate might have to say goodbye to their bonus and also, perhaps, their job. The only way to fix low-balling, Knight thought, was to get all the banks to act together.

A week before the *WSJ* article came out, on 9 April, her officials had told her that banks on the panel that contributed to the Libor average were clearly posting one interest rate as their Libor estimate but were then going into the market and paying a higher rate. The BBA had met the UK regulator, the Financial Services Authority, which wanted to pass on its concerns that Libor in US dollars may be subject to 'manipulation'.[4] And there'd been an article in the *Financial Times* by a former top Bank of England official, David

Rule, warning that Libor 'may not now be the best measure of short-term interest rates'.

She'd fired off an urgent memo to the board of the BBA, made up of the top-ranking bosses of the biggest banks in the City of London including chief executives and chairmen.

STRICTLY CONFIDENTIAL: MEMO
FROM: Angela Knight
TO: BBA Board
Re: CURRENT US DOLLAR BBA LIBOR RATES
Issue
The BBA is receiving increasing numbers of complaints from market participants that US dollar Libor is setting too low. A bank quoting a dollar rate is saying publicly: 'this is the rate at which I can fund myself'. If that bank then goes into the market and takes funds considerably above this rate it severely damages both the credibility of Libor and the credibility of the quoting bank itself. The BBA Libor team has been told that such mismatches between what a bank quotes and then later deals at are happening frequently and the discrepancy is often 20–30 basis points [...] If the reputation of BBA Libor is damaged, it will not do the wholesale interbank market any good and will encourage participants to look for an alternative benchmark. This may also add [to] the interbank market's dysfunctionality at the moment. If the interbank market benchmarks specifically from BBA are not representative, how can the market function?

Her memo went on to explain why lowballing was happening and why it was so hard to get any one bank to tell the truth.

To fix the problem without coordinated action between banks would require a single bank to break ranks with competitors. This is not going to happen because:

(i) if a contributor suddenly quotes a higher or 'more realistic' rate, it will immediately draw attention to itself and potentially start rumours about liquidity or solvency problems at the bank;

(ii) banks quoting BBA Libor use it as the basis for their internal and external funding rates. It might cost a bank's treasury if it increases its rates; and

(iii) when pressed, all contributors state that they currently quote accurate rates, genuinely based on their position. Rapidly changing their pattern of quoting could be seen as an admission that previous contributions were not accurate.

Angela Knight's plan was to convince the bank bosses to act together in an unprecedented collective move to raise the Libor average and bring lowballing to an end.

Recommendation
1. Coordinated action by a large number of panel banks, directed from the most senior level. Chairmen and CEOs should be apprised of the problem and request that their staff reflect the actual level of their current US dollar fixings when they contribute their rate. If we can orchestrate coordinated movement, no single bank need be out of line with the rest of the contributors.

2. If (1) does not succeed, we should consider amending our procedures to hold spot-checks on panel members to ensure they have dealt recently at – or very close – to the prices they contribute to the BBA Libor fixings at least at the headline rates. Failure to comply could result in expulsion from the panel. (There is currently no requirement for banks to deal at the prices they quote.)

Timing
We need to address this issue rapidly. Right now the reputations of BBA Libor and of the banks contributing to the fixings is being damaged.

The same day the *WSJ* article was published, 16 April, Knight was due to meet the chairmen and chief executives of the banking industry who sat on the BBA's board. Everyone from the top boss of HSBC to the chief executive of Lloyds Banking Group. Libor was on the agenda. As she read and reread the *WSJ* article, her resolve grew firmer. Something had to be done.

Someone had to take action to fix lowballing but no one else would. It was down to her.

Knight knew the banks had been lowballing almost as soon as the credit crunch began thanks to John Ewan, the BBA's Libor manager, who also first drafted her memo suggesting that the banks should 'orchestrate co-ordinated movement'.[5] Aged 32, sporting sideburns and slightly dishevelled sandy-coloured hair, Ewan had taken a degree from Bath University not in finance but biology. He had joined the bankers' trade body[6] two years earlier in 2005 after five years working at the Financial Times Stock Exchange (the firm that produces the FTSE 100 and FTSE All-Share indices that track the ups and downs of share prices on the London stock market), to take on the obscure but important-sounding title of 'Libor Manager'. At first the job seemed dull and nothing much happened. When it did, Ewan's role was almost like being a football referee. Occasionally he would take a phone call from a cash trader crying 'foul!', alleging that another bank was putting in a high or low Libor rate to try and nudge the average in their bank's favour. But it was almost always about tiny differences – a hundredth of a percentage point or two (on the money markets one hundredth of a percentage point, 0.01%, is called a 'basis point', or alternatively, simply a 'point'). He would call the bank in question, have a word with the trader's boss, asking if the rate was 'representative' of the interest rates the banks could pay that day to borrow cash. Could they prove it, for example by showing transactions where funds changed hands at that rate, or show him offers to lend at that rate? If the rate wasn't a 'true reflection', it would be corrected. A yellow card. If a phone call didn't do the trick, he would take it to the committee of bankers that ran Libor, the Foreign Exchange and Money Markets Committee (FXMMC).[7]

In the old-fashioned style of the City of London, the whole process of setting Libor each day was 'self-regulated'. The managers of the cash desks, where traders submitted their estimates of the interest rates they thought they'd have to pay to borrow cash, were also the ones who sat on the FXMMC. They were Ewan's sources of information about Libor and they were also in charge of it – older guys (there were few female traders on banks' cash desks) who knew how things worked.

Every year, Ewan would do a review, asking for the views of the banks on the panel that contributed to the Libor average (and other banks who didn't). How did they think the whole Libor-setting business was going? Some would comment that most banks were setting it commercially, adding three or four hundredths of a percentage point to the rates they were really paying to try and skim off a bit of profit (sometimes known as 'high-balling'). He was also told that banks would put in Libor submissions to suit their trading positions.[8]

Ewan took notes and passed the information on to his BBA bosses and to the team at the Bank of England that gathered intelligence on the markets, run by Bank of England executive director Paul Tucker. They were unsurprised and saw no reason to alert the regulators. No one at the Bank of England told Ewan they regarded it as improper, let alone criminal.

Ewan could have no way of knowing that, years later, his own witness testimony would be used by the Serious Fraud Office to help obtain a crucial ruling from the Court of Appeal. Following that ruling, a judge in the first trial for 'rigging' interest rates would sweepingly declare that all activity like that – any setting of Libor with commercial influence – was unlawful. And dozens of people would be prosecuted for something about which the Bank of England had been entirely relaxed.

On 9 August 2007, John Ewan's dull job started to get a little too exciting. After the decision by BNP Paribas to close its hedge funds due to losses on investments linked to defaulting US mortgages,[9] the market for banks to borrow and lend cash had seized up in fear. No bank knew how much it had lost on mortgages that borrowers couldn't afford to keep up. No bank wanted to lend money to other banks for fear that, sunk by losses on US mortgages, they wouldn't be able to pay it back.

If any commodity suddenly becomes scarce – in this case, cash – then those who most urgently need it will pay more. Its price should shoot up. The real price of borrowing cash – as measured by the Libor interest rate benchmark – should have been rocketing. But the banks didn't dare raise their Libor submissions. To do so would have been to admit how much they'd really have to pay to get hold of funds from another bank. If they did, it might look like they were desperate, sparking rumours that they were running out of cash.

The next day, 10 August, Ewan picked up a message from Clive Jones, who oversaw the cash desk at Lloyds Bank, and called him back at 10.19 a.m.

'Morning, Clive, it's John at the BBA here. Exciting times?'

'Er, yeah – interesting yes,' Jones laughed. Like many working-class boys who joined the City in the 1980s, Jones spoke with a strong east-end-of-London accent that sometimes got even stronger when he was under pressure. 'I just thought I'd give you a call cos I'm sure other people have tried to speak to you. And I just wanted to see if you had a view on Libors or if you'd heard anything or discussed anything with the Bank of England – the reason being is that obviously under the definition, as you know, it's where we can take cash in good size on or about 11 o'clock.[10] Now, right now there's nothing out there.'

With the credit crunch biting hard, banks were waking up to the fact that they'd lost vast sums on defaulting mortgages in the USA. But they had little idea exactly how much. Until they could work that out – something which would take months – they were hoarding cash. No bank dared to lend to other banks in case the bank borrowing the money, sunk by losses on investments linked to US mortgages,[11] was about to go bust. The fear was that if they did lend, they might never get their money back. Not a single commercial bank was lending. If a bank needed cash urgently, the only lender in the market was the Bank of England, through its emergency facility designed to help banks cover a temporary shortage of cash at the end of the day (known as the 'discount window'). The Bank of England offered to lend cash at a rate that was deliberately kept high enough, in normal times, to put banks off. Right now, its rate was 6.75%.

'So you could make a case,' Jones went on, 'for saying, "Well, now the only place where I could get money is by going down the window at the end of the day. So 6.75 is the Libor for all of them." Which isn't really the right thing to do, but equally if there isn't an offer, "where do you want the Libor set?" would be the question [...] Now I'm not really directly asking you that cos you couldn't say to us.'

Ewan knew what Jones meant. It was supposed to be a market rate – based on offers from other banks to lend hundreds of millions in cash at whatever interest rate they chose. It should be Jones, who saw those offers on his screen, telling Ewan what the rates should be. Not the other way round. But with no offers on the market, who could guess what the price was? The banks were like greengrocers who'd run out of apples and couldn't get hold of them at any price. Yet each day they had to state, truthfully, the price of no apples.

'So anyone who sets a Libor, it's not really based on the true definition cos there isn't an offer. Does that make sense?' Jones continued.

'Okay. Absolutely,' said Ewan.

'So Libors realistically should be significantly higher than they were yesterday.'

'Yeah, and they came up a long way yesterday but it wasn't reflective [of the cost of borrowing] was it?'

'No.' Jones asked if Ewan had spoken to the Bank of England about it. He hadn't. 'The point of my call is that at the end of the day we can set something where we think it should be but it's not consistent with the definition. And if things are being set like that, I think you should be aware of it and the fact that that is the situation – it should be consciously discussed between your guys there. Which to be fair is what you're going to do. Does that make sense?'

'Absolutely.'

Ewan called some other members of the FXMMC. If there was no cash on offer, the answer came back, they could base their Libor submissions on how much it might cost to borrow funds on other markets – like the foreign exchange markets. He called Jones again to pass that on. 'I guess, like, different banks will have different views and different ways of dealing with it at the moment,' Ewan offered, trying to be helpful.

'Yeah, don't get me wrong, we've probably put in something 5 or 10 points higher than yesterday. But realistically that's not real,' Jones came back. 'If you get challenged on that, you can't say, "That's where that bank could raise money," because we couldn't.'[12]

This was serious. Jones's own bank, Lloyds, had raised its estimate of the cost of borrowing cash by 5 to 10 points. But it was still far too low. Jones was telling the BBA that Lloyds was posting a false Libor rate – and warning that everyone else was, too.

The conversation between Jones and Ewan, recorded automatically (like all calls from banks' trading desks and from John Ewan's line at the BBA), was the first of many where the BBA was told that in the credit crunch, Libor was false. It was out of line with the definition that said it should be based on the real cost of borrowing cash from another bank.

Neither Ewan nor Jones could have had any idea of what would unfold in years to come. Ewan would become the star witness for the prosecution, supporting the SFO's case that it was unlawful to ignore the definition when setting Libor. Again and again, in criminal trials, he would testify that Libor should only be based on the cost of borrowing cash between the banks, in line with the definition. Yet here was Ewan, years before that, being told by Clive Jones, who sat on the FXMMC that ran Libor, that *anyone* setting Libor must be breaking that definition. The interest rates banks were putting into the Libor average, supposed to be a truthful reflection of what they'd have to pay to borrow cash, were simply being made up. They had to be, because there were no cash offers out there to base them on. And all the banks were doing the same thing: making up rates that were far too low to reflect what it was really costing to borrow cash. Ewan knew it didn't sound good. But he felt no impulse to pick up the phone to the police and alert them that the law was being broken. What was legal or illegal wasn't set out in any rules and Libor was unregulated. There was no law about Libor.

If Ewan didn't alert the Bank of England, someone else did. Five days after Jones warned Ewan all banks were lowballing, one of the top bosses at his bank, Mark Preston, was called to a meeting at the Bank of England, along with Jerry del Missier from Barclays, HSBC's top boss Stuart Gulliver, and senior directors Brian Crowe of RBS and Lindsay Mackay of HBOS. Paul Tucker was their host. The next day Preston sent a confidential email to a select few senior colleagues:

'Please only distribute on a strictly controlled basis,' he wrote. 'BoE [Bank of England] made it abundantly clear that if any details of our ongoing bank to bank discussions got into the press or the public domain, it would be us and not them who regretted it!'

The email went on: 'We (the banks) agreed that current Libors do not reflect where we can borrow decent size, and as such there was a case for us fixing Libors considerably higher (6.75% was referenced across the curve)'.

Following the meeting, the Libor average rose as banks sharply hiked their estimates of the cost of borrowing pounds sterling over three months. On 16 August, Lloyds and HBOS raised their submissions by 20 basis points; Barclays by 22 points; HSBC by 23 points and RBS by 25 points. After further hikes the following day, they were at, or close to, the target rate of 6.75%.

The email showed that Paul Tucker at the Bank of England and senior bankers at the biggest British banks knew that Libor was false from the start of the credit crunch. They also knew all banks were lowballing as soon as the credit crunch began. It was also evidence that senior bankers at some of the biggest commercial banks in London were colluding together to move

Libor with the blessing and at the urging of the Bank of England, starting in the middle of August 2007.

No juror in the later criminal trials of traders for Libor rigging was to see this email, or hear Ewan's conversation with Jones. Nor was it spelled out to any juror what some of the most senior bankers in the world did next, at Angela Knight's urging, following the plan drawn up by Ewan.

4

COLLUSION

To get to work every morning, John Ewan's quickest route was to catch a train from the suburbs of north London and join the hundreds of thousands of commuters pouring out of Liverpool Street station towards their offices in the City of London's square mile. A brisk walk of less than five minutes took him along one of its main arteries, Old Broad Street, past some excavated remains of a Roman wall to arrive at his workplace, Pinners Hall, a relatively modest neoclassical building four storeys tall, tucked away behind the mammoth London headquarters of Deutsche Bank. As he found his way up to the office on 16 April 2008 and spied a copy of *The Wall Street Journal*'s front page, he felt a flutter of nerves. This was going to be no ordinary day. The board of the British Bankers' Association, exclusively comprising top bank bosses, was about to hold a crunch meeting where, he hoped, lowballing would finally be tackled. It would be his job to take the minutes and be on hand with any information Angela Knight needed.

It had been Ewan, three weeks before, who first drafted the memo, suggesting the banks should 'orchestrate co-ordinated movement'.[1] Those were his words. But Ewan himself had first heard the idea that banks might collectively agree to raise their Libor rates from someone older and wiser who sat on the committee that ran Libor, a middle-aged senior banker from the north of England with decades of experience who'd always picked up Ewan's calls. He'd also been on the BBA's Libor committee years before Ewan arrived, even helping to write the definitions. It was the same senior banker, in fact, who'd passed on instructions to PJ from Barclays' top bosses forbidding him from setting a more honest Libor rate: Barclays head of group balance sheet management, Miles Storey.

But Ewan had only partially remembered what Storey's suggestion was. When he drafted the memo, he'd forgotten a crucial warning that went with it. That innocent lapse of memory was soon to lead some of the most powerful bankers in the world to take part in the kind of activity that would later be ruled to be against the law: conspiring to manipulate the Libor average for commercial reasons. What they would secretly arrange to do was very similar to what traders, accused of taking part in a criminal fraud conspiracy, would later be prosecuted and jailed for. But there was one crucial difference. It was on a much larger scale.

In the weeks and months before Angela Knight sent her 'Strictly Confidential' memo to the bank bosses on the BBA's board, John Ewan had been coming under growing pressure to get the BBA to fix lowballing before the situation spun out of control.

Storey got in touch with Ewan on Monday 3 September 2007, two days after Paul Tucker's instruction to del Missier that Barclays should lower its Libor rates (see pages 14–16 and 126–7). Early that morning, Barclays' group treasurer Jonathan Stone and Mark Dearlove had discussed how other banks were again posting spurious, low Libor rates. Dearlove and Lucas discussed it at a meeting on the thirty-first floor and later updated the Barclays Group Treasury committee, on which Lucas, Storey and Stone all sat. The real cost of borrowing funds on the market was rising but other banks were pretending it was still cheap. There was, apparently, no inflation in the price of no apples. Jon Stone understood from that meeting that there was a range of rates banks were posting – and that the thirty-first floor wanted Barclays to be at the bottom of it, not standing out at the top. Lucas was taking charge of the issue. Stone would convey his views to cash traders like PJ via Storey and Dearlove.

In passing on those instructions, both Miles Storey and Mark Dearlove knew that they were in effect ordering PJ to post false Libor rates against his protests. But they also knew that the top bosses above them thought that telling the truth by posting higher, more realistic rates was not worth it. Barclays would stand out from the crowd and its shares might bomb. And there was another small matter: the Bank of England didn't want it.

'Everyone else is keeping their head down and posting Libors that are so low it's ridiculous,' Storey confided to Dearlove. 'The trouble is, we look like complete sour grapes [...] if we say, well everybody else is posting too low.'

It wasn't sour grapes but the truth. The only way PJ could ever post higher, more accurate rates without his senior managers objecting was if he didn't stand out too much from the 'pack'. The other banks in the pack had to be stopped from lowballing and forced to raise rates to a more accurate level, and Barclays alone couldn't make that happen. But perhaps a trade body like the BBA could. After all, it owned the Libor index. Storey was tasked with contacting the BBA to expose the other banks' lowballing and try to get the trade body to do something. After talking to Dearlove he called John Ewan, who then wrote an urgent email to Angela Knight warning that all banks were posting rates based not on the cost of borrowing cash. 'This runs contrary to the definition of BBA Libor, which insists that rates are based on the interbank [cash] market. It is a dirty little secret that this is not always the case.'

Knight responded within minutes. 'This all looks a bit problematic. Convening the committee a necessity. Thanks, Angela.'

Later that week, the Foreign Exchange and Money Markets Committee that ran Libor met. From Barclays, Jerry del Missier and Bob Diamond also met Paul Tucker at the Bank of England. But no action was taken.

As the autumn weather grew cooler, Ewan started receiving a flurry of emails warning that lowballing was again getting worse. The Bank of England was hearing the same. Because the BBA knew that was happening and hadn't stopped it, it stood at risk of being seen to condone a huge fraud.

From Barclays' headquarters in Churchill Place, Canary Wharf, on 29 November, Storey took part in an emergency conference call with Mark Dearlove, Jonathan Stone, PJ and Colin Bermingham (see pages 18–19) where Dearlove told PJ that putting in a higher, more accurate rate would cause a 'shitstorm' and instructed him to lowball. Immediately after that, at 1.55 p.m., Storey picked up the phone:

'BBA, John Ewan speaking.'

'Hi, it's Miles from Barclays.'

'Hello! How are you?'

'Oh, interesting times as the Chinese would say.'

Ewan laughed. 'May you live in them, yeah.'

'Indeed. Umm, good old Libors [...] Umm, I know we've talked about this, you know, and where people are setting them versus the reality of prices in the market.'

'Yep.'

'I think this is getting... It's sort of raising its head again.'

'Umm-hmm.'

Storey picked out an example: the interest rates banks were claiming they would pay to borrow a large amount in dollars over a month. 'On the dollar 1-month, for instance.'

'Yep.'

'I think the highest setting today was, uh, five thirty [5.30%]. It's actually trading in the market at forty, fifty and sixty [5.40%, 5.50% and 5.60%]. And there are some people putting in settings of fifteen [5.15%].'

'Right [...].'

'But, you know, the divergence between where people are posting them for whatever reason and where they're actually trading [...] is beginning to sort of creep out of the woodwork [...] Well, the next question is what do you do,' Storey said.

'I am starting to, I must admit I am starting to hear this more often,' said Ewan.

'At the risk of being too emotive, manipulation, for whatever reason, is going to come out [...] I – I'm not going to say whether I think manipulation is or isn't going on, because I think that's far too difficult to point that out, but I do believe that Libors are being set lower than they ought to be.'

'Umm-hmm.'

'Because in the aggregate, banks are afraid to stick their heads above the parapet and post higher numbers because of what happened to us when we did. You get shot at. "Barclays has got a problem because it's posting higher Libors than anybody else." And that having happened, I think people are reluctant to post higher; and because no one will get out of the pack, the pack sort of stays low.'

Ewan let out a sigh.

'Now there's no way on earth,' Storey went on, 'that we as banks should go and talk to each other for instance and say, "Well, I'll set it ten higher if you do—"'

'Umm, hmm.'

'—because that's just as bad the other way round. Um. But – we had quite a long conversation with our money markets guys this morning before we decided where to set our dollar Libors. And dollars is the one that is most accentuated [...] That's where it's coming to a head.'

'I mean, uh,' Ewan sighed again, 'I'd like to head this off before it becomes an issue [...] I'm quite happy, for example, to write to all contributors but, I mean, it's very difficult for me – and there's no precedent of the BBA having done this – for saying "Oi, you lot!"'

'Yeah,' said Storey. 'I think [...] something from you guys ... But you know, the thing about this is: where is the enforcement of governance? And the answer is, there isn't any.'

The only way to enforce the rules, Storey told Ewan, might be to threaten to remove misbehaving banks from the BBA's panel of sixteen who contributed to the Libor average. 'I can't really see how we're going to enforce it unless we start to get heavy-handed and pull people. But – pulling people. I'm not sure what it would achieve.'

Another sigh from Ewan. 'Well, I mean, apart from anything else, I suspect if I did that, the first thing that would happen is that the, um, the chairman of the bank in question would drag our chief executive into his office—'

'Of course,' Storey sympathised, 'of course.'

'—and, um, give Angela a good dressing down. And then Angela would, um, tan my hide.'

Storey let out another sigh. He was asking a lot of a 32-year-old who was anxious not to annoy his boss. 'Exactly. I agree [...] But I do think [...] you need at least to be seen to be doing something [...] Longer term, if the market in and of itself decides that the rate is being manipulated – and infers manipulation from what may not be manipulation but people just being defensive and wanting to protect themselves ...'

'Mmm, yeah,' said Ewan.

Storey suddenly changed tone. 'I need to go, chief. I've got another call.' It was Mark Dearlove.

'So, did you have a chance to chat with the BBA or anyone like that?' Dearlove asked.

'I just literally came off the phone,' Storey replied. 'I was fairly forceful on it [...] I proposed to him, and he was receptive, that he'll have to go further up the tree, writing confidentially to all contributing banks, reminding them of what it's about and how it works and the risks.'

'Yup.'

'Now they can't say: "you're not pulling your weight and you're telling fibs".'

'Right, right.'

'But to make the point on that basis, I think it's a start.'

'Yup, yup, yup.'

'Will it change it? To be cynical, I don't think it will. And I said to him, you know, it's because we're all afraid to put our heads above the parapet and go higher.'

'Exactly.'

'So the pack of sheep are all milling around the middle, aren't they?' Storey liked to compare the lowballing banks, with their understated Libor submissions all bunched closely together, to a flock of sheep. 'Now what we really don't want to do is go down the route of, you know, three or four of us get to have some sort of conversation and say: "well I'll go 35 if you go 35".'

'Yeah, exactly right, exactly right,' Dearlove agreed.

'Because that's just as bad the other way round.'

Both Dearlove and Storey were anxious to do nothing to make matters worse. Yet the situation wasn't within their control. That qualifier they'd readily agreed to – no collusion between banks to move Libor up because that would be 'just as bad the other way round' – would be forgotten by Storey's protégé at the BBA. And the idea that banks could act together to push Libor back up to fix lowballing had already been planted in John Ewan's mind. As events developed, 'I'll go higher if you go higher' was exactly what some of the world's top bankers would soon agree to do.

A few minutes after the phone call with Storey, Ewan wrote to all members of the Foreign Exchange and Money Markets Committee that ran Libor, seeking their views. 'I am starting to receive more and more comments and queries on the levels at which rates are currently setting. These universally state that the rates are unrealistically low [...] I know that this is an issue in which Paul Tucker is interested [...].'

A week later, he had the answers back from the FXMMC members, few of whom did anything to reassure him. One answer stood out, from Jon Wood, an experienced trader who oversaw the cash desk at HSBC and, like many in the City, liked to swear for emphasis. 'There is no such thing as an accurate Libor [...] Be careful. You are treading on eggshells here [...] It's a bloody mess.'

Angela Knight, who could be direct to the point of intimidating, was now on the warpath. Ewan emailed a colleague. 'It's all going off. Angela has asked me to get in the head of Treasury for all contributor banks to give them a kicking.'

'Tin hats on then!' came the reply.

'Tin hats and plenty of spare underwear,' wrote Ewan. At the meeting, attended by Knight, Storey and twelve other senior bankers on the FXMMC, lowballing was discussed. Writing it up later, Ewan mentioned that Libor 'clearly isn't the rate at which banks lend to each other'.

But that was still what the banks' customers thought it was. They were also still relying on a false Libor benchmark to set the interest rates on outstanding loans worth trillions of dollars, as were hundreds of smaller US and European banks who, because of lowballing, were collecting repayments in dollar-denominated loans linked to Libor that were too low to cover their costs. Once again though, after the committee met, no action was taken.

Banks continued to post false, understated Libor rates throughout the winter, pretending to pay one, lower rate when submitting their Libor interest rate estimates for public consumption, but then taking up higher offers when they needed to borrow funds. But it was in the spring that it again became painfully obvious, even to those at the very top of the financial tree. In early March 2008 it emerged that Bear Stearns, the fifth biggest investment bank in the USA, was about to capsize under the weight of huge losses on investments linked to defaulting mortgages that (everyone now realised) would never be repaid. As Bear Stearns came close to running out of cash, the Federal Reserve Bank of New York was forced to step in to prevent it going bust. In renewed fear that the financial contagion was spreading, the money markets seized up. Banks, once again, were afraid of the scale of losses linked to US mortgages – too afraid to lend to each other. Central banks across the globe took co-ordinated action to offer funds to try and restore confidence. Once again, banks on the BBA's Libor panel didn't want to admit how much they'd really have to pay to get hold of cash, especially dollars.

John Ewan began receiving emails from European banks that were losing large sums.

'Look at the rates!!!' said one email to Ewan from an Italian bank. 'The only vaguely correct one is Barclays, posting the rate at which they are actually borrowing in the market!! [...] We are getting stuffed on the Libor fixed loans.'

'The real reason for low-ball rates is the huge tabloid exposure they risk getting,' said another. 'Like "Madonna Drunk at the Hippodrome" – next page, "Lloyds in Funding Difficulties".'

On 27 March, Ewan drafted a memo, marked 'Strictly Confidential' and addressed to Angela Knight and the BBA's Wholesale and Regulation team, that would later be redrafted to become Angela Knight's memo to bank bosses. Drawing on his conversations with Miles Storey, it set out a 'carrot and stick' approach to moving Libors up to where they should be. The carrot? 'If we can orchestrate co-ordinated movement, no one bank need be out of line with the rest.' The stick? The BBA would ask banks for proof they had actually borrowed money at the prices they claimed. If they couldn't produce that, they could be booted off the sixteen-bank panel, which (Ewan was assuming) would be highly embarrassing and very damaging to a bank's reputation.[2] On 28 March, he emailed to seek advice from a senior BBA colleague who'd previously done Ewan's job – an amiable former banker in his fifties with longish grey hair and a mischievous sense of humour named Alex Merriman. 'We need to act rapidly,' Ewan said. He wanted Merriman's advice but 'as this is extremely delicate reputationally, I'd rather not email the paper to you'.

On 3 April, Ewan and Storey attended a meeting at the Bank of England's Money Market Liaison Group, a committee of commercial bankers and central bankers that met regularly to discuss what was happening on the money markets, normally chaired by Paul Tucker but this time by his colleague Mike Cross, who listened as the bankers told him that it was difficult to submit accurate Libor rates when there was so little cash changing hands. In particular, the committee heard, 'US dollar Libor rates had at times appeared lower than actual traded interbank rates.'[3] Once again, the Bank of England was being warned of lowballing. Storey warned senior Bank executive Mike Cross he suspected traders were setting Libors with a direction from credit managers or liquidity managers. As a liquidity manager who had directed PJ to lowball, he was in a position to know. Storey was telling the Bank of England that senior managers like him, taking care of their banks' commercial interests (like its loan book or its cash position), were telling Libor submitters such as PJ what Libor rate to put in. Years later this would retrospectively be declared unlawful by a judge in the trials of traders for rigging rates. At the time, though, Cross felt no need to call the police.

A week later, Citibank published an analyst's note titled, 'Is Libor broken?' 'Libor at times no longer represents the level at which banks extend loans to others. We believe that Libor may understate actual interbank lending costs by 20–30 basis points,' the note declared. The public noise about lowballing was growing louder and the authorities on both sides of the Atlantic were starting to take notice.

On 11 April at 9.42 a.m. Eastern time (2.42 p.m. in London), a senior financial economist at the Federal Reserve, Fabiola Ravazzolo, phoned a reliable source on the money markets, someone she knew she could rely on to tell her the truth about Libor and Euribor. Back in August 2007, it had been Ravazzolo who'd received PJ's email warning about unrealistically low Libors, forwarded by Dearlove. Now, eight months later, she called another cash trader she knew from the past. It was a gentle, soft-spoken working-class guy from the south east of England with short, spikey, greying hair who sat on Barclays' trading floor close to PJ, trading not dollars but euros: Colin Bermingham.

'We strongly feel it's true to say that dollar Libors do not reflect where the market is trading which is, you know, the same as a lot of other people have said,' Bermingham explained. 'If we as a prime bank had to go to the market to borrow cash over three months, it's probably 8 to 10 basis points above where Libor is fixing [...] in the one year it would probably be about 20 basis points [above] [...] And I'm gonna be really frank and honest with you [...].'

'No, that's why I am asking you, you know?' chuckled Ravazzolo.

'You know we went through a period where we were putting in where we really thought we would be able to borrow cash in the interbank market, and it was above where everyone else was publishing rates. And the next thing we knew there was an article in the *Financial Times* charting our Libor contributions and comparing it with other banks and inferring that this meant that we had a problem raising cash on the interbank market. And our share price went down.'

'Yes.'

'So it's never supposed to be the prerogative of a money market trader to affect their company's share value. And so we just fit in with the rest of the crowd if you like [...] So we know that we're not posting, um, an honest Libor

[...] And yet – we are doing it, because, if we didn't do it, it draws unwanted attention on ourselves.'

Bermingham explained that without a doubt, if they'd based their Libor submissions on the interbank market for cash, they'd be posting higher. 'I mean it's true words to say we feel very, very uncomfortable with it [...] But the – the position we find ourselves in, is one where we can't really fight it.'

'I know, I know,' the Fed official said. 'You have to accept it. I understand. Despite [the fact that] it's against what you would like to do.'

'Yes.'

'I understand completely.'[4]

Colin Bermingham had alerted the world's most powerful central bank to lowballing, candidly admitting neither his bank nor any other bank was posting an 'honest rate' for borrowing dollars. The whistle had been well and truly blown. Would he have said that to the Fed if he'd believed it was criminal? Doubtful. Would Ravazzolo have said she understood the reasons completely if she'd believed she was hearing about a crime? Unlikely. Yet just like PJ, Colin Bermingham was to discover, to his great cost, that in exchange for his honesty, the US and UK authorities had a strange way of saying thank you.

Soon after Ravazzolo said goodbye to her old friend, a colleague of hers at the New York Fed's markets group circulated a briefing note to senior Fed officials, its board of governors and the US Treasury. 'Our contacts at Libor contributing banks have indicated a tendency to under-report borrowing costs in order to limit the potential for speculation about the institutions' liquidity problems,' it read. 'The data shows that over recent sessions some banks have paid as much as 10 per cent for overnight funds.' A senior official at the New York Fed, Bill Dudley (who later became its president), began to take a close interest in the Libor issue, later discussing it with Paul Tucker and Angela Knight. Both the Bank of England governor, Mervyn King, and Tim Geithner, then the president of the New York Fed and later US Treasury Secretary under President Obama, were kept informed.

On 15 April, a Fed official phoned the BBA and was reassured by Ewan's senior colleague Alex Merriman that the issue of lowballing was being discussed at its upcoming board meeting.

The same day, Prime Minister Gordon Brown met the top banks' chief executives in Downing Street for a well-publicised summit. In a newspaper article published a few days previously, Brown had gone public with a plea to banks to pass on a recent cut in the official interest rate by the Bank of England which wasn't, so far, getting through to ordinary borrowers. Newspapers reported how the interest rates banks charge each other to borrow money – a name new to the nonspecialist press known as 'Libor' – remained stubbornly high. Little did Brown know: far from being too high, Libor was already too low to reflect the real cost of borrowing money.

As Angela Knight prepared for her board meeting, the pressure had never been greater.

The directors who gathered at Pinners Hall the next day and seated themselves around the BBA's boardroom table were among the most powerful (and exorbitantly rewarded) bankers in the world. The chairman of the BBA's board, Stephen Green, was the chief executive of the global bank HSBC (he was also an ordained Anglican minister and had written a book titled *Serving God, Serving Mammon* about how you could use the financial markets not just for evil but for good). Board members present included the bosses of Deutsche Bank and Citibank in London; a future deputy chief executive of the UK's biggest bank, RBS; Dyfrig John, chief executive of HSBC in the UK; and Mike Fairey, deputy chief executive of Lloyds TSB. The global boss of Lloyds, Eric Daniels, phoned in to the meeting.

They discussed Knight's strictly confidential memo. The bankers on the board made it very clear to the BBA team attending the meeting: they did not want Knight's two key recommendations to come out in public. The minutes of the BBA's board meeting gave little away. Under item (v) on Money Markets, written up by John Ewan, were four sentences on Libor: 'All present agreed that setting accurate BBA Libors is reputationally important for contributor banks as well as the rates themselves. Board members asked for a list of members of the supervisory committee for the rates to be circulated, in confidence. In order to help quell uncertainty in the market, the BBA was asked to bring forward the scheduled annual review of BBA Libor. This will now take place on May 30th.'

But Ewan knew the bankers had secretly agreed to go much further than that. The real story of what happened that day can be revealed only because, as part of an evidence-gathering process prompted by the US authorities, the BBA handed over a large volume of emails and recorded calls from John Ewan's line. At the Libor-rigging trials of traders years later, the Serious

Fraud Office would seek to prevent that evidence being handed over in full to the defence, instead offering to disclose a 'representative sample'. When they were ordered to disclose all the documents, many of which were introduced in evidence, the journalists reporting the trial missed their significance. Assembled in a timeline, they reveal a very different story from the official version reported by the press in 2008.

Neither Knight nor Ewan was planning to tell journalists what actually happened. That was to be kept a secret to all but the closest associates of the BBA. Miles Storey had been in touch wanting to know how the meeting went. At 5.26 p.m., John Ewan called him.[5]

'Hello, Miles, how are you?'

'Guess ... Quiet, relaxed and calm.'

'That's very much how I find myself as well today,' said Ewan brightly.

'Exactly.'

'You've seen, I take it, the Bloomberg story?'

'Yeah, there's the Bloomberg and there's the *Wall Street*, but I've also had Angela's board memo forwarded to me as well because Hoffman's on the board [Gary Hoffman, vice-chairman of Barclays]. So – that I guess is your internal document from which the stories have emanated in one way or another?'

Ewan hastened to correct him. 'No, that's not the case, that's – that – that document has not gone anywhere outside of the BBA or the board [...] I mean actually ... Frankly my worst nightmare is that internal document.'

'Yeah, sure, no, yeah, I know, I appreciate that,' Storey sought to calm Ewan. 'And I'm not, I'm in no way commenting or accusing you guys of anything. I just wanted the clarity [...].'

'I mean we have a short-term reputation management issue that we will do our best to handle but I mean, as we all know, there is an issue with dollar Libors,' said Ewan.

'Yeah.'

'And the board agreed that needs to be addressed.'

Storey asked what had been discussed and what conclusions arrived at.

'Hmm,' said Ewan. 'The – I mean, uh, the central discussion was – I mean everybody who was at the Board recognised, you know, that this was an issue.'

'Mm-hmm.'

'And I think there was a recognition that this is one that is best dealt with quietly and, er, it needs to be dealt with at a high level. And so the board members were going to have a word with, um, the people who do, um, sort of quote the rates [...] So the idea is – try and investigate if there is anything that makes dollars unique or, and if that's not the case, see if we can gradually float the dollar rate slightly, gently, er – up.'

Storey took a deep breath. He was both hopeful and worried. Hopeful that if enough banks on the board had agreed to move Libor up, it could cure lowballing. But worried that if all the top banks had agreed to move the dollar Libor rate up, as he'd warned Ewan months before, that could be 'just as bad the other way round'. Illegal collusion to fix the price of borrowing dollars.

'Observations on that one [...] Who are the banks that are on the board?' Ewan told Storey most of them: HSBC, Deutsche Bank, Citigroup, Alliance and Leicester, HBOS, Bradford & Bingley, Lloyds, Standard Chartered. RBS also attended.[6] Eight of the board members attending the meeting were also on the panel that set dollar Libor – easily enough to move the average.

'OK [...] Do we have to be careful about quote "collusion", unquote?'

Now it was Ewan's turn for a sharp intake of breath. 'Uh, ye – uhhh – yeah ...'

Storey wanted to know – what steps had Ewan taken to prevent BBA board members being caught up in collusion? 'So my suggestion would be some sort of conversation with real practitioners, rather than whoever the board members are, about what the issues are [...] How will an HSBC, or an Abbey or an HBOS deal with it, given your suggestion was people would sort of go out and sort of have quiet words and comments and some sort of strategy would be arrived at? What mechanism, if any, did we think was going to be in place for that strategy to be "pulled together" – irrespective of my comments about things like collusion?'

Ewan sounded tense. 'Uh – didn't get that far.'

As Storey and Ewan spoke, news agencies were reporting that Libor had jumped by 10 basis points because of the BBA's warning that misbehaving banks could be 'thrown out of the pond' (meaning the panel of sixteen Libor contributing banks). No one had told the press what Ewan had just told Storey – that the board members were going to 'have a word' with the people who quote the rates (like PJ) to float the dollar Libor rate up.

'So one of the sort of silver linings to the cloud of the news story,' said Storey, 'is [that] it may serve our purpose a bit, to a degree anyway [...] if we see a little bit of Libor going up [...] So I would suggest that's a small positive and also without people quote "colluding" or whatever.'

'Hm,' said Ewan, sounding a little unsettled. 'Hmmm ...'

Storey was trying to find a way to avoid the members of the BBA's board being seen to act in concert to raise Libors, which could put them in the frame as what is known in competition law as a 'concert party' – an illegal price-fixing cartel. If the board members had been made aware of the issue in general, Storey explained, then Ewan could raise evidence of lowballing to the Libor submitters or their supervisors down the ranks, one by one. That might prevent a scenario, 'just as bad the other way round', where all the banks were fixing their Libor rates on instructions from their chief executives.

'Yeah, um—' Ewan was trying to come in.

'Not an easy thing to do. But that would get round the sort of collusion bit—'

'Sure, sure.' There was something Ewan needed to tell Storey.

'Just one piece, on each day, for each institution, including ourselves [Barclays],' Storey continued. 'Now you know where we [Barclays] have been historically and as far as we're concerned we're clean, but we're dirty-clean rather than clean-clean—'

'No one's clean-clean now, are they Miles?'

'No, because of the very fact of what happened to us. We were clean and it – the market, you know, the newswires, the market reacted accordingly. That's why we stepped away again,' Storey said, returning to his suggestions for how to avoid collusion. 'If you pick on the eight people who are board members, you find evidence of each one of those eight not doing it right and then [...] the soft conversation is with the board member.'

'Mm-hmm.'

'And I would suggest that you utilise the board member rather than a chairman/CEO approach.'

There was a long pause. 'Um ... sure,' said Ewan. 'In most cases, um ...'

'If they're one and the same ...'

'They're one and the same.'

Storey was stopped in his tracks, flummoxed. There was no way round it now.

'Um. OK. I wasn't aware it was at that level.'

'Yeah.'

'In that case, erm,' Storey stumbled, '... I didn't know it was all at that – that level ... so I apologise for that.'

'No, that's OK.'

'In that case, effectively – you, you know a co-ordinated thing through a CEO, a CEO or chairman bit. You know, the co-ordinated bit makes me nervous.'

No longer quiet, relaxed and calm, Ewan told Storey he'd need to think about what he'd said and talk to people within the BBA, then get back to him. It didn't at all sound good. For now, though, he could at least console himself that Libor was at last rising to more realistic levels. And at the very least, his boss Angela Knight was pleased.

The next morning, as the Libor submitters prepared to put in their latest estimates for how much it would cost their banks to borrow cash, Ewan was taking calls from banks angry about a report on Bloomberg, quoting a BBA colleague who'd said the BBA could throw banks off the Libor contributors' panel if they were caught quoting false rates. One was Clive Jones from Lloyds, who'd told Ewan eight months before that his bank's Libor quotes weren't real. Ewan hastily explained to Jones that the BBA had been 'quite extravagantly misquoted'. 'We are not in any way looking to try and conduct a witch hunt or interrogate panel members about their behaviour [...].'

'That quotation probably moved the market 10, 15 basis points yesterday. That's scandalous really, innit?' said Jones.

'Yes, it's not okay,' agreed Ewan. He didn't mention that the BBA board members had agreed to 'have a word' with their cash traders who quoted the Libor rates.

Fifteen minutes later at 9.31 a.m., Jones picked up a message to call his counterpart at HSBC, Jon Wood, who sat with Jones on the committee of bankers that ran Libor, the FXMMC. They knew each other socially; in fact, Wood and his colleague on the cash desk, Andy Fear, had been invited to a party at Jones's house the next Saturday. Like PJ, Jones and Wood had been annoyed for months that they couldn't post accurate rates because of the pressure not to be seen to be desperate for cash if they set their Libors above the pack. Now at last, Wood saw a chance to change that – if he could get others to agree. The phone rang.

'Clive! Hello, mate, how are you? I've got Mr Fear sat next to me. He says he's looking forward to drinking your cellar dry on Saturday.'

'Ah, right!' Jones chuckled. 'Gordon Bennett! Yeah – he can have a couple.'

'You best get down Majestic, mate,' laughed Wood, getting down to business. 'Hey mate, I want a word with you about Libors, funnily enough.' Lloyds's Libor submissions, like HSBC's, were around 2.73% – nowhere near the interest rates where cash was trading hands – much closer to 3%. 'So what I'm intent on doing is [...] posting much higher 9- and 12-month dollar Libors ...'

There was silence from Jones.

'Okay?' Wood went on, 'Probably 95 [2.95%], something like that. And it would be nice if somebody else would come to the party.'

Jones wasn't sure. If, like Ewan had just told him, the Bloomberg article was wrong, how would they justify it?

'Now I don't know whether everybody else will move or not,' said Wood. 'But that's what we're doing. And it's very justifiable. But I would rather be – if the press are going to get hold of it ...'

Jones got it. 'Oh, you don't want to move alone, that's the thing.'

'Well, you don't want to move alone. But if the press get hold of it, we say, "it's a proper fixing and this is why we did it. Everybody else is wrong". And we'd be right.'

Jones was worried. What if John Ewan put something out from the BBA denying the Bloomberg story about booting banks off the panel?

'They can't issue a denial [...] can't do anything [...] because they had the fucking – I read the board paper, mate.'

'You've done what, sorry?'

'I read the board meeting paper; I briefed our boss on the board paper. Angela Knight put a board paper up. The whole problem with this started with Angela Knight putting a resolution up saying that dollar Libor fixings were too low, people have complained and, you know, we need to do something about it. They can't issue a denial – it's fucking Item 4 on the board's agenda: "US dollar Libor fixings".'

'So which board's this? The BBA board?'

'The BBA board yesterday afternoon.'

'Ah, right. I didn't know that.'

'Yeah. So, you know, it's Angela Knight's started the fucking problem in the first place. So there's no way they'll issue a denial.'

'Right,' Jones said.

'I have their board resolution in my hand [...].'

'I'll speak to the dollar guys,' said Jones, 'and I'll give you a call back shortly.'

Less than fifteen minutes later, Jones called the HSBC cash desk to find Wood absent but the phone picked up by his colleague, Andy Fear. 'Y'know, Jon was talking to us about dollars – well, he was there with you. The boys [said], "Yeah, we can come some of the way." I don't know if we can go quite as high as he was thinking. I dunno, he was thinking 15 or 20 points. We were going to move it up – we were moving them up [by] about 10 or so; [now] we're talking about 13 or so in the 1-year?'

'OK.'

What Jones was telling the HSBC desk was that Lloyds would now raise its planned Libor submissions for borrowing dollars over twelve months by roughly 13 basis points (0.13%). Not quite as high as HSBC wanted. But higher than Lloyds had planned to before Wood called. It was exactly the sort of conversation that Miles Storey had been anxious to avoid.

After his call with Jones and the exchanges with Alex Merriman, Ewan was now worried. At 9.39 a.m., he tried calling Angela Knight, later texting her his concerns: 'Please see my text. Unwilling to put it in an email.' At 11.30 that morning, 17 April 2008, after Lloyds, HSBC, Barclays, RBS and the other banks on the panel had all put their estimates in, the Libor average for borrowing dollars over twelve months jumped by a startling 20 basis points. The 3-month rate also surged. Bloomberg published a story: 'The cost of borrowing in dollars for three months rose the most since August after the British Bankers' Association threatened yesterday to ban members that deliberately understate their borrowing costs,' it read.

But Storey had made it clear to Ewan: the 'threat' to remove banks from the panel was a toothless one. In the coming weeks, banks approached the BBA, asking to be removed. Putting in a false Libor rate each day to avoid bad publicity that might knock their banks' share price was something they could do without. But the BBA made no attempt to correct the story reported by the press: that it was the threat to remove them that had shifted dollar Libor up. It made the BBA look as if it had acted decisively. And of course, it made no mention of any agreement between the top bankers to have 'a quiet word' with the cash traders who quoted their dollar Libor rates, to orchestrate a co-ordinated upward shift in the official cost of borrowing dollars. Ewan emailed it to an amused Alex Merriman.

'Not an altogether negative story,' Merriman replied. 'Think again: we have done something positive to shake up the market, no matter what our – colluding – members think.'

Ewan panicked. 'Alex,' he emailed back. 'I think you might want to ask Richard or Dave [the BBA's IT staff] to retract and completely delete the email below. Of course your email is internal, but it would be too easy for any recipient to accidentally forward it out of the company. This sort of thing has happened to me before. I am paranoid about this, I know, but as we've seen lately, reputations can be tarnished without evidence at the moment.'

Now that she had something positive to say, Angela Knight had spent much of the afternoon briefing senior politicians including Treasury minister Yvette Cooper, and opposition Treasury spokespeople George Osborne and Vince Cable, telling them about the issues with dollar Libor and promising to review them, and that the BBA was 'acting quickly to restore stability'.

She emailed Ewan afterwards in response to his message earlier: 'John, the general point is that we have recognized an issue, informed accordingly, instigated a review and – hey, presto [...] there are competition issues I suspect ...'

But Knight's magic trick of 'orchestrating' a co-ordinated move upwards in dollar Libor didn't work for long. Just a few weeks later, the banks, once again, were lowballing. *The Wall Street Journal* and the *Financial Times* were noticing and reporting it. Worse still, the money broker ICAP was looking at publishing a rival index. The BBA's own commercial interest in 'fixing' Libor – the money it made from owning and publishing it – was, once again, in jeopardy. Knight fired off a furious follow-up memo to the bank bosses on the BBA's board.

'As you know we all discussed LIBOR at the Board meeting in April,' Knight wrote. 'Following that Board meeting, the announcement of the review and my subsequent letter to each of the contributors, the dollar Libor rate improved and by this I mean that it drifted up to a more accurate market rate. However, unfortunately it has not stayed there.'

Now, once again, brokers were telling the BBA banks were posting one rate as their Libor estimate of the cost of borrowing cash, then actually borrowing at a materially higher rate. Worse, she'd heard that banks were in contact with the broker ICAP to join a rival index they had set up.

'This fills me with concern. I was under the impression that the agreement was that we got accuracy into Libor through ensuring the rates that the contributing banks posted were accurate and on a continuous basis. I was not of the understanding that the accuracy was merely intend[ed] to last for a few days and that there was active consideration in providing an alternative[7] [...] Can I ask you again that you do what is necessary within your organization to effect appropriate rates to be set.'

The trouble for the BBA was that it wasn't supposed to be the chief executives or chairmen deciding what was the 'appropriate rate'. As a market rate, it was supposed to be set by the cash traders who could see what interest rates were being offered on the money markets, not by orders from above. And while the aim of the senior managers on the BBA's board was not to maximise the potential profit on their banks' trades, but to make Libor less inaccurate, they were still seeking to move Libor to take account of commercial interests – from the reputations of their own banks and the Libor brand to the BBA's income from it – all of which could be wrecked if lowballing went on.

In the years to come, thirty-seven traders would be prosecuted on the basis that they had requested (or agreed to make) small shifts in Libor submissions with their banks' commercial interests in mind. For them to be jailed, those requests didn't even need to have been carried out, let alone to have succeeded in moving the Libor average. Yet here was evidence that chief executives and chairmen on the BBA board whose banks contributed to the Libor panel had colluded to agree a much bigger shift in Libor. And they had done so with the BBA's commercial interest in preserving Libor, and the income that came from it, very much in mind. There was one big difference, though. In the case of the BBA, the agreement had actually succeeded in causing a huge shift in Libor.

Later in the year, on 10 October, as world leaders prepared to meet in Washington and Paris to discuss how to tackle the worsening banking crisis and civil servants summoned the bank chief executives to meet over the weekend in Whitehall, Miles Storey picked up a message from John Ewan and called him back.

'Hello, Miles, how are you?'

'Uh, I'm, uh, I'm alive,' was the glum response.

'Well, it's Friday. And it's a long weekend in the States.'

'Uh, yeah. So that just means more time for banks to fail.'

Ewan laughed. 'I've always said you're an optimist.'

'Well, you know, it's now a formally recognised risk: "Weekend Risk". Because the authorities act on the weekend.'

'Yeah, no I see what you mean actually, yeah ... Well I did hear one terrible joke from a trader which is: "This is worse than a divorce. I've lost half my net worth and I'm still married!"'

Storey laughed. '"Only half?" would be my response.'

Ewan asked him how he saw the market and the fixings. 'The interesting hint of the possibility of the chance that there might be a chink of light at the end of the tunnel, if it is a very long tunnel and a dark day,' said Storey. 'I think people are putting a lot of weight on what the G7 are or aren't gonna do.' They discussed the soaring cost of borrowing dollars and the fact that Libors weren't coming down, in spite of Gordon Brown's emergency measures announced two days before.

'So, is there much political or other rhubarb via her ladyship – like why aren't they coming off?' asked Storey, in an oblique reference to the interest taken in Libor by the Bank of England, traditionally referred to in the City of London as 'The Old Lady of Threadneedle Street'. Ewan said the nonspecialist media were again looking at Libor, including TV outlets.

'You know, whether the Libor is 4%, 5% or 6%, the fundamental point is people aren't lending money in term [i.e. for periods of longer than a week]. That's what it's fundamentally representing. We could all unilaterally drop it by 2% tomorrow and it sort of wouldn't change anything.'

'Yes.'

'But I have to admit,' said Storey, 'I have been thinking to myself, you know, if all the sixteen banks [...] got together and said, "Okay, we will slice a per cent off," even if it was, quote "fibbing", what do you think that would actually do to sentiment?'

Ewan sighed.

'Quite a lot,' said Storey. 'I mean, I'm not saying – obviously you wouldn't do it, but it would be dropped a per cent and everybody'd say, "Why?" and we'd just say, "We decided to change and move it."'

'At which point, two weeks later, we have to stop doing the quote, full stop,' interjected Ewan. 'Because everyone says, "Well, hold on, if that's the way it gets arranged, I'm sorry I don't want anything indexed to it."'

'Exactly. But you know, I was thinking about John Pierpont Morgan getting everybody in a room in a house in lower Manhattan and telling them, "You're fucking gonna do this,"' said Storey, referring to the US banker

J.P. Morgan's historic intervention to rally the market after the great stock market crash of 1929. 'You know, cos it's something that should not be dismissed out of hand in the current environment. Especially if it was in the context of: "Alright, well we're going to mark it down when some news comes out, even though there is no more money."'

'Yeah, the problem is – if that leaks, we're done for,' said Ewan.

'I know ... But then, you know what? When you say, "We're done for" ...'

'Yeah, okay ...' Ewan laughed.

'I mean, it would – you know. Do I think it's the right thing to do? No. But let's assume that everyone who contributes to Libor is a principled individual. So what's going to happen for that principled individual following the rules, to actually start cutting the Libors now?'

'Yeah, well, um, just – um, yeah, just between us,' confided Ewan, 'I mean, I was horrified at the – you know ... the ease with which I did shift the Libors when I simply spoke to, um, WestLB one time earlier this week. And you can see exactly where it happened.'

'Mm-hmm,' Storey responded, unsurprised. After a few minutes more discussing how Ewan might respond to a news inquiry, they ended the call and hung up. This time, Ewan wouldn't take forward Storey's ideas to the board of the BBA. But he had just admitted on a recorded line that, he, John Ewan, had succeeded in shifting Libor rates.

The evidence set out in this chapter has been in the possession of the US and the UK regulators and prosecuting authorities for a decade. It points to price-fixing and anti-competitive behaviour, as well as what is now regarded as unlawful manipulation of Libor by some of the world's most powerful bankers. Yet neither the US nor the UK authorities have chosen to investigate it, let alone start civil proceedings or prosecutions against the top bank bosses involved. In the later trials of traders for rate-rigging from 2015 to 2019, Angela Knight would not be required to appear as a witness for the prosecutors, the Serious Fraud Office. John Ewan, however, became their key witness, his testimony read attentively by judges as they made new law, retrospectively condemning Libor 'manipulation'. That law would be used to prosecute dozens of lower-ranking bankers, even as some bosses on the BBA's board sought to ensure that the real story, of collusion to manipulate interest rates at the top of the commercial banks, remained a closely guarded secret.

5

A POINT TO PROVE

On a bright spring morning in Washington DC, preparations were under way for the 2010 National Cherry Blossom festival, the annual celebration of the profusion of pink that decorated the capital's streets, parks and waterfronts as the weather warmed up. But for top US government official Gary Gensler, what captivated him that day wasn't sights but sounds. Sitting in his assistant's office on the ninth floor of the headquarters of the Commodity Futures Trading Commission (CFTC), on a downtown backstreet ten blocks from the White House, he huddled with members of his enforcement team around the only CD player in the building. They'd interrupted his tight schedule, insisting there was something he'd want to hear immediately: an incendiary audio recording, freshly dug up by investigators at Barclays Bank, indicating the Libor scandal went right to the top.

Gensler leaned in closer to the CD player's speakers and turned up the volume. 'The bottom line is you're going to absolutely hate this, and I've spoken to Spence about it as well, but we've had some very serious pressure from the UK government and the Bank of England about pushing our Libors lower,' said the upper-class English voice.

'So I'll push them below a realistic level of where I think I can get money?' protested his colleague.

As he listened, riveted, straining to make out the British accents, Gensler's eyes widened. His enforcement team hadn't been exaggerating. This was one of those watershed moments that come out of the blue one day and change not only your career but your life, forever. 'PJ, I'm on your side, 100 per cent. These guys don't see it. They're bent out of shape. They're calling everyone from Diamond to Varley to Jerry […] You and I agree it's the wrong thing to do […] I am as reluctant as you are. These guys have just turned around and said, "Just do it".'

If this wasn't a breakthrough, nothing was. The regulator Gensler had been appointed to run, the CFTC, was thought of as the runt of the litter of US financial watchdogs: toothless, barely capable of barking and safely ignored. There was even talk that it would be scrapped and folded into its far bigger and better-resourced elder brother, the Securities and Exchange Commission (SEC). But this tape was the kind of evidence that could be ignored by no one. This could mean the revival of the CFTC's fortunes, the start of the biggest investigation he or his colleagues had ever undertaken. Better still, it could give him a chance to turn the tables and prove his critics wrong. Feeling energised, Gensler turned to his acting head of enforcement – a tall, bespectacled New York lawyer with a salt-and-pepper beard and swept-back grey hair named Steve Obie – and told him to ramp up the Libor investigation. This was going to be big.

Describing himself jokingly as a 'short, bald Jew from Baltimore', what Gensler lacked in stature he more than made up for in energy. He let it be known that at 52, he ran marathons and climbed rockfaces for fun. Growing up in the sixties and seventies, one of five children of a businessman who sold pinball games and cigarette machines to bars around the town, he and his twin brother Robert had shown an early talent for numbers, which took them to the University of Pennsylvania's Wharton School at the age of 17. There, he'd managed to drop his weight to just 112 pounds to compete for the university rowing team as a coxswain – the aggressive little guy at the back of the boat who can steer it in exactly the direction he wants by barking orders at the much larger guys doing the rowing. The experience wouldn't go amiss regulating the banks.

Given the gravity of the wrongdoing suggested by the tape, Gensler couldn't keep it to himself. The criminal division at the US Department of Justice would love this. Their boss, Lanny Breuer, who'd become famous defending Bill Clinton at his impeachment hearings, was now under fire for being soft on Wall Street. He'd decided against prosecuting bankers who'd sold huge quantities of mortgage-backed investments, promoting them as safe, 'triple A-rated' securities, to investors all around the world.[1] The investments turned out to be worthless, costing investors hundreds of billions of dollars and triggering the credit crunch, the banking crisis and the recession that followed. His colleague in government tasked by President Obama with fixing the crisis, US Treasury secretary Tim Geithner, saw the growing calls to jail bankers for what they'd done as the 'Old Testament view'. But with so many losing their jobs and their homes, the press and the public were in no mood to forgive the banks. With Gensler's agreement, Obie picked up the phone to a colleague at the DOJ's fraud section, Robertson Park, and played him the recording down the line.

'Let's go back and challenge Jerry, Bob Diamond, all of those guys and go back to the Bank of England and say, "You guys are full of shit."'

'Holy Shit!' said Park.[2] This could make all the difference. On 26 April 2010, the fraud section of the DOJ launched a criminal investigation.

Gensler had every reason to push hard on Libor. He'd only just got the job running the CFTC after months of delay. When President Obama nominated him in February 2009, his appointment was furiously opposed by progressives on Capitol Hill. From their point of view, there were few people in Washington who more obviously personified how unhealthily close the right wing of the Democratic Party had grown to Wall Street. He'd been nominated just weeks after the global financial crisis had reached its peak and it was already clear that the mismanagement of the banks in New York and London had pitched the global economy into a calamity that was now wreaking havoc for millions of ordinary families across North America and Europe. The Great Recession was on. And Gensler, they thought, should bear a share of the blame for what Bernie Sanders called 'the greed, recklessness and illegal behaviour which have caused so much harm to the economy'.[3] A lifelong Democrat supporter, Gensler had practically grown up on Wall Street, clinching a job at the investment bank Goldman Sachs aged 21, rising to become a partner running the corporate financing arm, which had the lucrative job of minimising its clients' tax bills. He'd reportedly made $62 million before his former boss at Goldman, Robert Rubin, invited him in 1997 to join him as assistant Treasury secretary in Bill Clinton's administration. There he'd supported a key piece of legislation, the Financial Services Modernization Act, which de-regulated the banks, relaxing constraints on how big they grew and what activities they engaged in. The old restrictions on banks' lending, requiring them to set aside a substantial sum of capital in reserve for every loan they made, were loosened dramatically. As the amount banks were lending doubled and redoubled, it opened the way for a bonanza of outsized bonuses the like of which neither Wall Street nor the City of London had ever seen before. But by 2009, it was clear that the drive to 'modernise' had sown the seeds of a disaster. Deregulating the banks, the press now said with one voice, had opened a Pandora's box of irresponsible, unregulated lending led by executives who were all too aware that the more they lent, the bigger their bonuses would be. Much of the loose new money had gone into the housing market, pumping up a credit-fuelled price bubble across the Western world that burst in 2008 with catastrophic consequences: repossessions, mass unemployment and the worst recession since the 1930s.

When Barack Obama nominated Gensler to the CFTC job in February 2009, it was one blow too many for progressives like Senators Maria Cantwell and Bernie Sanders, who blocked his appointment. Their beef with Gensler wasn't just that he'd advocated policies that caused the financial crisis. He'd also been against policies that might have prevented it. Specifically, Gensler had opposed proposals to regulate a multi-trillion-dollar trade in financial contracts that had been labelled 'financial weapons of mass destruction' by the investment guru known as the 'Sage of Omaha', Warren Buffett. By 2008, that remark looked all too prophetic. They were at the heart of what financial author Michael Lewis would dub the 'Doomsday Machine' that caused the near destruction of the financial system. The weapons of mass destruction Buffett was referring to were financial contracts, once obscure but now traded on Wall Street and in the City of London in vast quantities, that went by the off-putting title of 'derivatives'. They were called that because you weren't buying or selling a real asset, like a house or a government bond or shares in the companies listed in the Dow Jones or FTSE 100. With derivatives, you could bet on the rise or fall in price of the asset the contract was 'derived' from, without actually buying the asset. You might, for example, bet on the movements of the FTSE 100, without buying the shares of the companies that made it up. Or you could bet on interest rates rising or falling, without having to borrow or lend any money.

Derivatives started as a sensible way to insure yourself against price movements that might ruin you. For centuries, farmers who'd sunk all their money into planting corn could be ruined if the market price dropped just before the corn were harvested. But since 1919 there'd been a way to insure against that risk. The farmer could go in the spring season to the new

Chicago Mercantile Exchange (CME) and strike a deal with a financier who promised to buy his corn in the autumn at a pre-agreed price. Come harvest time, if the market price of corn unexpectedly dropped below his break-even level, the farmer would avoid ruin. If, on the other hand, the market price suddenly rose, he'd miss out on the bumper profits. Instead, they'd be collected by the financier who, when the corn was delivered at the price agreed, could sell it on at the higher price in the market and make a quick profit. If, before harvest time, the financier got cold feet about the price of corn, he could sell on the insurance contract, known as a 'corn future', to another financier who was confident the price would rise. Soon, different financiers taking different views of where the corn price would go were trading the contracts every day on the CME.

Eventually, the market evolved and became decoupled from the underlying assets. There was no need for the buyer and seller to take delivery of the corn itself. They could just trade a contract whose value was derived from the corn price. If you bought lots of corn futures, you'd win if the corn price dropped. If you were the financier selling lots of them, you'd win if the price rose.

What banks and their business customers most wanted to insure against was the risk that interest rates might jump. If you, the borrower, had borrowed lots of money at a variable interest rate and were worried that rates might rise, you could buy an insurance contract known as a 'swap'. The contract would pay out if interest rates rose, covering the extra interest you'd have to pay. The more rates rose, the more the contract would pay out. It also worked the other way round. If rates fell, then whatever you saved in lower interest on your loan, you'd pay to the seller. It was designed to work out that you'd end up paying the same, no matter what happened to interest rates. Effectively, you'd have swapped a variable rate for a fixed rate. Like the corn futures, the swaps contracts were also bought and sold independently. One party to the contract would pay a fixed rate and receive a variable rate – meaning they'd be better off if interest rates rose. The other party would receive a fixed rate and pay a variable one – meaning they'd be better off if rates fell.

In the 1990s and 2000s, trading in swaps contracts mushroomed. Because most loans to businesses around the world had interest rates based on the Libor average (they typically charged Libor +1% or Libor +2%), it was a rise in the Libor rate that borrowers wanted to insure against. So whether swaps contracts made money or not, and how much, was based on movements in

Libor, up or down. As the market expanded, on any given day banks would be holding billions of dollars of swaps contracts that would make or lose money based on whether Libor rose or fell. On every bank's trading floor, it was now the derivatives desk where the big money was – and where ambitious traders like Ryan Reich wanted to work. The same traders, that is, who regularly got in touch with PJ, on the cash desk in London, asking him to tweak his Libor submissions high or low.

In May 2009, Gensler met Sanders with a message from the White House: the derivatives Gensler had fought to exempt from regulation ten years before, and which had played such a big role in causing the crisis, would now face a crackdown and be 'strongly regulated'. Offered such a significant promise, Sanders dropped his opposition to Gensler's appointment. After that, whenever Gensler spoke, the message was clear: he may have come from Wall Street but that didn't mean he was soft on the banks. In fact, the opposite. He put more energy into regulating the banks than any other regulator before him, spearheading new laws to control the multi-trillion-dollar trade in derivatives that had come to be thought of as the financial equivalent of the Wild West. Now, a year later, in 2010, with this evidence, the Libor investigation was shaping up to be another way for him to show he was no soft touch for his former Wall Street colleagues. In future, when bankers mentioned the name 'Gensler', it would be in a venomous tone of voice. But for the new sheriff, that was all to the good. The future of the CFTC, and with it Gensler's career, would from now on be staked on Libor.

Gensler would tell and retell the story of listening to the recording of the Barclays bankers for years to come, as he became progressively more famous for pursuing the banks for rigging interest rates. It was there on his Wikipedia page as a turning point in his career: 'Early in his tenure, Gensler listened to tape recordings of two Barclays employees as they discussed plans to report false interest rates in an effort to manipulate Libor.' But there was a problem with the anecdote. It covered up the elephant in the room, making it look like it was the lower-ranking bankers (PJ and Mark Dearlove) who had cooked up a criminal scheme. In fact, as Gensler knew, the whole reason for the call was that they were being instructed to post false Libor rates on instructions from their top bosses, the Bank of England and the UK government. But Gensler couldn't tell that bit of the story – not least because neither the CFTC nor any other regulator would ever pursue the people at the top of the system giving the instructions. That part didn't fit the narrative of a former Wall Street banker who was now being tough on Wall Street. That part would have to stay secret.

By the time Gensler heard the tape, lower-ranking officials at the CFTC had already been looking into Libor for nearly two years. They'd first picked up on the same *Wall Street Journal* article of 16 April 2008 that stiffened Angela Knight's resolve, which raised the tantalising possibility that banks in London were 'fibbing' about the real cost of borrowing dollars. Led by senior CFTC lawyers Steve Obie and Gretchen Lowe, they'd watched closely as the *WSJ* pursued the story in follow-up articles. The CFTC started reaching out to banks and their UK regulators. In London, though, the US watchdog's interest in Libor was far from warmly received. There were plenty of reasons why it wasn't in the interests of either the Financial Services Authority or the Bank of England to encourage a full-blown investigation into Libor. Nor, for that matter, was it in the interests of the Federal Reserve Bank of New York.

On the top floor of a modern fifteen-storey building in Canary Wharf, east London, overshadowed by the much taller skyscrapers housing HSBC, Citibank and Barclays, the FSA's chief executive Hector Sants sat in his glass-walled office, warily skimming through an inbox of emails filled with bad news. A tall, charismatic, upper-class stockbroker, educated at the elite Clifton College school in Bristol and Oxford University, Sants had spent thirty lucrative years in London and New York before joining the FSA in 2004, winning the top job three years later, just as the credit crunch began. He was first informed about lowballing just three weeks after PJ started blowing the whistle to anyone who'd listen. On 18 September 2007, his office was sent a summary of a note sent by one of his officials who'd attended a conference for traders. 'It is felt that Libor has issues at the moment [...] structural problems. Banks may enter rates but not offer at the rates quoted. Are the fixings real [...] ?' In October, November and December, Paul Tucker's markets division of the Bank of England sent the FSA numerous reports reflecting complaints, very similar to PJ's, that banks were paying much more in the markets than they were claiming in their Libor submissions. The Bank of England, which was in contact with Miles Storey and PJ at Barclays, even explained why lowballing[4] was happening. There was 'increased talk,' said one Bank of England report, 'that Libors were actually being understated given that banks did not want to post a rate above the pack'.[5]

Then there was the small matter of the time, in early December 2007, when Barclays' compliance director Stephen Morse had told the FSA that banks were putting rates in that were too low to reflect where cash was trading, and that it was staying at the top of the pack but no higher, and the FSA condoned that approach (see pages 24–6). FSA officials hadn't even viewed it as misconduct or worthy of escalation to the board. The British Bankers' Association was in charge of supervising the rate. But so unbothered was the regulator by the numerous lowballing warnings that, in 2007, officials neither phoned the BBA about it nor even sent them an email.

As the weeks had gone by, the warnings had become more explicit. By February 2008, Sants and other senior FSA directors were being told clearly by their own officials that Libors were being set at unrealistic levels, below the real market cost of borrowing cash. They'd also been warned of the huge implications because Libor was used to price loans and derivatives. The warnings were passed on to the Bank of England and the UK Treasury.[6] Yet to Sants and other officials, these warnings were showing market dysfunction, not wrongdoing. It was not until the Financial Services Act of 2012 that Parliament created an offence of interest rate manipulation.[7] No one in the UK authorities in 2008 had thought it necessary to report misconduct or launch an investigation, let alone contact the police to report a fraud.

On 27 March 2008, Miles Storey had spoken to the FSA in a routine call and again warned them that all banks, including Barclays, were lowballing. The official he spoke to wrote up a note of what he'd said that was circulated to the offices of Sants, the FSA chairman Callum McCarthy, other FSA directors, the Bank of England and the Treasury. No one raised concerns of wrongdoing.

The FSA in years to come would fine banks hundreds of millions of pounds for posting false Libor rates on the grounds that it was a very serious form of misconduct.[8] But in its Final Notices announcing those fines, the trail of evidence that showed how it had repeatedly condoned it, failing to launch an investigation or make inquiries or report it to the Serious Fraud Office, went unmentioned.

If posting false Libor rates amounted to misconduct, or worse, criminal behaviour, it was no less awkward for the top US authorities. The Federal Reserve Bank of New York had first been alerted to lowballing in August 2007, when PJ's email, 'Draw your own conclusions about why people are going for unrealistically low Libors', was forwarded to an official at the

New York Fed and a senior official at the World Bank.[9] The Fed did nothing. In September, PJ had told a Fed official that some derivatives desks might have too much of an influence over their cash desks' Libor fixings. Again, no action was taken. On 17 December 2007, PJ's friend and colleague in the USA, Bill Heym, had warned a Fed official that Libors were unrealistically low. No one complained to the UK authorities. Then there was the time when PJ's colleague on the cash desk, Colin Bermingham, spoke to senior Fed economist Fabiola Ravazzolo on 11 April 2008, admitting Barclays weren't posting an honest Libor and explaining why everyone was lowballing – something the Fed official said she understood completely (see pages 63–4). With the Fed at last awake to the issue, a briefing note based on that call was sent to the top bosses at the New York Fed including Tim Geithner and Bill Dudley. It was also sent to the US Treasury.

Nine days after her crunch meeting with BBA board members on 16 April 2008, Angela Knight discussed US concerns about lowballing at a meeting of bank chief executives at the Bank of England attended by John Varley, Paul Tucker and future Bank of England governor Andrew Bailey. She wanted the Bank of England to put its name to her attempt to get Libor into shape. But the Bank didn't want its name associated with the BBA review. It was supposed to deal with lowballing, but Paul Tucker was worried it wouldn't solve anything.

Later in 2008, less than a week before his instruction to lowball from the UK government and the Bank of England, PJ had warned a New York Fed official that dollar Libor submissions were 'absolute rubbish' and 'much too low' to reflect the soaring cost on the markets of getting hold of dollars in the midst of the worst crisis anyone could remember. Three days later, he'd even shown another Fed official the page on Bloomberg that proved lowballing was taking place (see pages 33–4). But the Fed's reaction wasn't to order banks to be more honest, or to alert the CFTC or SEC to his warning of false reporting. Instead, a few days later, the Fed was reportedly encouraging JPMorgan Chase to come into the market and make a below-market offer of cash to try and bring dollar Libor rates down even further. The duty of US officials, no matter what their rank, was the same as it was for anyone else working in the financial system. If anyone in the Fed, the FSA or the Bank of England had clear evidence of misconduct, they were required to report it to a regulator. If they had any reason to suspect criminal activity, they were professionally obliged to file a Suspicious Activity Report. But there was no evidence anyone had done so. The reason was simple. It wasn't obvious to anyone, American or British, that any laws had been broken.

Quite unaware of their own government's condoning of lowballing since the credit crunch began, CFTC officials told the FSA's director of enforcement, Margaret Cole,[10] that they had jurisdiction over Libor, even though it was an unregulated benchmark set in London. As Cole reported to colleagues, they believed the law that created the CFTC gave it oversight of false reporting of prices of any commodity in 'interstate' commerce, 'which in their view includes the world'. Dollars, CFTC officials argued, were a commodity. If the price of dollars – interest rates – was being falsely reported, they could act. On 10 September, the CFTC's law enforcement division emailed the BBA to say it was conducting a review into whether banks under-reported or misrepresented their rates. It wanted information about Libor. The BBA forwarded it to Margaret Cole. In the weeks that followed, CFTC officials wrote aggressive letters to US banks based in London who were on the dollar Libor panel and contributed their interest rate submissions to the Libor average, such as JPMorgan Chase and Citigroup. The watchdog was hungry, demanding traders' paperwork, their records of Libor settings and the names of the traders who put in their Libor submissions.

The timing couldn't have been more awkward. As the presidential election race between Barack Obama and John McCain picked up speed, the outgoing Republican president George W. Bush was under pressure not to be soft on Wall Street. His Treasury Secretary, former Goldman Sachs boss Hank Paulson, was preparing to pull the plug on Lehman Brothers, which would send the markets into a tailspin. With the notable exception of Barclays, banks were in no mood to admit what the crisis was doing to the real cost of borrowing dollars. Lowballing was now worse than ever before.

Angela Knight had told the CFTC in the summer that the BBA would be prepared to cooperate with their investigation if they went through the FSA and made a formal request. On 16 October 2008, just a week after Gordon Brown's big bailout announcement, the CFTC sent its formal request to the FSA. A few weeks later, John Ewan met two senior officials at the FSA who raised the CFTC's interest in Libor. 'In their view, the interest stems more from posturing for the domestic market, and in particular the CFTC's own standing in the anticipated US regulatory shakeout than any real worries about Libor,' he wrote. The FSA considered launching its own investigation but decided against it. Ewan later wrote to Angela Knight and her deputy at

the BBA, Sally Scutt. 'FSA also think that the CFTC claim to have any oversight of Libor may be rather tenuous. I also discovered that the FSA sees no
reason for a parallel investigation for a number of reasons – first in their
view we do not fall within their ambit and secondly, the market tells them
that Libor is not broken.'

The City of London's pushback against the US authorities had begun. In
spite of Angela Knight's promise to the CFTC to cooperate with a formal
request via the FSA, the senior bankers on the board of the BBA weren't
happy. It took until January for the BBA to send its formal response to the
Libor team at the CFTC. Before sending it, the trade body ran it past the FSA
to check it didn't disapprove. Its message was that the CFTC's investigation
was misguided. The BBA was now seeking legal advice on whether it was
obliged to forward any documents at all.

Even more awkward was the timing of the next watchdog to come sniff-
ing. It wasn't just the instruction to lower Libor from Downing Street on
29 October 2008 that no one was supposed to know about. It was much
bigger than that. Mark Dearlove and Jon Stone told the Bank of England on
4 November they thought there had been political pressure on French banks
to cut their contributions to Euribor, the equivalent of Libor for euros.[11] That
was corroborated by the data on what interest rates each bank had submitted. The French banks had suddenly, as one, dropped their submissions of
their estimates of the cost of borrowing euros in the days that followed the
co-ordinated central bank interest rate cut of 8 October 2008. The scale of
the drop – around 40 basis points – was bigger than any previous movement, including after 11 September 2001. It couldn't be explained by market
factors because the other banks in the same market – the market for borrowing and lending euros – had not been similarly affected (the German
banks, for example, hadn't moved). After Gordon Brown's meeting with
European leaders in Paris on 11–12 October, the Italian banks and Spanish
banks had done the same. Only the national central banks such as Banque
de France and Banco Italia were in a position to arrange co-ordinated moves
like that. There was evidence that the Swiss Central Bank, too, had ordered
rates down, and the Swedish government. The evidence suggested it wasn't
just the UK government and Bank of England, but Banque de France, and
other central banks and governments around the world, all co-ordinating
to get Libor and Euribor down.

On 5 November 2008, the UK's consumer protection watchdog, the Office of Fair Trading (OFT), held a meeting with the FSA. The OFT chief executive John Fingleton, an Irish economist who took his role as consumer champion seriously, had already earned the enmity of the banks with high-profile investigations into overdraft fees, credit cards and the mis-selling of unsuitable payment protection insurance, for which banks were currently being forced to pay billions of pounds in compensation to their customers. He told Sants the OFT was contemplating looking at Libor. With so many loans linked to it, if Libor were false, the potential for detriment to consumers or businesses was obvious.

Hector Sants promised to send the OFT the FSA's views about Libor and passed the issue down to the markets division, who emailed each other about it on 10 November. 'We would not be keen on an OFT investigation at the present time [...] The BBA has itself recently conducted a review of the Libor process and made some changes,' one email said. 'More importantly, the OFT would need to be very careful about the market (and political) implications of a decision to investigate Libor at the present time.' Their comments were forwarded to Sants the next day.[12]

The FSA's markets division wrote back to the OFT. 'This is not an area in which we consider that regulatory intervention is likely to be needed, given the recent changes the BBA has made. Are you aware of such work in progress or contemplated? We ought to discuss.' Staff exchanged emails on why the OFT was interested in Libor. They believed it had come out of discussions with the UK's top markets watchdog, the Competition Commission. The concern appeared to be the potential for collusion among submitting banks, to the detriment of consumers or other banks.

On 13 November, the OFT asked the FSA more directly if it was 'aware of any complaints about Libor in terms of how it is set?' Six days later, the FSA's answer omitted any mention of lowballing – of which, by now, top bosses and numerous members of staff were well aware. Instead, it referred to a particular case where a bank had not passed on a reduction in the central bank's base rate to its customers, hastening to add that the case was not related to the setting of Libor.

Just a day before that answer was given to the OFT, on 18 November, the Bank of England had sent the FSA a market conditions update making it clear once again that dollar Libor was false. The cost of borrowing dollars, it said, 'remains significantly more expensive than implied by Libor fixings'.

It was sent to Callum McCarthy; FSA banking sector director Tom Huertas; other FSA managing directors; and Hector Sants's office.

The following week the OFT got back in touch with the FSA, saying it was still 'doing some thinking on the Libor' and asking questions about the fixing process. It stayed interested until 12 January 2009, when Hector Sants signed an assertive letter to John Fingleton that had been drafted by his staff. 'On the subject of Libor, as I am sure you are aware, this is a process organised and run by the BBA. At the present time, the FSA would not encourage a further investigation into Libor as the BBA has recently conducted its own review of the process and made some changes. While these may not have been as far reaching as some have hoped, they did address concerns regarding the rate setting process and were accepted by the market,' said the letter.

'More importantly, we believe there may be financial stability implications of announcing an investigation at the present time, due to the Libor-OIS spread being such a key indicator of funding costs.'

Fingleton could have looked up 'Libor-OIS' spread and found it was simply the difference between official central bank interest rates and Libor. But the implication was clear: you're messing with dangerous forces. You could destabilise the financial system in the middle of a crisis.

The letter Sants signed helped to put the OFT off the scent. There was no further correspondence about Libor between the consumer watchdog and the FSA. The letter drafted for him by FSA staff had made no mention of the regulator's extensive knowledge, much of it coming from the Bank of England, of false Libor rates being submitted through lowballing. Nor did it mention months of contact with the CFTC, or their recently launched investigation. It was the first time the top of the British regulatory and financial establishment would cover up its knowledge of lowballing and seek to squash an investigation that might have serious political implications. But it wouldn't be the last.

6

LIP SERVICE

Jailed for conspiracy to defraud and sentenced to four years in prison, Jonathan Mathew had all too much time to regret the lies he'd told. Not the ones he'd been accused of telling – putting in false Libor rates when he was in his early twenties. He'd always set Libor honestly and wasn't guilty of the offences he'd gone to prison for, no matter what the jury had decided. He'd only started lying to try and keep his job, and then later to stay out of a US prison cell. In fact, some of the worst lies were in interviews with the Federal Bureau of Investigation (FBI) – who required confessions so he could become a government witness rather than a jailbird in an orange jumpsuit. But then later, as he put it, the Barclays Libor case was 'stolen' from the US Department of Justice by the UK's Serious Fraud Office. Jonathan had made confessions to avoid jail in the USA, only to be tried and convicted in the UK.

Few things are more honest than admitting to dishonesty in a criminal court when you're on trial for fraud. Jonathan's defence strategy looked brave. He'd repeatedly admit to having lied. The gamble was that the jury would recognise his newfound honesty and see his innocence of the crime he was charged with. But either they hadn't understood his defence, or they chose to ignore it.

I first met Jonathan, known to friends as Jon,[1] as he awaited the jury's verdict. 'I've been thinking of writing a book about this. The whole thing is unbelievable,' he told me. 'I mean, I was 23! I was getting paid six figures. I had more money than I'd ever dreamt of. We were going to all these top restaurants, strip clubs – I was like a kid in a sweet shop!' He told me he'd give an interview and wanted to speak out about what had happened. But that was only if he were acquitted. The day after he was found guilty, before the sentencing hearing, Jon and his father, who'd helped his young lad get a job at Barclays sixteen years before, came up to me as I waited outside Southwark Crown Court, just across the River Thames from the City of London, where he and four other former Barclays bankers had just stood trial for rigging Libor. Both father and son had been up all night and looked emotionally and physically shattered, with bloodshot eyes that suggested they'd both been in tears. Jon stepped towards me, tilted his head to one side and looked quizzically into my eyes as if I might have the answers. Then he asked me a bewildered question.

'How could this happen?!'

I'd spend the next five years searching for the answer to that question. A few days later, Jon was in a prison van, separated from his wife and baby, on his way to one of the roughest of Britain's Victorian jails: HM Prison Wandsworth in south-west London. It was the only time he'd ever been in trouble with the law.

Tall and thin with an angular face and retreating dark hair, Jon was 35 and had just started a family with his wife, Lorna, when he was found guilty in 2016. But the alleged criminal conspiracy he was accused of participating in dated back to 2005, when he'd just started, aged 23, as an apprentice trader on the cash desk at the headquarters of Barclays' investment bank division, Barclays Capital, in Canary Wharf. He'd spend every day learning the job from his boss, PJ, and return home every evening on the train to Billericay, Essex, to sleep in his childhood bedroom. Born deaf in his left ear and later diagnosed with dyslexia, he was intelligent and articulate but had struggled at school and didn't score well enough in his A levels to go to university. Aged 19, he started the job found for him by his dad, who also worked for Barclays, at the bank's e-commerce division. There, for modest pay, he'd print out presentations and do the photocopying, fetching breakfast and lunch for the team members. Keen to become a trader, he had to take the qualifying exam four times before he eventually passed. In 2004, he finally swapped photocopiers for a desk with eight screens surrounding it, two phone handsets and a black box with a microphone, a speaker and twenty buttons.[2]

There was no formal training; you learned on the job. At the desk next to his sat PJ, who was a generation older and taught him everything he knew. With a keen eye for detail, PJ wouldn't spare his feelings if he made a mistake. Once, when he did, PJ sent him a harsh-sounding email with a spoonerism for a title: 'Brick Dain'. 'I wonder about you sometimes,' PJ wrote. 'Did you really think that people would not notice ...? You should be looking to have a long career at BC [Barclays Capital]. To do so, however, you need to have a modicum of common sense and show that you are actually taking things into your thick skull.'

PJ may have been a hard taskmaster, but he was also a good teacher. On one of his screens, he taught Jon, was a database showing the trades he'd done. On another were his emails, while the rest would show prices currently being offered in the market or the headlines from financial news services such as Bloomberg or Reuters. The black box, Jon learned, allowed him to communicate with the people he'd speak to every day on permanently open phone lines, the money brokers. He'd press one of the buttons, lean into the microphone and ask, for example, what the broker on that line would quote him to borrow a 'yard' (a billion dollars), to be repaid one month later. The broker would answer, their voice coming out of the speaker, with a 'price'. On the cash desk, the prices were the interest rates other banks were offering to borrow or lend cash. The brokers, who worked for external firms such as Tullett Prebon, ICAP or Tradition, acted as middlemen,[3] helping a bank that wanted to borrow cash to find someone offering to lend it[4] and arranging the deal.

It was the brokers who kept their ears pinned to the ground and knew best what was going on in the market. For decades, City traders had come from two contrasting types of background: the 'Toffs', who tended to come from privileged upper-middle-class backgrounds and were often destined for management; and the 'Barrow Boys' (so-called after the upright barrows that street market traders once used to sell their goods), who were typically working class, light on education – and lightning quick with numbers. The brokers, normally Barrow Boys, were a little further down the City's pecking order from the highly paid traders whose business they relied on.

As everyone on the trading floor knew, everything that was said over the speaker system or the phone lines was recorded and kept on file. It was partly so that trades could be agreed and executed at speed with no need for signatures or paperwork (which was done later by the back office staff). But it also meant that anything the traders said could be monitored and listened back to by anyone in the bank, including the compliance department whose job it was to make sure the traders played by the rules.

After less than a year learning from PJ, Jon was allowed to trade cash, meaning he borrowed and lent large sums of money at a time. He'd bid to borrow funds at one interest rate that he'd quote to the brokers; and he'd offer to lend at a slightly higher one, two or three hundredths of a percentage point higher (0.01%, one hundredth of a percentage point, was known as a 'basis point', or less formally a 'point' or a 'tick'). Most of the work was making sure the different parts of Barclays had the funds they needed to lend or invest, which they'd borrow from the cash desk. It acted like a Treasury for the rest of the bank. Throughout the day, the other departments of Barclays would come to the cash desk to borrow funds. That would then determine how much money Jon needed to borrow from other banks. Suppose he needed to borrow $100 million. He'd press one of the buttons on the box, ask for a price and the broker would give him two interest rates: one that was the best interest rate in the market if he wanted to lend (the bid) and one that was the best he might borrow at (the offer). If the offer was right, Jon would give the broker the go-ahead. The broker would check whether the sum he wanted to borrow was within the lender's credit limit for Barclays. If so, the deal was done, and the broker would then tell him who was lending the money – the counterparty – and supply details of the deal.

First, Jon was allowed to trade only in the smaller currencies, where less money was at risk, like Canadian dollars, Swedish krona or the Swiss franc. Then later, when he'd learned how to do it, PJ relied on him to look after the much larger US dollar book when he was away. The stressful part of his job was making sure the bank had enough money to fund its activities, so that at the end of each day, it had borrowed the same as it had lent and wasn't short of cash. Libor took up only a few minutes each morning.

At 7 a.m. each day, Jon would call a broker to find out what interest rates other banks were offering to borrow and lend at (their bids and offers) over different lengths of time. You could borrow overnight or over a week. You could borrow over one month, two months, three, four, five, or six months, or over nine or twelve months. By hand, he'd fill out a list, in two columns of a paper grid, of all the bids and offers for each time frame. Later, at 11 a.m., he'd phone a broker for their guidance on where they thought Libor would fix for each period. They'd run through them, leaving out the initial figure for the sake of verbal economy. For example, the broker might say, 'On the overnight we've got 91 [2.91%]; on the 1-week it's 94 [2.94%] and on the

1-month 98 [2.98%] ...' Jon wrote down those Libor rates in a third column on the same grid.

Crucially, the different brokers he spoke to each had different customers offering to lend cash. Each of those customers were offering to lend at slightly different interest rates. So, the brokers wouldn't quote him exactly the same Libor figure. One might quote, say, 3.65% to borrow dollars over three months, while another would quote 3.64%, and another 3.66%. That created a narrow range of rates, no more than 2 or 3 points wide (0.02%–0.03%), from which Jon could choose his Libor submission. Because he knew from the brokers that he could realistically borrow at any of the rates they'd quoted, anything within that range would be a valid answer to the Libor question: 'at what rate could you borrow cash at 11 a.m.?' If someone in the bank wanted a high Libor, he could put in 3.66%. If they wanted it low, it could be 3.64%. On trading floors across London going back to the 1990s, it was normal, everyday practice. Libor submitters like PJ or Jon would fine-tune their Libor estimates to suit their banks' commercial interests, up or down by no more than a point or two, within the narrow range of interest rates where they could borrow funds on the market. If someone asked PJ or Jon for a Libor outside the range of interest rates where cash was trading, they'd refuse, saying something like 'sorry, can't do that'.

In the interest rate-rigging scandal, this narrow *range* of accurate rates would turn out to be the devil in the detail – the thread which, when pulled, would start to unravel the whole idea that the traders on trial were guilty of misconduct in the first place, let alone criminality. The lawyers investigating – first the external lawyers appointed by the banks then the lawyers at the Commodity Futures Trading Commission and the US Department of Justice – didn't consult independent market practitioners before they decided for themselves the rights and wrongs of Libor and Euribor. That meant they didn't fully understand it until it was too late. They'd already spent years investigating, shaking down the banks for billions of dollars in fines and starting criminal proceedings, all on the understanding that shifting Libor submissions high or low to suit a bank's commercial interests was 'self-evidently' corrupt. The CFTC and DOJ decided that any request for Libor rates to be put 'high' or 'low' must be improper because there could only be one genuine, accurate answer to the Libor question, 'at what rate could you borrow'? In fact, there was always more than one genuine, accurate answer that could be given. There was nothing self-evident about it.

Years later, on both sides of the Atlantic, prosecutors at the rate-rigging trials were so worried it might destroy their cases against the traders, they'd resort to denying the existence of any 'range'. But the lawyers were in denial of a simple and basic economic fact. There was never only one honest price you could set. There was always a range.

Suppose you wanted an estate agent to quote you a price on your home. If they came back to you saying, 'it's worth £253,419 pounds and 26 pence', you'd probably, and quite rightly, doubt their honesty. No house can be priced to the penny. However wide or narrow, there's a range. An honest estate agent would look at the prices recently paid for houses in your area with the same number of bedrooms and there'd be a range of prices – say between £240,000 and £260,000. If they were frantically busy, they might quote £240,000 to put you off so that you'd go to another agent. If things were quiet and they wanted your business, they might quote £260,000. Nothing dishonest there. Whenever a business quotes a price, it's almost never solely about the cost of the underlying commodity. It also takes account of other commercial considerations, like their need to manage their orders or their wish to improve their profits. Think of a lemonade stand that cuts its prices on a cold day; or an airline that offers a discount if you book ahead; or an electrician who charges more on a weekend. Far from being dishonest, it's simply normal commercial practice.

Of course, an unscrupulous estate agent could quote you a house price way higher than the range where he really expected it to sell, just to reel you in, then gradually beat your price down when no one made an offer. That would be the estate agent's equivalent of a Libor submission out-side the range, the dishonest 'outlier' that competitors protest about. Unfortunately, neither the CFTC nor the DOJ nor the SFO ever investigated whether the Libor estimates Jon or PJ submitted were outside the range of interest rates where their bank could borrow cash. The data was there if they'd wanted to look. But they hadn't understood that that issue – whether it was inside or outside the range of accurate rates where cash was trading – was the crucial one. So, they didn't bother to check. Instead, they simply assumed that any request to tweak a Libor submission to suit the bank's commercial interests must be corrupt. It was an error with monu-mental consequences.

It wasn't until August 2005, when he was covering PJ's US dollar trading book while he was away, that Jon received his first request from a trader about Libor. It came from Stelios Contogoulas, an energetic swaps trader from Greece with dark eyebrows and receding hair who would often give Jon a friendly nod or smile if they passed each other on the second floor of Barclays Capital's headquarters in Canary Wharf. Aged 33, Stelios was nine years Jon's senior and had started in IT before switching to become a trader. He now worked closely with the swaps desk in New York, covering for them in London in the hours when Wall Street was closed.

'Hi Jon, we would really like to have low 1M US dollar Libor fixing and high 3M US dollar Libor fixing for the next couple of weeks. Any help would be greatly appreciated,' said the email.

'Hi Stelios, I'll do my best for you. Thanks,' was Jon's reply.

'Thanks a lot for that. I appreciate it. Have a great day,' wrote Stelios.

Jon hadn't seen an email like this one before and didn't know how to respond. But he didn't want to annoy Stelios so he was paying him 'lip service', telling him what he wanted to hear without really meaning it. That day he did what he'd always done, what PJ taught him to do – putting in rates based on the Libor figures the brokers had quoted to him. The figure he put in as his estimate of the cost of borrowing dollars over one month was higher than any other bank – the opposite of what Stelios had asked for. His 3-month figure, too, was in the middle of the sixteen contributing banks, ignoring the request from Stelios to go high.

When PJ came back from holiday, Jon told him about the email. He hadn't known what to do with it, so he'd ignored it. 'We get these requests from traders from time to time,' PJ said, telling Jon they should take a 'firm first' approach. 'We should help these guys out as long as the rate we put in can be justified,' PJ said. It was justified if it was inside the range of Libor rates quoted by the brokers.

Jon didn't get requests for tweaks to his Libor submissions on the New Zealand dollar or the Swedish krona. Few traders had a lot of money at stake in those currencies. But when PJ went away on business trips or on holiday, he'd leave Jon notes about the New York swaps traders' positions, such as 'Swaps desk are looking for high 1-month and low 3-month Libors'; or 'Swaps have a preference for low 1-month and high 3-months if that suits.' To Jon, who'd soaked up everything PJ told him, the phrase 'if that suits' had a clear meaning. It meant 'if it is within the range'.

From 2005 to 2006, Jon continued to get requests from Stelios, passing on information about whether the New York swaps desk would like Libor to be set high or low.

'It's me again (as if you couldn't guess)', said one. 'Thanks a lot for yesterday. Really appreciate it. If possible (and I stress the IF) a high 1M, low 3M would be great [...] Thanks in advance again. Coffees are on me today.'

'I'll do my best for you,' replied Jon.

'Thank you, sir. Much appreciated.'

This time Jon didn't pay lip service. Stelios had said 'if possible', which to him meant 'if it's within the range given by the brokers'. Checking with the brokers to confirm it was, he put his estimate of the cost of borrowing dollars over one month at the top end of the narrow range from the brokers. For his 3-month Libor submission, he put in an estimate at the bottom end of the brokers' range. The next day Stelios sent him an email: 'Superstar! I'm going to get some Itsu[5] today. Can I bring two or three take-away boxes for you and your group over there?'

'You are a gentleman, sir,' Jon emailed back. 'You'll always find a taker for sushi on this desk.'

Later that year, another email from Stelios explained that the New York desk had a big trading position that would lose money because it was the 'reset' day, when variable rates on the swaps contracts would move up or down depending on what happened to Libor, making or losing the bank large sums.

'Hi (again),' said Stelios. 'We're getting killed on our 3M resets. We need them to be up this week before we roll out of our positions. Consensus for 3M today is 4.78 – 4.7825. It would be amazing if we could go for 4.79. Really appreciate your help mate.'

Jon checked if the requested submission was within the range from the brokers. It was. He adjusted his Libor submission upwards. 'Happy to help,' he replied.

'How do you guys prefer your lattes? Skinny or regular?' asked Stelios.

'Skinny's excellent,' replied Jon.

'Four waiting for you on PJ's desk.'

'Thank you. Just got back to desk. Very kind of you, dear boy.'

The next request from Stelios, a few days later, made it very clear that he didn't mind if Jon ignored him. 'If it's not too late, low 1M and 3M would be nice, but please feel free to say "no". Coffees will be coming your way either way just to say thank you for your help in the past weeks.'

'Done, for you, big boy ...' replied Jon.

'Hehe, thanks,' wrote Stelios. Stelios liked to joke around; a little office banter helped the day go by. Later, when he'd been lured away to a better-paid job at the US investment bank Merrill Lynch, Stelios stayed in touch with his former colleagues via the instant messaging system on the Bloomberg computer terminals that all the traders used. One Barclays trader he knew well, often sharing a car into work with him, was Don Lee, an American swaps trader of Korean descent who worked on Barclays Capital's trading floor in Canary Wharf, on a desk close to PJ's. One morning, Stelios had a big trading position that would lose money if the Libor average didn't go lower. At 7.12 a.m. he messaged Lee. 'Where do you think 3M LIBOR will be today?'

'PJ thinks 38.'

'Wow ... unchanged!!!!!!?????? Short dates have rallied by three-quarters of a basis point [...] so I take it he's going unchanged? If it comes in unchanged I'm a dead man haha.'

'I'll have a chat,' Lee replied.

PJ put in his Libor submission to borrow dollars over three months at 5.375 – half a point lower than he'd said earlier.

At 11.29 a.m. Stelios messaged Lee again. 'Dude I owe you big time. Come over one day after work and I'm opening a bottle of Bollinger! Thanks for the Libor.'

'No worries!!!' wrote Lee.

Later, when Jon covered the dollar book for PJ while he was away on business trips or holidays, there were requests directly from the swaps traders in New York. Among them were Alex Pabon, Jay Merchant and Ryan Reich. 'For Monday we're very long 3M cash here in New York. Would like the setting to be as low as possible. Thanks,' said one request from Ryan Reich soon after he'd joined the swaps desk in 2006.

'You heard the man, Jon,' wrote PJ, forwarding the email to Jon. 'Ryan, I am off on Monday but Jon will take notice of what you say about low 3M.'

'Thanks,' replied Jon. He put in a calendar entry in Microsoft Outlook with an alert for the following Monday morning. 'USD 3 mth Libor down.'

Once, on 19 December 2006, Ryan had sent a request via instant messages to PJ because the New York swaps desk had a big trading position that would benefit from a lower Libor fix. 'Can you pls continue to go in for 3m Libor at 5.365 or lower [...] Until the [...] year end.'

PJ: 'Will do my best sir.'

PJ had forgotten about it for the first two days, submitting rates of 5.37% and 5.375%. Then on 21 December, Ryan forwarded their earlier email exchange to remind him. 'Whoops,' PJ replied, then forwarded it to Jon, who was covering his book while PJ was off for the Christmas holidays. He set a calendar entry for every day from 22 December until 1 January 2007 with a reminder 'SET 3 MONTH US$ LIBOR LOW!!!!!!' Jon then set rates in the following days of 5.36%, 5.365%, 5.35% and 5.369% to the end of year – very close to what Ryan had asked for.

Other requests came from another swaps trader who worked alongside Ryan in New York, Jay Merchant. In one of them he clarified a garbled email to Jon that he'd been copied into by his colleague, Alex Pabon. 'What our verbose friend Alex means,' wrote Jay, 'is can you please put in the 1m fixing below 5.08 if possible as it would help our position greatly.'

'Leave it with me, thanks,' Jon wrote back. He checked if the request was 'possible' – meaning within the range for 1-month Libor given to him by the brokers. It was. Jon met the request and tweaked his Libor submission.

A few seats away, one of the very few women on the trading floor, a reserved Danish cash trader in her early twenties with long blonde hair named Sisse Bohart,[6] had a similar daily chore to perform. Because she traded in euros, the traders sometimes made requests for tweaks to her estimates of the interest rate Barclays would pay to borrow euros, which she submitted into the process for setting Euribor. Just as PJ taught Jon, she followed the example of her boss, Colin Bermingham, who tried to help out the swaps traders with a shift of a basis point or two if the bank had a big interest – as long as it was within the range where cash was trading. The requests came in from swaps traders a short distance away on the trading floor, including a French-speaking Moroccan trader called Philippe Moryoussef, and a quiet young Italian trader, Carlo Palombo. Forty-six banks contributed their interest rate estimates to the Euribor fixing, so it was hard to see how it might influence the overall average, even if you could convince other banks to move in your preferred direction. But it was only an email to the cash desk that took a minute. Even if it only made a difference of one thousandth of a percentage point or less, it was still worth doing, just in case it might help.

All told, from 2005 to 2007, there were twenty-eight requests from the swaps traders for Jon to tweak his Libor submissions. The polite-sounding emails and messages, with their offers of coffee as thanks, would be used a decade later to send him to jail for taking part in what prosecutors said was an international criminal fraud conspiracy with Jay Merchant, Alex Pabon and Ryan Reich. The weird thing was, he'd never met them.

When the credit crunch struck in August 2007, setting Libor became very hard for Jon or any other Libor submitter to get right. It was supposed to track the cost of borrowing cash in the interbank market. But because of the fear stalking the market caused by huge losses on subprime investments, no bank was lending. It was supposed to be based on the market interest rates where banks were offering to lend cash. But now, there were no offers. On the interbank market, no cash was changing hands. As Clive Jones had explained to John Ewan almost as soon as it started, you couldn't set Libor based on real transactions because there weren't any. It was no longer the case that all the banks' Libor submissions would be bunched together, a point or two apart. Setting Libor became, in the words of Jon Wood of HSBC, a game of 'pin the tail on the donkey'.

No longer did any trader bother to get in touch with PJ or Jon to ask for adjustments to their Libor submissions. There was no point in Ryan Reich or Jay Merchant asking for Barclays' Libor submission to be tweaked high or low by a basis point or two, just in case it might help to nudge the average by a fraction of a point in the direction that would suit the bank's commercial interests. The Libor average was 20 to 30 basis points lower than the interest rates where cash was really changing hands. It would be like trying to fine-tune a car when the wheels had come off.

What PJ and Jon knew was that banks were still borrowing dollars via the foreign exchange markets and paying prices that made lowballing obvious. The effective interest rate banks ended up paying using that route was much higher than anyone was declaring as their Libor rate. If they really could borrow dollars on the interbank market as cheaply as they said they could, why on earth would they go through the foreign exchange markets to pay more? It meant their Libor submissions for the cost of borrowing dollars on the interbank market, which were much lower, had to be false.

Jon had a ringside seat as PJ furiously campaigned to make Libor more honest. Almost every day, he overheard him on the neighbouring desk, 4ft away, ranting on the phone to Ryan Reich or whoever else would listen about how other banks' Libor submissions were 'fucked'. Jon had only to look at his screens or call a broker to see that PJ was right. You simply couldn't borrow cash as cheaply as the other banks were pretending they could. But Libor submitters at other banks were taking their cue from the 'run-throughs' – the brokers' guidance each morning for where Libor would set. And that guidance was far too low.

Unbeknownst to Jon, the Bank of England was taking a close interest in exactly the same thing. On 27 November 2007 at 1 p.m., a member of Tucker's markets intelligence team, Andrew Shankland, wrote an email to colleagues reporting that both Barclays and Deutsche Bank were lowballing and giving their reasons why: 'Both Barclays and Deutsche noted that they don't want to be seen as the first bank raising Libors/Euribors higher when compared to the rest of the market in case the market perceives that they are in trouble.' His email reported how the broker Tullett Prebon thought Euribor was artificially low and should be 7–12 basis points higher. Then it added the following:

'Confidential – Tomorrow Prebon are either going to black out their screen and show no prices or move their screen prices higher to see if it has any influence on Euribor fixings.'

The next morning Shankland's colleague Ben Wensley emailed saying comment was frequent that derivatives desks have an 'undue influence' over the fixings. It was also 'definitely true that banks are wary of being outliers, fearful of being higher than others in case it tarnishes their name'. He added: 'It will, though, be interesting to hear any reaction if Prebon temporarily remove their rates, although I'm not sure it will endear them to their clients.'

Later that morning, Shankland reported back: 'While it may just be coincidental, today's Euribor fixings came in around 3bps [3 basis points or 0.03%] higher today which is similar to the increase in Euro Deposit seen on Prebon's Reuters page [...] Whether it is a coincidence [...] the Euribor fixings did mirror the Prebon increases.'

The next day he followed up. 'There was a similar scenario today with the Euribor fixings. Prebon raised their screen prices by at least 3bps to "reflect a more realistic market valuation of where quality banks could borrow money", and whether coincidental or not, the Euribor fixings mirrored the increases seen on Prebon's screen. Most fixings, with the exception of the 1-month, are up around 3bps today.'

In the context of the later criminal prosecution of rate-rigging, the implications of the email chain were striking. The UK's central bank was looking on as a broker tried an experiment to see if they could move the Euribor rates up by changing their guidance on their screens about where Euribor rates would set. Eight years later, Tom Hayes would be condemned for attempting to move Libor by getting brokers to change their guidance. No one could prove he'd been successful. Yet here was the Bank of England, supervising an experiment to shift the Euribor average which looked like it had been successful – twice. Clearly, no one at either Prebon or the Bank of England thought of it at the time as punishable misconduct. If they had, they would hardly have been writing it down in emails to each other. Certainly, no one at the Bank of England thought it appropriate to call the police.

At the height of the banking crisis in October 2008, Jon joined in blowing the whistle on lowballing to the authorities, telling an official at the New York Fed, 'I am sure you know Peter Johnson, who is on a one-man crusade about these Libors, and rightly so to be honest [...] We are still setting our Libors – certainly in dollars and all the other currencies – where we think we can get the cash in the market.'

Throughout the credit crunch, Jon had overheard PJ, Colin Bermingham and the other traders on the cash desk trying to work out why other banks were lowballing. One reason was 'reputational risk' – the risk Miles Storey told the Financial Services Authority about that if a bank like Barclays stuck its head 'above the parapet' by posting a truthful, higher Libor submission, it might get 'shot at', as Barclays had in the summer of 2007, with negative media coverage and a plummeting share price to go with it. Another reason, they speculated, was that in some banks, the Libor submitter sat not on the cash desk but on the derivatives desk. They could be putting in Libors to suit their swaps trading, keeping it low to benefit their banks' commercial interests instead of basing it on the market for borrowing cash.

Since PJ and Pete Spence received their instructions from on high, the traders on the cash desk had got used to a third reason: Libor was too low because central banks wanted it low. Across the City of London, traders discussed how Libor was lower for political reasons, rather than because it was cheaper to borrow money. On 10 February 2009, a colleague asked Jon why he was posting a Libor rate higher than the rest of the market. 'Because there's a huge dislocation between Libor and where cash is offered in the market,' he told the colleague. 'I think everyone's paying the same for cash. We're just setting our Libor where we think it's fair.'

'Okay – and the reasons why these other guys aren't posting at these higher levels?'

After a year and a half of lowballing, Jon was almost bored of explaining it. 'I dunno. Same excuse as before. It's not being set by money market traders; it's being set by interest rate swap traders. You know: reputational risk; pressure from central banks. That's – I wouldn't use that last one cos it's, sort of – having a go at central banks.'

If you worked as a trader, speaking out against central banks was one way to jeopardise your career. As Jon was about to find out, talking to American investigators was another.

7

CONFIRMATION BIAS

Across the giant trading floor from the desk where Jon Mathew was talking to his colleague, in an area walled off by a partition, half a dozen newly qualified young lawyers were rifling through thousands of paper documents and digitally sifting hundreds of thousands of emails and Bloomberg messages. They'd begun a gargantuan secret task, codenamed 'Project Bruce', to find what the Commodity Futures Trading Commission had asked Barclays (and other banks) to search for.

It could have been an even less manageable job. At first, the CFTC had wanted all the banks that contributed to the dollar Libor average to search for anything that mentioned the word 'Libor'. So central was Libor to the bank's business that that would have meant hundreds of millions, if not billions of documents. Even with a much bigger team, the bank calculated, it would have taken decades to go through them. There was no computer software that could be relied on to identify misconduct. Nor, however, was the judgement of human beings flawless when it came to discerning between genuinely bad behaviour and accepted commercial practice.

After exchanging emails with the bank, Steve Obie's team at the CFTC agreed to give Barclays much more specific search terms, narrowing it down to a more manageable size. But it still meant millions of documents to search through, most of which went straight onto the 'irrelevant' pile. In the early months of Project Bruce, the team was looking solely for evidence of lowballing. That was what the CFTC was interested in: evidence of false reporting of commodity prices so that it could take action under its false reporting statute. *The Wall Street Journal* and *Financial Times* had written about allegations of false reporting of the cost of borrowing dollars since soon after the credit crunch started to bite in 2007. The CFTC was simply looking to prove it.

In 2009, Barclays was the only British bank ready to spend the millions of dollars required to pay external lawyers to go through its records. Executives had made what looked like a shrewd move in response to the CFTC's inquiries, hiring a US law firm – McDermott Will & Emery – one of whose partners, Greg Mocek, had until very recently been the CFTC's director of enforcement. A tall, 46-year-old attorney from Louisiana with receding fair hair, square-rimmed spectacles and a confident style, Mocek had already won kudos for pursuing the British energy company BP on criminal charges of manipulating the price of propane fuel, used to heat up to 7 million rural homes in the USA, where traders were caught on tape discussing whether they could 'control the market at will'. BP had settled it by means of a deferred prosecution agreement, paying a $303 million fine. To Mocek, Libor looked like an even worse example of Brits manipulating prices. He'd been in charge of the 150-strong team of lawyers in the enforcement department at the Commodity Futures Trading Commission when his staff, led by his friend Steve Obie, had written to the London-based banks, the British Bankers' Association and the Financial Services Authority, only to meet stiff resistance (see Chapter 5). When Mocek left the CFTC in September 2008 to join McDermott Will & Emery, Obie had stepped into his old role running the enforcement division. Obie and Mocek would stay in touch, smoothing the flow of information from Barclays' internal investigation to the Libor team at the CFTC.

Mocek took the view that it was better for Barclays to cooperate because US agencies often showed much greater leniency if you did. Executives at Barclays felt the bank had been on the right side of the argument, given all those times in 2007 and 2008 when everyone from PJ to Miles Storey to Bob Diamond had raised red flags about other banks' lowballing to the FSA, the Bank of England or the New York Fed. So they agreed to cooperate with the CFTC and spend the millions of pounds it would take to fund Project Bruce. But Mocek didn't know about the new atmosphere at the CFTC because he'd left before Gary Gensler arrived. Under him, it was to prove far less lenient than he'd predicted.

At first, the team of young lawyers was searching only for evidence of lowballing. As more was discovered, the CFTC's list of search terms grew to include the names of individuals involved such as Peter Johnson, Jonathan

Mathew and Ryan Reich. Significantly, it didn't include any individuals ranking higher than Mark Dearlove and investigators were only permitted to search through data from Barclays Capital, the investment bank division. Barclays Group, the parent company headquartered down the road at Churchill Place, Canary Wharf, which ran the retail bank that catered for consumers and small business customers, was a separate regulated entity. That meant the team wasn't allowed to search the email accounts of executives on the thirty-first floor of Churchill Place who worked for Barclays Group, such as Chris Lucas, John Varley and Bob Diamond. The only time they'd see their emails was if they were copied into someone else's email chain at Barclays Capital.[1]

The young lawyers turned up every day at Barclays Capital's headquarters on North Colonnade, Canary Wharf, and sifted thousands of documents each, helped by Barclays' compliance department under Stephen Morse. When they found something significant, the investigators would send it to Mocek, who'd pass it through to his former colleagues. It was difficult for them to know if the emails and messages they were looking at showed misconduct. Libor was unregulated and there were no laws or written rules to be observed or breached. Instead, they were slowly picking up what seemed to be the rights and wrongs of Libor as they went along. The most relevant evidence they found came from the cash desk where Jon and PJ worked. In material like the internal email list PJ frequently wrote to, 'Rates Europe', he was the one who was most vocal about 'dishonest' Libor fixing.

The Project Bruce team began to get the gist. You should set Libor based on where cash is trading at 11 a.m. The other banks were understating what it was costing them to borrow cash and they damn well shouldn't be – as PJ's emails and messages made clear. And it shouldn't be set by derivatives desks, he said, who might be inclined to submit it based on their own swaps trading linked to Libor. That wasn't in the BBA's definition, PJ kept saying. The investigators checked the definition (something traders on the market rarely did). Libor was 'the rate at which an individual contributor panel bank could borrow funds, were it to do so by asking for and then accepting interbank offers in reasonable market size, just prior to 11 a.m. London time'. Nothing there about derivatives.

As the investigation progressed, the team came across dozens of emails and messages mentioning Libor which didn't quite fit the lowballing pattern highlighted by *The Wall Street Journal*. Most of them were from before the credit crunch, in early 2007 or 2006. Then they looked further back in time, to 2005, and found more. With these emails, it wasn't about Libor rates being submitted much too low on instructions from senior managers in case it led to bad publicity that might knock the bank's share price. Instead, the messages showed requests from derivatives traders. They seemed to be asking for PJ or Jon to move Libor in any direction – high, low, or even unchanged. Sometimes they even specified the rate they wanted. There were dozens of puzzling messages, quite a few of them sent from the swaps desk in New York to PJ:

'Hi PJ, please can you put in a low 1M and 3M LIBOR for us Friday. Thanks very much, Jay.'

'Hi Peter, all three of us here in New York have the same 3M LIBOR position, i.e. long. Keep your fixing low. It would be greatly appreciated.' That was from a New York swaps trader named Alex Pabon (pronounced 'Pay-bon').

Then they came across many more, relating not to Libor but to its European equivalent, Euribor. It worked in a similar way, asking banks to estimate how much it would cost them to borrow euros, cutting out the highest and lowest estimates and averaging those in the middle. The young lawyers unearthed hundreds of messages from swaps traders asking for banks' estimates of the cost of borrowing euros to be submitted 'high' or 'low' in the hope that it might help to nudge the Euribor average up or down.

Some of the messages made it very clear that the traders stood to make or lose money depending on where Libor or Euribor went. Like this one from Ryan Reich to Jon Mathew:

'Please go for 536 LIBOR again today. Very long and will be hurt if a higher setting. Thanks, Ryan.'

'Yeah, sure. 3s?' replied Jon (checking that Reich meant his 3-month Libor submission).

'Yes.'

It seemed to show that Reich was asking for Libor to be set at 5.36% to help his trading position, which would lose money if Libor were too high. The same trader was in touch again a little later.

'Please set 3M Libor as high as possible today.'

'*As high as possible*'? Now that looked corrupt.

Alas, neither Jon nor PJ was there to explain what 'as high as possible' really meant. Ryan knew Jon couldn't just submit any old high rate to suit the bank's swaps trading. What he meant by 'as high as possible' was short-hand for 'as high as possible within the range where cash was trading'. But because the traders might become the targets of their investigation, the lawyers weren't asking any traders to explain the messages they were look-ing at. They saw the emails and heard the recorded calls of PJ, Pete Spence and Colin Bermingham, who were making it very clear that it shouldn't be derivatives desks that decided what Libor rates should be submitted. Yet here was documentary evidence – emails – that clearly showed derivatives traders asking for a favour.

Without knowing the essential background, the lawyers and compli-ance officials investigating Libor for Barclays began to become convinced they were unearthing evidence of a whole new category of wrongdoing. But there was a problem they hadn't thought of. They were taking what PJ and others had been saying about dishonest Libors during the crisis and applying it to trader requests pre-crisis, without realising the fundamental difference. Lowballing during the crisis meant putting in false rates that were way outside the range of interest rates where cash was trading. With trader requests pre-crisis, it was the opposite: the adjustments PJ or Jon or Sisse were making to their Libor submissions were accurate, well within that range. Oblivious to that crucial distinction, the compliance officials and American lawyers were breaching an old scientific principle dating back to the beginning of the Enlightenment. If you have a theory, look for evidence that might prove it wrong. Otherwise, the danger is that you only look for evidence to confirm your theory. You only see what you want to see. The investigators were finding misconduct where they hoped to find it. At first, though, they could only see the requests from the swaps trad-ers. They didn't yet know for sure if the Libor submitters like PJ or Jon had accepted them.

When Jon was called to his first interview with the investigators, a con-ference call with Mocek's firm, it lasted only twenty minutes and was all about whether the bank had engaged in misconduct in the financial crisis – lowballing. At first, neither PJ nor Jon felt any sense that they, personally, were in trouble. It was the bank that was being investigated, not them as individuals. And as their emails and recorded calls would show, the orders had come from the top.

Unlike PJ, Jon would rarely challenge authority or behave in a confrontational way. Unfailingly polite with his colleagues and still, at 28, one of the younger people on the trading floor, he'd always tried not to ruffle feathers, taking his cue from older, wiser people who seemed to know what they were talking about. He also felt very lucky to have his well-paid job and was ready to do or say whatever was needed to keep it. Survival was paramount.

On 30 September 2009, Jon was working as normal on the trading floor of Barclays Capital's offices in Canary Wharf when he received an unexpected call from compliance. He needed to attend a meeting downstairs, immediately. He'd been given no warning of it but guessed it was bound to be about the CFTC's ongoing investigation into Libor. Descending the grandiose circular staircase to the ground floor, he found his way to a large meeting room where he was surprised to find eight people awaiting him, some from compliance and some from Barclays' legal department. From the USA via a conference phone, Greg Mocek and his colleagues at McDermott Will & Emery dialled in.

Most of the questions were about lowballing in the financial crisis. He explained why he and PJ had thought the other banks were lying. There was no way any bank could borrow cash at the cheap interest rates where they said they could. He knew it for sure because whenever he tried to borrow dollars, the only offers to lend were at much higher interest rates. Then, just as the interview drew to a close, Jon was blindsided by an unexpected question. One of the investigators fixed him in the eye. Did anyone ever influence his Libor submissions?

'No,' said Jon. He searched his memory. For such a long time, all the talk about Libor had been about lowballing. If anyone had influenced his Libor submissions it was senior managers, and later, central banks, who were seeking to ensure Barclays didn't stand out too high above the rest of the pack. He'd forgotten all about the requests from the traders in New York, tiny by comparison, which had stopped happening as soon as the credit crunch began more than two years before.

'You didn't take requests from swaps traders into account?' demanded the investigator.

Jon repeated that he didn't think so. Frowning, the investigator leafed through a ring binder of evidence, took out a few sheets and showed them to him. They were printouts of messages he'd exchanged with Ryan Reich.

Reich: 'Please go for 536 LIBOR again today. Very long and will be hurt if a higher setting. Thanks, Ryan.'
Mathew: 'Yeah, sure. 3s?'
Reich: 'Yes.'

And there was another, sent by Ryan Reich on 6 August 2007:

Reich: 'Please set 3M Libor as high as possible.'
Mathew: 'Sure. 5.37?'
Reich: '5.36 is fine.'
Mathew: 'Okay, sir.'

The question was now insistent and pressing, like a cold blade of accusation held to his throat: 'When you set your dollar Libor rates, did you take requests like this one into account?'

Jon looked carefully down at the exchanges and what he'd said in reply to Ryan. The messages had nudged a distant memory of swaps traders in New York making requests. It looked like an obvious matter of fact. 'Yes, I probably would have taken them into account,' he agreed, still looking at the documents.

As he slowly looked up again, Jon was taken aback by the reaction of the investigators. They were staring at each other, eyes wide and mouths half open, leaving him no room for doubt that they were shocked by what he'd just said. He looked again at the expressions on each of their faces with a rising sense of anxiety. There was no doubt about it: they clearly saw these emails as trouble and thought they'd found something bad – very bad. The interview was terminated immediately.

As he left the meeting room, stunned, Jon tried to stay calm. But his heart was pumping faster, and his anxiety was turning to panic. It was the first time anyone had suggested that when he accepted requests from traders to tweak his Libor submissions he was doing anything wrong. He tried desperately to think back to the traders' requests from years before. He could remember adjusting his Libor submissions a tick or two up or down. But he didn't remember having any feeling at the time that he was doing anything against any rules. Could it really be that he'd been doing something bad all that time? After all, he was only doing his job the way he'd always done it, the exact same way PJ had told him to!

Visibly shaken, Jon slowly made his way back up the staircase to return to the trading floor. He had to talk to PJ, immediately. 'I've just had an interview,' Jon told him, the tension in his voice betraying how worried he was. 'The swaps traders' requests seem to be a problem.'

'OK,' said PJ, noticing how panicky he was. 'Let's go outside and talk.'

As they emerged from the building into the late summer sunshine on North Colonnade, a cool breeze was blowing in from the open water next to Canary Wharf. PJ turned away from the wind to light up a cigarette, took a drag on it and asked Jon what had happened in the interview. Jon told him he'd forgotten all about the requests from the swaps traders. When he was shown evidence of them, he'd told them he'd taken them into account. From the reaction of the people in the room, they seemed shocked.

Both Jon and PJ were struggling to take it on board. What was going on here? Who was being investigated – all the banks that were doing the lowballing? Or them as individuals, for something tiny? The investigation was already casting a shadow over their lives, as if a giant oil tanker was heading towards them and they couldn't get out of the way. They knew it was going to be very difficult to stop – and feared they were going to get sucked under.

'You know, I've thought long and hard about this,' said PJ. 'We're good guys. We wouldn't have done anything wrong.'

Only Jon Mathew has given a public account of what came next in the conversation, which he would use, unsuccessfully, to defend himself. The following is his version, told on legal advice when he was on trial and doing his best to stay out of jail. He wouldn't go as far as to claim that PJ explicitly ordered him to lie. Instead, he said, he felt 'under pressure' from PJ not to tell the truth. According to Jon, PJ said: 'We wouldn't have taken these requests into account. We'd have ignored them – wouldn't we.' Jon's claim was that when he tried to interrupt, PJ cut him off, repeating, 'We're good guys. We would have ignored these requests. We wouldn't have done anything wrong.'

Jon's story was that he interpreted PJ's reaction to mean that his boss wanted him to lie about accepting the trader requests. Before that day, he said, he hadn't ever thought that taking trader requests into account when setting his Libor rates was bad. It was the fact that PJ reacted as he did, together with the shocked reaction of the Project Bruce team, that made him think, for the first time, that he'd been wrong to oblige the traders' requests.

At the cash desk a few days later, PJ showed Jon some messages he'd exchanged with the traders. He'd been going through the data showing where he'd put his Libor submissions on the days when traders made a request for a high or low Libor. They showed that he'd never posted a Libor submission outside the range of interest rates where cash was available – meaning that whether or not they'd accepted the requests, they were still accurate rates. And much of the time he hadn't done what the traders had asked for, or alternatively had just carried on submitting the same rate because it happened to coincide with what they'd asked for. According to Jon's account, PJ brought up the data on a Bloomberg computer terminal, showing where each bank had put their Libor submissions on that date. 'Look we're within the pack,' he said. 'I ignored them – I didn't act on it ... Lip service, right?'

For a split second, according to Jon, he even wondered briefly if his memory was playing tricks on him. Maybe he really had ignored them? But then he remembered the coffees, the banter, the sushi. This wasn't a matter of misremembering one or two emails. He'd spent too much time building relations with the swaps desk, with PJ's approval. He even remembered mentioning to PJ in his annual appraisals that he'd been really useful to the swaps desk. 'But what if the Libor submissions show you've actually done what the request asked for?' Jon asked PJ. 'How can you defend being asked to do something and then actually doing it?' PJ told him he could say it was 'subjective' and just a coincidence.

Feeling under pressure from PJ, according to Jon's evidence at trial, he decided he would lie to investigators, telling them that when he appeared to accept a trader's Libor request, he was only paying them lip service. He'd keep up that lie throughout 2010, telling it to the bank's lawyers and compliance officials, the CFTC, the FBI, the SEC and the FSA.

In cognitive psychology and criminology, 'confirmation bias' is defined as 'the tendency to interpret new evidence as confirmation of one's existing beliefs or theories'.[2] Evidence that appears to confirm your theory is given great weight and evidence that would contradict it is played down.

The old-fashioned name for it is 'wishful thinking'. You think something is true because you want it to be true. You believe it, not so much because the evidence forces you to, and more because you'd like to.

The CFTC's belief was that it was investigating the false reporting of the cost of borrowing dollars, as measured by Libor. If the evidence it found didn't show false reporting, it would be outside the CFTC's jurisdiction and the time and money it had spent investigating Libor would have been wasted. The evidence from lowballing was much stronger than the trader requests, with Libor rates being submitted that were obviously false. On some days banks were posting one rate as their Libor submission, then paying another, very different rate. But it was extremely awkward to pursue. Gensler's team already knew that the top fraud prosecutor at the US Department of Justice, Lanny Breuer, was very cautious about the collateral damage that could be done to confidence in the financial system by going after a commercial bank or its top executives, let alone a sovereign government – even when there was clear evidence that the blame belonged at the top. The lowballing evidence that the CFTC was accumulating pointed to senior bank executives, central bank officials, even governments. If they went after a sovereign institution like the UK government or the Bank of England, it wouldn't be merely undiplomatic. It could cause a renewed loss of confidence in the financial system and quite possibly a renewed financial crisis. Even going after the 'controlling minds' of the commercial banks could open them up to huge claims from business customers with loans or other products linked to Libor, potentially crippling them financially and triggering further bailouts. No one wanted that. But these trader requests, on the other hand, this they could do something about!

The CFTC could use them to fine banks for misconduct and the DOJ could pursue these lower-ranking bankers criminally, without the risk of bringing down the whole financial system. It was true that the messages asking for high or low Libors looked a little humdrum and routine – not your normal evidence of crime. And it was odd that the traders had left such a trail of evidence of misconduct when they knew their messages were monitored and their lines recorded. But that, investigators wishfully decided, was because this rotten practice had become so deeply embedded; it was every bit as criminal as lowballing and no less so for being done openly: a casual, everyday contempt for the rules.

Alas, in their eagerness to believe they'd uncovered further, prosecutable wrongdoing, no one at the CFTC (or the SEC, DOJ or SFO) did the arithmetic. It was true that the Libor average could move a little if Barclays' submission went from being towards the top – say the fifth highest – to being the lowest out of the sixteen banks contributing. One of the banks that had been excluded, just below the middle eight, would now be included in it, dragging the average down slightly. The CFTC had worked that one out. But they hadn't noticed that the maximum shift in the Libor average that a move like that could achieve was only one eighth of a basis point – or one eighth of one hundredth of a percentage point (0.00125%). Compared to the 50 basis points that PJ had to move when the instruction came down from the UK government and the Bank of England, it was tiny. The Libor instruction from the top was 400 times the size. That was why PJ and Jon had been fuming about lowballing. Unlike the fine-tuning involved in accepting trader requests, which might or might not make a small difference to the Libor average, lowballing truly counted. It meant the Libor average was clearly false.

Following Jon's interview, after months of getting nowhere, the CFTC team had what looked to them like confirmation of misconduct from one of the very people who submitted Barclays' dollar Libor rates to the BBA. Greg Mocek had heard Jon Mathew admit it. It wasn't just that the swaps traders in New York were making requests for changes to Libor rates. In his interview on 30 September 2009, Jon Mathew had confirmed he'd taken those requests into account.

Attending a conference in London a week after Jon's interview, Mocek and Obie met for a drink at the Grosvenor House hotel on Park Lane. 'I've been looking into Libor,' said Mocek. 'You're not going to believe what I've found.' They'd accumulated hundreds of emails that supported the CFTC's worst suspicions. Libor was being routinely manipulated every day, he told Obie. 'It was just like ordering take-out.'

Mocek was now convinced of it: they'd discovered a whole new type of Libor malfeasance. In January 2010 he gave a presentation to his former colleagues in Washington. According to reports based on interviews with the Libor team at the CFTC,[3] he noted how hard Libor had become to set since the credit crunch and the lack of rules, which meant traders couldn't be expected to know what to do. But, he added, his client, Barclays, had also been shocked to identify some 'rogue elements' and would 'deal with them without mercy'. By 'rogue elements', he meant the New York swaps desk that had been in touch with PJ and Jon Mathew between 2005 and 2007: Jay Merchant, Alex Pabon and Ryan Reich.

The 'Old Testament view' hadn't gone away. It just didn't apply to the guys at the top.

Hearing that the CFTC was back on the warpath about Libor, Barclays executives moved to put some insurance in place. The CFTC were clearly convinced now that requests from traders to alter Libor submissions amounted to misconduct. If executives could show they'd already investigated it and disciplined the individuals involved, they couldn't be criticised for condoning it. Appointing external lawyers to investigate alleged misconduct was a standard tactic for banks defending themselves against regulators. You could win a reduction in the size of any future fine because you were 'cooperating'. And you could ensure there were no unpleasant surprises for executives.

In February 2010, Jon Mathew was away skiing when he received a call from Mark Dearlove, instructing him to cut short his holiday and fly back to London immediately to attend his third interview about the Libor investigation, this time by the top 'magic circle' law firm appointed to defend Barclays in London, Clifford Chance. As he returned to London, Jon grew increasingly worried. The US authorities were now obviously focusing on the trader requests and had decided it was wrong to take them into account. PJ was much more senior and better connected than he was. Since his interview the previous September, Jon had had a growing anxiety that he could end up being scapegoated, blamed as the culprit of misconduct and sacked to take the pressure off the rest of the bank. Afraid of losing his job, he started trying to use the interviews to shift the blame away from himself.

In late March 2010, the Project Bruce investigators had a breakthrough. They came across an email from Peter Johnson to Mark Dearlove, sent on 29 October 2008 at 3.57 p.m., less than fifteen minutes after Dearlove's instruction:

Following on from my conversation with you, I will reluctantly, gradually and artificially get my libors in line with the rest of the contributors as requested. I disagree with this approach as you are well aware. I will be contributing rates which are nowhere near the clearing rates for unsecured cash and therefore will not be posting honest prices. I am not sure that the BBA definition of libor would accept this approach. Today for instance the only cash offer in 3 months has been Chase Nyk [Chase Manhattan bank, New York] who is offering at 4%. Please do not tell me that 3.42% was the correct rate as we both patently know that it was not. I will continue to keep a record of where money is or is not offered in the periods. COF spreads [cost of funds spreads – the difference between Libor and the interest rate the cash desk charged internally to other departments to whom it lent money] will have to go up massively in USD to compensate for fixing Libor rates unrealistically low.

They also came across another email two hours later by PJ's colleague who submitted Libor for pounds sterling, Pete Spence:

As per the telephonic communication today with Mark Dearlove, I have been requested to reduce the Sterling Libor rates to be more in line with the 'Pack'. As I understand it, this is an instruction either by senior management and/or the Bank of England. I voiced my views as below but as such will comply with the request and [...] it will take me a week to comply. But it should be noted that this will be breaking the BBA rules with regard to the setting of Sterling Libor rates (i.e. a reasonable amount offered in the market in the period concerned) and as such the breaking of such rules will happen until the instruction demanded by senior management will be rescinded or the BBA rules are changed.

Only after finding those emails did the Project Bruce team start listening to all the audio recordings from PJ and Pete Spence's lines. It was then that they discovered the recording, less than twenty minutes before the email was sent, of Dearlove's instruction to PJ from the UK government and the Bank of England. Within hours, Greg Mocek at McDermott Will & Emery had heard it. A CD with a copy of the recording was sent to Anne Termine, the CFTC lawyer now in charge of the Libor investigation day-to-day, who brought it to Steve Obie, who brought it to Gary Gensler (see pages 77–9).

Soon after, in April 2010, Greg Mocek met Margaret Cole in Canary Wharf. They'd got to know each other when they were both directors of enforcement attending international conferences for regulators. Now representing Barclays, Mocek played her the recording of the Dearlove–PJ instruction. The implication was serious and obvious: lowballing and false Libor rates weren't just the result of instructions from Barclays' senior management. Both the Bank of England and the UK government had been involved; if the FSA did not drop the investigation into Barclays, officials at the Bank and UK government would also be implicated. To Mocek, this was a smoking gun that the FSA couldn't ignore. Cole, who'd never seen eye to eye with the Americans about Libor, wasn't ready to either drop the investigation or use the tape to go after the Bank of England or the government. Frustrated, Mocek wouldn't let it go, needling Cole with follow-up emails, reminding her of what she'd heard. It didn't go down well. To Cole, she and Greg Mocek may have known each other personally, but he was now representing Barclays, and being far too 'cloak and dagger' about it. She also had her doubts about the competence of Mocek's former colleagues at the CFTC. When he sent one email too many, an indignant Cole got in touch with Barclays' general counsel, Mark Harding, saying she wasn't sure Mocek was representing his client's interests very well. Within days of their conversation, McDermott Will & Emery were no longer representing Barclays in the USA. Another US firm, Sullivan & Cromwell, would take over. Compliance would no longer report directly to the Barclays' board; Barclays' legal department was taking charge.

With the CFTC now joined by the SEC and the DOJ launching a criminal prosecution, the Americans were changing up a gear. Until now, the FSA had continued to resist launching its own investigation. But now, with the SEC and FBI on board, the Libor investigation was no longer just an obscure Washington commodities regulator trying to punch above its weight. Two years on from the first contact about Libor from the CFTC, the UK regulator was now ready to join in. The US Libor 'bus' was revving up, ready to accelerate. Neither Barclays nor the BBA nor the FSA could press the brakes. From now on, it would only be a case of who'd be able to get out of its path, and who would get thrown under.

8

A TANGLED WEB

Sometimes, hiding something you've done can make it seem worse than it really is.

In June 2010, PJ and Jon were informed that the US government wanted a formal interview with each of them. Then in November, the US authorities arrived in force. Granted, the benchmark interest rate at the heart of this scandal might be called the 'London Interbank Offered Rate'. But to the Americans, this was their territory. It was, after all, about manipulation of the price of borrowing *their* currency: US dollars.

Jon was interviewed first, on 18 November at the headquarters of the Financial Services Authority at 25 North Colonnade, Canary Wharf, a short walk down the road from the headquarters of Barclays Capital where he worked. Waiting for him in a large meeting room were eighteen people, including two from the Commodity Futures Trading Commission, two FBI agents, three from the US Department of Justice, three from the Securities and Exchange Commission, three from the FSA and five lawyers, two of them representing him in the UK and three in the USA. From the CFTC, Anne Termine was there along with her colleague Steve Tsai. For the US DOJ, Robertson Park came with two colleagues. The lead FBI agent, Mike Kelly, led the questioning and the vast majority of the questions were about lowballing. But Jon was surprised how many questions there were about trader requests. Asked again if he'd felt 'uncomfortable' when he'd received the first trader request from Stelios Contogoulas, Jon's answers implied that it was all about the British Bankers' Association definition of Libor. 'I don't remember my exact feelings at the time, but it wasn't, you know, it wasn't in the definition. Yes, I mean, it's not a nice position to be in,' Jon told the investigators. 'I thought enough to raise it with PJ – so I was uncomfortable with it. I do remember doing that [...] Again, sorry to harp back to the definition, but it's, you know, it's not in the definition. It's not something that I'd ever taken into account when setting Libor, what swaps traders or what any trader's view has been on Libor so, you know, instantly it makes you feel uncomfortable.' As Jon would later admit, it wasn't true. It wasn't just that he wasn't uncomfortable; when the trader requests came in, he'd never read the BBA definition.' No one at the bank had ever given him a copy of it to read.

'But you continued to get requests?' asked Kelly.

'I received only a couple,' said Jon.

Towards the end of the day, when Jon's interview wrapped up, his place in the hot seat was taken by the man he'd been seeking to blame. Over the rest of that evening and the whole of the next day, PJ was grilled by the FBI, revealing to everyone present that he'd come under pressure to 'keep his head below the parapet', meaning that he had to keep his Libor submission no higher than 10 basis points (0.1%) above every other bank contributing to the Libor average. That meant he was putting in Libor rates below what he'd really have to pay to raise cash. Senior management, in other words, had instructed him to post false Libor rates.

The lead FSA investigator, Joanna Howard, asked who he meant when he referred to pressure from 'senior' management. Mark Dearlove and Miles Storey?

'I would call "senior management" people above Miles and Mark.'

'So could you just clarify who in senior management you were talking about?' asked Howard.

'I believe it was people higher up than Jon Stone, Mark Dearlove and Miles Storey ... You know, people very senior in Barclays Bank.'

'Can you give any specific names?' asked Howard.

'People on the thirty-first floor.'

'And what does people on the thirty-first floor mean?'

'That means the extremely senior people in Barclays Bank. I mean the top people in Barclays Bank.'

'And when you say the top people, who are you talking about?'

'Chris Lucas, finance director of Barclays Bank,[2] people like that.'

'And was there anybody else apart from that?'

'I can't specifically recollect.'

PJ explained that he'd escalated his concerns not only to senior management but to central banks. His colleagues had raised it with the FSA – and the regulator seemed to think the approach Barclays was taking was reasonable in the circumstances. 'I talked to the Fed about it, I talked to the Bank of England about it, I talked to a lot of people about it and I didn't feel I had anything to hide,' he said. 'I was concerned that we weren't setting them high enough. I was aware that there was pressure from fairly high up in the bank not to be too much of an outlier, and I raised my concerns and I made sure, well I found out that they had been, taken to the BBA and the FSA.'

'Okay,' said Kelly.

'So I felt – "comfortable" isn't really the right word – but I felt that I was … in the comfort zone about where I was setting my Libors, even though I wasn't actually sure that I was setting them totally correctly.'

Kelly brought up an email PJ sent to Dearlove on 4 December 2007.

> I am feeling increasingly uncomfortable [...] My worry is that we (Barclays and the contributor bank panel) are being seen to be contributing patently false rates. We are therefore being dishonest by definition and are at risk of damaging our reputation in the market and with the regulators ...

Kelly didn't want PJ to think the FBI was pointing the finger at him. 'I think it's very well established, that you were under extreme pressure from management, pressure that you openly and frequently communicated your concern with, alright? So I want you to understand that this isn't [...] missing that point in any way whatsoever and that we're looking at this and saying, "Isn't it true that you alone filed patently false submissions?" That's not the direction I'm trying to take this conversation. But I do want to make sure that I understand. Is there an acceptance or an understanding on your part that there was a time that you were, in your own mind, submitting rates that you knew to be patently false?'

'I was concerned that it was becoming the case,' said PJ.

Kelly pressed him; the numbers he was submitting were something other than what he'd have put if he'd had a free hand?

'That's correct.'

'Okay,' said Kelly. 'Then let's just understand. That free hand – not having a free hand – that you're talking about is pressure from management?'

'Yes.'

PJ's role in the interview shifted repeatedly from being a potential defendant to being an expert witness, coaching his interviewers through how Libor worked, and back again. After much further questioning, Kelly wrapped up the interview at 4.30 p.m. 'Alright. I think we have exhausted ourselves for the amount of time that we have available. I would like to thank you very much for your time, you've been very helpful. You've brought a lot of context to the documents that we had, and I really appreciate your candour and your willingness to work with us on this, so thank you very much.'

'Okay, thank you.'

'The time is now 4.30 and this is the end of our interview with Peter Johnson,' said Howard.

But it wasn't quite the end. Within an hour, the US agencies changed their minds and asked PJ to go back on the record. There was something they hadn't yet asked about – something so highly confidential that PJ wasn't supposed to be discussing it with anyone. No one was meant to know.

At 5.26 p.m., the interview recommenced, recorded (as the rest of it had been), on to a CD. 'Notwithstanding that the interview was ended at the end of disc two, the parties have agreed that the interview should be continued on the same basis,' said the FSA's Joanna Howard, asking everyone there to identify themselves for the tape. This was one chance to get the truth on the record and PJ had made up his mind to come out and say it.

'What I'd like to do,' Mike Kelly began, 'is turn the focus to the period in late 2008 where the pressure from an external source was identified to you. Could you just give us in your best description, what was communicated to you, what your understanding was of what was communicated to you – as far as where the pressure that was coming in late 2008?'

'I was effectively being told by the Bank of England to put my rates down,' said PJ.

'Okay. Who in the Bank of England, if you know, was the source of that pressure?'

'I was of the understanding that it was Paul Tucker.'

So how did this differ, Kelly wanted to know, from the pressure from senior management starting in August 2007?

'This was a directive from an external source where I was being told to push my rates lower, no matter what the circumstances [...] Even if I felt that rates were going up generally, I would have to put rates down [...] Before, you know, if rates were rising and I wanted to be above the pack, they were happy for me to do that. If rates were falling a little bit and I still want to be above the pack they're happy for me to do that. [Now] the rising and falling rates environment made no difference, I was just being told to get rates down [...] I was just thinking, I just don't believe that rates should be coming down.'

Agent Kelly pulled out an unofficial transcript of Dearlove's call to PJ on 29 October 2008 and showed it to PJ. 'Right,' he said. 'Did you have any understanding as to why this pressure was being put upon Barclays?'

'I'm not sure, excuse me. I'm not sure that it was being put just on Barclays.'

'Okay? Who else did you think, was being pressured?'

'We understood that the French banks had been told to get their rates down. It's not in this transcript, but we understood that's what had happened.'

'Okay,' said Kelly. 'So some French banks were also being pressured?'

'We had heard, yes.'

'You had heard. And what entity was pressuring them?'

'We believe it was the Banque du France.'

'The Bank of France?

'Yes.'

'So the national bank of the respective country?'

'Yes.'

'Okay,' said Kelly. 'So with regard to the Bank of France pushing on the French banks, what currency or what Libor is it your understanding they were pressuring them to lower?'

'That would have been Euribor or Euro Libor.'

'If we go to the first exchange here,' Kelly picked up. 'Mr Dearlove, at the bottom of his first statement, says, "The bottom line is you're going to absolutely hate this and I've spoken to Spence about it as well, but we've had some very serious pressure from the UK government and the Bank of England about pushing our LIBORS lower." You've mentioned the Bank of England already, there is a reference here to the UK government?'

'Yes.'

'Do you have an understanding as to what part of the UK government?'

'I have no idea.'

'Further down at the bottom of this first page, three lines up from the bottom, Mr Dearlove says, "PJ, I'm on your side, 100 per cent. These guys don't see it. They're bent out of shape. They're calling everyone from Diamond to Varley." Do you have an understanding who "they" and "these guys" and "they're" are referring to?'

'I have no absolute knowledge,' said PJ, 'but my assumption was – is – the UK government or Bank of England.'

'Okay. And in reading this, and if you have a recollection of the call or the event as it happened, is it your understanding that the direction came through senior management?'

'Yes.'

'And Diamond and Varley are members of senior management?'

'Yes,' said PJ.

'Okay so I think your final takeaway is the fourth line up from the bottom, "I'm going to get to the top of the pack, I'm not going any lower than that." How about that? Is that – was that your plan, was that your intention coming out of this conversation?'

'I didn't feel I had much choice; this was a directive from the Bank of England as far as I was concerned. I just didn't really feel I had much choice at all, and you can see I wasn't happy about it.'

'Right okay,' said Kelly. 'So you voice your concern – that's very clearly stated here, it's very clearly stated in the email we're going to look at next – but still you felt that you were compelled to oblige – is what it sounds like you're saying?'

'Yes,' PJ replied.

'Okay. And just to clarify: you're going to get your Libors down regardless of where you normally set Libor?'

'I am going to do what I am being told to do by the Bank of England.'

'And you're not just going to be looking at transactional data, you're going to be getting your Libors down regardless of the transactional data?' asked Bob Tripp.

'Yes, I'm going to do what I've been told to do by, in my view, the supreme monetary authority in the land. I don't feel particularly good about them.'

Kelly asked PJ about the email he'd sent after Dearlove's call. 'And in this you appear to outline your-your discomfort with the request at hand, but acknowledge that as you say, "I will reluctantly, gradually and artificially get my Libors in line with the rest of the contributors as requested"?'

'Yes.'

'Is that consistent with what you – what you did?'

'My Libors came down.'

'Okay, but you go on to say that you "disagree with this approach. As you are well aware, I will be contributing rates which are nowhere near the clearing rates for unsecured cash and therefore will not be posting honest prices. I am not sure that the BBA definition of Libor would accept this approach." I guess it's clearly written here but I just want to make sure I understand your frame of mind – that your understanding was that you were going to have to change, lower your Libors, in a manner that was not in line with the BBA definition of Libor?'

'Just nowhere near in line,' said PJ. There was one thing which had given him comfort, he said. In late October, just before he'd been given the instruction by Dearlove, a sudden change took place on the money markets. It had been weeks since there were any serious offers to lend cash. But then one of the few big Wall Street banks strong enough to survive the banking crisis without taxpayer help, Chase New York, had all at once come into the market and started offering to lend – a significant event. Anne Termine said she had information that Chase was offering funds at 4.68% but had put its Libor submission of the cost of borrowing at 3.25%. PJ confirmed there were rumours surrounding Chase at the time. 'What were they?' asked Termine.

'That the Fed had asked it to lend money into the market.'

Before the interview wrapped up at 7.30 p.m. on a Friday evening, PJ had given the US investigators names, dates and figures – all they needed to investigate, expose and prosecute what had every appearance of an unprecedented financial scandal. It involved top bank bosses, central banks and governments across the Western world pressuring him and others, in some cases against their protests, to change their Libor submissions in a way that violated the BBA definition, to serve the commercial interests of the banks – the very same actions for which traders would later be jailed. He'd pointed the US authorities to the Bank of England, the Banque de France and the Fed, supplying all the evidence and investigative leads the FBI, CFTC, SEC and DOJ could have wished for to set about proving that in truth, the blame for interest rate-rigging lay emphatically at the top of the financial system.

But alas, just like the tape of his instruction from Dearlove, PJ's interview with the FBI and the regulators would be buried. All the important information it contained would be hidden not only from Parliament, the press and the public, but from the juries at the rate-rigging trials in London.

Soon after their interviews, PJ took Jon out for a drink to discuss what they'd said to the US and UK regulators and the FBI. Jon didn't mention what he'd told them about PJ, or that he'd said he believed trader requests were 'inappropriate'. PJ was talkative, saying he was very happy that it was out of the way and pleased with how he'd done. It seemed like the investigators had liked and believed him; and best of all he'd finally seized the chance to tell the truth to the US civil and criminal authorities, who, unlike their UK counterparts, might actually do something about it.

What PJ didn't yet know was that it wouldn't be the regulators and criminal investigators in that room who would decide his fate. It would be the young man sitting opposite, drinking the pint he'd just bought for him.

The DOJ did follow up on what PJ had said. Three months after his interview, on Monday 28 February 2011, Jerry del Missier turned up with a team of lawyers at the DOJ's offices at 1400 New York Avenue Northwest in the centre of Washington DC, less than 400m from the White House. He'd agreed to fly over from the UK to give the US authorities an interview for their investigation into the rigging of Libor and Euribor. It began at 9.47 a.m. and the questions came from the same lead investigators who'd spoken to PJ and Jon, the DOJ's Robertson Park and FBI agent Mike Kelly. Nearly two hours into the interview, they were discussing an email del Missier had sent to Mark Dearlove and his boss John Porter on 1 September 2007, recounting a phone call he'd just had with Paul Tucker. Something unexpected had come up. Park asked to stop the interview for a couple of minutes to speak to his top legal adviser. 'Going off the record here,' said Kelly. 'It's 11.35.' Fifteen minutes later they resumed.

'This email appears to recount a meeting or a call that you had with Mr Tucker. Is that accurate?' asked Kelly.

'Yes,' replied del Missier. He and Tucker had discussed the *Financial Times* splash that had got Tucker so worried, headlined 'Anxious Market Catches Barclays Short of £1.6 billion', reporting how Barclays had had to use the Bank of England's emergency lending facility, the 'discount window'.

'It appears in the middle portion of your email,' said Kelly, 'where it says, "Separately we had a discussion about Libor rates. We agreed that this is a non-story that was typical of the sort of stuff that the press was pursuing in the search for sensational headlines." Do you have a recollection of having any additional—of anything else being said about Libor rates during that meeting with Mr Tucker or during that call?'

'Yes. Mr Tucker said that we should get our Libor rates down.'

'And how did that come up in the call?' asked Kelly.

'Well, so the call was ostensibly about the two instances that we'd had of going to the window of the facility and symptomatic of kind of the way things were evolving. He was going around talking to all of the British banks to say, "Be extra careful to not let this kind of thing happen again." In essence, he was saying, "This is not, kind of, normal markets, you shouldn't be managing without margins for error so please don't let these things happen, because, you can see, the impact on market sentiment and confidence is quite extreme."

'I don't know how we got on the subject of Libor rates, whether he raised it or if it was a subject that came up because of some of the press in and around the time. I don't recall that, sir. But we got into a discussion about Libor rates. And I don't know how we jumped into the section of the conversation where he made the statement, "you should get your Libor rates down". But it came up as part of the overall conversation about Libor. And my statement that this was a non-story was a statement that Libor rates weren't symptomatic or indicative of any financial health – and that is what is conveyed here.'[3]

'So did he give you an indication that he was telling all the other British banks he was meeting with that they had to get their Libor rates down as well?'

'He didn't say.'

'And did you protest the statement in any way?' asked Kelly. 'How did you respond to the statement?'

'I told him that we called the market where we saw it. There wasn't much of a discussion after that,' del Missier told Kelly.

A few months later, Mike Kelly and Bob Tripp of the FBI, Luke Marsh and Nicole Sprinzen of the DOJ and Anne Termine of the CFTC travelled to London to interview Paul Tucker on 2 June 2011, at the offices of the FSA in Canary Wharf, where his role in Libor was discussed. His interviewers had already heard about his instruction to del Missier on 1 September 2007. But when they later came to fine Barclays for rigging Libor, neither the CFTC nor the DOJ nor the FSA would mention it. Neither the defendants nor the juries in the later trials of traders for rigging rates would ever get to see a full transcript of the interview.

At the end of 2010, PJ wrote in Jon Mathew's appraisal: '2010 has been a demanding year for Jonathan. He has had to spend a considerable amount of time and energy on Project Bruce. I know that this has been extremely stressful. Jonathan is to be congratulated on the way that he has not allowed this to affect the standard of his work. He has displayed enthusiasm and initiative and has made a big contribution to the team effort.'

But there were significant things Jon was keeping from PJ. For more than a year, he'd been reinforcing the US investigators' view that trader requests were 'inappropriate' and blaming the practice on PJ. He'd kept up the story that they only paid 'lip service' to trader requests for high or low Libors and didn't help them by putting in Libors 'high' or 'low'. But it was becoming harder to make it hold water.

First were those bits of evidence that were awkward to explain away. When Jay Merchant, Alex Pabon, Stelios Contogoulas, Ryan Reich and others had asked for Libors to be submitted high or low, neither PJ nor Jon had said, 'I'll see what I can do', as you would if you were paying lip service or 'fobbing someone off'. It was more committed – like what Jon had jokingly said to Stelios Contogoulas: 'Done, for you, big boy ...' Then there were the notes PJ had written for Jon when he went away, such as 'swaps desk are looking for high 1-month and low 3-month Libors'. Why bother if they were only going to fob them off?

The hardest one to explain was an email exchange that Agent Kelly had brought up, from Ryan Reich to PJ, copying in Jay Merchant on 14 December 2006: *'For Monday we're very long 3M cash here in New York. Would like the setting to be as low as possible.'*

P. Johnson: *'I am off on Monday but Jon [Mathew] will take notice of what you say ...'*

PJ had tried to explain it away as a fob off. But within a few days of PJ and Jon's interview, the Project Bruce team unearthed a small but devastating piece of evidence. They'd discovered the reminder Jon had entered on his Outlook calendar to make sure he wouldn't forget Ryan's request the following Monday (see page 100), with a note accompanying the alert saying 'USD 3M Libor down.'

Soon after his interview with the US authorities, Jon received a call about it. He arranged a meeting with his lawyer, who agreed to meet Barclays' lawyers on 16 December. At the meeting, Jon again tried to shift the blame. Whenever Libor was set for US dollars, he said, PJ was always involved – even when he was away and Jon was covering for him – because he gave him detailed briefings and instructions about how to set it. Barclays' lawyers asked him about the inconsistency between what he'd said in the meeting in September 2009, when he'd told shocked investigators he'd probably accepted traders' requests, and what he'd been saying since then. Jon kept up his story that he'd only provided lip service but said the calendar entry was an exception; PJ had asked him to set a Libor and he'd done so.

But even that story wasn't going to hold water long. Jon had made more than one use of his Outlook calendar reminders. Soon, the Project Bruce team discovered one he'd created in November 2005, setting an alert for 19 December to remind him that Barclays' most senior trader John Porter had a trade that would benefit from a low Libor average: '3M Libor 4.53 J Porter Long'. Then there was the time in December 2006 when PJ had received a request from Ryan to set his 3-month Libor estimate low and then forgotten about it, saying, 'Whoops. Was away from desk,' when he realised. He'd then forwarded the request to Jon. Why would anyone say 'whoops' for overlooking something they'd never meant to do in the first place? There was a calendar entry for that too, set every day from 22 December to 1 January 2007, with a note saying, 'SET 3 MONTH US$ LIBOR LOW!!!!!!'

It didn't make sense to set up a calendar entry, every day for more than a week, just to pay lip service to a trader. As Jon put it, 'You can't justify setting a calendar entry to remind yourself to ignore an email request.' Worse, the part of their defence that was true – that trader requests weren't that big a deal – was undermined by the new evidence. It was becoming impossible to hold the line. The story about lip service was falling apart.

Then, in the spring of 2011, Jon learned something even more alarming that made him afraid not only for his job but for his liberty. The DOJ employed a textbook move – the same move it had used to great effect, for decades, against every criminal gang from the Sicilian mafia to the Mexican drug cartels. Turn the heat up high enough on the little guys – and they'll put their bosses in the frame. Officials in Rob Park's team at the DOJ got in touch with Jon's lawyers to say they believed he'd been lying. He had taken trader requests into account and made false statements when he put in his Libor submissions. Jon could now face charges not only for manipulating Libor but for obstruction of justice. It was no longer just Barclays Bank that the US authorities wanted to pursue. They were now interested in him, personally.

In the City of London and Canary Wharf, the US justice system is regarded with horror. Unlike the generally light punishments in the UK, where sentences for white-collar crime rarely exceed ten years, in the USA it's punishable by long jail sentences that can run into decades. The widespread belief in the City is that once the DOJ has decided you've done something wrong, you don't have much of a chance. It was well known that more than 90 per cent of those prosecuted are convicted, mostly because they have agreed to a 'plea bargain': submitting a guilty plea in exchange for a reduced or suspended sentence. Those who choose to go to trial are only rarely acquitted; so if you want to fight the DOJ's accusations, you take a big risk that, with the wrong jury, you could spend a large chunk of your life in a rough US jail. If the judge were to sentence you to fifteen or even thirty years, you wouldn't be released on good behaviour halfway through as you would in the UK; you'd serve most or all of it. Jon was now staring into that abyss.

In the witch hunts of seventeenth-century England, women suspected of witchcraft were sometimes tied up and thrown into a pond to see if they would sink or swim. If they sank, they were innocent; if they swam, they were guilty and would be hanged as witches. There was a flavour of that in the dilemma Jon now faced, the same dilemma faced by thousands of others before him who'd gone through the US justice system. Either admit to wrongdoing, in which case he might just avoid jail; or maintain his innocence, in which case he'd be very likely to spend a long time in a US prison. British prosecutors will tell you, mostly privately, that they wouldn't want the US system in the UK. It may be true that plea bargaining can cut the cost of investigations and prosecutions. Instead of building a case, prosecutors simply find what they regard as evidence that someone has done something illegal, threaten them with a huge jail sentence, offer a plea bargain and require the 'cooperator' to testify against anyone else who protests their innocence. But in this carrot and stick approach, the stick of a long jail sentence is so frightening, and the carrot of no jail time so

appealing, that it creates a huge incentive to go along with the DOJ story –
their theory of what the crime is and who is guilty – regardless of whether
that theory is right. So overwhelming is that incentive that if the DOJ has
misunderstood something – or if their case against you is misconceived
– it can be against your interests to say so. Faced with the likelihood of
decades in a US jail, most defendants will say whatever the DOJ wants to
hear. And that can mean they give unreliable evidence. It's the same reason
that evidence extracted by torture is unreliable. Eventually, the victims of
torture will say whatever their captor wants to hear, whether or not it's
true. Or, to put it another way, they will pay 'lip service'. And that lip service
can include confessions of dishonesty, confessions made not because they
are true but because they appease the DOJ.

Jon discussed it at length with his lawyers. If he maintained his innocence, he was heading for a trial where the odds were stacked against him,
threatening to wreck his life by forcing him to spend years in a US penitentiary, thousands of miles away from his family or friends. But if he came
forward and told the truth, the whole truth and nothing but the truth, he'd
be offered a non-prosecution agreement, escaping any risk of jail.

To Jon, who was very scared of being prosecuted in the USA, it was 'a
complete no-brainer'.[4] There was no need to think hard about what to do; it
was obviously in his self-interest to cooperate. But there was a catch. When
the DOJ asked him to 'tell the truth, the whole truth and nothing but the
truth', it was clear that they already had their own view about what the
truth was. It meant going along with a view that he hadn't believed at the
time – that accepting trader requests to adjust his Libor submissions was
wrong. It also required him to give the DOJ a witness statement that pointed
the finger of blame at his bosses, starting with his mentor and teacher, the
man who'd taught him everything he knew about trading since he started,
aged 23, six years before: Peter Charles Johnson, also known as PJ.

In May 2011, Jon and PJ went out for a pint of beer after work. It would be
the last time. Unlike in their previous discussions, PJ was now far from
bullish about the investigation. According to Jon, his mood was dark. He
mentioned that their colleague on the cash desk, Pete Spence, had travelled
to the USA and had been stopped at the airport and had his bags searched
– something PJ connected to the Libor investigation. PJ said he was never
going to travel to the USA again. Jon told PJ nothing about the discussions

he'd been having with his lawyers. The US authorities had ordered him not to tell his employer.

To the US investigators, Jon's admission that he lied when he said he was only paying lip service to the traders' requests was further confirmation of a view they'd formed very early on: that all trader requests about Libor and Euribor were wrong. Why lie about something unless there's something bad to hide? That view was given further support by what Jon had said in November 2010, that he'd felt uncomfortable about the traders' requests way back in 2005.

The trouble was that it wasn't true. Jon had only started to think trader requests were problematic in the first place because of the reaction of the internal investigators at his September 2009 interview, from US lawyers and compliance officials who had clearly already decided for themselves, without any input from traders, that granting requests for 'high' or 'low' Libor submissions was wrong. Before that, Jon had heard or seen nothing to suggest that they were anything other than fine. The investigators had created their own reality, their own version of the rights and wrongs of Libor. Like other traders in years to come, Jon, faced with the threat of a long jail sentence in the USA, was simply fitting into it. Now, to seal the deal with the DOJ, Jon had to give the US authorities what they wanted: further confirmation that accepting trader requests was wrong and evidence of who else had been involved.

In July 2011, executives at Barclays discovered, to their horror, that their employee Jonathan James Mathew was about to become a cooperating US government witness, prepared to testify against his boss and the New York swaps traders in criminal proceedings. Both Jonathan and PJ were called to human resources and informed that they would now be put on paid leave. There was no set date for when they might return to the trading floor, and it was quite possible that they never would. From that moment on, both of them knew their lives had changed for good.

In early August 2011, Jon and his lawyers flew to Washington DC to attend what is known in the USA as a 'proffer' interview, where he'd have to admit to wrongdoing and offer evidence to implicate PJ and others. The carrot dangled before him was a full non-prosecution agreement if he gave the DOJ what it wanted. On 3 August, Jon and his lawyers made their way from their hotel to the DOJ offices in Washington – the same offices where Jerry del Missier had given an interview five months before. They were led to a room where Jon was greeted by some of the same investigators he'd lied to eight months before at the FSA in Canary Wharf. They included Anne Termine, the lead investigator for the CFTC, Rob Park, who led the investigation for the DOJ, and Mike Kelly and Bob Tripp from the FBI. Police officers armed with what looked to him like sub-machine guns stood guard as he nervously sat down and prepared to try and give the DOJ what they were looking for. It was frightening and intimidating, but Jon also knew this was his main chance to save his future. If he got it right, he'd be on the witness stand, comfortably far away from the dock, giving evidence against his former colleagues and bosses as the United States Department of Justice put Barclays bankers on trial for rigging interest rates.

The FBI had struggled to believe Jon's evidence the previous November, not least because he'd claimed he'd only received a 'couple' of further requests from traders. They'd been through his emails and messages, counting twenty-eight of them. And they'd compared both his and PJ's Libor submissions to the requests, 'high' or 'low'. About 70 per cent of the time, they calculated, the submissions were in line with the requests. Now, with the calendar entries telling a tale, Jon was forced to admit he'd lied to the DOJ when he said he'd ignored the traders' requests – an obstruction of justice for which he could have been jailed.

This time he told them, truthfully, that PJ had instructed him to help out the traders. He told the FBI that he'd accommodated the swaps traders' requests, moving his Libor submission in response to them – and couldn't recall a time when he didn't do so.

Jon also told the US authorities that when the traders made a request there would have been a range of interest rates where cash was trading. When he got a request, he'd generally move his submission a tick up or down if the number could be justified.

But there was a problem to be overcome. The truth, as Jon knew, was that there was nothing to choose between any rate within that range. Any of the slightly differing Libor rates given by the brokers was a legitimate answer to the Libor question, 'At what rate could you borrow cash at 11 a.m.?' But to prosecute trader requests, the DOJ needed to be able to say that they were wrong. It was no good for them if anyone could defend accepting a Libor request on the grounds that it was within a legitimate range. And to win the non-prosecution agreement, Jon had to make a confession.

What Jon now said was that as a young trader, he'd 'bought into' PJ's approach which involved PJ's own 'abridged' definition of Libor – a definition that (wrongfully) included trader requests. He'd understood that honouring them was for the greater good of the bank, even though swaps traders were not covered in the definition of Libor.

The investigators asked Jon if his Libor submissions honestly reflected his view of Libor. Jon replied that at the time, he never questioned whether the number he submitted was his honestly held opinion. But looking back on it now, he couldn't say that it was. Then he went further. As he reflected on it, he said, without the swaps traders' requests he would have submitted a different number. And the number he ultimately submitted was therefore not consistent with the BBA definition of Libor. He was then asked if he thought his rates were accurate. He hadn't thought it at the time, Jon said. But as he considered it today, they weren't.

What Jon had given the DOJ was an idea that there were two numbers. One number was his genuine perception of the interest rate at which he could borrow money. And the other was the rate he put in following a trader's request. Based on what Jon was now saying, one was within the BBA definition, the other wasn't.

The effect was to create an artificial dividing line. In logic, it would be called a 'false dichotomy' – like the lyric from 'Human' by The Killers that asks, 'Are we human – or are we dancer?' You're assuming it must be either one thing or the other, when the truth is that it could be both. Jon was telling the US investigators that his Libor submission must be either his genuine perception of the rate at which he could borrow, or a rate intended to advantage the swaps traders' positions. The truth was that as long as it was within the range where cash was trading, it could be both at the same time – both helpful to the traders' positions *and* a genuine, accurate perception of the cost of borrowing. Yet that false dichotomy would soon be used to create new law that would retrospectively criminalise trader requests in order to prosecute traders on both sides of the Atlantic Ocean. Including Jon himself.

For now, though, he had successfully performed the ultimate lip service – telling the US regulators and criminal investigators exactly what they wanted to hear.

Over the next three months Jon waited, desperate that he might yet be sent to the USA and prosecuted for obstruction of justice or fraud, or both. Once, the phone rang and PJ's name popped up on the screen. But he left the phone to ring, unanswered. Then, three months later, in November 2011, he too heard what he had been dying to hear. The DOJ were offering him a non-prosecution agreement. He wouldn't be charged in the USA, either for obstruction of justice, or for manipulating Libor. 'Waiting for that was an immensely long, dark period of my life and it meant everything to me that they believed me and that they weren't going to prosecute me,' he later said. It was a 'massive sense of relief'. He'd succeeded in avoiding a fate that threatened to destroy his life. What he hadn't counted on was that the US authorities might not keep ownership of the case. Someone might steal it from them.

Neither Jon nor PJ had told the whole truth and nothing but the truth about trader requests, partly because it was obvious the US authorities had already made up their minds that they were wrong. They were damned if they admitted it – and now they were damned because they didn't. To the CFTC, SEC and DOJ, the two of them must have been lying to hide something important. And because of Jon Mathew's efforts to go along with the DOJ view and shift the blame to PJ, they now had a cooperating witness who was ready to admit the requests were inappropriate and testify against his former colleagues.

The unfortunate effect was that it confirmed the US investigators in their view that trader requests must be corrupt and distracted from the real, original wrong that PJ had worked for more than a year to expose. He'd now told the FBI, the US regulators and the FSA the truth, on the record, pointing to a huge fraud ordered from the top of the financial system – lowballing in the financial crisis. But in spite of voluminous evidence, including contemporaneous audio recordings, the DOJ would never attempt[5] to put anyone in the dock to answer for it. Instead, the US authorities were now emboldened to pursue Libor 'rigging' wherever they found evidence of traders attempting to influence Libor submissions for commercial reasons.

Jon Mathew had supplied Gary Gensler's CFTC, the FBI, the SEC and the DOJ with their nitroglycerin. Now they were preparing an explosion.

9

DIAMOND GEEZER

On Wednesday 27 June 2012, the BBC TV news machine had its top story all planned out. It's not often that a historic piece of news – like one about the Queen shaking hands for the first time with the former commander of the Irish Republican Army (IRA), Martin McGuinness – gets knocked off the top slot by a story about banks. But the press releases from the Financial Services Authority and the US regulators had ignited a powder keg of suppressed public anger.

'Tonight, Barclays is engulfed by a new banking scandal,' announced presenter Huw Edwards over the drumbeat at the top of the *BBC News at Ten*. 'The bank is given record fines of £290 million for lying about the interest rate it paid on loans. The chief executive Bob Diamond is to waive his bonus, but he's facing calls to resign.'

'If Bob Diamond had a shred of shame, he would resign,' said a clip from Liberal Democrat peer Lord Oakeshott, putting the boot in. 'He hasn't – so if the Barclays board has an inch of backbone, they'll sack him.'

Since the banking crisis of 2008, the Western world had been through its worst economic crisis in eighty years. Millions had been thrown out of work and hundreds of thousands had lost their homes while the banks were bailed out from the consequences of their own gross incompetence, at a cost to taxpayers of hundreds of billions of dollars. By 2012, it looked like the UK and USA were in a 'double-dip' recession – a renewed economic contraction that threatened to bring further job losses and home repossessions. As the cult musician Tom Waits put it in his song 'Talking at the Same Time', 'We

bailed out all the millionaires / They've got the fruit / We've got the rind.'
The living standards of millions of ordinary families were falling. They were
now being told by the government that they would have to endure years of
austerity and cuts to public services to repair the public finances. Yet the top
bankers whose greed and recklessness caused the crisis had walked away
with their giant bonuses and pensions intact. After RBS had to be rescued by
the government at a cost of £45 billion, its culpable chief executive Sir Fred
Goodwin had been stripped of his knighthood, becoming ordinary 'Fred'
again but keeping a pension of £342,000 a year.[1] The previous year, after
Prime Minister David Cameron demanded that young people who took part
in the London riots of August 2011 be locked up, a 23-year-old student had
been jailed for the maximum sentence of six months for theft. His crime was
to steal bottles of water worth £3.50 from a shop in Brixton, south London,
at 2 a.m.[2] By contrast, for actions that did real harm to the livelihoods of
millions of working people, few bankers had lost their jobs, let alone their
liberty. No one in authority seemed to want to punish the banks for all the
damage their mismanagement had done to the economy. Now, at last, the
regulators on both sides of the Atlantic were confirming a widespread suspicion. The bankers had rigged the system in their favour.

The BBC's business editor Robert Peston pulled no punches. 'It's a scandal engulfing huge global banks, many of them operating in the City of
London,' his report began. 'Today, Barclays became the first to be punished,
paying £290 million in penalties – the largest ever imposed by American
and British regulators.'

'We view this conduct as extremely serious as reflected in the level of
penalty which we've imposed on Barclays – by a significant margin, the
highest penalty we've imposed on a firm for misconduct in the past,' said
Tracey McDermott, acting director of enforcement at the FSA, in the first
clip in the report.[3]

'Barclays attempted to manipulate interest rates called Libor and
Euribor,' Peston went on. 'They're supposed to show the average rates paid
by all banks when lending to each other. And they really matter because
they set the prices for investors and banks in enormous transactions. And
the manipulation of these rates may also mean that the mortgage rates paid
by millions of us *weren't right.*'

It was hard to work out exactly how the misconduct had hurt ordinary
mortgage borrowers. Like every other journalist covering the story, Robert

Peston had taken the point, sprinkled throughout the press releases from the Commodity Futures Trading Commission, the US Department of Justice, the Securities and Exchange Commission and the UK's Financial Services Authority, that Barclays had submitted false estimates of interest rates to the Libor average. And the regulators laid it on thick, pointing out that loans and financial products worth $350 trillion were linked to Libor – five times the value of everything the world produced in a year – and that it was a big influence on the cost of mortgages and consumer loans. So, the rigging of Libor and Euribor meant interest rates were too high, surely? No, in the case of one kind of manipulation identified in the press release, they seemed to be talking about rates being too low (lowballing). That would mean the mortgage payments were cheaper! Nor was it clear how the other kind of misconduct, these 'trader requests', had affected the interest rates paid by consumers. Most of the emails referred to changes in Libor esti-mates of a hundredth of a percentage point or two – too small to alter the average monthly mortgage payment by more than a few pennies. And the rates were being manipulated down as well as up. So, you couldn't say 'the mortgage rates paid by millions of us were too high'. To be accurate, the most you could say was that the mortgage rates 'weren't right'.

But forget the details for a minute (thought many of us journalists), just look at the quotes! They could make a difficult, detailed story like this come alive. Across national newspapers from *The Daily Telegraph* to *The Guardian*, reporters enthused about the press releases to their editors. Because it was the regulators saying it was wrong, no one could sue you for repeating what they'd said. The announcements from the FSA and the US authorities were doing something that official press releases from regulators rarely did: illus-trating the misconduct with emails showing the actual words the traders had said to each other when they were going about their wicked business. It was true that most of the quotes looked disappointingly dull given the size of the fine, involving polite-looking requests in technical language about 'low 1M' and 'high 3M', not exactly what you'd expect a crook to say. Yet a few of the messages leaped out at you. A quote from a bad banker doing bad things was already gorgeous. If it was funny, even better.

'Now a tiny difference in the Libor or Euribor rate could determine whether a bank like Barclays would make a big profit or a loss on these massive deals,' Peston explained in front of a big screen graphic. 'So, Barclays traders had a powerful incentive to try to manipulate these rates in collusion with traders from other banks. This is what Barclays traders said in emails, when their counterparts elsewhere asked them to rig the market: "Always happy to help," said one. "Done, for you, big boy," and, "I owe you big time. I'm opening a bottle of Bollinger."'

Case closed. Or alternatively – opened.

All around the media, the story caught fire as journalists were drawn in by the power of an irresistible quote. The *Daily Mail* reported on calls for a criminal investigation following the release of 'devastating emails which show how bonus-hungry traders promised each other bottles of Bollinger champagne to fix the figures which affect millions of homeowners and small firms'.[4] Journalists remembered how, just after he'd become chief executive at the start of 2011, Bob Diamond had faced demands from MPs to give up his bonus after taking home £18 million in 2010. He'd refused, saying, 'There was a period of remorse and apology for banks. That period needs to be over.'[5] A few months later he'd been invited by the editor of BBC Radio 4's morning radio news programme, *Today*, to give a newly instituted annual business lecture. He'd concluded that banks could be 'good citizens'.[6] But he'd added, 'I'm mindful of what was said to me three years ago: "Bob, think about the fact that no one will believe you."'

To many British newspaper readers and TV viewers, Bob Diamond, with his American accent, bleached white teeth and vast pay and rewards package, epitomised the bonus-driven culture of entitlement in the City of London and Wall Street, in which bankers had progressively become more outrageously overpaid, and more detached from the rest of society, since the City of London was deregulated in October 1986. Reports said he'd received at least £120 million from his time at Barclays, and probably much more. Ever since Barclays ducked out of the 'balti weekend' of 11–12 October 2008[7] and raised money privately from the Gulf state of Qatar, allowing it to avoid nationalisation and keep the bonuses rolling in, relations between the regulators and the bank had been poor. Always regarded askance by some in the Treasury and the Bank of England who didn't like his unabashed American style, he now fitted well into his appointed role: the cultural archetype of the greedy, irresponsible bank boss. Now Prime Minister David Cameron was weighing in, saying Bob Diamond had 'some serious questions to answer'.

'I'm determined that we learn all the lessons from what happened at Barclays. People have to take responsibility for the actions and show how they're going to be accountable for those actions. And it's very important that goes all the way to the top of that organisation,' Cameron said.[8]

In a furious delayed reaction to what had happened in 2008, politicians, reporters and regulators were surfing a tidal wave of political outrage that was now breaking over not just Barclays but the whole banking industry. True, the record-breaking fines imposed by the regulators were not officially about going after the unpunished culprits of the financial crisis. But in Parliament, that was exactly what many were thinking, including the prime minister's right-hand man who ran the UK's public finances, the Chancellor of the Exchequer. 'It is clear that what happened in Barclays and potentially other banks was completely unacceptable – and was symptomatic of a financial system that elevated greed above all other concerns and brought our economy to its knees,'[9] said George Osborne.

'The government says traders were motivated by greed, lying to increase bank profits and improve its finances. We'll be asking how this could have happened,' said the TV news that evening. 'I do want to see criminal prosecutions and I do want to see those who've done the wrong thing – those who've committed what I think are atrocious acts – brought to justice,' said a clip from the leader of the opposition Labour Party, Ed Miliband.

'Regulators tell me criminal prosecutions of individual bankers in New York and London are likely,' Robert Peston added. 'Today saw the most serious slump in bank share prices since the financial crisis of 2008/09 – caused, say many, by the light shone on bankers' greed-induced recklessness.'

The presenter turned to the BBC's political editor Nick Robinson. 'Nick, lots of condemnation tonight but people will want to know if anyone's actually going to get punished?'

'Well, they will indeed and that's why I think the politicians are trying so hard to catch up with the public's anger,' said Robinson. 'When the prime minister arrived here in Brussels, he talked about accountability at the very top of Barclays. Ed Miliband, the Labour leader, talked about prosecutions, as you've heard. The public that they know want to see either people losing their jobs or, if criminality is proven, losing their freedom – going to prison, in other words.'

But there was a problem with that, Robinson added. There was no law that made what the traders had done a criminal offence. In Parliament that day, the Conservatives had been blaming the previous Labour government for failing to regulate the City, while Labour MPs were blaming the

Tories for deregulating the City under Margaret Thatcher in the 1980s. 'Now people watching at home, I suspect, don't really care whose fault it is. What they want to see is prosecutions,' said Robinson.

'Certainly, the politicians are hopeful that although there's not a specific offence, it may be possible for the Serious Fraud Office to bring prosecutions under general fraud legislation,' said Robinson. 'What is true, I think, is this: that the public know that in the United States, you have seen bankers on what they call the "perp walk". In other words, with policemen alongside them, often with their wrists shackled. All we've seen in Britain so far – the worst for any banker – is a man losing his knighthood.'[10]

About half an hour later, on the popular television talk show *Question Time*, the actor and TV presenter Tony Robinson denounced bankers in the strongest terms for the way they'd acted before, during and after the financial crisis: 'They blew it – and then they come back to us and say "Oh, can you bail us out now for hundreds of millions of pounds?" We give them the flipping money and they don't lend it to us even though they've promised to do so,' said Robinson to loud applause, his voice rising, 'And all the time, in the background, they're committing acts which in any other business, I think would be seen as criminal.' More loud applause. Speaking for the government, Conservative cabinet minister Justine Greening said, 'It does show this culture of greed that has clearly sprung up within the banking industry. We will look at how we can introduce criminal sanctions to take action on this sort of behaviour. They're not there at the moment,' she added, blaming the previous Labour government for being lax. 'In terms of what happens with these particular individuals, the FSA is talking to the Serious Fraud Office already about whether we can look at sanctions that are in place now to tackle what's already happened. But I think going forward we do need to look at criminal sanctions and I think that's long overdue.'[11]

The chief executive of City of London brokerage Tullett Prebon, Terry Smith, agreed with Robinson. 'Seeing what's happened with this Libor scandal, this rate-fixing scandal that's broken today, it must be very difficult for ordinary people looking at that. If you defrauded somebody on your mortgage application, you would probably go to jail. This action that has been taken almost certainly affected the price that you pay for your mortgage. So why isn't anyone going to go to jail?'[12]

From the start, the criminal prosecutions that would later send traders to jail were prompted not by complaints from victims of a fraud,[13] followed by a police investigation and a careful review of the evidence, but by a political firestorm. In the regulators' detailed final notices that accompanied their press releases, the traders' emails and messages were anonymised, referring to 'Trader C' (Stelios Contogoulas) or 'Manager D' (Miles Storey). In the succeeding days and weeks, reporters would be assigned to try and find out who they were, but Barclays was bound by its settlement with the authorities not to reveal their names, either on or off the record. The DOJ was planning to put the traders in jail. If their names were revealed, the traders' lawyers would be able to apply get any trial dismissed on the grounds that the regulators had created prejudice against them. It meant that in this media frenzy, the unnamed 'greedy traders' were being found guilty in public without any opportunity to defend themselves. Righteous anger at the irresponsibility and greed of the banking industry, if directed at the banks' top bosses who'd recklessly led their banks into trouble, was well justified. But it was now finding expression in public condemnation, less of the overpaid senior managers and more of a group of unnamed traders – for emails and messages which their denouncers didn't fully understand. No one in newspapers, radio or TV was giving the traders' point of view on what those very quotable emails really meant.

Every financial hack wanted a piece of the story. That night I'd been invited to speak, as presenter of the BBC's early morning daily financial radio programme, *Wake Up to Money*, at a corporate event held by a division of Lloyds Banking Group at the Landmark Hotel, near Marylebone station in central London. Reading the extraordinary newspaper articles, I thought I'd have some fun with 'the Libor scandal', as everyone was calling it. 'Just imagine what Gordon Brown must be thinking!' I said to the audience. 'All those billions he spent in the financial crisis trying to get interest rates down, when all he really had to do was pick up the phone to a Barclays trader and say – "Hey, I've got this bottle of Bollinger [...]."' It fetched a decent laugh. I wouldn't find out until years later just how close it was to the truth.

Looking back, with the benefit of the evidence presented at court or leaked to the media since then, the press releases of 27 June 2012 appear in a whole new light. The detailed statements accompanying them, containing the quotes from emails that caused the uproar (known as Statements of Fact or Final Notices[14]) were the result of months of complex negotiations between three US agencies (the CFTC, DOJ and SEC), the UK's FSA and Barclays' legal department, leading to a 'settlement' where the admissions of misconduct and the fines were agreed. For the bank, negotiations were overseen by Bob Diamond's lieutenant, Rich Ricci, assisted by the top lawyer for Barclays Capital, Judith Shepherd, with the settlement signed off by Mark Harding, the General Counsel for the parent company, Barclays Group. On the US side, Assistant Attorney General Lanny Breuer and James McJunkin of the FBI's Washington Field Office took the credit and the responsibility for the announcement in the first paragraph of the press release. Before publishing the notices, the UK regulator was also required to consult any person or body named in the statements, such as the Bank of England or the British Bankers' Association, who had to be given the opportunity to challenge anything they disputed in the regulator's early drafts.

For the lawyers involved on Barclays' side, the priority was to protect their client's survival, first by ensuring the bank itself wasn't put on trial by the DOJ. Second, if possible, no board directors should be in the frame. If someone on the board were implicated, that could mean a 'controlling mind' of the bank was culpable, potentially exposing the bank to a huge swathe of expensive litigation that might well push it into bankruptcy.

After Jon Mathew's proffer interview, the bank, as a corporate body, had faced the same 'sink or swim' dilemma that Jon Mathew had confronted. If Barclays didn't confess to wrongdoing, the DOJ would launch a full-blown criminal prosecution, which could lead to a trial that put both the bank and at least one senior director in the dock. A British bank, charged with fraud in a US court, wouldn't have much chance of acquittal. A criminal conviction of a bank for fraud would be a first in British history and would almost certainly lead to the bank's demise. If, on the other hand, the bank admitted to wrongdoing, it could secure a non-prosecution agreement. Whatever the bank executives and lawyers may have privately thought about the trader requests, to avoid a prosecution, admitting to wrongdoing was imperative.

Already, by the time the notices were published, a new narrative about Libor 'rigging' was taking shape. The truth was that lowballing was on a far greater scale than any trader requests. It meant that the Libor average was materially false, causing large losses to smaller banks in the USA or Europe that had lent money to customers with repayments tied to Libor, but were not on the panel of sixteen banks contributing to the Libor average. During the crisis, they were the victims of lowballing because they couldn't collect enough in interest to cover their costs. By comparison, the trader requests were tiny and there was little or no evidence that any of them had actually succeeded in shifting the Libor average. No one had identified any victim of trader requests. Unlike lowballing, no one had even complained to the FSA about them. Yet in the press releases from the DOJ, the trader requests were coming first, the lowballing later.

'According to the agreement, Barclays provided Libor and Euribor submissions that, at various times, were false because they improperly took into account the trading positions of its derivatives traders [trader requests] or reputational concerns about negative media attention relating to its Libor submissions [lowballing],' said the DOJ's notice. It said 'according to the agreement' because, as MPs had noted (and Nick Robinson reported), there was no law to refer to. There weren't even rules written down to show it was improper to take trader requests into account. The rights and wrongs of trader requests had been decided, not by reference to any laws or rules at the time the requests were made, or by Parliament or Congress, but retrospectively, in negotiations between the US authorities and the bank.

'According to the agreement, an individual bank's Libor or Euribor submission cannot appropriately be influenced by the financial positions of its derivatives traders or the bank's concerns [...] When the requests of traders for favorable Libor and Euribor submissions were taken into account by the rate submitters, Barclays' rate submissions were false and misleading [...] For this illegal activity, Barclays is paying a significant price,' the DOJ release went on (without referring to any laws, British or American, that showed it was illegal at the time). The release acknowledged the bank's 'extraordinary cooperation' and confirmed it would not be prosecuted, a reference to the resources Barclays had poured into investigating and defending itself since the CFTC had sent its request for information more than three years earlier – an estimated £100 million.[15] Without Barclays' cooperation, from Project Bruce to the huge sums it was now spending on corporate lawyers, the CFTC, DOJ, SEC and FSA wouldn't have had their fines and their final notices. Now Barclays was paying fines of $453 million (£290 million). But no board directors were implicated. The cost would be borne by Barclays' shareholders, from pension schemes to life insurance companies to retail investment funds. No board director would pay a financial penalty, or face disciplinary procedures from either the bank or the regulators.

In a public statement, Gary Gensler took credit on behalf of the CFTC: 'Banks must not attempt to influence Libor or other indices based upon concerns about their reputation or the profitability of their trading positions. The CFTC has and will continue vigorously to use our enforcement and regulatory authorities to protect the public, promote market integrity, and ensure that these indices are free of manipulative conduct and false information.'

The press releases gave an unusual reason why the Libor rates Barclays had submitted were false, a reason that would later be used by the courts on both sides of the Atlantic to prosecute trader requests. They were 'false because they improperly took into account the trading positions of its derivatives traders'. In other words, it wasn't inaccuracy in PJ or Jon's Libor estimates that made them false: it was the fact that a trader had asked for them. The CFTC and DOJ had formed their own views of what was 'improper', based not on any law or rule at the time the requests were made, but on two confessions of wrongdoing that had been made under threat of prosecution in the USA: from Jon Mathew in his proffer interview; and from the bank itself in its agreement with the authorities. No greater authority than that was cited for condemning the conduct. The judges in the British and US courts[16] would later follow their lead.

There was a lot the DOJ and the regulators knew that never made it into their press releases, or the detailed statements that accompanied them. None of the four agencies fining Barclays mentioned, even in anonymised form, what Jerry del Missier had told Mike Kelly and Rob Park at his interview at the DOJ in Washington in February 2011 – that Paul Tucker of the Bank of England had told him that Barclays should get its Libor rates down on 1 September 2007 (see pages 15–16 and 126–7). Neither the DOJ, nor the FSA, nor the other regulators mentioned what PJ had told all of them, about the Libor and Euribor instructions from central banks and governments in October 2008. The regulators had corroborating evidence in the shape of contemporary audio recordings, emails and public information on what happened to each bank's submissions. But there was no sign they'd investigated it. Nowhere was there any information about the US central bank, the Federal Reserve Bank of New York, asking Chase New York to intervene and offer to lend dollars at rates far below the market to get Libor rates down.

The DOJ, CFTC, SEC and FSA all had access to the audio recordings and emails where Dearlove, Stone, Storey and Morse made it irrefutably clear that it was the board of directors of Barclays who were directing what PJ and the other cash traders did with their Libor and Euribor submissions,[17] backing up what PJ had told all of them on 19 November 2010, namely that by 'senior management' he meant executives on the thirty-first floor of Barclays Group headquarters, where Bob Diamond and John Varley worked, including the bank's finance director Chris Lucas. They also showed that the bank's group chief executive John Varley was clearly aware of the low-balling issue and that Paul Tucker had told him Downing Street had been involved. Yet the releases made no mention of the evidence indicating it was the board of Barclays, the Bank of England and later the UK government that was the source of the directions passed down to PJ and others to lowball.

The FSA politely avoided embarrassing its non-executive director, the deputy governor of the Bank of England, by omitting from its press release any mention of Paul Tucker's conversation with Bob Diamond on 29 October 2008. But it did get a mention, with names and job titles removed, on paragraph 176 of the detailed Final Notice[18] that went with it. In their negotiated settlement, the US and UK regulators and the Barclays' lawyers had to deal with the awkward file note written by Bob Diamond, sent on 30 October to del Missier and Varley, recounting the conversation and saying, 'Mr Tucker said the levels of calls he was receiving from Whitehall were "senior" and that while he was certain we did not need advice, that it did not always need to be the case that we appeared as high as we have recently.' But nowhere did the press releases or detailed statements mention the evidence that top UK government officials in Whitehall and Downing Street played a role in pressuring Barclays to lower its Libor rates. Instead, there was an account which didn't mention the UK government and let both the Bank of England and Bob Diamond off the hook – if you were credulous enough to take it at face value.

The FSA's Final Notice acknowledged 'an instruction to reduce Libor submissions given by senior management on 29 October 2008', but added: 'This instruction was given following a telephone conversation between a senior individual at Barclays and the Bank of England during which the external perceptions of Barclays' Libor submissions were discussed. No instruction for Barclays to lower its Libor submissions was given during this telephone conversation. However, as the substance of the telephone conversation was relayed down the chain of command at Barclays, a misunderstanding or miscommunication occurred. This meant that Barclays' Submitters believed mistakenly that they were operating under an instruction from the Bank of England (as conveyed by senior management) to reduce Barclays' Libor submissions.'

The Statement of Facts from the DOJ, an outcome of the same negotiations between regulators and bank lawyers, told a similar story.[19] When you filled in the names, the story negotiated by the lawyers filtered out all the toxic elements that might have put the UK government, the Bank of England or Bob Diamond in the frame. The euphemistic phrase 'external perceptions' avoided mentioning what Bob Diamond and Paul Tucker would later admit: that they were really talking about the views of top government officials in Whitehall. The story prepared for public consumption was instead that one unnamed senior manager (Jerry del Missier) had given an instruction to reduce Libor rates and that unnamed Libor submitters (PJ and Pete Spence) had acted on it, lowering their Libor rates in violation of the BBA definition in the mistaken belief that the Bank of England had instructed them to. But it was all a misunderstanding. When one senior manager (Bob Diamond) told another (del Missier) about his conversation with the Bank of England, he hadn't understood it as an instruction. And in the detailed statements agreed as part of the settlement with the DOJ, SEC, CFTC and FSA, their names would remain unmentioned.

By 2012, top regulators on both sides of the Atlantic, from Gary Gensler to Margaret Cole,[20] had known for two years about the recorded phone call between Dearlove and PJ saying the bank had come under 'very serious pressure from the UK government and the Bank of England about pushing our Libors lower'. The DOJ, SEC, CFTC and FSA knew the phone call also referred to other central banks, including the European Central Bank. All of them had a seat at the table in November 2010 when PJ went through the transcript of the call with them and told them about the involvement of the Banque de France and the Fed. There was separate evidence about the Swiss central bank and the Bank of Japan. A quick google search would have reminded anyone checking out PJ's information that the central banks were already coordinating cuts in their official interest rates, including on 8 October 2008, when six central banks dropped their rates at once,[21] the same day Gordon Brown announced his £50 billion plan to recapitalise stricken banks. Added up, it pointed to an international initiative to get Libor and Euribor down, either by making cash cheaper to borrow through emergency lending schemes, or by simply ordering it down.

Yet none of the regulators' public statements referred to it. The lawyers' explanation for Bob Diamond's file note – that it was all a misunderstanding – was already wafer thin. Had the DOJ not covered up the Bank of England's earlier interventions in Libor setting on 1 September 2007, it would have been even less plausible. Dearlove's information about his meeting with Tucker at the Bank of England earlier in October 2008, when Tucker warned him that Barclays should lower its Libor rates because it was getting attention from the government, would have blown it apart. The FBI, DOJ, FSA, CFTC and SEC had been told about that meeting, too. But they would never mention it, not in their press releases[22] or in any public forum since then. The DOJ, the FBI, the CFTC, the SEC and the FSA were all knowingly allowing important, historic facts, about central bank manipulation of benchmark interest rates all around the world in the middle of the worst financial crisis since the Great Depression, to be kept from the public.

In terms of the injustice that flowed from it, it was a cover-up like no other. If seeking to obtain movements in the Libor average, not justified by similar movements in the real cost of borrowing cash, truly was unlawful, then the evidence given to the US and UK regulators pointed to two very important conclusions. First, that the Bank of England, the Fed and the FSA had for months condoned the 'illegal' behaviour because they were repeatedly told about the submission of false, lowballed Libor rates by numerous commercial banks and did nothing to stop it.[23] Second, that the Bank of England had itself engaged in the same misconduct on a much greater scale than the traders, starting in August 2007 through to October 2008.[24] The evidence also suggested the Banque de France played a similar role to the Bank of England in the crisis. Other central banks and governments were also implicated in evidence seen by the regulators.

If getting more than one bank to change their Libor submissions to try and move the Libor average really did amount to illegal collusion, then the evidence suggested that the Bank of England, the Banque de France and the BBA had far more to answer for than any trader. Not only were the shifts in Libor that they were seeking far larger than anything any trader could have dreamed of – at least 160 times[25] the size. The other big difference was that they hadn't been merely attempting to move the Libor average: unlike the traders, they'd succeeded.

Yet in the final notices and statements of fact published by the DOJ, the CFTC and the FSA, almost all the evidence they'd gathered that was awkward for central banks and governments was left unmentioned.

Nevertheless, the material that remained in the press releases was incendiary enough to light a fire that stubbornly refused to burn itself out. At Barclays, the in-house communications directors and a team of external public relations consultants wracked their brains for any means they could think of to dampen it down. They'd told the BBC and others that it was unfair to single out Barclays just because it was the first to be fined. Deutsche Bank of Germany, UBS of Switzerland, Citigroup of the USA, and Lloyds and RBS were also being investigated. In newspapers and on TV, the point was made repeatedly: it wasn't just Barclays. Nonetheless, as the only bank so far to be named on the record by the regulators, it was Barclays that was being pilloried. The external communications consultancy, Brunswick, urged the bank to draw the sting of public anger by making an apology. But the bank's lawyers weren't prepared to apologise for everything they'd been accused of. The regulators were conflating two separate things – trader requests and lowballing – by calling both 'manipulating Libor'. With lowballing, the Bank of England had, repeatedly, instructed Barclays to lower Libor – and the FSA had okayed their approach! Diamond reluctantly agreed to use the word 'sorry' in a public statement:

> The events which gave rise to today's resolutions relate to past actions which fell well short of the standards to which Barclays aspires [...] I am sorry that some people acted in a manner not consistent with our culture and values.

But saying sorry for other bankers' actions didn't sound like a proper apology. Bankers tended to defend their exorbitant rewards by saying that the high pay came with heavy responsibility. That meant the buck should stop at the top. After the furious debate in Westminster and the prime minister's intervention, Barclays' PR team privately started to doubt that Bob Diamond could survive the public outcry. In a letter to Andrew Tyrie MP, chair of the Treasury committee of MPs in the House of Commons, he offered to appear before the committee the following week and did his best to 'spin' the story away from the bank's senior leadership.

'These traders had no way of knowing whether their actions would ultimately benefit or detriment Barclays overall. They were operating purely for their own benefit,' he wrote.[26] It suited the narrative that the bank wanted to propagate but the second sentence couldn't possibly be true. The traders' bonuses were linked to the profits that the swaps desk, or the cash desk, made for the bank. There was no other way they could make money from any shifts in Libor. If they made bigger bonuses, it could only be because they'd made bigger profits for the bank.

The letter pointed out that 'various individuals within Barclays raised lowballing externally with BBA, FSA, BoE [Bank of England] and Fed'. But it didn't mention the main individual who'd blown the whistle as loudly as possible at the start of the credit crunch and campaigned for more than a year for honest Libor rates: PJ, whom the bank's senior executives and lawyers had put on paid leave nearly a year before and were now preparing to throw under the Libor bus.

Over the weekend, *The Sunday Times* reported that David Cameron's government had said it would order 'a review of the Libor market that would examine the case for a criminal investigation of the individuals responsible', to report back that summer.

'If Bob Diamond believes it is enough to give up a bonus, he is living in a world of his own,' wrote one of the paper's columnists, Dominic Lawson.[27] 'Now that the City is run along the American principle that everything not actually illegal is fine, it is perhaps old-fashioned to hope for a return of what used to be called "the governor of the Bank of England's eyebrows" [...] The governor would need to do no more than indicate to the board of Barclays it really would be in the bank's own interests if Mr Diamond were to decide it might be time to move on [...] If the City has not altogether lost its sense of self-preservation, it will organise the necessary execution.'

The Barclays PR team had worked hard over the weekend on a communications strategy aimed at defusing the crisis while keeping Bob Diamond in his job. On Monday 2 July, Diamond wrote to employees saying he was 'disappointed and angry' about the regulators' findings. He argued it was his responsibility to remain in his post to make sure such misconduct never happened again. Barclays chairman Marcus Agius announced he would leave the bank, giving a public statement that 'Last week's events have dealt a devastating blow to Barclays' reputation [...] The buck stops with me and I must acknowledge responsibility by standing aside.'[28] But the buck was still travelling.

The UK government tried to show it was getting to grips with the public's anger by announcing a parliamentary inquiry into banking. The Labour Party was opposed, demanding a full-blown, judge-led independent public inquiry, along the lines of the Leveson Inquiry that investigated phone hacking by the British tabloid press. 'Politicians investigating bankers will not command the consent of the British people,' said Ed Miliband. 'The British people will not tolerate anything less than a full, open and independent inquiry. They will not tolerate the establishment closing ranks and saying we don't need an inquiry. They want a light shone into every part of the banking industry – including its dark corners.'[29] But it was in vain. Closing ranks is exactly what the establishment would do in the weeks, months and years that followed. That night, as the political uproar raged on, the Barclays PR team were called back in to work at 10.30 p.m. Everything had changed. The attempt to defuse the situation with the resignation of Marcus Agius had failed. They'd now have to work all night to prepare a statement. Bob Diamond was going.

The conversations that Diamond had before he gave up the fight and resigned from his lucrative position remain an information black hole, even ten years later. The Bank of England chief cashier Andrew Bailey, who ran the Bank's Prudential Regulation Unit, and the chairman of the FSA, Adair Turner, had decided to speak to Marcus Agius on Monday afternoon, after he had resigned as Barclays chairman. Turner told Agius, 'I'm sure you are considering whether you can continue with Bob Diamond as CEO.' He made it clear that they hadn't found anything against Bob Diamond. But he added, 'You have to think about whether he (it was very clearly "he") is the right person to lead the substantive change which is required in the culture [of Barclays].'[30] The regulator wasn't proposing to withdraw his registration or question his fitness as a director. Given what he knew about the Bank of England's own role in the Libor scandal, he could have hung on, ignored the governor's raised eyebrows and continued to fight. His willingness to go, giving the impression that he was accepting responsibility for the misconduct, even as the US authorities were planning criminal prosecutions, has never been fully explained.

At 7.35 the following morning, Tuesday 3 July, in an official announcement on the London Stock Exchange, the news broke that Bob Diamond had resigned with immediate effect. In an unheard-of reversal, Marcus Agius was going back to be the chairman of the bank, just one day after he had stepped down, to lead the search for a new chief executive. Bob Diamond gave an emotional statement: 'No decision over that period was as hard as the one that I make now to stand down as chief executive. The external pressure on Barclays has reached a level that risks damaging the franchise. I cannot let that happen. I am deeply disappointed that the impression created by the events announced last week about what Barclays and its people stand for could not be further from the truth.'[31]

But Barclays' consent to Bob Diamond's departure came with a sting in the tail. On its website, the bank published a memo that it had prepared for MPs on the Treasury committee.[32] As with the letter a few days earlier, the memo began by focusing on the traders' conduct. Then came the big reveal. Barclays showed the world evidence that the deputy governor of the Bank of England, Paul Tucker, had been involved in encouraging the very same misconduct detailed in the press releases from the regulators:

> As one would expect, Barclays (including Bob Diamond and Jerry del Missier) was in close contact with the Bank of England and other Authorities about the liquidity crisis generally. On 29 October 2008, Bob Diamond received a call from Paul Tucker, the Deputy Governor of the Bank of England. The substance of the call was captured by Bob Diamond via a note prepared at the time.

A copy of the file note dictated by Bob Diamond was appended to the memo.

'The Bank of England told us to do it', screamed the splash headline on the front page of the conservative newspaper, *The Daily Telegraph*. 'The Deputy Governor of the Bank of England encouraged Barclays to try to lower interest rates after coming under pressure from senior members of the last Labour government, documents disclosed yesterday. A memo published by Barclays suggested that Paul Tucker gave a hint to Bob Diamond, the bank's chief executive, in 2008 that the rate it was claiming to be paying to borrow money from other banks could be lowered. His suggestion followed questions from "senior figures within Whitehall" about why Barclays was having to pay so much interest on its borrowings, the memo states.'

The memo gave the following account of the 29 October call from Tucker to Diamond, fitting in to the accounts in the FSA's Final Notice and the DOJ's statement of facts but now supplying names:

> Bob Diamond did not think he had received an instruction from Paul Tucker or that he gave an instruction to Jerry del Missier. However, Jerry del Missier concluded that an instruction had been passed down from the Bank of England not to keep Libors so high. He passed down an instruction to that effect to the submitters.

In the narrative negotiated by Barclays' legal department, Jerry del Missier was carrying the can. The memo said the FSA had investigated Jerry del Missier personally in relation to these events and closed the investigation without taking any enforcement action. Soon after the memo was published, it was announced that del Missier was also resigning. It was rumoured that when he learned that the buck was stopping with him, del Missier turned up at the bank with an 'army of lawyers'. Three weeks later, it would emerge that a 'golden goodbye' payment of £9 million had been agreed.[33]

Barclays' memo also claimed that when 'less senior managers' (Dearlove, Stone and Storey) gave instructions to Barclays submitters to lower their Libor submissions in 2007 and 2008, 'the origin of these instructions is not clear'. Yet Barclays' legal department, which approved the memo before it was published, had overseen the investigation which unearthed contemporary written and audio evidence that Barclays' approach to Libor was being directed by Barclays Group's finance director Chris Lucas (see pages 19–20 and 56) and that Bob Diamond and John Varley were aware of the issues. All three sat on the group's board.

You don't choose to lie to a parliamentary committee if you want to keep your career or your reputation. The jeopardy is too high. If you're caught out, you could, at least in theory, be prosecuted for the crime of contempt of Parliament. But in a highly political interrogation that would be watched closely by the FBI, there was sometimes a tension between the story prepared by your lawyers that took care of your own interests and what really happened.

Ahead of the hearings in front of the Treasury committee into Libor rigging, the senior bankers who testified were careful to take legal advice. The difficulty was that the lawyers knew the US authorities were preparing criminal prosecutions. They had to keep their clients out of the frame. Anyone who admitted to knowledge or approval of what the US authorities had judged to be misconduct would be within their sights, at high risk of losing their career or spending a large chunk of their life in an orange jumpsuit.

Bob Diamond may have resigned but a commitment to answer MPs' questions was still a commitment. As he prepared for the hearings with his lawyers, there were two things he had to avoid. First, putting himself in the frame by appearing to admit he knew what was going on when the bank was 'manipulating' Libor or Euribor. That meant he could make no admissions that he had known about either trader requests or lowballing before the investigation had delivered its results. Second, he had to avoid contradicting anything the bank had agreed in its settlement with the US authorities and the FSA. Given how involved those negotiations had been, that was far from easy.

On Wednesday, 4 July 2012, a chauffeur-driven car pulled up in a prohibited space on Victoria Embankment, on the west bank of the River Thames near Westminster Bridge. Bob Diamond got out and made his way, accompanied by an aide, through a dense crowd of reporters and flashing cameras towards the revolving doors at the entrance to Portcullis House, the newly developed wing of the Houses of Parliament. After a few minutes just inside its glass-fronted walls clearing security, he made his way up to the room on the first floor that housed the Treasury committee. He was well dressed, carefully groomed and, above all, well briefed. If he showed that he was every bit as angry as the MPs, it might take the spotlight off the lowballing that led to the top and instead turn it firmly on to the traders. The Barclays PR team had picked up on a word used a week earlier by *Daily Mail* columnist Alex Brummer to condemn the traders' behaviour: 'reprehensible'.[34]

Within a few seconds of the start of the hearing, Diamond was blaming the traders. Asked why he had resigned, he said: 'Wow. I love Barclays. That's where it starts. I love Barclays because of the people [...] I worry that the world looks at Barclays and a small group of traders, or group of traders, who had reprehensible behaviour, and that that is being put on Barclays in a way that is not representative of the firm that I love so much [...] My decision to resign was that my leadership and questions about my leadership have been a part of that. The best way I think I can help bridge Barclays from the turmoil of being the only one out [...] and prevent the damage to the reputation that has happened over the past week, was to step down but to continue to come here and answer the questions of the Committee. I love Barclays, but I also will tell you, for almost twenty-five years I have been a part of the financial services industry in the UK. I have developed great relationships with regulators at the Bank of England, at the FSA and the Treasury. I have loved my time here. This is a great place to work.'

'I am glad that you can say that on the 4th of July,' said the thin, bespectacled Conservative chair of the committee, Andrew Tyrie, who'd won a reputation for his sceptical, forensic questioning of witnesses.

'The note from Mr Tucker says that he felt your Libor returns could be lower, doesn't it?' asked Tyrie.

'He felt that our Libor rates relative to the other fifteen posters—'

'Could be relatively lower. Yes?'

'Yes,' said Diamond.

'Why then, on page two of your note to this Committee yesterday, did you say that you don't believe you received an instruction?'

'I did not believe it was an instruction,' said Diamond.

'So what was it? A nod and a wink?'

'The most important thing of that note to me, chairman, was the comment that there was a perception in Whitehall that our rates were high.' Diamond explained that he'd been worried that the government officials might wrongly think the bank wasn't able to get the funds it needed to go on – and therefore might nationalise it.

'I just want to be clear. You don't think you received an instruction; you don't think that it was even a nod and wink, even though it reads that way to almost everyone who looks at it?' said Tyrie. Diamond told the committee he didn't think it was an instruction.[35]

'What I want to know is, how did Jerry del Missier get this wrong, when you had just been talking to him?' asked Michael Fallon MP. 'How did he believe it was an instruction, either from the Bank or from the public authorities?'

'Michael, with apologies, I can't put myself in Jerry's shoes,' said Diamond, falling back on the FSA's official version of events.

Diamond was telling the same barely credible story that Barclays' legal department had carefully negotiated with the DOJ, CFTC, SEC and FSA. MPs and the public were being invited to accept that these two senior executives, Diamond and del Missier, who'd worked as friends and business partners for over a decade, spoke to each other several times a week and had both been talking to Tucker at the Bank of England about Libor for more than a year, somehow miscommunicated in such a way that they'd ended up doing something unlawful – a manipulation of Libor submissions fifty times the size of anything the traders might have achieved – by mistake. Bob Diamond hadn't meant to pass on an instruction from the Bank of England. Jerry del Missier had just got the wrong idea and given an instruction when he shouldn't have.

Even on the basis of the material already published by the regulators, the story was difficult to believe. Without mentioning his name, the statements referred to the email that Pete Spence had sent on 29 October 2008 to his boss John Porter and others after receiving Dearlove's instruction to lower his Libor rates, saying the instruction would be breaking the BBA rules.[36] Then the rates had stayed lower for weeks. Apparently, neither Porter nor any other executive had been bothered enough by this terrible mistake, this open breach of the rules, to report it back up the chain of command. If both PJ and Pete Spence dropped their Libor estimates by 50 basis points on the basis of a mistake by del Missier, it would have become immediately obvious the next day in the published Libor submissions, to which Diamond, del Missier, Tucker and Downing Street all had access – and which had recently been the focus of the intense attention of civil servants such as Jeremy Heywood, then head of the policy unit in Downing Street, and Tom Scholar, then second permanent secretary to the Treasury. Yet there was nothing in the evidence to indicate that anyone, either in the bank or in the government, had run around in the days following that, horrified that Libor had come down in violation of the BBA definition. Instead, the regulators' findings[37] acknowledged that del Missier had reiterated the instruction to lower Libor rates a few days later, just after the Bank of England cut its official rate. No one had thought it should be reported to the regulators, let alone the police.

The MPs asked about the FSA's reference to the concerns of senior managers at high levels about negative publicity, which led to less senior managers (Storey, Dearlove) instructing submitters to lowball their Libor rates. Who were the senior managers? Diamond said they were group treasury. But as the evidence trail known to the regulators made clear, Jon Stone, Barclays' group treasurer, had continually sought the view of Lucas, Diamond and others on the thirty-first floor of Barclays' headquarters (see pages 18–20, 24 and 56).

Then Diamond said something that would later prompt accusations he'd misled Parliament. After spotting in the regulators' statements the fact that the lowballing instructions from senior management had started more than a year before 29 October 2008, Conservative member David Ruffley asked a pointed question.

'Can you tell us when you discovered that this lowballing activity was going on?'

'During the investigation.' Bob Diamond's answer was unusually terse.

'So you did not know it was going on when you spoke to Mr Tucker on 29 October 2008?'

'No,' said Diamond. 'That would have been before the investigation. So I was not aware of it.'

'Okay,' said Ruffley. 'When did you discover? You say in the course of the investigation. What month approximately?'

Diamond stalled, talking generally about the US investigations and when they began, but Ruffley wouldn't let it go. 'Forgive me, I don't wish to be rude in interrupting, but give me an approximate date when you discovered this lowballing – which is the subject of the FSA notice; that is why you have been fined and that is ultimately one reason you have lost your job, Mr Diamond – was going on. Simple question. Approximately?'

Again, Diamond stalled and again, Ruffley pressed. 'With respect, for the third time, what month did you discover that lowballing was going on? Just give me a date.'

'This month,' said Diamond.

That would become the headline that night on the evening TV news. 'The former Barclays boss denies knowing about rate-rigging until this month.' What Diamond said met the need to stay out of the sights of the criminal division of the DOJ. But it wasn't true. There was contemporaneous evidence from emails to audio recordings, familiar to investigators at the US authorities and the FSA, that contradicted what Diamond had just said (see Chapters 1 and 2). Yet none of the investigators at the FSA, the CFTC, the SEC or the DOJ wrote to the committee to correct the record.

Bob Diamond has been asked repeatedly about these statements to the Treasury committee and has insisted he never misled Parliament.

'Do you think the role of banking in our society should include a more puni-
tive regime, such that wrongdoing by people acting recklessly or deliberately
to mislead markets should lead to custodial sentences for bankers?' Ruffley
asked Diamond. 'It requires a straight "yes" or "no". What do you think?'

Diamond was now on safer ground. 'I think that people who do things
that they are not supposed to do should be dealt with harshly. I think they
should go through due process. We have been through a process ourselves
of dealing harshly with people. David, when I got the results of this investigation – and when I read the e-mails from those traders, I got physically ill.
It is reprehensible behaviour. If you are asking me should those actions be
dealt with—absolutely.'

Former Barclays banker Andrea Leadsom went further, contradicting the
government's statements that there were no laws to prohibit what the traders had done at the time. 'Surely you must realise how enraged people are
at the criminality? You talk about reprehensible behaviour, but it is actually
criminality,' said Leadsom (without referring to the laws or evidence that
brought her to such a firm view).

'The behaviour was appalling,' Diamond responded. 'The behaviour was
absolutely appalling and as soon as we knew it—it has been eradicated.
When we discovered this, some traders had already left and some were
removed immediately.'

'And how many have gone to prison?'

'I understand that there will be follow-up criminal investigations on certain individuals.'

'And you would support that?'

'It's not up to us,' said Diamond. 'But we are certainly not going to stand
in the way of it.'

Across Westminster at Number 11 Downing Street, the Conservative
Chancellor of the Exchequer George Osborne was making plans. Members of
the former Labour government were clearly involved, he thought. And after
making inquiries he'd confirmed that there was a big effort in the crisis to get
Libor down. If the trail led up to Downing Street and the former prime minister Gordon Brown, the blame for Libor rigging could be pinned on Labour,
damaging his political opponents. Privately, he'd urged the Bank of England
to come clean, but he was meeting resistance. Now he was talking to the new
director of the Serious Fraud Office, David Green, about arranging millions of
pounds in extra funding to investigate and prosecute Libor rigging.

Just after Barclays published its memo about Diamond's conversation with the Bank of England on 29 October 2008, Paul Tucker had asked the Treasury committee if he could appear to give his side of the story. Regardless of Labour's concerns about the risk of an establishment cover-up, its calls for a judge-led public inquiry into the banking industry were voted down as David Cameron's coalition of Conservatives and Liberal Democrats ordered their MPs to oppose it. It would now be left to MPs and the SFO to investigate a scandal that had already been heavily condemned, but only lightly understood. And Barclays was preparing to deal with the traders. Harshly.

10

THE SERIOUSLY FLAWED OFFICE

'Equality before the law is a fundamental principle of the rule of law as we know it. Everyone is subject to the same laws, no matter who they are, and is treated equally by the courts.'[1]

(Baroness Brenda Hale, President of the UK Supreme Court, 29 October 2018)

At a desk on the top floor of the headquarters of the Serious Fraud Office in Elm Street, central London, David Green peered at the window on his computer screen showing Bob Diamond's appearance in Parliament. The SFO's new director had spent much of the past week reading newspaper coverage and listening to the radio as politicians, journalists and members of the public demanded that bankers be prosecuted. The Chancellor of the Exchequer George Osborne had assured him millions of pounds in extra funding would be made available to ensure the SFO had enough resources to take on the rigging of Libor and Euribor. In the race to catch up with the public's anger, the baton was being passed to Green.

He'd approved a 'holding statement' as early as 2 July 2012 after repeated mentions in Parliament and on TV that discussions with the SFO were under way. 'The SFO are considering whether it is both appropriate and possible to bring criminal prosecutions,' it said. 'The issues are complex and the assessment of the evidence the FSA has gathered will take a short time, but we hope to come to a conclusion within a month.' But after Bob Diamond's appearance in Parliament on 4 July, the political pressure was irresistible. Two days later, the SFO announced that David Green had formally accepted 'the Libor matter' for investigation. This would be the biggest inquiry the SFO had ever undertaken.

But there was a problem. Keen to prosecute the 'rigging' of dollar Libor, the US Department of Justice had declared the bankers' conduct 'illegal', sparking the uproar in Westminster. But as government ministers had repeatedly said in public, there wasn't any law in the UK at the time that the traders appeared to have broken; and Green was yet to work out whether the conduct described in the regulators' statements could be covered by existing criminal offences.

Square-jawed with receding brown hair, Green had the well-groomed look typical of the close-knit, clubby world of barristers specialising in white-collar crime, favouring dark brown or navy suits that covered a pronounced paunch. Aged 58, he'd started his career in defence intelligence before going into private practice and more recently becoming head of prosecutions at Her Majesty's Revenue & Customs, pursuing tax evaders and earning a reputation in court as a 'bruiser'. When he took the job as SFO director, Green knew that he might soon be sipping, like his predecessors, from a poisoned chalice. After a series of botched investigations and embarrassing lawsuits that threatened to cost the UK Treasury millions of pounds in compensation, the home secretary, Theresa May, wanted to scrap the SFO and fold it into a new National Crime Agency.

The SFO had come under severe criticism from the new Lord Chief Justice of England and Wales, more commonly known as John Thomas, who'd rebuked it for 'sheer incompetence' in an earlier case, that of the Iranian-born property tycoons Vincent and Robert Chenguiz. White-haired and ruddy faced, Thomas (now elevated to a life peerage in the House of Lords, Baron Thomas of Cwmgiedd) was very much an insider in the privileged social class that dominated the London legal establishment. Educated at Rugby, one of England's top private schools, before attending Cambridge University and becoming a barrister in 1969, Thomas had been on the Court of Appeal for twelve years. While regarded by his peers as charming and intelligent, he was also known for his irritable outbursts. Thomas would remain the most senior judge in charge of the judiciary through most of the UK's seven rate-rigging trials from 2015 to 2019.

In London's legal community, as rumours circulated that the SFO would soon need a new director, David Green was seen as a strong candidate. He'd later tell an anecdote recalling how, unsure if he wanted to apply, he went to see a former Attorney General, Lord Goldsmith,[2] to ask for his advice. Goldsmith went quiet. 'David, I don't know what you're worried about,' he said. 'You couldn't make it any worse.' That was why Green thought it made sense for him to take over an organisation at a low ebb. 'The only possible trajectory,' he would later say, alluding to a well-known pop lyric, 'was in an upward direction.'[3] By the end of April, Green had been appointed.

There was something Green had chosen not to mention in the official press releases about the Libor investigation. Just over a year previously, the SFO had already considered whether to investigate Libor and Euribor and decided against it. Since it met a brick wall at the Financial Services Authority,[4] the Office of Fair Trading had never quite lost interest in interest rate-rigging and had brought evidence to the SFO in 2011, urging it to consider a criminal inquiry. Having watched the SFO's budget dwindle under austerity measures since the 2008 crash, Green's predecessor Richard Alderman thought the FSA, which had far greater resources, was better placed to pursue it criminally and sent the case on to the regulator. The FSA had the capacity to pursue criminal investigations,[5] and it was already across the evidence for the purposes of fining Barclays and other banks. But for some reason unclear to Alderman, it wasn't keen.

At Andrew Tyrie's Treasury committee on Monday, 9 July 2012, the Bank of England's deputy governor Paul Tucker was granted his request to give his side of things. The first questions he was asked were about Bob Diamond's file note.

'Can I just clarify,' asked Tyrie. 'Was one of the "senior figures" referred to in there Sir Jeremy Heywood?'

'Yes,' replied Tucker.

'Who were the other senior figures?'

'The person I spoke to most in Whitehall during this period was Tom Scholar at the Treasury. The other senior officials that I spoke to less frequently from time to time were Jon Cunliffe in the Cabinet Office and very occasionally Nick Macpherson at the Treasury.'[6]

The implications were serious. In October 2008, Jeremy Heywood was Gordon Brown's principal private secretary and had just become his chief of staff at 10 Downing Street. In one word, Paul Tucker had just confirmed his involvement. Tom Scholar was the number two civil servant at the Treasury, which coordinated the government's emergency measures in the crisis. The Cabinet Office was the arm of government that sat above the other departments and the whole civil service, accountable to the prime minister. Heywood, Scholar, Cunliffe or Macpherson might be able to clarify whether Downing Street had pressured Barclays to lower its Libor rates. But the MPs on the inquiry would never ask them that question.

MPs on the committee kept getting the same answer from different witnesses to the same question: 'When did you know about lowballing?' Answer: 'Not until I saw the results of the investigation.' It was almost as if they were all following the same legal advice. All the committee's witnesses were by now familiar with the regulators' announcements that spelled out how Barclays traders understated the interest rates they were paying to borrow dollars, putting in false Libor submissions under instructions from senior management to avoid bad publicity – and therefore a plunging share price. It was only since the crisis that it had become widely known as 'lowballing' but it was clear what the term referred to. Three days after the SFO confirmed it was launching a criminal investigation, it was Paul Tucker's turn.

'In your recollection,' asked Labour MP Andrew Love, 'when was the first time that Libor was raised as an issue in relation to low-balling?'

Tucker cupped his hand behind his right ear and squinted, apparently mishearing the question. 'To ...?'

'Lowballing,' Love repeated.

'Erm ...' Tucker looked down and shuffled his papers. 'The ...' There was a protracted pause before he looked up, opening his arms as if he were appealing to the committee to believe him. 'I mean, I wasn't aware of allegations of, of, lowballing until ... the last few weeks,' he said, scratching his left forehead and glancing to the right.[7]

'You will know, from the FSA and other reports,' said Love, 'that lowballing was going on, and had been for some considerable period of time before the events that we focused on – almost a year?'

'We did not realise,' said Tucker, looking down. 'We did not realise.'

A week after Paul Tucker's evidence to Parliament, the MPs had another witness helping them get to the truth. Jerry del Missier wasn't signed up to the party line. His memory of events didn't chime in with the official version negotiated between Barclays' legal department, the US authorities and the FSA. Having bought into the story that it was his fault that Barclays had lowballed after the Tucker phone call – his misunderstanding of what Diamond had said – MPs were almost too hostile to take in what he had to say. Asked what Diamond had said to him on 29 October 2008, del Missier replied, simply enough: 'He said that he had a conversation with Mr Tucker of the Bank of England, that the Bank of England was getting pressure from Whitehall around Barclays – the health of Barclays – as a result of Libor rates, that we should get our Libor rates down, and that we should not be outliers.'[8]

'And what did you say when you passed [on] that instruction?' asked Andrew Tyrie.

'I relayed the contents of the conversation that I had with Mr Diamond, and fully expected that the Bank of England's views would be incorporated in the Libor submission.'

'Did you know that this lowballing of submissions was illegal at the time?' asked David Ruffley.

'No, it did not seem an inappropriate action, given that this was coming from the Bank of England.'

'Did not seem an inappropriate action? But the US Department of Justice has said it is illegal in its findings. That is why Barclays has been fined. It was illegal. Why are you telling us, in slightly different terms, that it did not seem inappropriate? It does not sound as if you know your job [...] You have read the US Department of Justice judgment. Isn't that true?'

'Yes, I have.'

'Yes, it is true, isn't it?'

'No, sir.'

Ruffley was losing patience. Surely Jerry del Missier wasn't contradicting the DOJ? 'I am going to quote what the US Department of Justice says: "Barclays' illegal activity involved manipulating its submissions for benchmark interest rates in order to benefit its trading positions and the media's perception of the bank's financial health." So we are talking about that; the perception of the bank's financial health [...] It is illegal, isn't it?'

Del Missier's answer was precisely worded: 'The manipulation of Libor is illegal according to what you have just read.'

'According to the US Department of Justice. What we are trying to get at here, Mr del Missier, is that you were unaware that the instruction – would you call it an instruction that Mr Diamond gave you? – to procure lowballing of Libor submissions at Barclays. It was an instruction, wasn't it?'

'Yes, it was.'

'Now, you weren't aware that that was an illegal activity that he was asking you to bring about?'

'I disagree that it was an illegal activity.'

'So you are disagreeing with the Department of Justice.'

Andrew Tyrie intervened, 'Do you consider it to have been improper?'

'No, I don't.'

'So you are taking issue with the Department of Justice's conclusions, when in paragraph 48 it describes this as "the period of improperly lower Libor submissions"?'

'I base my judgment, Mr Chairman, on the role that the Bank of England plays, in the context that the world was in. It did not strike me as improper in late October 2008.'

'Okay,' said Tyrie. 'But you are taking issue with the Department of Justice on that point, aren't you? It is saying that it was improper, and you are saying that it is not?'

'No, sir. I am merely telling you how I looked at it in October 2008.'

'Then you did not consider it improper [...] Do you now agree with the Department of Justice, or disagree with it?'

'I am certainly not going to disagree with the Justice Department,' said del Missier.

It was precisely at that point – disagreeing with the US Department of Justice – that attempts to be completely honest about 'rigging' interest rates broke down. For everyone who might have wanted to tell the truth, the fear of losing your career or spending a large chunk of your life in a US jail, incarcerated thousands of miles away from your loved ones, got in the way.

Nevertheless, aware that lying to Parliament was a crime, Jerry del Missier repeatedly contradicted the account negotiated between Barclays' legal department and the DOJ. He recalled no misunderstanding on his part. Diamond told him Paul Tucker had given an instruction.

Jerry del Missier told them he'd had a follow-up conversation a few days later with the money markets team[9] where he again relayed the instructions from the top.

'Who on the money market desk – which person – did you give the instruction to?' Andrea Leadsom asked. 'Who is the head of the money market desk?'

'Mr Mark Dearlove,' said del Missier.

'Mark Dearlove. And what exactly did you say to him?'

'I relayed the conversation that I had had with Mr Diamond.'

'No, what exactly did you say to him?'

'I said, "I've spoken to Mr Diamond. He's had a call from Mr Tucker." I alluded to the pressure – the political pressure – around Barclays' health, as demonstrated by our Libor rates, and that we should get our rates down and not be an outlier.'

'So you explicitly instructed him to bring the Libor rate submissions down?'

'I passed the instruction along, yes.'

'Okay. So if we bring Mark Dearlove before this Committee, he will absolutely corroborate that, will he – that that is exactly what you said to him?'

Del Missier said he didn't know what Dearlove would say. Leaked internal Barclays documents indicate that Dearlove would have corroborated del Missier's version – and also would have added his evidence about Tucker's instructions direct to him earlier in October. But he would never be called.

The same day, the committee heard from the governor of the Bank of England, Sir Mervyn King, with his deputy Paul Tucker sitting alongside him along with the FSA chair Lord Turner.

Michael Fallon asked Sir Mervyn, 'Governor, at what point did the penny drop with you that Libor was not just dysfunctional but was actually being manipulated dishonestly?'

'There were two dates,' Sir Mervyn replied. 'I was informed of the allegations that Barclays had made in connection with the conversation between Mr Tucker and Mr Diamond in April 2010, but the first I knew of any alleged wrongdoing was when the reports came out two weeks ago.'

'I just want to be clear,' said Fallon. 'You had no suspicion until two weeks ago that anything had been going wrong in the Libor market?'

King was adamant about what he had been told. 'No, we have been through all our records,' replied King. 'There is no evidence of wrongdoing or reporting of wrongdoing to the Bank.'[10]

None of the MPs on the committee had access at the time to the Bank of England's confidential records, some of which I've subsequently obtained.

They show that, as early as 14 August 2007, a German bank, Landesbank Hessen-Thuringen Girosentrale, told one of Paul Tucker's staff that Libors were 'totally distorted, 25–30 bps away from where they should be'. On 20 August 2007, another bank, Landesbank Baden-Württemberg, told the Bank of England it believed that other banks 'may be manipulating Libor and SONIA fixings'.[11] Two days later, Deutsche Bank warned the Bank of England about lowballing, saying banks were setting Libor 'artificially low to allay market concerns'.[12] A month later, another of Tucker's officials made a note of a call where the Dutch bank ABN AMRO said that Libor quotes were 'still to some extent fictitious'. On 22 February 2008, an executive at Clydesdale Bank told the Bank of England that 'something needs to be done to stop banks quoting too low'.

Fallon's questions were about a troubling email from the New York Fed sent to King and Tucker by its boss Tim Geithner at a time after the Fed had heard from Colin Bermingham that Barclays, like other banks, was 'not posting an honest Libor' because it might draw unwanted attention (see page 63–4). The email sent the Fed's recommendations for changes to how Libor operated, including 'procedures designed to prevent accidental or deliberate misreporting'.

King told MPs that at no stage did anyone at the New York Fed raise concerns that they had actually seen or had evidence of wrongdoing.

'So he was suggesting a section entitled "We should eliminate incentives to misreport" because there was not any misreporting going on. Is that really credible?' asked Fallon.

'Of course it is credible. When you design any self-reporting scheme, you have rules to prevent misreporting. That is not the same as saying you have evidence that there is misreporting, and nor did the Fed or anyone else send us any evidence of misreporting,' said King.

Later in the committee's session, Labour MP John Mann asked the Bank of England governor: 'You appear to be still in denial that it was known that Libor rigging was going on – the lowballing – when it was patently obvious to everyone that it was known. Why are you still in denial over that? Wouldn't it help the situation if the Bank of England, along with the FSA, recognised that lowballing had failed to be spotted because you had other priorities because of the economic crisis? That honesty might give us some credibility in going forward and dealing with this crisis.'

But King didn't think it would help. 'No, is the short answer,' he replied. 'The slightly longer answer is that there is a world of difference between people saying they do not know how to submit when they are doing Libor submissions because the market is dysfunctional [...] and deliberate misrepresentation of the submissions with a view to a financial gain, either private or institutional [...] I did not say that fraud was restricted just to the rogue traders. It was also true that there was deliberate misrepresentation by Barclays in the submissions. On that, we had no evidence of wrongdoing. None was supplied to us. The evidence you cite – there were plenty of academic articles that looked into it and said that they could not see in the data any evidence of manipulation. I say again, if you go back to the inquiries that the regulators made, it took them three years to work out and find the evidence of wrongdoing. If it was so obvious and all in the newspapers and everyone was talking about it, one might ask why everybody did not say, "This is wrong." The reason was that it wasn't wrongdoing. It was a market that was dysfunctional and was not operating in any effective way.'

No one on the committee asked the obvious follow-up question. The FSA, whose chairman Adair Turner was sitting next to King, had just fined Barclays £59 million for misconduct – wrongdoing – in relation to lowballing. If it really wasn't wrongdoing, why had Turner's FSA levied a fine? And why had the DOJ called it 'illegal'?

Not only had Paul Tucker's markets division received numerous complaints about banks posting Libor submissions below where cash was trading, it had also passed them on to the FSA. During the crisis, Bank of England officials wrote eighteen market intelligence reports and updates that touched on lowballing and sent them to the regulator. It had even explained to the FSA why lowballing was happening – because banks were afraid of bad publicity if they stood out from the pack.[13] That was precisely the reason both the FSA and DOJ had called it 'manipulation' – something that both agencies had said was misconduct.

The Bank of England was also told early on about trader requests. On 1 October 2007, one of Tucker's team at the Bank of England sent a paper to Paul Tucker, copying in Mike Cross, titled, 'Why are Libor rates high?' It contained the following: 'A contact told us (in strict confidence) that derivatives desks will call cash desks before their Libor submission if they have positions on that would benefit from higher/lower Libor.' That was another contemporary report of what the FSA and DOJ would later fine as misconduct (also known as 'wrongdoing').

Another confidential note was even more explicit. It summarised bilateral meetings between Paul Tucker, Mike Cross and two other Bank of

England officials with the treasurers of banks and fund managers between 28 October and 7 November 2008. The note said the Bank of England had been told 3-month Libor was regarded as an imperfect indicator of conditions on the money markets because of a lack of activity and 'accusations of manipulation to game derivatives markets'. Yet as he sat there, listening to King, Tucker said nothing to correct him.

Was Parliament misled? MPs were being told that the Bank of England had checked all its records and found no reports of wrongdoing. In fact, its confidential records indicate that from August 2007 it was hearing allegations of manipulation, lowballing and misreporting of Libor – the very same misconduct for which banks were fined billions of dollars. The Bank of England has never shown those records to Parliament.

Both Paul Tucker and Jerry del Missier had given the committee investigative leads which, for any inquiry determined to get to the truth, cried out for further investigation. Diamond and del Missier were flatly contradicting each other. For the committee to get to the bottom of it, the next steps were obvious. Go to the top and bottom of the chain of command. Call as witnesses the cash traders who submitted Libor and Euribor: PJ, Pete Spence and Colin Bermingham. Del Missier had also repeatedly mentioned Dearlove, whose evidence about Tucker's instruction to lower Libors earlier in October would have exploded the wafer-thin story about a 'misunderstanding'.

A committee following the natural lines of inquiry would have spoken to the architects and supervisors of the settlement between Barclays and the authorities: Rich Ricci, Judith Shepherd, Mark Harding and the relevant officials from the US and UK regulators. Or they could have pursued it to the top to find out whether there had indeed been pressure from Whitehall by asking the top officials who might know. Paul Tucker had supplied them with names of the 'senior Whitehall figures' he was in touch with: Jeremy Heywood, Tom Scholar, Jon Cunliffe and Nick Macpherson. The evidence, even that which was already before them, pointed to the involvement of not just the Bank of England but 10 Downing Street, where, at the time, Jeremy Heywood was Brown's principal private secretary and chief of staff. The committee could also have called Gordon Brown.

But for the MPs' inquiry into interest rate-rigging, none of those witnesses were called. Neither Brown nor the top civil servants were asked about their involvement in trying to get Libor and Euribor down. All the top bank executives, including Mark Dearlove and Stephen Morse, were 'lawyered up' and ready to give evidence if asked. But the committee's chair, Andrew Tyrie, never invited them to testify. No one among the witnesses who did appear before the committee mentioned the Dearlove call – even though it had been known of in regulatory circles for two years and was a big part of the reason why the DOJ had launched a criminal inquiry.

Soon after Sir Mervyn King's evidence, Parliament went into 'recess' – its long summer break – and the public outcry over the rigging of interest rates started to die down. When it published a report on its hearings only a month later, on 18 August 2012, the MPs' inquiry into this matter of great public interest was strangely curtailed, titled 'Fixing Libor: Some Preliminary Findings'. The word 'preliminary' suggested more to come. But there would never be a full report.[14]

The findings of Tyrie's committee went along with the official version of events negotiated between Barclays' legal department and the US authorities, including the highly questionable story that let the UK government, the Bank of England and the board of Barclays Bank off the hook. What happened on 29 October 2008, the MPs' report allowed, was a 'perceived' instruction that came down to PJ and Pete Spence to lower Libor by 50 basis points. It wasn't real but was all the product of a misunderstanding. In the concluding wording, approved by Andrew Tyrie, you could detect a hint of the natural scepticism that anyone who read the official story would feel: 'If Mr Tucker, Mr Diamond and Mr del Missier are to be believed,' the report concluded, 'an extraordinary, but conceivably plausible series of misunderstandings and miscommunications occurred. The evidence [...] describes a combination of circumstances which would excuse all the participants from the charge of deliberate wrongdoing.'

Lots of stories are 'conceivably plausible'. But that's a long way from being believable or accurate. The big question never answered by the MPs' unusually short inquiry was whether the official version was true or not. Its concluding phrase, '*if* Mr Tucker, Mr Diamond and Mr del Missier are to be believed' failed to disentangle their differing accounts, to seek corroborating evidence or to decide which account was the more credible. After only six weeks, the only inquiry into interest rate-rigging ordered from the top, tasked with getting to the bottom of things, had ended on an 'if'.

Every word of the dubious story negotiated between the regulators and the bank's lawyers to deflect the blame for rate-rigging away from those at the top of the financial system had been swallowed whole by Andrew

Tyrie's committee. The traders, by contrast, would struggle to get anyone to listen, let alone believe them.

Within weeks of Bob Diamond's appearance, Barclays sacked PJ, Jon Mathew, Colin Bermingham and most of the other remaining traders on its staff implicated in interest rate 'rigging'. Devastated after thirty-one years of loyal service, PJ tried to appeal on the grounds that he'd already been disciplined over trader requests with a written warning, but to no avail. Then Barclays went further, cutting defendants off from any legal support. That threatened to ruin them financially because of the huge sums it would cost to pay lawyers to defend them.

The outcome of the disciplinary process for Mark Dearlove was very different. During his disciplinary hearing, he was asked why he'd accepted Jerry del Missier's instruction to lower Libor on 29 October 2008. Dearlove came back with an unexpectedly forceful answer. This had to be seen in context, he said, telling them of his meeting at the Bank of England earlier in October 2008 when Tucker said the bank's Libor rates should be 'put down' because they were getting attention in 'the West'. Barclays' legal department was now fully aware of this and other persuasive evidence that contradicted the story it had negotiated for public consumption. But Barclays' legal department never wrote to the Treasury committee to correct the record. Fortunately for the Bank of England, that part of the story was kept quiet.

Dearlove was promoted to run Barclays' operations in Japan. Miles Storey, who'd resigned from Barclays in late 2008, got a new job as treasurer at Clydesdale Bank, later taken over by Virgin Money. After Bob Diamond's departure, the board of Barclays appointed Antony Jenkins as chief executive, the new broom who was going to clean up Barclays' sullied image. To underline his determination to change the bank's much-criticised culture, one of Jenkins' first moves was to appoint a senior regulator to become its new head of compliance and government and regulatory relations, a man with the ideal public profile to show the bank's determination to sort itself out: the outgoing chief executive of the FSA, Hector Sants.

In deciding what cases to pursue, David Green publicly declared that what mattered was no longer to do with the scale of the fraud: he was concerned to protect the good name of the City of London. His criteria for taking on a serious fraud case were 'cases that undermined UK plc in general and the City of London in particular'. He was less interested in the amounts of money the victims of the fraud had lost, or how much the perpetrators had made.

That was just as well. In spite of all the talk in the press about how interest rate 'manipulation' affected ordinary borrowers, no victims had come forward to complain that they'd lost money because of it.[15] And in the four years since the Commodity Futures Trading Commission began inquiring into Libor and the two years since the DOJ got involved, no one had worked out how much money had been lost as a result of the alleged misconduct. Indeed, in the case of trader requests, it wasn't at all obvious that anyone had lost any money at all. The nefarious deed identified in the press releases was that swaps traders were *attempting* to nudge the Libor average in their favour. No one had shown that they'd succeeded. In spite of pouring huge resources into the investigation over four years, the US authorities hadn't delved deep enough into the data to work out if all the tweaks to Libor and Euribor submissions made by PJ, Jon Mathew, Colin Bermingham or other submitters had made any difference to the Libor or Euribor average. Nor was it easy to prove the core offence of fraud.

The Fraud Act 2006 required prosecutors like Green to show a defendant had made a misrepresentation, dishonestly saying or implying something false that was intended to make money for himself – or to cause actual or potential economic harm to someone else.[16] To show PJ or Jon Mathew had made false statements when putting in their estimates of the cost of borrowing, the authorities would have had to show they were putting in Libor submissions that were materially inaccurate, outside the range of interest rates where cash was trading that day. Before the credit crunch, there was no evidence that they had done so. As PJ kept telling Jon Mathew in 2010, the submissions data supported the opposite view; that they'd stayed within the range of accurate rates where they could borrow cash. After August 2007, they'd posted false rates – but only because of pressure from above, which they'd done their best to protest about while blowing the whistle to the authorities.

There was another problem. What would it take for you to break the law at work and risk prosecution? A coffee? A glass of champagne? A box of raw fish? That was what the traders had offered each other by email. To prove a fraud, Green needed more than that. To make a credible case that the

Libor and Euribor submitters were engaged in fraud when they accepted a request from swaps traders, you'd have to show they made money from it, or at least hoped to do so. But submitters like PJ and Jon Mathew could not possibly have made money from accepting the requests. Their bonuses were linked to how the cash desk did – not the swaps desk. And in the case of swaps traders like Ryan Reich or Jay Merchant, the amounts they might have made through higher bonuses if their requests succeeded in nudging the Libor average to benefit the bank were tiny compared to their six-figure salaries. So much for the claim that rate-rigging was the work of greedy 'rogue traders'. It only made sense if you never did the arithmetic. On any realistic view, it was much too little to motivate anyone to jeopardise a lucrative trading career by taking part in a criminal enterprise.

For Green, it was a serious problem. With no victims, no credible estimates of the amounts of money lost, no obvious false statements and little or no gains for the perpetrators, it would be very difficult to prosecute the traders, as politicians had told Nick Robinson they hoped would be possible, under general fraud legislation such as the Fraud Act 2006. He had to find a way through. An old friend of his from the community of lawyers who prosecute white-collar crime, a senior barrister named Mukul Chawla, came up with a solution. In other legal systems, such as the French and German systems, crimes had to be prohibited by statute, a law deliberately made, to be prosecuted in court. But in the UK system, there were also 'common law' offences, meaning laws where rights and wrongs had been decided not by Parliament passing a law but by the decisions of judges in cases down the ages, setting precedents that became law in future. Under the common law, there was an offence of 'conspiracy to defraud', where more than one person agreed to do something dishonest that might make them money at the expense of others. All they would have to convince a jury of was two things: that there was an agreement and that there was dishonesty. There was no need to demonstrate losses for the victims or gains for the perpetrators. There was no need to put a victim on the witness stand. All you had to show was that the defendants had agreed to do something, and then convince a jury it was dishonest. So vulnerable were perfectly honest defendants to conviction under the offence of 'conspiracy to defraud' that lawyers had campaigned for its abolition to the professional body in England and Wales tasked with updating and improving the law, the Law Commission. But given the political pressure he was now under to make a success of the rate-rigging prosecutions, that wasn't about to put David Green off.

With lowballing, the evidence to demonstrate that instructions from the top resulted in false statements was replete. The SFO had access to emails and audio recordings where submitters like PJ, Pete Spence and Colin Bermingham openly complained that they were being instructed to submit Libor or Euribor rates that clearly broke the rules, rates that were 'dishonest' and 'patently false'. It would have been straightforward to corroborate what they were saying by comparing the interest rates they'd submitted with the interest rates where cash was changing hands on the day in question, either on the cash markets or on the foreign exchange markets. That would have shown submissions of interest rates far below the range where cash was trading. There was also clear evidence, in emails disclosed by the British Bankers' Association, that there were victims among the smaller European banks who'd complained to John Ewan that they were getting 'stuffed' because Libor and later Euribor were too low. It was clear that Barclays, like the other banks, had procured a financial advantage through lowballing because it had avoided the 'beating' it would have taken (meaning bad publicity leading to a lower share price) had it allowed the likes of PJ, Jon Mathew and Colin Bermingham to give their honest view about the real cost of borrowing cash. Unlike trader requests, lowballing did fit what you'd need to prosecute under the Fraud Act 2006: a misrepresentation (false Libor and Euribor submissions) that led to a gain and that was being openly labelled dishonest by both PJ and Colin Bermingham. But in 2012, Green showed no sign of wanting to pursue all the lowballing evidence that implicated the banks' top bosses and central banks and governments.

The SFO would later defend itself from the charge that it had gone after traders down the ranks and ignored evidence pointing to the top by saying it 'followed the evidence as high as it went where there was a realistic prospect of conviction'. But what exactly was meant by 'the evidence'? David Green was aware that the bundle of evidence that came to the SFO, collated by Barclays' US lawyers Sullivan & Cromwell, was far from comprehensive. It came from the searches of Barclays records carried out for the CFTC by Project Bruce. The SFO knew the US watchdog was interested only in manipulation of Libor in dollars, not pounds sterling; there was likely to be a vast wealth of additional evidence in the records related to lowballing of sterling Libor that it had not yet seen. Project Bruce was not allowed to search the email accounts of Barclays Group executives such as John Varley, Bob Diamond or Chris Lucas; they would only come across their emails if they were included on email chains with more junior staff. The evidence produced by Sullivan & Cromwell for the CFTC had also had key documents filtered out of it, such as emails involving the bank's lawyers that were covered by the lawyers' obligation of confidentiality to their clients, also known as 'legal professional privilege'. That meant the bank's lawyers were unlikely to be implicated and all their advice to top executives was excluded.

You had to stop and think to digest the implications. Barclays, according to the four regulators whose public notices had led to the SFO investigation, was the culprit of interest rate-rigging. That was why it was paying the fines. Yet much of the evidence the SFO was relying on was produced by lawyers appointed and paid for by Barclays, who could see their ultimate duty as being to protect the bank's interests. No serious investigator would be happy to stop there. It was true that the evidence implicating the board of Barclays, the Bank of England, the UK government (and other central banks) wasn't yet a slam-dunk case. It was arguable that the Bob Diamond file note and the Dearlove phone call weren't enough in themselves to prove the lowballing ordered from the top. But like other bodies tasked with investigating crime, the SFO had a statutory duty to pursue all relevant investigative leads. In other words: to find out more. On any genuine attempt to find out all the relevant facts, those leads were far too strong to ignore.

David Green had access to all the evidence set out in Chapters 1–4 of this book. The SFO could listen to the audio recordings from PJ's line showing he'd been ordered to lowball, with instructions passed down via Jon Stone, Miles Storey and Mark Dearlove, first from the top of the bank, then from the Bank of England and the UK government. But the SFO showed no interest in investigating that before it brought charges against the traders down the ranks. For the first four years of the biggest inquiry the SFO had undertaken, Green didn't even instruct the team investigating Barclays' Libor rigging to interview Dearlove, Storey or Stone.[17]

Given what the Diamond file note, Jerry del Missier's evidence and the Dearlove call suggested, the gaps in the evidence at the top of the chain of command were obvious. Faced with that, a determined investigator keen to get to the truth would have wanted to dig: to find out about what was said to Tucker by Heywood and Scholar in October 2008; to find out what was said to Jerry del Missier and the other bank executives in August and September 2007; to learn more about the coordinated moves of banks in the Eurozone before and after Gordon Brown met European leaders on 12 October 2008. Using the evidence that it already had access to, the SFO could have sought a court order forcing Barclays' legal department to carry out searches of the email accounts of senior executives. That would have built its evidence about the serious kind of interest rate-rigging, the one that cost victims large sums: lowballing. It could have interviewed members of the Barclays' board, senior civil servants and politicians to find out the truth about lowballing in the crisis.[18] But David Green chose not to pursue it.

Neither Green nor his successor, Lisa Osofsky, would ever go to court to try the evidence implicating the top of the financial establishment in rigging interest rates.

As an SFO source put it to me, 'going after the top guys would have taken years. The SFO needed a result quickly, so it could turn around to the government and say, "Look we've scored a success" and ask for more funding.' Bluntly, prosecuting the traders was simply easier. Someone else – the banks' lawyers – had done the spadework.

With Theresa May threatening to abolish the SFO, Green had staked its reputation on the rate-rigging trials.[19] Now, he began to work out whom to charge. To prove a conspiracy to defraud, the SFO needed both ends of it: the swaps traders who made the allegedly dishonest requests and the submitters on the cash desk who agreed to carry them out. Among the swaps traders who'd made the requests were Ryan Reich, Stelios Contogoulas, Alex Pabon and Jay Merchant.

Among the Libor submitters Green decided to prosecute were PJ and Colin Bermingham: the very same traders who'd tried to blow the whistle on lowballing. The key prosecution witness, the man tasked by the SFO with setting out the rights and wrongs of Libor in public, would be John Ewan.

11

THE MAN WHO COULDN'T LIE

'December 10th, 2012. That was the last time I had a good night's sleep. A slumber that descended into contented darkness about which you recall nothing and awake from recharged and relaxed. From that date onwards sleep became a disturbed mix of anxiety, panic, fear, nightmares and cold sweats.'

(Tom Hayes, letter to the author from HM Prison Lowdham Grange, Nottinghamshire, 2017)

At 7 a.m. on 11 December 2012, Tom Hayes and his wife Sarah were fast asleep in bed when they were suddenly awoken by a loud and unfriendly sounding banging. Tom wondered whether it might be the builders, arriving early for once. Their home, a Surrey doer-upper, was in the midst of renovation. 'No, it's not the builders,' said Sarah. 'Someone's trying to knock on the front door.' He could hear cars outside honking their horns. Josh, their 14-month-old son, started to cry. As Sarah went to check on him, Tom drew up the blinds and peered out of the window into the freezing winter morning. Instead of the builder's van, a line of unmarked cars was crowded into the driveway, tailing back to the street outside. Police, some in uniform and some in plain clothes, were getting out of the cars and gathering in front of the entrance to their house.

Another series of bangs, even louder this time. Sarah went downstairs to open the door but it wouldn't move. 'Tom!' she called out. 'The bolt's stuck!' Tom jogged downstairs in his boxer shorts and reached up to release the bolt and open the front door. A plainclothes detective thrust a warrant in his face. The 32-year-old former UBS trader stared at the document in disbelief as the officer told him he was under arrest, on suspicion of conspiracy to defraud. 'Show me that!' said Sarah. One of the police officers at the door started moving to enter the house but then stopped, startled, as Sarah raised her arm and held a flat hand a few inches from his face. She looked him straight in the eyes.

'You – can wait.'

Sarah knew from her legal training that they had to give you enough time to read the warrant. Urgently, she scanned the document as the crowd of police officers looked on. The section listing the charges against him didn't make sense. But all the legal requirements had been met and the judge's signature was there. They were going to have to let them in.

Around twenty-five people, including detectives, police officers and lawyers from the Serious Fraud Office, entered their house and started looking around and taking photographs. As Josh crawled around the floor looking bewildered and lost, the detective read Tom the allegations that had led to his arrest. 'I couldn't really take them in,' Tom said. 'The officer went on and on. "Conspiring with James Gilmour." Who is he? I thought. I grabbed at the word "Libor". The officer pronounced it Leebor, not, as it should be, Lie-bor. "Yeah, all right. Whatever," he snapped when I corrected him. If they can't pronounce it, they can't understand it, I thought, this just needs some explanation, it will all be fine.'

But Sarah could already see this was about something much bigger than Tom's actions as a trader. 'When are you going to leak this?' she asked one of the SFO officers.

'There'll be an announcement today, 4 p.m.,' came the reply.[1] As Sarah had guessed, Tom's arrest had been planned as a public event.

Minutes later, he was dressed and ready to get into a police car to be driven the 20-odd miles to Bishopsgate Police Station in the City of London, where he'd be held ahead of an interview with the SFO. Just as Tom was about to leave the house, he saw Josh eating a piece of toast in his highchair and walked over to pat him on the head. 'I'll see you later, buddy,' he said in his best dad voice, as if everything was fine. But inside the back of the police car, Tom wondered what the hell was going to happen.

Placed in a cell at the police station with a metal toilet and a cardboard-thin mattress, he paced up and down, every now and then pressing a bell to call the custody officer so he could order a cup of tea. As he gingerly sipped from the small plastic cups, Tom had plenty of time to reflect. He ruefully considered the fact that he was just opposite the very building where his trading career had begun; the headquarters of what was once called Greenwich NatWest.

Tom had severe Asperger's syndrome, but he wasn't diagnosed until he was an adult. He'd grown up in a small, terraced house in Shepherd's Bush, west London. His parents, Nick and Sandy, had separated when he was only 4 years old. Money had always been an issue in the Hayes household; bailiffs once came banging on the door after his dad fell behind with the bills. As a result, Tom swore he'd always have enough cash. He became obsessed with collecting coins he earned from various odd jobs, stacking them in neat piles by denomination. He also carried a backpack filled with his most precious possessions, as if ready to go on the run at any moment, lest the bailiffs show up again.

Once Tom became interested in something, it absorbed him totally, like the football team Queens Park Rangers (QPR), whose Loftus Road Stadium he could see from his bedroom window. He followed them obsessively and collected football stickers, arranging them in peculiar displays. He was also obsessed with toy soldiers but, above everything else, Tom loved numbers. An inspirational maths teacher, Ruth Molden, taught him Pythagoras' theorem when he was only 6 and he'd enjoyed maths ever since. People were fallible, difficult to understand, deceitful. But numbers were simple, straightforward, either right or wrong. They told the truth.

Tom grew up in a family that was politically engaged. His dad, Nick, was a TV executive who, in the early 1990s, had been editor of the flagship documentary strand on independent television, Granada TV's *World in Action*. In 1985, when Tom had just started school, a *World in Action* film was broadcast[2] that questioned the safety of the convictions of six Irish men who'd been coerced by police into making false confessions that they'd carried out the bombings by the IRA of two Birmingham pubs in 1974, which killed twenty-one innocent young people, enraging the press and public.

Their interrogation, prosecution and convictions took place amid a huge public outcry. The Court of Appeal turned down their appeals following the first programme. But then, in a book by the journalist Chris Mullin and a 1990 drama-documentary watched by 10 million people titled *Who Bombed Birmingham?*, the programme makers had gone even further, identifying and interviewing the real culprits, an IRA cell known as the Balcombe Street Gang. In 1991, the six men's sentences of life imprisonment were dramatically overturned and a new body was set up, the Criminal Cases Review Commission, as politicians recognised that the Court of Appeal was an insufficient safeguard to prevent serious miscarriages of justice. What Nick could never have known at the time was that his own young son would himself later end up making a false confession of crime – and would later apply to the very same body.

While Tom was still a schoolboy at Chiswick Community school, his mother, Sandy, worked as a researcher for Gordon Brown when he was an up-and-coming opposition politician in the early 1990s. He rapidly ascended the ranks of the Labour Party to become Shadow Chancellor, the opposition spokesman on financial matters. Tom would sometimes pick up the house phone and Brown would ask him how school was going before Tom called out for his mum. After the Labour leader John Smith died in 1994, Brown's work intensified. Once, Sandy was away from home for so long helping Brown prepare for the Budget that the Labour politician, perhaps feeling some guilt towards the teenage boy and his brother, bought him a present: the *Oxford English Dictionary* ('Just what every 15-year-old wants,' said Tom). Later, after Labour took power under Tony Blair in 1997 and Brown became Chancellor of the Exchequer, he offered Sandy a chance for her 17-year-old son to come and work for him. She decided against even telling Tom about the offer because she thought he wouldn't fit in with Brown's politics. Instead, Tom, while studying engineering at Nottingham University, opted for an internship at investment bank UBS. He was soon fascinated. Especially by derivatives, which involved placing massive bets on the future value of various commodities, or on benchmarks like the FTSE 100 or Dow Jones.[3]

While some members of Tom's family were in the media and politics, others worked in the City of London. Tom was close to his grandfather who'd had a long career as a stockbroker. His uncle, Chris Salmon, had also embarked on a successful career in the City as an economist, joining the

Bank of England and later rising through its ranks to become private secretary to the governor, Sir Mervyn King,[4] during the financial crisis.

Against the wishes of his parents, Tom told them he was going to become a trader, and as soon as he graduated, he took a job at Royal Bank of Scotland, just across the road from Bishopsgate Police Station. Tom's ability to spot patterns in huge amounts of data won him attention and it wasn't long before he was making a name for himself as a trader thanks to his tireless and obsessive dedication and his accurate predictions about where dozens of different products, rates and markets were headed.

He both loved and hated his job as a trader. 'I mean, it's a little bit like *The Hunger Games*, you know. It's very, very competitive, very dog-eat-dog. Very, very stressful. Lots of times you'd go to work and you're feeling physically sick. It's like going in for an exam every single day and you don't know what the questions are going to be. You don't quite know what the market is going to throw at you. You're under pressure and the markets are open 24 hours a day. So that stress doesn't abate at 5 o'clock. The transparency in trading is like no other job. There's nowhere to hide: if you lose money, you've got a big red number in front of you. And that's on the basis of your decisions. On the flip side, if you make money, again, that's also on the basis of your decisions, so you can take full credit for it. It can be brutal to you, but it can be very rewarding as well.'

Tom was headhunted, first to a new job with the Royal Bank of Canada and then later by UBS, who offered him $138,000 per year plus a first-year bonus of nearly $500,000, along with free accommodation in Tokyo. He didn't speak the language, didn't like the food, and preferred to head straight home after work. The occasional visit to a Western-style burger bar was about as exotic as he let his social life get. Although earning well, Tom didn't spend. He showed no interest in high living, expensive trinkets or even new clothes. What he enjoyed wasn't so much the money as winning in the markets. He created huge, predictive programmes using Microsoft Excel spreadsheets which instantly told UBS – while taking into accounts hundreds of variables and their relationships with one another – which trade in any given situation would benefit UBS. Tom felt more connected to his software than any human.

His programmes set, he began trading in derivatives connected to Japanese interest rates in September 2006. Tom focused on derivatives that would be profitable, if on a particular date, the difference in interest rates between two countries widened or narrowed by the tiniest of margins, just hundredths of a percentage point. On the most volatile days, he'd go from being down $4 million for the day to being up $4 million. It was a little bit like being a professional sports person, he'd later say. You had a number of very good earning years while you were young, when you also got very, very stressed. Burnout rates in trading were high. So, you had to make the most of it while you were still able to withstand what it was doing to you, mentally and physically.

A key part of Tom's role at UBS was to manage the risks being taken by the swaps desk in Tokyo. That was what buying and selling derivatives like swaps was all about. The bank's loans were priced based on the Libor benchmark, typically Libor +1%, so that if the Libor benchmark were 3%, the bank would charge 4% interest. If it had made a large volume of loans at yen Libor +1%, it would collect less income if the rate fell. To offset that risk, the bank could enter swaps contracts where you'd receive a fixed rate and pay a variable one – contracts which would rise in value if yen Libor dropped. That meant the risks to the bank attached to the loans had been 'hedged'. As a result of the swaps contract, in other words, the bank would lose less money if yen Libor fell.

Over time, the swaps desk had accumulated thousands of trading positions, some of which might benefit from a higher yen Libor and some from a lower. Like other swaps traders all around the world, Tom would work out, each day, what the bank's net position was and whether it would be better for the bank to have higher or lower Libor rates. Then he'd get in touch with the cash traders who submitted the Libor rates for UBS and ask them for a high or low yen Libor submission. It might or might not make a difference to the published Libor average that the banks' trades were linked to. You couldn't know it would work. But as a trader, Tom had a duty to the bank to do anything and everything he could think of to help the bank make money and to limit any losses. It was worth the effort of making a request, just in case it helped.

Swaps traders in London, Tokyo or Zürich would typically put in their Libor or Euribor requests verbally, either by calling out across the floor to the cash desk, a matter of a few metres away, or by walking over. 'Where do we want the Libors today, mate, high or low?' was a common question across the City of London at 11 a.m. In some banks, such as Deutsche Bank, senior managers had even rearranged the seating plan on the trading floor to make it easier for the swaps traders to make their requests, putting the derivatives desk right next to the cash desk. But because of the time difference between Europe and Tokyo, the cash traders wouldn't always be at their desks when Tom worked out which way his bank was 'facing'. That meant that unlike other swaps traders, he had to make his Libor requests via email or via the Bloomberg messaging system. Something about his Asperger's made him unusually thorough about it. If, for example, the bank's net position was the same as it had been the day before, he wouldn't leave it alone for a day or two. He'd send an email like clockwork, every day. During his time at UBS, he sent hundreds of similar emails and messages, each as dull as the others, all asking the cash traders to submit high or low yen Libors. Those same dull emails would later be used to condemn him.

Tom took the practice of trying to obtain commercially advantageous Libor submissions further than others. Whereas most swaps traders were aware you could ask your own cash desk for Libor submissions to be put in high or low, Tom had worked out how the traders on the cash desks usually arrived at their Libor submissions. Like Jon Mathew, they'd pick up guidance from the brokers just before 11 a.m. as to where they thought the Libors would be, known as 'run-throughs' (see pages 94 and 101–3). For example, Jon Mathew might press a button at his desk to ask a broker from ICAP at 10.50 a.m., 'Where do you reckon the Libors will be this morning?' And the broker would reply, 'We've got Ones at 3.70 [their Libor estimate of what it would cost to borrow cash for one month at 3.70%], Twos at 3.75 [3.75% to borrow cash for two months], Threes at 76 [3.76%], Sixes at 78 [3.78%], Nines at 80 [3.80%] and 81 in the 1-year [3.81% to borrow cash for a year].' Often, cash traders like Jon were just repeating the guidance from the brokers. If you could get the brokers to shift their guidance higher or lower, you could influence not just your own bank's submissions, but those of all the banks who asked the brokers for their Libor guidance. If it might boost the chances that Libor would go in the direction that would help his bank, it must be worth doing. Tom's Asperger's made him a stickler for the rules. He knew Libor. There was no law or regulation, and nothing in any code of conduct, that said you couldn't do that.

As one of the biggest traders in the yen swaps market, Tom knew he brought a lot of business to the brokers he spoke to, such as Darrell Read at ICAP, and Noel Cryan at Tullett Prebon, whose key benchmark of success was how much commission they made. That was what determined the size of their bonuses. The brokers went to all kinds of lengths to keep big traders like Tom happy, wining and dining them and flying them to conferences or sporting events like the World Cup or the Olympics and doing whatever Tom wanted to keep the business rolling in. Seeing a trading opportunity, Tom started taking advantage of his position with the brokers on behalf of his bank. The brokers he spoke to, like Noel Cryan, dealt with swaps. There'd be another desk at Tullett Prebon that dealt with cash and gave out the run-throughs every morning at 11 a.m. to the likes of Jon Mathew and PJ. So Tom started asking Read, Cryan and others to have a word with their cash desks and ask them to shift their guidance up or down a tick or two. It was one way among many of trying to boost UBS's trading performance and manage its risks, which wouldn't do much in itself to change the amount of money the swaps desk made. Shifts in Libor would make up a maximum of 5 per cent of the profits or losses on the bank's trading book that Tom ran. But the way he saw it, even if it could only make a small difference, it was worth trying. 'I made calls and sent hundreds of messages openly, on recorded phone lines and on emails that I knew were being monitored. And I did it with abandon because I didn't think I was doing anything wrong.'

Over the course of his time at UBS, Tom made more than 950 daily requests to cash desks to submit yen Libor high or low, and multiple requests to his brokers to have a word with their cash desks and get them to shift their guidance. His tone towards the brokers could be rude and bullying, sometimes threatening to 'pull their line' if they didn't help him out, meaning the line of credit that enabled the broker to keep doing business with UBS. The brokers – such as Read and Cryan – would pay him lip service, pretending they were doing what he'd asked just to keep him happy. But they didn't see him as doing – or asking for – anything wrong or illegal. Tom could never quite tell if his requests to the brokers had made any difference to the yen Libor average. Nor, it would later turn out, could the SFO. But that wasn't enough to put the SFO off prosecuting him.

It was while he was in Tokyo that Tom met a bright young finance lawyer who was on a three-week holiday with a friend after completing her qualifications, Sarah Tighe. He first spotted her sunning herself on a lounger by the pool of her hotel and plucked up the courage to walk up to her, sit down and start chatting. 'He was dressed in the full England football kit. I know – sexy, right?' Sarah said, laughing. 'There was something different about him; it was attractive.' Tom wasn't a party animal like some traders, often eschewing alcohol for hot chocolate on after-work trips to the pub. The toxic masculinity of some London trading floors, where there were frequent invitations to strip clubs or parties involving cocaine and prostitutes, wasn't for Tom. He'd rather stay at home, cook sausages and watch the football.

As they got to know each other better, he realised that along with her blonde good looks, she was astute, outgoing, fun. Sarah, too, found herself growing more attracted to him: nice looking, intelligent, interesting. Even his Aspie streak was appealing; there was a complete absence of the sort of guile that was all too highly prized among some lawyers. He was incapable of duplicity – the most honest person she'd ever met.

Both of them were making money in the world of international banks, yet both often felt out of place in their surroundings. Both found the pomposity of some senior bankers and lawyers ridiculous. They were both very good at their jobs. But the world of highly paid bankers and lawyers, most of them from privileged backgrounds and educated the expensive way, felt to Sarah and Tom like someone else's world. Neither of them felt in the least inclined to suck up to their bosses or fit in with the painfully conformist, absurdly hierarchical culture of the banks.

Born into a working-class family in Tamworth, a market town 11 miles north-east of Birmingham, Sarah always knew her own mind, especially when it came to bullies. At school, she once confronted a girl who'd been bullying her sister all the way through primary school. The school kept putting them in the same class, even when they moved to senior school. Sarah had a blazing row with her, shouting at her to stay away from her sister, and was taken to see the head of year. 'Everyone else involved cried and apologised but I refused. They said I would be in big trouble. But I said I would never apologise to the person who had bullied my little sister so badly and I was categorically not sorry. And I would take whatever punishment they needed to deal out in order to cover up their own failure to address bullying in their school. I said I didn't care if they called my parents or the girl's parents, and I would explain it to anyone who asked – including the headmaster and the governors and the newspapers.' She was only 13 years old.

Sarah and Tom had something else in common. From the age of 24, long before she met Tom, she'd started work as a solicitor arranging finance for big infrastructure projects such as power stations, wind farms and solar parks. They'd be financed by a consortium of banks, each lending a share of a syndicated loan with an interest rate that was benchmarked to Libor. The terms and conditions would typically specify an interest rate of Libor +1% or Libor +2%. 'That was why I knew Tom was innocent. I didn't need any convincing because I could see it was all wrong from the start. I knew how Libor worked and the charges didn't make any sense. The whole case was bullshit,' she said.

By the time they got married, Sarah was all too aware that things had gone wrong at Tom's workplace. The problem was not that he was over-reaching himself out of some excessive greed for a larger bonus. In fact, he'd turned down an opportunity to make much more. In the global financial crisis, after Lehman Brothers collapsed, there was huge volatility – meaning much bigger opportunities for a trader to make profits by shifting money from one market to another. In the year of the Great Recession 2008/09, Tom had his biggest ever trading year. At one point, the bottom line of his trading book, the 'profit and loss' (known as 'P and L') was up by $169 million. He'd been offered millions to join Goldman Sachs but turned it down, preferring to stay at UBS where things would be less pressured. Tom was fully aware that the US authorities were investigating false Libor submissions in the crisis, investigations ordered by senior management to protect their banks' solvency. It was well known that the Commodity Futures Trading Commission had been looking into that since October 2008 and he guessed that UBS was probably also being investigated. But that didn't put him off making requests of the UBS Libor submitters in Zürich or those doing a similar job at Citigroup. He wasn't asking for false Libors, way outside the range where cash was trading. He was asking for rates to be submitted high or low within an accurate range of rates where offers were being made. To Tom's precise mind, sharp with numbers but a little deaf to corporate politics, the investigation was never going to touch him for the simple reason that he'd never asked for a false rate to be put in.

In December 2009, Tom left UBS, exasperated that the bank had decided not to pay him or any other traders a bonus in the wake of the crisis, when he'd played a blinder helping the bank to trade its way through it. As usual, there were plenty of banks keen to hire him and he chose Citigroup's Tokyo office. There, he continued to make Libor requests every day, openly on emails and messaging systems that he knew were being monitored. His bosses knew what he was doing. But on 6 September 2010, less than two weeks before his wedding, Tom was on the trading floor of Citigroup in Tokyo when he was tapped on the shoulder and told that the chief executive, Brian McCappin, wanted to speak to him. At a meeting with McCappin and other senior Citigroup staff, Tom was told he was being sacked. 'So, I sat down and then they started reading out, like, how I was getting fired for attempting to manipulate LIBOR and TIBOR and all of those things. And I said to him [McCappin], "Well, it's sort of ironic that you're firing me given that you were involved in it up to your eyeballs as well." And the Head Legal Counsel quick as a flash said, "He didn't have any trading positions," and I said, "Well, that's not really true, is it? As a CEO he's responsible for every trading position the bank's got." But, so I said, "Well, look, I mean, this is, obviously, bollocks. How much are you going to pay me to go quietly?" You know, like, as in – otherwise I'm going to make a real fuss about this.'[5]

Tom was sent out of the meeting to wait in another room. 'Then they came back and said I could keep $3 million that otherwise I would have had to return.[6] They gave me a standard reference, not a reference that said I'd been sacked for gross misconduct. And largely, I was content with that, because I had other banks who wanted to hire me.'

Tom's dismissal sent a shockwave across trading floors around the world. Until then, no one had been fired for making Libor requests. 'At the point I was fired, no one believed I was fired because of Libor, because no one could comprehend that that was even a sackable offence, let alone a criminal offence. I was saying to people, "I got fired because of Libor," and they said, "No, you got fired because you lost some money at Citi". It's true that I did lose some money at Citi, but that's not why I got fired. I literally had to persuade people that Libor was the reason.'

Sarah was furious with Citigroup, telling Tom he should sue for unfair dismissal. The episode was enough to cast a pall over Tom and Sarah's wedding, just two weeks later. But they had money now and Tom knew his skills were in high demand; he should soon be able to get another job. He'd had expressions of interest from Barclays, Deutsche Bank and Bank of America Merrill Lynch.

Then Tom discovered that, for now at least, even that escape route was cut off. He spoke to the head of rates at Barclays, Harry Harrison, who told him, according to Tom, that they'd have liked to hire him but explained that the Libor issue was getting too hot; the regulators were putting the banks under pressure to sack people. The other banks interested in hiring Tom were also holding off.

Tom figured the politics of the Libor investigation would take a while to settle down. He'd have to take a break from trading for a while. In January, Sarah discovered she was pregnant. Trying to look to the future positively, he applied to do a one-year master's in business administration course at Hult, an international business school headquartered in Cambridge, Massachusetts, with a branch in London, to start the following autumn. He hoped to return to trading when the course was over.

In the summer of 2011, a few weeks before the course began, Sarah and Tom went to University College Hospital in central London for a routine ultrasound scan – the first time they'd see their baby. As they waited in the scanning room, Tom's phone rang. On his phone screen, it looked like the call was coming from Kazakhstan. It was a young former colleague of his at UBS, whom he'd personally trained, named Mirhat. He told Tom he was being questioned by the FBI about what they'd done when they were trading together with Libor. What should he say? 'I don't know. You can blame me if you like,' said Tom, walking out of the scanning room to take the call. 'I'm your manager; I trained you in everything you did.' Tom knew the investigators would talk to his managers, who knew everything he was doing and were happy with it, so he was happy for Mirhat to pass the blame up the chain.

But overhearing Tom on the phone, Sarah suddenly sensed danger. Rushing out of the scan room behind him, she frantically tapped him on the shoulder and waved to interrupt him. Tom broke off for a second. Looking straight in his eyes, she said urgently: 'You must tell him that he must tell the truth.' Tom did as Sarah said.

Sarah was already doing a demanding full-time job. But she was now also taking on a second one as a criminal defence lawyer for her husband. It would take up huge amounts of her energy in the coming years, even as she brought up their baby. Later, Tom received another call from Mirhat. This time he told Tom the FBI was investigating. He said he was worried about some emails to do with Libor.

'I have these documents; what should I do with them?' he asked.

'I don't know what you should do with them,' said Tom. 'Do what you want with them. You know, if you want to throw me under the bus and blame me, that's fine. I was your manager. And I'll take responsibility for that, because I'll be saying exactly the same thing.'

Tom and Sarah later discovered that the calls hadn't come from Kazakhstan, though they may have been routed through the central Asian country. Mirhat was calling on a recorded line from the Washington field office of the FBI. He'd been offered a non-prosecution agreement and was trying to help the FBI entrap Tom. If he'd said, 'don't tell the FBI' or 'destroy the emails', Tom would have been facing an obstruction of justice charge on top of conspiracy to defraud. Do not pass Go, do not collect £200, go straight to jail. Sarah's advice to say 'tell the truth' had protected him.

Meanwhile, unbeknownst to Tom and Sarah, UBS's external lawyers were working behind the scenes, first with the US authorities and later with the SFO. In the months leading up to his arrest, a lawyer paid for by the Swiss bank, Osma Hudda of Gibson Dunn, was shuttling back and forth every week between her firm and the SFO headquarters as its team of investigators tried to gather evidence. UBS refused access to thousands of relevant documents at its headquarters in Switzerland, where the Libor submitters who accepted Tom's requests sat, citing Swiss secrecy laws. That evidence might have shed more light on senior management knowledge, enabling the SFO to pursue the investigation higher up the chain. It might also have shown evidence that was exculpatory for Tom. But despite all the evidence regulators already had seen that showed senior management ordering low-balling and condoning trader requests, it was never disclosed. It was just the same as it had been with Barclays, where almost all the evidence against the traders came from Sullivan & Cromwell, an external firm paid for by Barclays to represent it in the CFTC's investigation. The vast majority of the evidence the SFO had against UBS and Tom Hayes had first been sifted by the bank and its lawyers. In spite of George Osborne's 'blockbuster funding', designed to give the SFO the resources it needed for an independent investigation, it had little-to-no success investigating and uncovering new evidence on its own account. That enabled the banks' external lawyers to exert a significant degree of control over what evidence the SFO had, and therefore whom it prosecuted.

On 11 December 2012, as Tom sat in his cell sipping tea at Bishopsgate police station, recalling everything that had happened, he thought back to the uproar in the news in the summer, when the Barclays settlement was published. There'd been so much opprobrium for bankers; so many calls for traders to be prosecuted. Those MPs on the Treasury committee like David Ruffley and Andrea Leadsom, accusing unnamed traders of 'criminality' and 'atrocious acts'; Labour MP Clive Efford denouncing the banks and their traders for 'treason'. That public anger towards bankers was now being directed on him. There was an old term for it, going back to Old Testament times. He'd been set up to become a scapegoat.

The police searched Hayes's house for nine hours, flicking through photo albums and going through the family's cardboard boxes, as yet unopened since they'd moved in. Tom's phone, all the computers in the house, along with hard drives, memory cards and USB sticks were taken as potential evidence. Sarah put on a calm exterior for Josh's sake but was terrified of what the future might hold.

Tom was told that he'd been charged with conspiracy to defraud – of being the linchpin of an international conspiracy in which he'd bribe brokers, traders and Libor setters to alter their Libors so that he, along with other traders, could make millions in bonuses, hurting millions of ordinary people in the process.

'But that's not how Libor works,' Tom thought. 'That's not even what I was trying to do. They just don't understand.'

Not even Tom's fellow traders had understood what he was doing. 'It's too complicated, they've missed the point,' he thought desperately. 'If they would just let me explain.'

Before entering the interview room, however, Tom's lawyer recommended that he respond with 'no comment' to any questions from the SFO. It was much better to provide a considered written response later. Then it would all come out. Talking now would change nothing. Tom had to be patient. Let the detectives do their job; he should go through the motions, get bailed and then he could sort this mess out.

Hours passed as the officers went through hundreds of pages of evidence, quoting from recorded calls and emails. In one 2006 call, Tom had explained to a broker how easy it was to move Libor: 'Just give the cash desk a Mars bar and they'll set wherever you want.'

Other calls sounded more serious, such as this one, in 2008.

Tom: 'I don't care right – just get me any fucking trade which pays you basically, mate. If you keep fixes unchanged, I'll do a humongous deal with you. If you keep it as low as possible, I can do that. I'll, of course, support and pay you [...] $50,000, $100,000, whatever you want, all right?'

Broker: 'All right.'

Tom: 'I'm a man of my word.'

Broker: 'I know you are. No, that's done, right, leave it to me.'

Anyone would have to admit that this call sounded bad, that Tom was offering huge commissions to any brokers who could influence Libor. But Tom remembered this call, and it was exceptional. He'd made it when he was doing his utmost on the trading floor to help save UBS in September 2008, just after Lehman Brothers folded. What he was offering in commission wasn't a bribe; it was in line with agreements negotiated by his managers, who were paying the brokers by the deal because the normal trading wasn't going on.

'Still got another bloody seventy-five pages of this, yeah?' Tom said, his frustration boiling over. When the seemingly interminable interview was finally over, at 8.30 p.m., one of the officers asked if there was anything Tom would like to say.

'Not at this stage,' he replied. 'I'm biting my tongue.'

Tom knew that this was just a big misunderstanding. He was only one trader out of hundreds, if not thousands, who tried to ensure that Libor submissions were set to suit their bank's commercial interests, every working day of the year. Everything would be fine. These detectives just didn't understand how Libor worked, that was all.

That night, once Tom arrived home, he talked over the charges with Sarah. They agreed that everything would be cleared up once Tom presented his side of the story. The emails and phone recordings looked and sounded dodgy to untrained eyes and ears, but they were actually just the visible sign of a normal, routine commercial practice, of quoting prices with a company's commercial interests fully in mind. Far from Tom being a rogue operator, the requests were often on the orders of senior managers and all of them knew it was going on. Far from banning it, many senior managers encouraged it. Libor was just another trading tool. If the SFO wanted to prosecute Tom, then they'd have to prosecute every trader on the planet.

Tom spent the next week working out how he would explain to the SFO why they'd got it wrong. They were interpreting his requests for high or low Libors as corruption when they were nothing of the sort. There was always a narrow range of accurate interest rates where you could raise cash at 11 a.m. The requests were for Libor submissions to be put in high or low to suit the bank's commercial interests – within that range. Without that, what would a request for a 'high Libor' even mean? How high exactly? That was something that submitters on the cash desk would never ask, because they knew the range of interest rates where cash was trading and the swaps traders didn't. His plan was simple: explain to the SFO why everything they believed about Libor was wrong. It was so clear to him that they'd entirely misconceived the whole case. If only he had enough time, he could explain it all and stop this train in its tracks.

But he would never get that opportunity. Eight days after his arrest, Tom's world collapsed.

On the afternoon of 19 December 2012, Tom was sitting at home at the breakfast bar in their kitchen, glued to a window on his laptop showing Bloomberg TV. He was feeling encouraged – or at least, comforted. That morning at 7 a.m. the regulators' announcements had been published: 'UBS fined £160 million for significant failings in relation to LIBOR and EURIBOR'. Tom combed through the Final Notice from the Financial Services Authority. Loads of references to 'Trader A' whom he recognised as himself. 'More than 80 documented External Requests were made by Trader A to at least six External Traders seeking to influence the JPY LIBOR submissions of four other Panel Banks,' it said in paragraph 52 (b). 'At the request of Trader A, Brokers altered the information that those screens were showing and inserted false market information,' said paragraph 62.

But then there was evidence showing what senior managers knew about influencing the Libor fixing. Paragraph 98 showed UBS managers themselves ordered it, just as Barclays had. And paragraph 99 said they knew what Tom was doing: 'A number of Managers knew about and accepted the practice of manipulating submissions in certain LIBOR currencies and EURIBOR: At least four Managers were directly involved [...] At least three further Managers were aware [...] At least four Senior Managers were aware [...].'[7] To Tom, this was vindication. The Final Notice said the bank knew about it: it was their policy. It also showed they'd helped him implement that policy by negotiating the first set of payments to the brokers. If the SFO came at him with the same evidence, he'd be able to point to the Final Notice. His top bosses knew all about what he was doing.

But Tom's hopes for a fair outcome didn't last long. Early that afternoon, Bloomberg TV switched to a press conference in Washington DC hosted by the top law enforcement official in the USA, Attorney General Eric Holder.[8] Alongside him were officials from the CFTC and the FBI, and Lanny Breuer, who ran the criminal division of the US Department of Justice. Holder knew Lanny Breuer well from earlier days when they'd been partners at the upmarket US law firm Covington and Burling, where some of their biggest clients were banks.[9] Like Breuer, he'd been criticised for being too soft on Wall Street. On top of the failure to prosecute executives for selling the instruments that caused the credit crunch,[10] banks had been caught using fabricated paperwork and forged signatures on an industrial scale to turn mortgage borrowers out of their homes, leading to fines totalling $25 billion from attorneys general at the state level.[11] But not a single banker had been prosecuted for that either.

Now, at last, Holder and Breuer were seizing the opportunity to silence anyone who said they were soft on the banks. UBS had agreed to plead guilty to criminal conduct – a 'scheme to manipulate the London Interbank Offered rate' – and to pay a total of $1.5 billion to avoid prosecution. 'The non-prosecution agreement [...] reflects the department's determination to rigorously enforce federal financial criminal laws and underscores our willingness to bring criminal charges under these laws,' said Holder. 'By causing UBS and other financial institutions to spread false and misleading information about Libor, these alleged conspirators defrauded the company's counterparties of millions of dollars and they did so primarily to reap increased profits and to secure bigger bonuses for themselves.'

The top lawyer in the US government was laying out the crimes as fact, with very little sense of any presumption of innocence. Surely, Tom thought, it couldn't be him that Holder was referring to? He'd played no part in the internal investigation at UBS. No US investigator had ever spoken to him. 'Former UBS traders.' Could that mean him?

Then it was Lanny Breuer's turn, calling it 'one of the most significant scandals ever to hit the global banking industry [...] The bank's conduct was simply astonishing [...] UBS, like Barclays before it, saw fit repeatedly to fix Libor for its own ends, so UBS traders could maximise profit on their trading positions and so that the bank would not appear to be vulnerable to the public during the financial crisis. In addition to UBS Japan's agreement to plead guilty, two former UBS traders – Tom Alexander William Hayes and Roger Darin – have been charged in a criminal complaint unsealed today with conspiracy to manipulate Libor. Hayes has also been charged with wire fraud and an antitrust violation.'

Tom's jaw dropped. 'Sarah!' he called out. His voice sounded strange, unlike his normal tone. 'I've been charged in the US!'

Sarah rushed to see what Tom was watching. They listened in horror as Breuer went on, forehead glistening under the bright lights of the press conference. 'There was nothing – nothing subtle – about these traders' alleged conduct [...] Make no mistake: for UBS traders, the manipulation of Libor was about getting rich.'

Sarah felt her legs turn to jelly and grabbed the back of the chair Tom was sitting on to steady herself, another hand on the kitchen counter. 'Oh my god!' she thought to herself. 'This is going to happen and there's nothing I can do. They're going to do this to him, and I can't change it!' She turned to look at his face, staring open-mouthed at the screen, recalling everything she knew about her husband. She wasn't sure if he could handle it – facing police interrogation, being prosecuted, having to defend himself in public. She almost wished it could have been her instead: she was much tougher. He wasn't built for this stuff: he couldn't communicate. Then it dawned on her: *That's why they picked him, isn't it? It's disgusting.*

Sarah's instincts were now ringing alarm bells at full volume. This was going to destroy their lives. 'I had a ringing sound in my head and I couldn't see properly. I was seeing black and white dots; my vision went all fluid.' As the nausea welled up, Sarah rushed to the kitchen sink and vomited.

'As one broker told a UBS derivatives trader,' Breuer went on, 'Quote – "Mate, you're getting bloody good at this Libor game. Think of me when you're on your yacht in Monaco, won't you?"' As he struggled to utter casual London slang in an uptight New York accent, his demeanour filled with derision for these hitherto unknown British felons, it almost sounded sinister. There was no sign that the number two lawyer in the USA realised the irony. What he was condemning was, literally and figuratively, a joke.

Minutes later, Tom spoke to his lawyers. How much chance would he stand of being acquitted if he were extradited to the USA? More than 90 per cent of prosecutions end in a plea deal, he learned. But after a public condemnation like that, the chances of striking one that kept him out of prison were slim; he'd clearly been lined up as a target. So if he went all the way to trial? Defendants were only rarely acquitted. So what would the maximum sentence be if he were convicted? Fifteen years – or maybe thirty. And he'd serve almost all of it. Unlike in the UK, there were no tariffs that allowed you to be released halfway through. Tom was facing spending much of his adult life in jail, thousands of miles from his wife and son.

From that moment on he was focused on only one thing: avoid extradition at all costs. There was only one way to be sure: get prosecuted in the UK, not the USA. 'I was desperate for them to charge me,' he said. 'I'd flipped from being absolutely adamant that I was going to go and defend myself, to absolutely adamant that I needed to go and incriminate myself.' Tom's lawyers set to work. But nothing was going to happen overnight.

As 2013 began, Tom's anxiety started to get the better of him. Stressed all day and all night, he struggled to get to sleep and when he did, he slept briefly and badly. Nightmares plagued him and he'd often wake up drenched in sweat. Frightened by the size of his legal bills, he tried to make more money spread betting. He'd made a million pounds trading for himself as a 'day trader' since he'd left Citigroup. But since the arrest, continual sleep deprivation had left him with no judgement. His trades and his spread bets were all cock-eyed, driven by wishful thinking. He lost all the money he'd built up. Mentally and emotionally, he was a wreck. Tom withdrew into himself, becoming uncommunicative. Sarah couldn't get through to him. The combination of sleep deprivation and extremely high stress levels robbed him, and the three of them, of any calm. He crashed the car. One cold winter night in early 2013, Sarah saw him in the garden in the middle of the night, out in the snow in only his boxer shorts, standing in front of a tree. It looked like he was drawing something on it. When she put on a coat and came out to help him, she saw that he was rocking back and forth, tracing repetitive patterns with his finger on the tree's bark. She recognised what she was seeing from what she'd read about his Asperger's. It was 'comfort behaviour'. Tom was undergoing a nervous breakdown.

Sarah wanted to help Tom all she could. She would end up going all the way as his informal criminal defence lawyer. But he was now almost like a zombie, incapable of performing even the simplest task. She could see he was in no emotional state to look after Josh and she needed to work, now more than ever. Yearning for some stability and sanity, she moved back in with her parents, taking Josh with her but assuring Tom she'd keep trying to help him in any way she could. She knew why he was desperate. He was innocent and the whole world was against him.

Knowing how urgently he needed to avoid extradition, Tom's lawyers at Fulcrum Chambers had found a way. Under the Serious Organised Crime and Police Act of 2005 (SOCPA) there was a witness protection programme. It was designed for 'supergrass' witnesses exposing the misdeeds of major organised criminal networks such as drug gangs or terrorists. But if Tom could show he was going to give prosecutors what they needed – a confession and real evidence of wrongdoing by others – he could become the Crown's star witness and receive a reduced sentence in exchange. In his case, that meant condemning his fellow 'co-conspirators': the brokers at ICAP, RP Martin and Tullett Prebon whom he'd asked to help him try to get the Libor average up or down. For his cooperation, he might spend fourteen months in an open prison, wear a tag for another four and a half months and then he'd be free. He'd also get to keep much of the money he'd made.

It would make it easy for the SFO. Pursuing common law charges of 'conspiracy to defraud', all that was needed was one guilty plea and a conspiracy was proved. For the SFO, still under threat of abolition from Home Secretary Theresa May, it was also good politics. With Tom as their star witness, it would be the SFO, not the DOJ, that would lead the prosecution of the rigging of the London Interbank Offered Rate, with the trials taking place in London. It would mean that the ugly spectacle of bankers in the City of London being put on trial in New York could be avoided. It would also spoil the party for Eric Holder and Lanny Breuer at the DOJ.[12] Too bad for them.

But for Tom there was a problem. If he were to get charged in the UK, he'd have to be useful as a prosecution witness, fitting in with the prosecution's version of events. That meant he'd have to tell three big lies. One, a guilty plea – a false confession of wrongdoing which he didn't believe: that he'd conspired dishonestly to try to obtain false Libor submissions. Two, a lie about the rules of Libor: that it was against the rules to procure or make submissions that took account of a bank's commercial interests – when, in fact, there were no rules. Three, a lie about more than twenty fellow defendants in the alleged 'conspiracy' to help the SFO jail them – that they'd done something dishonest and fraudulent by helping him. And lying didn't come naturally to a guileless man with Asperger's.

In the spring of 2013, Tom went every day to Interview Room 1 in the SFO's new offices in Cockspur Street, near Trafalgar Square, to give a total of eighty-two hours of what were known as 'cleansing interviews', going through all the Libor requests he'd made. He had to try to fit in with the preset narrative. There'd been a criminal conspiracy. He was guilty. Trader requests were wrong. Allowing commercial interests to influence Libor submissions was dishonest and against the rules. Even as he was letting that narrative be rehearsed by the SFO interviewers, he was inwardly thinking, 'This just isn't true.' No such rule had ever existed. And he didn't believe it was dishonest. The confession he'd have to make was false. To escape extradition, he was being required to create an alternative reality.

'It was frustrating being asked questions in those interviews. Where I wanted to give one answer, and I'd have to give another. Sometimes someone would make an astute point, and I would want to say, "Yeah, you're totally right." So it doesn't make any sense, does it? And I'd have to give a different answer. It was so frustrating.'

Tom's lawyers grew so concerned that he wouldn't make sufficient admissions of guilt – particularly that it was against the rules to allow any commercial influence – that they drafted an Aide Memoire for him: a text that he had to keep referring back to, to ensure he made the confession required.

'A panel bank's submission should not be determined by, or reflect, the bank's own positions/trading interests,' the note said. 'I accept that I was influencing a rate that was intended to be completely independent and devoid of any influence other than that of an independent submitter. Clearly, I did this to benefit the bank's positions. I accept that the system in which I participated was fundamentally dishonest in relation to the way LIBOR submitters were influenced.'

Tom uttered that last line once; that was all the SFO was getting. 'I had to say, "Oh, well, it was obvious we should have done this," and, "We shouldn't have done that." But actually, it wasn't obvious because not only was it not against the rules: it was totally in line with the rules.'

At the end of May 2013, the SOCPA agreement that Tom's lawyers had worked to secure was nearly ready and the warped good news that Tom had longed for, that he would be charged with conspiracy to defraud in the UK not the USA, was within his grasp. But when he finally achieved his goal, there was something that stuck in the craw.

At the end of May, Tom got a call from his lawyers. To his supreme relief, the good news was that the SFO had confirmed it would charge him in the UK – his dearest wish. But the agreement had been that the SFO would announce it was charging him in the autumn – September or October. Now, his lawyers told him the SFO wanted to bring forward the announcement that he'd be charged to 13 June, just two weeks away. It was timed to coincide with the publication of a report by the parliamentary inquiry set up in the wake of Bob Diamond's resignation: the Parliamentary Commission on Banking Standards, chaired by Andrew Tyrie. The SFO was supposed to be independent, taking its decisions to charge based on the law and the evidence. But this made it seem all too obvious to Tom. It was all about how it looked. He was a pawn in a political game.[13]

'The optic was great,' said Tom. 'Like – "oh, we've got this parliamentary report into banking standards", and, "oh, look, we've charged somebody!" But what that did was destroy any degree of trust I had in the Serious Fraud Office at that point, which was not fantastic in any case. At that point, I couldn't believe anything they said.'

Sure enough, on 13 June 2013, the Parliamentary Commission on Banking Standards published its report, the very same day that the SFO announced that Tom Hayes was being charged. 'The irony is I was supremely grateful to be charged. I felt like I'd been diagnosed with cancer and I'd just been given the all-clear,' said Tom. His mental health improved. He was able to make decisions.

'That's when the anger started building. Because I thought: this is just a joke. I've been forced into these false confessions and now I've been charged. And now I'm going to plead guilty to this. And now I'm going to be forced to lie about my co-defendants.'

Sarah had watched Tom go from being almost incapable of functioning to being much more his old self. But the result of that was he was now so incandescent with rage he was, again, almost impossible to live with. It was affecting his mental health now in a different way. One day in late 2013, she came out of the bedroom with Josh to see Tom on the landing, pulling out his hair and eyebrows. Sarah stopped. 'What's going on?'

'Sarah, I'm going to have to lie under oath about myself and other people. And I'm worried about committing perjury if I do this SOCPA thing.'

'You can't do that, Tom – you shouldn't and you can't. You need to get a second opinion about your case and see if you can fight it. The SFO are going to go as hard as they can on you. But I'll support you.'

Tom called the London barristers, Furnival Chambers, and got through to the clerk, who told him they didn't do 'direct access' work, only through solicitors. 'Wait,' said Tom. 'I'm Tom Hayes, the Libor guy. Just google me.'

At the top of the google list, of course, were articles about Tom being the first to be sacked and arrested over Libor rigging. For once, Tom's newfound infamy worked in his favour. The clerk arranged a meeting a few days later with one of their leading criminal defence lawyers, Charlie Sherrard QC. Tom took a few documents to the meeting and a draft statement prepared by Sarah. It was meant to be mitigation for his sentencing after the guilty plea he'd been planning to make. 'This isn't mitigation,' said Sherrard. 'This is a defence. You shouldn't be pleading guilty to this.'

Tom felt a sudden wave of hope. For the first time, a new vista opened up for him. Here was someone who thought he could fight it, who wanted him to fight it. He didn't have to plead guilty, give false witness against others and go to jail. The SFO wouldn't like it. Nor would anyone else who'd been expecting him to help save the City of London's reputation by becoming the Crown's star witness. By deciding to defend himself and plead not guilty, Tom was sticking an emphatic two fingers up to David Green and the rest of the legal and political establishment. He knew he was risking a longer sentence. But it felt right. Because for the first time in months, Tom would be able to tell the truth.

12

THE RINGMASTER

Overlooking the River Thames at the east end of the City of London is a royal castle that's long been a symbol of the way the British state of the past would mete out 'justice' to its enemies. Visitors to the Tower of London learn about the two heirs to the throne aged 12 and 9 who died after being imprisoned there in the late fifteenth century before Richard III became king; the jailing and beheading of Henry VIII's wives Anne Boleyn and Katherine Howard; and the excruciating torture and execution, approved by King James I, of the man who in 1605 tried to blow up Parliament, Guy Fawkes. In the history of British justice, in addition to cruelty and torture, there's also another recurring motif: the hanging judge. The most notorious in history is Judge Jeffreys, who occupied the top judicial office of Lord Chancellor and sentenced at least 160 people to death after a West Country rebellion against James II, including one woman he sentenced to be burned at the stake just for sheltering some of the rebels. After James was overthrown by William of Orange, Jeffreys begged to be held in the Tower to protect him from a mob who were threatening to show him 'the same mercy he had ever shown to others'. He was never to leave his voluntary captivity and died within its walls. When the yeomen who guide tourists around the Tower recount that horrible history, it is always with a tacit understanding that that confusion between justice and a cruel kind of vengeance, that state-sanctioned indulgence of some of our least civilised impulses, is safely consigned to the past. Of course, in modern-day

Britain, we no longer do things like that. These days, we don't use the justice system to crush people. Or do we?

Just across the river on the south bank, a short walk from Tower Bridge, is an ugly six-storey 1970s building with a red-brick exterior and only a few brown-tinted windows where the modern, apparently more civilised, version of justice is carried out. With an interior that was notable, after years of 'austerity', for its threadbare carpets, foam-upholstered seating and peeling paint, Southwark Crown Court is nevertheless the hub of the UK's efforts to prosecute white-collar crime in the City of London and Canary Wharf – a concrete reminder of how little successive governments have been prepared to invest in bringing genuine fraudsters to justice. It's not that there's a shortage of genuine white-collar criminals. It's just that the capacity of the police to investigate fraud has been so chronically underfunded that very few of them end up in court.

On Tuesday, 26 May 2015, a bright but cloudy spring morning, I was assigned to Southwark Crown Court to help cover the opening day of the trial of Tom Hayes. Because he was the first banker to be prosecuted since the 2008 financial crash, it was the lead story on the news throughout the day, as my colleague Emma Simpson reported how he'd been branded 'the ringmaster' of a criminal fraud conspiracy, 'motivated by pure greed'. Despite confessing dishonesty in interviews with the Serious Fraud Office, said the prosecutor, he now claimed that what he was doing wasn't dishonest.

If a show trial is defined as one where you need a ticket to get in, the Hayes trial was a veritable circus. I was the reporter outside doing the hourly 'lives' for the BBC News TV channel, staying with the camera crew as it captured pictures of the 'perp' and his wife Sarah exiting a cab and walking the 30m you had to walk in front of the flashing cameras of the paparazzi before disappearing through the revolving door at the entrance to Southwark Crown Court.

In four further live spots on the news, I reported quotes from Mukul Chawla as he gave his opening speech inside. This was a very simple case at its heart, he was saying. The jury would simply have to decide whether Tom Hayes acted honestly or dishonestly. Unacquainted as I then was with the history of Tom's case, what I was really thinking (but not quite saying on camera) was, 'He's confessed to dishonesty. If that's the only issue in the trial, how on earth can his lawyers defend it?'

Later that afternoon I was warned that the 'greedy ringmaster' was about to emerge from court. Get the crew ready! He'd clearly had legal advice not to speak, so I was trying to work out how to get him to give us some words – any words. As he emerged from the covered entrance to the court building with Sarah in support, here was my chance to get a soundbite on tape. Tom and Sarah stopped to allow the bank of photographers to take their pictures. What might tempt them to say something? I know ...

'Tom,' I called out as he and Sarah stood there on the steps of Southwark Crown Court, enduring their moment of hell. 'Are you being unfairly blamed for the Libor scandal?'

It was almost a taunt.

Tom didn't answer but something else happened. Sarah's eyes widened and she looked straight into my eyes. She wasn't speaking, wasn't even nodding, just staring at me, stock-still, almost frozen. There was something in the way she looked at me, wordless but full of urgent meaning. Suddenly, I felt a chill. What she was communicating with that urgent look was unequivocal. 'Yes,' it said. 'Just what you said. That's exactly the story. Something awful is happening. And by the way, Mr Reporter: this is no game.'

My mind starting racing.

Oh.

My.

God.

Really?

What I wasn't aware of in 2015 was that there was an unusual reason why Mukul Chawla could narrow down the issues for the jury to just one question – whether Tom Hayes had behaved dishonestly. Against all convention, most of the crucial factual issues in the trial, such as whether he deliberately broke any rules, had not been left to the jury to decide. They had already been decided by judges. Judges, that is, who were all too aware of the political context of the trials. Everyone in the small community of white-collar crime barristers in London knew that the interest rate-rigging cases were being brought by an SFO fighting for its survival that had staked its reputation on the outcome of the Libor trials. Everyone also knew that after the public and political outcry of 2012, the SFO had stolen the prosecution of Libor away from the US Department of Justice, insisting that the

British courts were just as capable as the American ones of cracking down on white-collar crime.

Seven months earlier, in a pre-trial hearing on 7 October 2014, Tom had shared a courtroom for the first time with the judge assigned to his case, a 66-year-old evangelical Christian with long grey sideburns whose official title was 'Mr Justice' Jeremy Cooke. He'd appeared shocked to learn that Tom Hayes intended to plead not guilty and actually fight the case. The rules of this game were supposed to be well established by now. Just like Barclays, Tom's former employer UBS had admitted wrongdoing, agreed a fine and signed a non-prosecution agreement with regulators on both sides of the Atlantic. That had happened nearly two years before. Since June 2012, banks had paid $5 billion in fines for rigging interest rates.[1] How dare the defendant claim there was nothing wrong in what he did!

Tom's legal team had submitted a written summary of his case, pointing out there was no rule written down to say the bank couldn't consider its commercial interests – such as its traders' derivatives position – when putting in its Libor estimates of the cost of borrowing cash. So, in Tom's many requests for high or low Libor rates, no rules had been broken. Therefore there had been no unlawful act, and no criminal offence. The SFO's case, his lawyers had argued, should be thrown out. The argument was potentially fatal to all the rate-rigging trials, upon which so many millions of pounds had already been spent. If Tom's lawyers had succeeded in convincing a judge of that, then his trial, and also those of all the other defendants the SFO was planning to prosecute, would fall apart.

This particular judge, though, seemed in no mood to be convinced. Far from keeping a judicial open mind and considering the case on its merits, Cooke gave every appearance of having decided already that this Tom Hayes character was guilty. He spent much of the hearing pressuring Tom to change his plea. 'Let me be absolutely blunt,' he said to Tom's barrister. 'The time has come for you to give – and you may well have given such advice already, I know not – extremely robust advice to your client. There remains credit to be obtained for a plea which will self-evidently diminish the closer the trial gets.'

In London's legal community, it was rumoured that Cooke, who'd replaced the original trial judge, had been 'helicoptered' in to preside over the trial. A leading member of the socially conservative Lawyers Christian Fellowship (slogan: 'Love Mercy'), Cooke could be seen as a good fit for the trial because he was experienced as a commercial judge. But he also had a reputation as a hardliner given to harsh sentencing, not least because of cases like that of Sarah Catt, whom he'd sentenced to eight years in prison after she pleaded guilty to self-inducing a late-stage abortion. The appeal court overturned Cooke's sentence, describing it as 'manifestly excessive'. But Cooke, it would turn out, hadn't lost his weakness for imposing excessive sentences.

Mukul Chawla's suggestion that the SFO could prosecute Libor under the common law offence of 'conspiracy to defraud' had reduced to the very minimum what the prosecution had to prove. There was no need to bring a victim to the witness stand or identify any ill-gotten gains. He merely had to convince the jury that defendants had dishonestly agreed to do something unlawful. But the SFO still needed to show what the unlawful thing was. The way the SFO approached that was to accuse Tom (and his co-conspirators at the money brokers RP Martin, ICAP and Tullett Prebon) of deliberately disregarding the 'proper basis' for setting Libor. But what did that mean? When there were no rules written down about Libor, what was the 'proper basis'? What rules had been broken?

The thrust of Tom's defence case was that the hundreds of requests that he had made for Libor estimates to be submitted high or low hadn't broken any rules. Therefore, there was no crime. He was simply looking to get colleagues to put in commercially advantageous Libor estimates of the cost of borrowing, within a permissible range of offered rates.

Faced with a detailed defence statement, Cooke was infuriated. Staring straight at Tom, Cooke declared he was acting like a 'gambler' because he wanted to plead not guilty and take his chances with a jury. 'Your client,' he told Tom's barrister George Carter-Stephenson, 'if I understand the mentality of City traders (which I like to think I do from my experience) is probably, by nature, a gambler. As I see it, the points that have been raised, which supposedly are points of law, in your note go nowhere at all. I am likely so to direct any jury if we get that far.'

Cooke had apparently decided Tom's defence case went nowhere at all before he'd heard the legal arguments in court. 'I would expect more defendants to see the light, to be frank, and to plead. But we will see. We know that some of the Barclays defendants are thinking on those terms. At least one has pleaded. It is all straightforward on the material. The sooner that people get the message the better: to take whatever credit is open to them.' Seen from Tom's side of the courtroom, Cooke could hardly have made it clearer that before Tom's trial got under way, he'd effectively already made up his mind. It was all 'straightforward'. Guilty.

Forbidden to speak in the proceedings, Tom could only defy this pressure from the judge to submit himself voluntarily to imprisonment by shaking his head. That seemed to anger Cooke even more. To Tom, watching Cooke's face reddening and his voice rising, it felt like he was being shouted at by a judge determined to lock him up. 'It is an open and shut case on the e-mails,' Cooke raged. 'I say that because it is. There is no way round that [...] If he wants to put before a jury that defence in circumstances where he had already admitted dishonesty in the interviews and where, by the ordinary standards of right-thinking people, at least in my view – though it is, of course, a matter for the jury – it is self-evident that there was dishonesty.'

In the rate-rigging trials, judges kept on using that phrase. 'Self-evident'. It meant no further evidence need be offered. The conclusion was so obvious, apparently, that it could be drawn without evidence. Yet the same points Tom's legal team were making – that he hadn't broken any rules – would later be accepted in another case by the higher courts in the USA, who would decide requests like his broke no rules and therefore didn't amount to criminality. The US judges were senior lawyers with great experience in white-collar crime cases who clearly thought the issue of dishonesty was far from 'self-evident'. But that wasn't until seven years later. For now, in 2014, Cooke appeared confident the Court of Appeal would uphold his approach.

Tom's team applied to have Cooke recused on grounds that he was biased and had shown a closed mind ahead of the trial. But the recusal application was heard by Mr Justice Jeremy Cooke, who decided he did not need to recuse himself. Just because his remarks had not been qualified, he said, did not mean they were incapable of qualification. Tom discussed with his lawyers whether to take it to the Court of Appeal. But they took the view there was no point.

In the pre-trial hearings, there was now a clear and crucial issue between the SFO and Tom's defence team. Tom, they agreed, had made hundreds of requests to the guy who submitted yen Libor at UBS headquarters in Switzerland, Roger Darin.[2] When a bank's Libor submitters on the cash desk were putting in their estimates of the cost of borrowing cash to the Libor setting process, were they allowed to take a bank's trading positions into account? Or not?

Cooke rejected any idea that it was within the rules to put in a rate that suited a bank's commercial interests, within a range of interest rates where cash was being offered on the markets. The issue, he ruled, was 'not whether the rate put forward could be justified by one method or another'. It was whether Tom 'was seeking to defraud by procuring the submission of rates which did not reflect any genuine view on the rate, but instead represented a rate which would advantage him and his employers in the trades that he had concluded'.

Tom's legal team applied to challenge Cooke's ruling at the Court of Appeal. The SFO argued that anyone submitting interest rate estimates of their bank's cost of borrowing cash to the Libor setting process had a legal duty to ensure it was on the 'proper basis' – meaning in line with the British Bankers' Association definition[3] that said it should be based on the interest rates on offer to lend cash between banks. There was an unwritten rule, apparently (though no practising trader had ever heard of it before), that it was wrong to allow a bank's commercial interests to influence any Libor submissions.

With so little evidence to support that key premise for prosecuting the traders, the SFO needed someone to buttress its case. The logical choice would have been an independent swaps trader, someone from another bank who'd done the same job as Tom. But as an SFO insider told me, there was a problem. They'd talked to dozens of experienced traders whom they'd thought might agree to be expert witnesses. Not a single one of them was suitable. Why? Because each and every one of them had at some point themselves been involved in making or receiving a 'trader request'.

At that point, a naïve observer might think, the SFO should have stopped, re-examined its case and asked whether it was actually seeking to imprison people for something everyone was doing because it was normal commercial practice. But the government had given the SFO millions of pounds extra to bring the rate-rigging trials. Much was expected. The SFO ploughed on, its prosecutorial steering wheel impervious to bends in the road.

Instead of calling as a witness an independent swaps trader actually working in the market, the SFO decided the witness whose testimony would help the courts to determine the law on Libor would be the Libor manager of the BBA, John Ewan. It took weeks to draw up his witness statement. Ewan told the court it was 'impermissible and wrong' for a derivatives trader to try to move his bank's Libor submissions to suit its trades. Had he been aware of that taking place, Ewan said, he would immediately have raised it with the committee governing Libor,[4] the Foreign Exchange and Money Markets Committee, in order to put a stop to it.

'At no point during the Relevant Period did I or the BBA have any suspicion that this type of behaviour was taking place,'[5] Ewan wrote in his sworn witness statement in November 2014. 'My view is that had any of the members known about this type of behaviour, they would have acted upon it immediately because they would have considered it wrong. I never got the impression that any member of the FXMMC was involved in [it].'

It wouldn't be until years later, when Tom was going through thousands of pages of evidence on the bed in his cell at Lowdham Grange high-security prison, that he came across a document that had been disclosed in US court proceedings but not in the UK. It was a transcript of a 2011 telephone conference call involving John Ewan and other members of the FXMMC, where Ewan had discussed just such 'behaviour'. But he hadn't acted upon it immediately as he'd said he would. 'Deutsche Bank put down their Libors,' he told the FXMMC members in the transcript. 'RBS put up their Libors so I don't know if this was on the back of any derivatives trading going on. I'm happy that the rates are representative, so from that point of view I'm fine.'[6] Both RBS and Deutsche were on the FXMMC; yet from the minutes, there appeared to be no action from the committee. Nor had anyone felt the need to call the police.

The Court of Appeal never saw that document before they ruled on the law on Libor. And it never made it into Tom's trial. The lead judge on the panel of three that would decide the law on Libor was Lord Justice Nigel Davis. Tom's barrister Neil Hawes argued that on any given day there was a range of interest rates, 1 or 2 basis points wide (0.01% or 0.02%), that a Libor submitter (like PJ or Jon Mathew) might pick from to arrive at their estimate that day of the interest rate they'd have to pay to borrow cash – their Libor submission. There were no rules to say that submissions couldn't be put in high or low within that range of accurate rates to suit a bank's commercial interests.

In January 2015, Davis wrote a judgment forcibly rejecting the Hayes camp's arguments. 'If a panel bank makes a submission then it is under an obligation to do so genuinely and honestly as representing its own assessment. Not to do so is potentially dishonest. The judge regarded that as self-evident. So do we,' wrote Davis. 'That the figure could be within a range provides no answer if the figure actually submitted does not represent the genuine opinion of the person submitting that figure.'

But the Court of Appeal judges were making a crucial – and controversial – assumption. Both Cooke and Davis were copying the same false dichotomy Jon Mathew had offered to the DOJ in 2011 (see page 134). *Either* a Libor estimate was a genuine opinion about how much it would cost his bank to borrow cash *or* it was influenced by the bank's commercial interests. The unspoken, untested assumption – unsupported by any law, written rule or expert testimony – was that it couldn't be both at once. The Court of Appeal, in other words, was ruling that no Libor submission could be *both* a genuine answer to the question 'At what interest rate could you borrow cash?' *and also* commercially advantageous to a bank. No one, apparently, could be both a human and a dancer.

Tom's legal team had tried to argue the SFO was wrong to try to bring in a rule that no one had heard of before that a panel bank couldn't let its commercial interests affect its Libor estimates of the cost of borrowing cash. But the Court of Appeal flipped that on its head, saying there was 'no indication that a bank was free to take its own commercial interests into consideration'. That, Davis wrote, 'comes close to saying likewise that because bad faith has not been explicitly excluded, then bad faith may be allowed: which of course is quite ridiculous'.

There was a problem with that reasoning too. Davis was clearly assuming that taking account of a bank's commercial interests was 'bad faith'. But that was precisely what was being disputed – whether or not seeking a Libor interest rate estimate that suited a bank's trades was wrong. This Court of Appeal judge was making an assumption that pre-judged the outcome. In logic going back to classical times, it had a name: Davis was committing the fallacy of *petitio principii*. In modern English, he was 'assuming the conclusion'.

Tom's legal team applied to take the ruling to the Supreme Court. But in the UK, in a criminal case, the Court of Appeal can block the path to the Supreme Court by refusing to certify that its ruling involved a point of law of general public importance. Led by Lord Justice Davis, that is what the Court of Appeal did. It wouldn't be the last time.

The implications of the ruling were profound and, perhaps, unintended. As it was interpreted by prosecutors in the trials that followed, the Davis ruling meant that if a bank allowed any whiff of its commercial interests to taint its Libor submission, that was against the law. Defence lawyers pointed out that it had absurd consequences. As the Bank of England had been told by the BBA as far back as 2005, every Libor submission every day was in fact set not at a rate the bank thought it could raise cash at, where the best offer in the market was, but slightly higher. As Jon Mathew later explained, the rates banks put in as their Libors were always 3 to 4 basis points above what it might actually cost them to borrow cash in order to build in a little room for profit when the cash desk lent money on internally to other departments of the bank. That meant that every Libor submission, every day, had been subject to commercial influence. Davis and his colleagues had just rendered every Libor submission, every day, unlawful. Not only that, it meant anyone who sought to influence Libor with commercial reasons in mind was doing so unlawfully. Because of the way English common law works, that law, although only 'clarified' in 2015, would apply to everyone who'd tried to influence Libor in the past. The fact that no one had thought that at the time, or that the rules hadn't been written down, didn't matter.

What Lord Justice Davis may or may not have realised was that in making a sweeping ruling that appeared to outlaw any commercial influence on the setting of Libor, he and his Court of Appeal colleagues were not just outlawing requests from the traders. They were also outlawing the actions of the board of Barclays, the key prosecution witness John Ewan, the board of the BBA, the Bank of England, the European Central Bank, the Federal Reserve and the UK government – all of whom had sought to influence Libor with commercial reasons very much in mind. And the regulators, who had known banks were influencing Libor for commercial reasons for years but had done nothing to stop it, had condoned this apparently unlawful activity. The sweeping new law on Libor applied no matter who the actors were. Tom Hayes, Peter Johnson, Mark Dearlove, Miles Storey, John Ewan, Angela Knight, Stephen Green, Bob Diamond, Paul Tucker and Gordon Brown – all were subject equally to the same law.

Or at least they were *in theory*.

In the trials that followed, the Davis ruling was used by prosecutors to say 'any commercial influence' on Libor submissions was unlawful and defendants were condemned to prison on that basis. But the SFO's application and enforcement of that sweeping law was highly selective. In spite of clear evidence that the BBA, the Bank of England and the UK government had sought to influence Libor for commercial reasons, and on a much greater scale, no one senior in the banks was prosecuted, let alone a regulator or a government official. Only traders and brokers were brought to trial, based on the evidence handed to the SFO by Barclays, the other banks and their lawyers.

At Tom's trial in June 2015, John Ewan gave evidence to match his witness statement, that he hadn't known about traders seeking to influence Libor submissions, and that had he heard of it, he would have tried to stop it. All the evidence of John Ewan's knowledge of lowballing especially, but also of trader requests, including the episodes set out in Chapters 3 and 4 of this book, was in a bundle of five folders containing just over 2,000 pages of evidence. So revealing was it that the SFO tried to prevent its full disclosure at trial, arguing it should be allowed to disclose only a 'representative sample'. In a rare victory for the defence, Cooke ordered its full disclosure. Ewan was grilled about it extensively on 8 and 9 June by Tom's lawyer Neil Hawes. But, as it turned out, it was all for nothing. Cooke wouldn't allow him to use it in his closing speech.

Tom could prove that what he was doing – making requests for high or low Libors – was approved of and expected by his bosses. The SFO said that was no excuse, assuring jurors they didn't have to worry that he was being unfairly scapegoated; this was just the first trial of many. But Tom's bosses would never be brought to trial. The SFO failed to obtain a large volume of evidence from UBS headquarters in Zürich, which the bank refused to disclose on the grounds of Swiss banking secrecy laws, but which might have been exculpatory for Tom. Tom's lawyers wanted to bring evidence to prove that the regulators knew about traders' requests and didn't regard it as misconduct if the rates their banks put in were within a range of interest rates where cash was being offered. The Financial Conduct Authority (FCA), as the Financial Services Authority had been renamed, had just made such a decision in the case of a senior manager at UBS who sat on the FXMMC that regulated Libor, Pete Koutsogiannis, who was exonerated after the regulator heard his requests were for Libors to be high or low within that range. But Mr Justice Cooke wouldn't allow that FCA decision into Tom's trial.

Rather than bringing in another trader who'd done the same job as Tom to give evidence, the SFO appointed an 'expert witness' who had never worked in the relevant area. Saul Haydon Rowe had worked as a trader but knew very little about the derivatives traded by Tom and not much more about Libor. He had even warned the SFO that he lacked relevant expertise. He testified that he didn't recognise the term 'permissible range', undermining Tom's defence. But long after Tom's trial, it would emerge that he wasn't really expert at all.

As he took to the witness stand before the jury of seven men and five women, Tom was resolved to tell the truth because, as far as he was concerned, it was obvious that the truth was on his side. But his Asperger's didn't help him. 'I'm not always the best at expressing my emotions [...] I don't think it helped me as a witness,' he said. 'I felt I was engaged in some sort of intellectual battle of chess with the prosecutor. So rather than coming across cutting a sympathetic figure, much like the brokers did, I came across as brittle, maybe somewhat arrogant, a bit haughty, and not compassionate and human. And that didn't help me when I was being painted as this very callous, greedy individual.'

Tom was trying to fight the charges with logic. But it's a well-known aspect of Asperger's that sufferers find it harder to empathise – to put themselves in others' shoes. He was only weakly attuned to the less rational, emotional side that experienced prosecutors know is crucial if you're going to win: namely, how the members of the jury might be feeling. Each time Mukul Chawla suggested Tom was making Libor requests because they could make him a great deal of money, his logical mind went down the same path. If he could get hold of his trading book, he could do an analysis to show how little of the money he made came from making requests for Libor to be set high or low. In the mind of an Asperger's sufferer, his trading book would offer numerical certainty, and with it, the means to disprove the accusation that he was acting out of 'pure greed'. But the SFO refused to disclose his trading book. Each time the issue came up, Tom explained that he could deflect the accusation that the requests were so important to him – part of an international fraud conspiracy – if only he could have his trading book. After he'd mentioned it nine times, exasperated members of the jury sent a note to the judge saying they hoped they wouldn't hear about the trading book any more.

Then, in the middle of the trial, something extraordinary happened. The Bank of England had been watching the Hayes trial closely. On 4 June 2015, it wrote to the court asking Mr Justice Cooke for copies of transcripts of the trial, which he agreed to give. While George Osborne had urged the central bank to come clean about its role in Libor, the Bank of England had decided against that. Freedom of Information requests would be consistently rejected in the succeeding years. But to the Bank of England, there was a serious risk that some of its secrets might emerge in evidence disclosed to the Hayes defence team. Then, on 10 June, the Bank's media team briefed the press, in the middle of the trial, that its governor Mark Carney would use his annual set-piece Mansion House speech that night to demand tougher sentences for 'rogue traders'. The headline in *The Guardian* read: 'Mark Carney to warn rogue City traders they should face 10 years in jail'. 'The Age of Irresponsibility is Over says Bank of England Governor as he Demands a Crackdown on Rogue Traders,' shouted *The Daily Telegraph*. The *Mirror* headline was: 'Bent bankers and crooked city traders to be jailed for 10 years'.

In his speech, Mark Carney would publicly demand that the government should change its sentencing guidelines to raise the maximum jail term for 'rogue traders' from seven to ten years. It didn't quite say, 'We want a long sentence for Tom Hayes.' But without naming him, it was about as close as you could get. The BBC headline was, 'Carney seeks tougher sentences for "irresponsible" traders'.

To the Hayes defence team, this was highly prejudicial. The jury might read these articles and be swayed by the strength of feeling coming from the governor of the Bank of England and reported all over the press. Tom felt it was a clear attempt by the Bank to influence his trial. All the newspapers were demanding tougher sentences for 'rogue traders' and everyone knew that at that point in time, that meant him. Tom's lawyers considered applying to have the trial dismissed on the grounds of prejudice. But Cooke declared after reading them that he wasn't 'unduly troubled'. It was a high bar to get a trial dismissed on the grounds that the Bank of England appeared to have tried to influence it. But if he needed any public encouragement to impose a harsh sentence on Tom Hayes, Cooke now had plenty of it.

Mukul Chawla was careful not to state during the trial that he disputed the existence of a range of permissible rates from which an accurate Libor rate could be selected, high or low. Had he done so, it would have become an issue in the trial, allowing Tom's lawyers to bring evidence and call their own expert witnesses. His line of attack on that key plank of Tom's defence was to point out that no one at the time seemed to talk about a 'permissible range'. In cross-examination, Chawla confronted Tom with an exchange of messages he'd sent from his desk at UBS in Tokyo to a junior trader in Zürich, who was submitting the bank's Libor rates in place of the normal submitter, Roger Darin. It's one of a number of passages in the trial where the tendency of someone with Asperger's to take things literally becomes obvious. Chawla read out the exchange: *'My name is Tom. I work on the securities side [...] Do you have any fixings today? Roger and I generally co-ordinate, i.e. sometimes trade if it suits, otherwise skew the Libors a bit.'*

'Help us, Mr Hayes,' said Chawla. '"Otherwise skew the Libors a bit"? What does that mean?'

'Set towards one side of the range or the other,' Tom replied.

'Why couldn't you say that? Why do you use the word "skew"?'

'Well, that's what mathematically "skew" means.'

'Skew is a word, isn't it, which represents "manipulate"?'

'No, that's completely wrong,' said Tom. '"Skew" is just – something is asymmetric. "Skew" is just a mathematical, financial term. It's not a manipulative term. It just refers to an asymmetry.'

'You say to him: "Great. Do you have any 6M fixes today?" He carries on: "So personally go for high ones at the moment." You say: "Yes, I think so. Great. I'm paid too. Really need high six-month fixes till Thursday". Does it say anywhere here "within the range"?'

'No, but, as I've said, you know, the range exists,' said Tom. 'I'm not going to constantly refer to something everybody knows exists.'

'Did you know that he knew it existed?'

'Well, I mean, look, let's say I'm talking about the Earth, I'm not going to say "the Earth, which is round" every time I write about the Earth. It's a given that the Earth is round.'

In his closing speech Chawla attacked the idea of a range, denying that such a range existed. 'Members of the jury, you may think, when you strip all this down to its essentials, that the thing Mr Hayes was thinking about was how to make the most money possible. That's not a crime. Let me be clear about that. You're a trader in a bank. That's your objective, but you do it honestly.

'Mr Hayes, on the other hand, was willing to use whatever means, including blatantly dishonest means, to achieve that goal. As he told you, he wanted to get an edge, wherever he could maximise his opportunities. That's what it was all about. It was nudging the market to his benefit, about rigging the rates in order to do so. The reality is that range was not mentioned contemporaneously in the terms that Mr Hayes describes – as it simply did not exist.'

Chawla offered the jurors a seductive argument, to be copied by many of the prosecutors who followed. They didn't need to get bogged down in all the technical details. 'Essentially this case, like so many criminal cases, boils down to issues of honesty and dishonesty,' said Chawla. 'In doing what he was doing, were Mr Hayes's actions honest or dishonest? We suggest on behalf of the prosecution that it is patently clear that in relation to each of these eight counts on the indictment you can be sure that his actions and intentions were nothing more and nothing less than dishonest.'

Judges are meant, by law, to direct juries to decide each factual ingredient of the alleged offence, such as: Did Tom know the rules? Did he deliberately disregard them? Did he knowingly make a misrepresentation? Only if they're convinced beyond a reasonable doubt of those factual matters are the jurors meant to decide if a defendant has behaved honestly or not. He was accused of *deliberately* disregarding the proper basis for setting Libor. In later Libor trials, the courts would decide the prosecution had to prove defendants deliberately disregarded the rules – meaning that they knew what the (unwritten) rules were and deliberately chose to flout them – before deciding the bigger issue of whether they'd been dishonest. In those later trials, prosecutors couldn't get past that first base, and defendants were acquitted in a matter of hours. But in Tom's trial, Cooke decided there was no need to leave that up to the jury. He'd decide as a matter of *law* that what Tom did was not honest, regardless of how he understood the rules at the time. What counted, he decided, was not whether the high or low rates Tom had requested were within a range of justifiable figures. Even if they were within that range, they wouldn't be genuine if they'd been in any way influenced by the bank's commercial interests.

Cooke set out a plan for the close of the trial where the key judgement on the facts belonged to him, Cooke, not the jury. He proposed to give the jury the following directions, telling them as a matter of law that if there'd been any attempt to influence the Libor rates for commercial reasons ('we'd like a high Libor today pls') then it wasn't genuine and therefore wasn't lawful: 'If a submitter considers that there was a range of possible figures which could be submitted, each one of which was justified as a subjective judgment on the information that he had, and then submitted a figure within that range which took into account such commercial interest of the bank or any other bank or person, even if the submitted figure did not differ from the figure which would have been submitted without taking such commercial interests into account, the submitter would not have made a genuine assessment of the bank's borrowing rate in accordance with the Libor definition.'

Tom's lawyers tried to dissuade Cooke from giving those directions, arguing they went far beyond what the Davis judgment had said. The Court of Appeal had said that all matters of fact were still at play. Yet Cooke was deciding matters of fact as matters of law. It was him, not the jury, who was deciding if a 'genuine' rate was being put in. Cooke dismissed the defence's objections.

But that wasn't the only problem. Cooke's rulings created an absurdity. A submitter like Jon Mathew might actually do a deal to borrow cash at, say, 3.15% at 10.30 a.m. In that case there could be no doubt then that if they put in '3.15%' as their Libor rate, it would be a genuine, accurate answer to the question, 'At what interest rate could you borrow cash?' But if a few minutes later – say at 10.45 a.m. – Stelios or Ryan asked Jon to put in that same accurate rate, 3.15%, it would suddenly become *illegal* to submit it. Because it didn't differ from the figure which would have been submitted without any commercial influence, it would, on Cooke's directions, be against the law. The trader's request would have 'polluted' Jon's accurate answer and made it unlawful. For putting in an accurate rate, a trader could go to jail!

Worse, it could happen even if the rate Jon was putting in was not only accurate, but the same as yesterday. He might put the same, accurate rate, every day. But if at any point a derivatives trader had asked him for that unchanged, accurate rate he'd suddenly find himself outside the law. Even for putting in an accurate, unchanged rate, a cash trader could be jailed. Was that really the result the courts wanted?

Cooke refused to change the jury directions and his words became law. As of 2023, it remains the case. If a cash trader wants to put in an accurate interest rate as his Libor estimate of the cost of borrowing, based on actual interest rates where he's just borrowed cash, he can go to jail – simply because someone else in the bank has asked him to submit that rate.

One of the most obvious moves for Tom's lawyers to make was to show the jury the evidence that suggested the Bank of England condoned and was also engaged in lowballing, a much bigger form of misconduct involving shifts in Libor interest rate estimates of ten, twenty or even thirty times the size Tom was hoping for. The point was obvious. If it wasn't seen as dishonest for those in authority to condone or even engage in a much larger form of rate-rigging, how could Tom be jailed for it? But Mr Justice Jeremy Cooke would frustrate them.

It was established law that jurors were supposed to ask two questions to decide whether what Tom did was dishonest.[7] One was an objective question: was what he did dishonest by the standards of ordinary, reasonable people? The second was about his state of mind: did he *know* that what he did was dishonest (by the standards of ordinary, reasonable people)?

You might think that if you're asked to decide whether ordinary, reasonable people might think something dishonest, one thing you might consider was whether the people at the time who had an informed view, from central banks to regulators, thought it was dishonest. Tom's defence barrister Neil Hawes planned to argue that if you wanted to know whether ordinary people thought it was dishonest, you might inform your judgement by looking at what the Bank of England thought. The SFO hadn't disclosed to Tom's defence team the incendiary audio recording from 29 October 2008 between Dearlove and PJ – itself a material non-disclosure of highly relevant exculpatory evidence. But there was still plenty of persuasive evidence[8] that neither the board of Barclays, nor the FXMMC that ran Libor, nor the BBA, nor Banque de France, nor the ECB, nor the UK government thought it was dishonest to seek to influence Libor for commercial reasons.

However, in his summing up of the case, Cooke directed jurors that if they thought what Tom had done was dishonest by ordinary, reasonable standards, it didn't matter if the FXMMC, the BBA or the Bank of England took a different view. The jury was told to disregard whatever anyone else in the market thought if it differed from their own assessment of what ordinary people thought. All the wider circumstances – about how everyone else using Libor didn't seem to think it was against the law to influence it – the jury wasn't allowed to consider in assessing whether Tom had been dishonest or not.

Cooke should have directed the jury that they had to be convinced by the prosecution that Tom was both aware of *and* deliberately disregarded the 'proper basis' for setting Libor. There was plenty of evidence that Tom thought what he was doing was justified because others in the market were doing the same thing, or because his employers and others encouraged it. But Cooke directed the jury that even if they decided Tom thought his actions were justified, that that had no bearing on whether he was acting dishonestly.

For the prosecution, Mukul Chawla kept repeating the point. All that counted was whether they thought what Tom was doing was dishonest by the standards of ordinary, reasonable people like them.

And that issue seemed sewn up. In his eighty-two hours of interviews with the SFO in 2013, Tom had never signed a witness statement. But it appeared he'd confessed in those interviews to dishonesty. The SFO prosecution team was worried that Tom's lawyers would apply to exclude the interviews from the trial on the grounds that they were obtained under duress (because of his fear of extradition). But Tom's lawyers never tried that. He tried to explain that he'd made false confessions of dishonesty to avoid being extradited to the USA. But it tied him up in knots. A false confession seemed no less dishonest than the dishonesty it was apparently confessing to. And this was a trial all about honesty. With a cruel, tangled logic, the conundrum would all but seal Tom's fate.

With evidence excluded, experts who weren't experts, matters of fact determined by judges not the jury, and no requirement for the prosecution even to convince the jury he deliberately broke any rules, the odds were already stacked against Tom. But he remained hopeful, to the last minute, that the justice system would deliver the right result. The jury left the courtroom to begin its deliberations on Monday, 27 July. By the end of the week, it still hadn't reached a verdict.

'That weekend, I was looking at holidays, I thought the very worst it would be was a hung jury. I didn't think I'd necessarily be acquitted, but I thought it would be hung. And I fancied my opportunities and challenges at a second trial. Having gone through the first trial, I understood what was going to be thrown at me.'

But then, just after 2.30 p.m. on Monday, 3 August, the verdict came back on the first of eight counts of conspiracy to defraud.

'How do you find the defendant?' Cooke asked the jury's foreman.

'Guilty.'

On the BBC News, the presenter Ben Brown gave the headlines at 3 p.m.: 'City trader Tom Hayes has become the first trader to be found guilty by a British jury of rigging interbank interest rates. He's been found guilty on all eight charges.' At first it was reported that Tom Hayes could face 'up to ten years' in prison. But Jeremy Cooke had other plans. His sentencing remarks were already written. The hearing happened almost immediately, comfortably in time to prepare a report for the *BBC News at Six*.

'The sentence I am imposing is one of fourteen years in all,' said Cooke.

Tom, who'd been allowed to watch the trial from the lawyers' benches because of his Asperger's, was in the dock for the first time.

'When they found me guilty and I was sentenced, it was just like I was in a dream. I just sat there looking at myself reflected in the bullet-proof glass. And I just remember the faces of my mother and my wife. When he— When he announced that sentence, I just looked at them, and I looked at their faces. And I'll never forget those faces.' Tom paused for a moment recalling it. 'Yeah … You know, the pain when he said fourteen years was just … and actually, in some senses, they reflected the pain that I should have been reflecting but wasn't able to. Because I was just numb.'

Tom was being given a longer sentence than some defendants get for killing someone.[9]

'There is no separate standard of dishonesty for any group of society,' said Cooke, with no trace of irony in his tone. It was no excuse to point to lowballing. 'The fact that others were doing the same as you is no excuse, nor is the fact that your immediate managers saw the benefit of what you were doing and condoned it and embraced it, if not encouraged it.'

('Oh, so that didn't matter? My bosses knowing and approving made no difference?' thought Tom as he listened, struggling to stay steady. 'How can that not be important?')

'The conduct involved here must be marked out as dishonest and wrong and a message sent to the world of banking accordingly [...] The reputation of Libor is important to the City as a financial centre and of the banking industry in this country. Probity and honesty are essential, as is trust which is based upon it. The Libor activities, in which you played a leading part, put all that in jeopardy.'

There it was. Tom's sentence was about sending out a message. It wasn't all about the law and the evidence or the gravity of the wrongdoing. It was about reputations. Or put more simply: politics. Tom was being made an example of.

'I can see little by way of mitigation,' said Cooke, 'though your counsel has said all that could possibly be said on your behalf, referring to your age, family life, and the ethos in which you operated, as well as to the Asperger's Syndrome with which you were diagnosed shortly before trial, which was agreed to be of no relevance to the issue of dishonesty.

'The maximum sentence is ten years for a count of conspiracy, which is generally recognised as too low. The starting point for a Category A case of high culpability based on a loss figure of £1 million is seven years. The figures here exceed that by a distance and the number of counts must drive the sentence up.' No one had shown that anyone lost more than £1 million because of the requests Tom made. But numerical exactitude meant more to Tom, perhaps, than it did to Jeremy Cooke.

'You will serve up to half your sentence in custody before you are released on licence: you must abide by the terms of the licence and commit no further offence or you will be liable to be recalled and you will then serve the rest of the sentence in custody [...] You will go down.'

Tom was led out of the dock by the police officer, through the door at the side of the dock that he'd hoped never to enter. It led to a sealed corridor. He was left for a while in an austere room where he got his first taste of what it was like to be incarcerated. It contained only an unhygienic toilet and a metal bench covered with graffiti. Soon after, he was taken downstairs to a tiny, windowless cell.

'Then my lawyers came down and saw me for about ten minutes and I said to them, "I'm scared." And I ... was put in the van. And I huddled up as far as I could into the corner, because I knew people would be trying to take photos of me in the van. And the last thing I wanted was a photo of me in my most desperate moment. So, no one got a photo of me inside the van, thankfully. And I mean, at the very start of my sentence, I was very much like – it wasn't happening to me. My body's self-defence mechanism was to just shut down and just make it like a dream. And what I found actually was the first sort of year-plus in prison, I wandered around in my little bubble, like it wasn't really me. Like it wasn't really happening.'

Tom was first admitted to the Victorian high-security jail, HM Prison Wandsworth – notorious for its violence, vermin and high suicide rates.

Sharing a cell with two others, he had only half an hour each day out of his cell for exercise. Sleep was nearly impossible. With his guard constantly up, one of his hardest moments was the first family visit, with Sarah, his brother, Robin, and his mum, Sandy.

'There was this feeling of just absolute desperation. Those people who you love and who love you, and you get sixty minutes with them, and then they're gone. And then you're back on the wing with the noise and the smell and the violence, and the terrible food. And the lack of exercise, lack of natural sunlight, lack of grass, lack of trees. It's amazing how much you really come to appreciate nature when it's taken from you.'

After just under two weeks, Tom was transferred to HMP Lowdham Grange, near Nottingham. That was less alarming than Wandsworth. But the atmosphere was tense. 'There's a large number of bad people in prisons; there's a large number of good people, but there's still a large number of bad people. The worst thing about prison is you can't choose who you're locked up with. And you're locked in a cell for twenty-three and a half hours a day with two other guys. They might be doing drugs. They might have killed someone.

'In prison you're constantly feeling on edge that you might be randomly attacked at any time. The attacks varied from a straightforward scrap to people having their throats slit with the lid of a tuna tin. I've seen the air ambulance arrive in prison several times. And no matter how protected you feel, those random acts of violence can just happen in an instant. I suffered massively from night terrors and extreme fear in the night – not being able to sleep properly. That's something that continues to this day, you know, I can't sleep well. I have nightmares.'

It was a few weeks before either Sarah or Tom was ready to bring their 4-year-old son Josh to see what they'd taught him to think of as 'daddy's new place'. 'I remember his first visit,' said Tom. 'And he was saying to me, "Daddy, can I see your bedroom?" and, "Daddy, I want to stay with you." And I was just in floods of tears. And I just had to tell him he couldn't. And I remember reading a book by Shirley Hughes, you know, on that first visit, and I could barely read it because I was crying so much.'

Sarah was resolved as she never had been. She knew Tom was innocent. It was obvious to her the offences he'd been jailed for were nonsense. To lock him up and make him a scapegoat for the Libor scandal, those judges had done nothing less than make up a crime out of nothing. The way she saw it, he'd no more acted criminally than any of the many bankers she knew. He was supposed to be going to jail because he was dishonest. But Tom – her Aspie husband – wasn't dishonest: he was the most honest man she'd ever met. Yet here he was, his face all over the newspapers as the poster boy for 'bad bankers' everywhere, when in fact he was an Asperger's sufferer who couldn't communicate. He had been bullied and brutalised by the DOJ, then by the SFO and then by the judges. She knew there were thousands out there who'd worked in the City who must know these 'crimes' were made up – just a wilful misreading of evidence of what was actually normal, widespread, harmless City practice. There must be thousands who must sympathise and see through this nasty scapegoating exercise.

Sarah knew what and whom she was up against. White-collar crime barristers and judges from David Green to Jeremy Cooke to John Thomas. The Bank of England, perhaps, along with senior civil servants in the Treasury. The heart, in other words, of the British establishment. But she also knew how strong she was. Recruiting the help of her parents to look after her young son Josh, Sarah was going to do everything – and when she said everything, she meant *everything* – to get him out of there.

To give Tom hope, Sarah founded an online website, the Tom Hayes Support Group. Thousands of followers joined, many of them via Twitter accounts that didn't give away their identities. Sarah poured her energy into what was not a second job but a third, alongside working as a finance lawyer and bringing up their son. She'd wake absurdly early and stop working absurdly late, ploughing through court documents, briefing journalists, trying to raise money.

Newcomers to the campaign weren't necessarily told a secret; although she was strong, she also needed support. Desperate for any connection he could rely on, Tom was leaning on her to an extraordinary degree. In his cell at Lowdham Grange, he had a phone. His mind would go round and round, worrying the same point over and over. Maybe if he said this at appeal; and maybe they could say that. Each time he wanted to fight what was happening to him, there was only one thing that made sense. Call Sarah.

Tom would call Sarah thirty to forty times a day. Sometimes he'd call at 2 a.m. Sometimes at 4 a.m. Once, Sarah tried to ignore his calls, just to get some respite. But within hours, she got a call from Tom's brother, desperate because Tom was suicidal and sounded like he was going to kill himself.

It was her sentence too.

Sarah and Tom's lawyers stretched every sinew to try to get his conviction overturned. On 1 December 2015, his appeal was heard by three senior judges. One was Lord Justice Brian Leveson, famous for leading the inquiry into phone hacking that put newspaper tycoon Rupert Murdoch and some of his inner circle on the ropes. The Lord Chief Justice, John Thomas, made sure he was on the panel. The third judge was Dame Elizabeth Gloster. At the hearing, Tom's barrister Neil Hawes protested that Cooke had blocked the jury from considering key evidence about whether what he did was dishonest by the standards of reasonable people at the time – about all the circumstances, from the regulator's lack of any action at the time, to the BBA's knowledge of and lack of objection to commercial influence on Libor submissions, to the disinclination of the Bank of England or FSA to say Libor needed regulation. Thomas pushed back. Hawes's argument seemed to hinge, Thomas said, on bankers having their own standards of honesty and dishonesty? Far from it, Hawes said: 'In judging standards of reasonable and honest people, you have to have regard to the conduct of the market [at the time].' Tom's team complained that key evidence, from his trading book to the records from UBS in Switzerland that would have shown whether managers there thought it was dishonest, was unfairly excluded from the trial. And how could Cooke impose a longer sentence on the basis of the harm caused, when the SFO had never been able to quantify how much anyone had lost because of Tom's participation in a fraud conspiracy?

The appeal panel went into discussions. Sometimes the Court of Appeal takes only a matter of minutes – sometimes weeks. This time the three judges agreed, within days, to uphold Tom's conviction. But it took much longer to decide upon his sentence. Well-placed observers suggested there was a deep split on the panel about Cooke's fourteen-year sentence, longer than any that had been imposed on any other white-collar crime defendant in living memory. One of the judges was understood to think it was grotesque and should be halved to seven years but John Thomas insisted fourteen years was appropriate. The dispute lasted nearly three weeks. Eventually, Tom's sentence was cut, but only to eleven years.

'However,' said John Thomas's judgment, 'this court must make clear to all in the financial and other markets in the City of London that conduct of this type, involving fraudulent manipulation of the markets, will result in severe sentences of considerable length which, depending on the circumstances, may be significantly greater than the present total sentence.' For Thomas, the man in charge of all the courts of England and Wales, it was all about sending a message. The British courts could be severe.

As Tom awaited appeal, the trial had begun at Southwark Crown Court in November 2015 of the co-defendants named on his indictment as parties to Tom's international conspiracy to defraud. They were six brokers Tom had worked with every day from three firms of money brokers – ICAP, RP Martin and Tullett Prebon. One was Tom's main broker Darrell Read, along with Danny Wilkinson, Colin Goodman, Noel Cryan, Jim Gilmour and Terry Farr. Much of the evidence against them consisted of messages and recorded phone calls where they seemed to be agreeing to Tom's requests that they should 'have a word with the cash desks' to try and get them to shift their guidance for where Libor rates were going to set.

This time the SFO prosecutor Mukul Chawla had less luck. The defendants were able to prove they'd been on holiday when some of the alleged crimes had taken place. Members of the jury cast their eyes heavenwards when defence counsel revealed that the SFO didn't have any proof that Cryan had passed on Hayes's requests to get his cash brokers to change their guidance on where Libors would set. In fact, Read and Cryan said, they'd worked against Hayes. If anything, they were in a conspiracy against Tom.

The brokers' defence lawyers made much of the fact that as money brokers, the defendants were all working-class boys at the bottom of the City of London's hierarchy. Yet now they were being expected to bear the blame for the Libor scandal when in fact there was evidence that the Bank of England had been involved.

The jurors started smiling sympathetically as the defendants left the courtroom each day. On 27 January 2016, the verdict took less than a day for all of them: not guilty. Outside, a juror, wiping a tear from her eye, embraced the joyful wife of one of the defendants. On the steps of the court, Noel Cryan spoke out about how they'd been treated.

'We've been scapegoated in the whole thing. I mean they've gone to the bottom of the food chain – six yen brokers answering the Libor question –

really? If there's things to be answered, we're not the ones who should be answering the questions. The SFO need to ask themselves, should they have wasted that much time and money bringing this case against six money brokers? I don't think so.' This time it didn't make the TV news bulletin. 'Brokers acquitted' evidently wasn't as strong a story as 'brokers jailed'.

Tom now stood convicted of a conspiracy to defraud in which no one could prove an actual fraudulent transaction had taken place, or identify a victim who'd lost money, or how much had been lost, or whom he was conspiring with. A 35-year-old with severe Asperger's was now serving an eleven-year prison sentence for conspiring to commit a fraud with no one else but himself. If Tom really was the ringmaster of a conspiracy, it was a conspiracy of one.

13

THE SUSHI CONSPIRACY

'Why would I, as a trader who could make hundreds of thousands at the bank by just doing my job, suddenly decide to throw all that away and commit a crime for the sake of – nothing at all? It's absurd. It's Alice in Wonderland! Yet here I am. They can just forget about me and leave me to rot in jail.'

(Jay Merchant, phone call from HM Prison Highpoint North, Suffolk, England, 23 February 2017)

On 27 June 2014, Paul Tucker leaned forward to grasp the two handles on either side of the ornate, red-cushioned stool just in front of the raised platform at the far end of the Ballroom in Buckingham Palace. He placed his right knee on the cushion and gently lowered his weight on to it. Bowing his head low and savouring the moment as the flat blade of a lightweight sword touched briefly and benignly on each shoulder, he held still for just a second longer to hear the long-awaited words uttered by then heir to the throne, Prince Charles.

'Arise, Sir Paul.'

Given the choice, he'd have preferred to be governor of the Bank of England. But usually that came with a knighthood anyway. It was the Libor scandal that had wrecked what should have been the climax of Paul Tucker's career. In November 2012, the UK's top finance minister, the Chancellor of the Exchequer George Osborne, had ruled him out and doubled the governor's salary to attract a politically safer choice, the Bank of

Canada's outgoing governor, Mark Carney. For years, the governorship was supposed to have been Tucker's for the taking. The newly titled Sir Paul still cherished the hope that one day he might yet revive his high-flying career as a central banker and win the top job. But in the meantime, here at least was some consolation that his three decades at the Bank of England hadn't been wasted: a ringing official endorsement from the symbolic heart of the British establishment, the Royal Family.

Whatever Paul Tucker was thinking at that ceremony, it's a safe guess that the fates of others of lowlier status, whose careers had also been trashed by the Libor scandal, weren't uppermost in his thoughts.[1] Just a few weeks earlier, the media had for the first time learned the names and seen the faces of the hitherto unnamed 'greedy' former Barclays traders who'd been so roundly condemned in public in 2012. Two were American – Ryan Reich, from New York, and Alex Pabon, from Houston, Texas – and one was an Indian dual citizen with a British passport resident in New York, Jay Merchant. These were the 'rogue elements' at the bank's derivatives desk that Barclays' external US lawyers had apparently been shocked to identify in 2009 and had vowed would be dealt with 'without mercy'; the same evil-doers that Bob Diamond had promised would be dealt with 'harshly'; the very same gang condemned by politicians for 'atrocious acts' of 'criminal-ity' and 'treason'. The three of them flew across the Atlantic, voluntarily, to face charges at Westminster Magistrates Court in central London. At the time when the alleged offences began in 2005, Ryan was 23, Alex was 25 and Jay 34. Now they were nine years older. Their first taste of the British jus-tice system consisted of two brief court hearings where they saw their case listed in the traditional form: 'Regina v. Stylianos[2] Contogoulas, Jonathan Mathew, Jay Merchant, Peter Johnson, Alex Pabon and Ryan Reich.' Regina meant the Queen. The Royal Family was knighting Tucker: but it was prosecuting them. The former Barclays traders attended two court hear-ings, first at Westminster Magistrates Court and then at Southwark Crown Court, where they confirmed their identities and their intention to plead not guilty. They said nothing further and a few days later returned home to the USA. So far, at least, it was fair.

It wasn't until April 2016, when their trial at Southwark Crown Court began, that the public and the media would finally get to hear the detailed evidence of their wickedness. By the time I turned up for the prosecu-tor's opening speech on 5 April, I'd been leaked some confidential internal documents that showed that knowledge of and involvement in interest rate-rigging went right to the top of Barclays Bank. I was already suspicious that the traders were taking the rap for something much bigger, ordered from somewhere much higher. But I was cynical enough to be entirely prepared to believe these overpaid traders were probably guilty too. I remembered the public outcry in 2012: the bottle of Bollinger; the funny quotes like 'Done, for you, big boy'; the way our worst suspicions about the greed of the banking sector were officially confirmed by US and UK regulators. Here, at last, you could see the people, look at the faces of these monstrous villains, report the compelling story of their misdeeds. Throw a few rotten tomatoes at the bad guys in the stocks and the pillories.

But then I started listening to the evidence.

If they were criminals, they weren't very smart. There were no smoke-filled rooms, no muttered threats of violence, no 'burner' phones. Their crimes seemed to have been arranged on emails, instant messages and phone calls recorded and monitored by the compliance department of Barclays Bank. Some of them had never met each other before. Jonathan Mathew was meeting his three USA-based co-conspirators for the first time at court on the first day of the trial. Some of them hadn't even spoken on the phone. Yet, somehow, they were engaged together in a transatlantic fraud conspiracy?

Then there was the question of their motive. Why would these bankers, absurdly overpaid as they were, jeopardise their lucrative careers by taking part in a criminal conspiracy, when they could make plenty of money without taking any legal risks at all? The prosecution's answer to that question was easy. They wanted even more. 'This case is about employees of Barclays Bank rigging for their own advantage what is in fact a global benchmark interest rate. In doing so, they were driven by money. Their goal was to make more profit on their trading and, as you will see, honesty and integrity were matters which were entirely expendable,' said the lead barrister for the Serious Fraud Office, James Hines, opening the trial.

The defendants who'd worked in New York included Jay Merchant, Alex Pabon and Ryan Reich; in London, Stelios Contogoulas, Jon Mathew and Peter Johnson (PJ). Just as with Tom Hayes, the evidence against them consisted of requests made of the Libor submitters on the cash desk (Jon and PJ) to submit 'high' or 'low' Libor estimates in the hope it might shift the Libor average in a direction that would help their swaps trades, which went up or down in value with movements in Libor.

The SFO hadn't ever worked out if the traders' requests had succeeded in shifting the Libor average, let alone how much money they might have made if they did. And the prosecution had to admit that in relation to at least two of the defendants, there was very little evidence that they had made any money at all from the criminal conspiracy they were being prosecuted for. PJ and Jon Mathew were on the cash desk. No matter how many requests they accepted from traders like Ryan or Alex or Jay or Stelios, any shifts in the Libor average they might have helped to obtain could only affect the profits made by the derivatives desk, not the cash desk. There is no way the trader requests that made up all the evidence of the SFO's criminal conspiracy could have affected their bonuses. So where was their criminal motivation? Why would they take the risk of behaving criminally?

Well, what about those seemingly tell-tale emails reported on the news in 2012? The bottle of Bollinger? No. Those words came from Stelios. He had never purchased it. The Bolly wasn't real. The quote that Robert Peston and the rest of the media had so enjoyed repeating was just a bit of office banter, nothing more than a silly joke. It was the same with 'Done, for you, big boy'.

The following was read out in court, in earnest, as evidence of a criminal conspiracy. Stelios: *'If it's not too late, low 1M and 3M would be nice, but please feel free to say "no". Coffees will be coming your way either way just to say thank you for your help in the past weeks.'*

Jon Mathew: *'Done, for you, big boy ...'*

Stelios: *'Hehe, thanks.'*

Do criminals, egging each other on in a fraud conspiracy, really talk like that? It 'would be nice' but 'please feel free to say no'? Do they promise coffees even if their co-conspirators don't cooperate? Because they don't really mind if their fellow criminals help them out – or not? Aren't the stakes a bit higher than that in a lucrative transatlantic fraud? Come on. The exchange with Stelios was entirely lacking any sense of naughty boys breaking the rules, let alone any properly sinister atmosphere. Surely the prosecution could offer something more incriminating than that?

Well yes. There was the sushi.

Here a word of explanation is needed. Because Libor was set at 11 a.m. in London, 6 a.m. Eastern Standard Time, swaps traders in New York such as Alex, Jay and Ryan would often send emails with their Libor requests the night before. It was the job of Stelios Contogoulas in London to look after Barclays' dollar swaps trading positions while New York was still sleeping.

Whereas, under the stress and pressure of the day's trading, Alex could be a little blunt, Stelios was mindful that if he asked PJ or Jon Mathew to tweak their Libor submissions, there was nothing in it for them. It wasn't really a core part of their job and they'd be perfectly entitled to refuse to help. He was asking a favour. If he wasn't nice about it, they might just tell him where to go. Brought up in the famous Greek tradition of generous hospitality, being nice and friendly came very easily to Stelios, who'd make sure he thanked PJ or Jon properly for helping the New York desk out, either by lavishing them with compliments like 'superstar!' or 'you're a true gentleman!', or by offering a modest treat like a cup of coffee. In public relations or management school, they'd call it 'building a relationship' – the little extra positive energy that you put into your job that might be noted in your annual appraisal. But now those emails were being used as evidence by the Crown's prosecutor to try to condemn both Stelios and Jon to jail.

In his opening speech making the case that they'd been 'cheating' and 'stealing', James Hines asked the jury to look at a string of emails from ten years before, including the exchanges where Jon Mathew had tweaked his Libor submission to help Alex Pabon's swaps trades linked to Libor and Stelios wanted to thank him (see page 98).

'Superstar! I'm going to get some Itsu today, can I bring 2–3 takeaway boxes for you & your group over there?' wrote Stelios.

Seven minutes later, not wanting to make Jon wait too long, he sent a quick sushi update. 'Going to get it now, be back in 5 minutes.'

The next page in the jury's bundle of evidence of the criminal conspiracy of interest rate-rigging was an email back from Jon, now a little less hungry.

'That was awesome. A big thank you from everyone on the desk ...'

'No problem. A big thank you from us as well.'

Stelios had clearly bought plenty of sushi.

James Hines was keen not to put too much evidential weight on something as delicate as sushi, lest it be ridiculed by defence lawyers. They did their best anyway. 'Are you setting a dishonest rate for some sushi?' said Jon Mathew's defence lawyer Richard Clegg in the driest of tones.

'No,' replied Jon.

'It's plain that you offer on occasion to send coffee or Itsu to Mr Johnson and those working with him; yes?' said one barrister to Stelios on the witness stand.

'Yes.'

'Why did you do that?'

'Just to show my appreciation for their help.'

'Was it an effort to pervert and corrupt Mr Johnson?'

'Absolutely not.'

'Was it a bribe or a reward for misconduct, as far as you were concerned?'

'No.'

From the bewildered look on the jurors' faces, I wasn't the only one in the courtroom who couldn't quite believe what I was hearing. Was the Serious Fraud Office, well – serious? Did it really think this exchange was evidence of a criminal fraud conspiracy?

The keenest barrister for the SFO, Emma Deacon, was determined to make it sound fishy.

'The submitters, Peter Johnson and Jonathan Mathew. In acting on your requests, in taking them into account, did you consider that they were helping you out?'

'Yes,' said Stelios. 'They were accommodating potentially the requests, yes.'

'They were doing you a favour, weren't they?'

'Yes.'

'Because we see them peppered throughout your e-mails, don't we – little thank-yous?'

'Yes.'

'Coffees and Itsus and the like?'

'Yes.'

'You were rubbing them up the right way, weren't you?'

Stelios had never heard that expression. 'Sorry, what does that mean?'

'Getting them on side, Mr Contogoulas.'

'I was just being appreciative and thankful.'

'Keeping in their good books?' Deacon's tone was very arch.

'In their good books? It's just a way for me to say thank you.'

'Yes, but it wasn't thankyou just for the sake of it, was it? It was thankyou in the hope that they would carry on doing what you wanted, wasn't it?'

'Well, if buying them coffee might do that, then why not, yeah,' said Stelios. Now he was really sounding like a criminal.

'You thought it might help to get more of the same, didn't you?' said Emma Deacon, with an air of contempt.

'I don't remember thinking anything like that,' said Stelios.

To Stelios, Libor was a clerical task that he'd hardly thought about, except for at the start of the day or at around 11 a.m. The way he saw it was that it was a 'free option'.

'You could do it – ask for a high or low Libor submission. It was perfectly proper. If it worked and helped to nudge the Libor average your way, great. If not – it didn't matter. No downside. So you might as well do it in case it works. That was it! I was just doing my job and thanking them afterwards. That was all. A tiny part of my day.'

The prosecutors didn't want to hear it. It wasn't meant to be something mundane and clerical, this business of rigging Libor. The SFO was trying to prove what the US Department of Justice had said in 2012, that these requests were illegal: an international fraud conspiracy!

Stelios would later say that throughout the investigations and trials, 'I felt like I was in this really bad movie. You know it's something really – if you'd told me ten years ago this would happen, I'd have said, "You're mad!"' As a trader in his early thirties, he'd spent two minutes a day on Libor. But now, aged 44, he'd spent more than five years trying to explain to investigators, prosecutors, judges and juries why he'd bought coffee and sushi.

PJ had told the DOJ and other regulators on 17 November 2010 that he was 'extremely self-critical'. It was that unusually strong wish to keep up high standards for himself and be honest and truthful that had driven him during the financial crisis to convince his bosses and, in turn, senior management that when Barclays set its Libor rates, they should put in estimates as close as possible to the interest rates at which cash was actually being borrowed and lent. His firing in 2012, after thirty-one years at Barclays, was a devastating blow. He hired lawyers to protest that he was being punished twice for the same offence (accepting trader requests to tweak his Libor submissions) after having had a written warning in 2010 that had expired. But the politics were now poisonous. Having said, so publicly, that they were dealing with traders harshly, Barclays executives were determined to fire him.

With PJ, as with all of those prosecuted, the SFO's decision to charge him wrecked his life. But it was in one respect a relief when it came, because he no longer had to worry about the risk of being prosecuted in the USA. Like Tom Hayes, he was advised that he might serve up to thirty years in a

US penitentiary. Like Tom Hayes, he'd become a shadow of his former self, barely able to function. He couldn't see any way out of his situation and had thoughts of taking his own life. Unlike Tom Hayes, but very much like others who were prosecuted, he tried to seek relief from the constant stress in alcohol.

PJ had money saved up from a very well-rewarded job. But if he defended himself, that money could disappear very quickly on expensive lawyers. Everything he'd worked for over an otherwise successful career spanning three decades, including the financial security he hoped to pass on to his children and grandchildren, could be lost. He'd gone through almost all the requests and still believed no one could say he had posted an inaccurate rate before the financial crisis. After that point, during the crisis, he was clearly posting false rates, but it was also clear from all the phone calls he'd made and emails he'd sent that that was very much against his wishes and protests. Yet, based on what banks had paid fines to the regulators for, that wasn't what counted. If he'd at all adjusted his Libor submissions based on a trader's request, so it seemed, he'd engaged in misconduct. And there were one or two emails that were more awkward than others to explain.

On Friday, 10 March 2006, for example, Stelios had got in touch with PJ: 'Hi mate. We have an unbelievably large set on Monday,' he wrote. Just like variable rate mortgages, the interest rates on the swaps contracts traded by the New York desk didn't go up and down every day. They'd typically reset every three months on a set date – some of them on the third Wednesday of the month in March, June, September and December. That was when the dollar Libor rate counted most for the swaps desk.

'We need a really low 3m fix,' wrote Stelios. 'It could potentially cost a fortune. Would really appreciate any help, I'm being told by my NYK that it's extremely important. Thanks S.'

PJ wrote back saying that brokers were saying the 3-month dollar Libor rate was likely to fix at 4.90.5 or 4.91. He was planning to submit 4.90.

On Monday at 7.48 a.m. Stelios emailed PJ again:

'Good morning. The big day has arrived ... My NYK were screaming at me about an unchanged 3m libor. As always, any help wd be greatly appreciated. What do you think you'll go for 3m? Thanks, S.'

'I'm going 90, although 91 is what I should be posting.'

'I agree with you and totally understand. Remember, when I retire and write a book[3] about this business your name will be written in golden letters ... And you'll have an open invitation to my bar in the Greek Islands he he.'

'I would prefer this not be in any books!' wrote PJ.

'Ha ha ok,' replied Stelios. 'I'll go get some Itsu today for lunch, they do these nice takeaway boxes. Do you have any preferences? I'll bring 3–4 along for you and a few of your colleagues.'

'Don't worry about it!' said PJ, uninterested, as yet, in sushi for lunch.

'Well I'll bring something anyway and if you don't want it you can leave it,' said Stelios.

At the trial the prosecution made the most of this email chain – one of their best pieces of evidence of the international fraud conspiracy. 'There can't have been any doubt at that stage about whether Mr Johnson wanted any of this in the public domain,' remarked James Hines, prosecuting. 'That reference to "book" gives a bit of insight, doesn't it, into the clear knowledge that what they're doing must never really see the light of day?'

Long before the trial, PJ's lawyers had gone through all the evidence forensically, comparing his emails with the Libor rates he'd put in on the relevant days. Their conclusion was that as it stood ahead of the forthcoming trial, this email chain, and one or two others where he had clearly adjusted his Libor estimate in response to a request, an act now held to be unlawful, would make it more likely than not that he'd be found guilty. If he took his chances with the jury then, whatever the outcome, there'd be a huge legal fight, both before and during the trial, funded out of his savings. If the trial went against him, he was likely to get a long sentence – perhaps seven years or more. If on the other hand he pleaded guilty, he'd get a reduced sentence, most of which he could probably spend in an open prison where it wouldn't be impossible for his family to visit. He could negotiate a confiscation agreement that enabled him and his wife, Liz, to stay in the family home. He might get sentenced to four years and have to serve two. If, on the other hand, he pleaded not guilty, he'd likely be stuck with giant legal bills and might have to sell the family home to pay them; and he might nevertheless go to prison, possibly for a lot longer. That was what tipped the balance. It was the lesser of two evils. Hope lay not in the courts finding the right result; it lay in accepting the wrong one. After talking it over with Liz, PJ made up his mind. His lawyers notified the SFO he'd decided to plead guilty. In October 2014, PJ attended court and voluntarily gave the SFO its first interest rate-rigging conviction.

There was an irony that wouldn't be lost on those who knew PJ as he prepared to go to prison in the summer of 2016. In accommodating trader requests, he'd hardly acted out of greed. It could have no positive effect on his bonus. Beyond accepting the odd skinny latte from an insistent Stelios, he'd declined even the modest inducement to criminal conduct of an Itsu box. Yet he was pleading guilty because he'd gone '90' when he should have gone '91'. Because of that tweak of one basis point, which could have no financial benefit to PJ and which still represented an accurate estimate of the cost of borrowing cash within one hundredth of a percentage point, he'd become one of the few public faces of bank 'corruption', jailed for the very scandal he'd originally tried to blow the whistle on. Yet in that lowballing scandal, there was clear evidence from his own recorded phone line and emails that the pressure on him to lie about interest rates – the pressure to engage, against his vehement protests, in a huge fraud – came not from traders but first from the board of Barclays, then from the Bank of England, then from the UK government including the Treasury and Downing Street.

PJ would have been one of few defendants who could have revealed an explosive story about his own experience – a story of a cover-up at the highest level of the financial establishment on both sides of the Atlantic, a story of top-level knowledge of, and culpability in, the lowballing fraud. He could have told the world that the FBI knew all about it. The DOJ, the SFO, the FSA, the Fed, the Bank of England, the UK government – they all knew. They'd covered it up and kept it from the public. PJ might have said much of that on the witness stand. But now, partly because he'd pleaded guilty, much of the evidence that might have revealed that extraordinary story would never be brought into the traders' trials.

Sitting on the press benches in the spring of 2016, a simple but deeply shocking thought kept running through my head. No one at the SFO or the DOJ seemed to have done some very simple arithmetic. When you did, it shed a blindingly bright light on the whole prosecution on both sides of the Atlantic of interest rate 'rigging'. The charge of 'conspiracy to defraud' that PJ had pleaded guilty to and that threatened to send Stelios, Jay, Ryan, Alex and Jon to jail, was all about tweaks in Libor submissions of only one hundredth of a percentage point. The SFO had offered no proof that the tweaked rates that PJ or Jon had submitted were outside the accurate range of interest rates where cash was on offer. The Libor instruction from the top, by contrast, was for a shift in PJ's Libor submission more than fifty times the size. Yet that fraud, the one involving properly false, obviously inaccurate rates that PJ had tried for more than a year to expose, would never be brought to trial by either the US or the UK authorities. Instead, PJ, the original Libor whistleblower, was about to go to jail for emails where he'd agree to do colleagues the occasional favour involving shifts in his Libor rates of one hundredth of a percentage point, with no losses, no victims and no greater reward than some sushi he didn't even want.

14

BETTER NOT CALL SAUL

'It's ridiculous. These were emails and conversations from ten years ago and there was nothing wrong – we were just doing our jobs. We just always thought someone would eventually realise [...] what bullshit this all is!'
(Texan defendant Alex Pabon, two hours before sentencing,
Thursday, 7 July 2016)

When we first turned up at Southwark Crown Court for the Barclays Libor trial, the producer working with me, Ramzan Karmali, took one look at the jury and whispered, 'They're going to convict, aren't they? You can tell.' The twelve jurors had been whittled down from an original pool of more than thirty. They were in for a three-month trial. Many in the wider pool who were in professional jobs had been able to avoid serving on this jury on the grounds that they couldn't stay away from work for that long. The jury was then made up of those who had no such excuse. As the case unfolded, some of them didn't look very engaged in what was being said by the barristers. One juror stood out, a New Zealander who'd reportedly worked at a bank's IT department. Throughout the trial he had an almost permanent half-smile on his face. Maybe he was enjoying being on a jury that might lock some bankers up for fraud? He would become the jury's foreman.

Ramzan thought the jury would get the overall point that some bankers were being tried for fraud by the Crown. But they'd be less likely to understand the complicated defence. The defence case was technical and boring – an argument about rules that didn't exist and a narrow range of interest rates in an abstract place called 'the money markets', inaccessible to ordinary mortals. The prosecution case, by contrast, was sensational, an invitation to punish greedy bankers up to no good who were paid far more than most jurors could dream of – and they were repeatedly assured by the prosecution not to worry if they didn't fully understand the detailed evidence.

Hines was keen to simplify matters. 'It really is no different to stealing,' he said. But in a normal trial for theft or burglary, there'd be a victim on the witness stand. As with the other trials, there was no victim. Hines explained that it wasn't for the prosecution to prove a fraudulent transaction took place. Because they were trying the offence of conspiracy to defraud, they only needed to show the traders had agreed to do something dishonest. The courts had already decided it was unlawful to seek to influence Libor for commercial reasons. The crime, apparently, was the agreement. All the prosecution needed to show was one person uttering the words, 'can we have a high Libor?' and another answering 'yes'. Boom, there it was in that one-word answer: a criminal conspiracy to defraud. No need to show victims, or losses, or that Libor actually moved as a result of its alleged 'manipulation', or the criminals' alleged gains.

Just in case the jury still didn't understand, Hines simplified further. The Libor rate was meant to be 'independent', he said. 'The reason why the Libor rate must be independent of you and me, if we're dealing on the basis of it, is obvious, isn't it? I'm hardly going to enter a trade with you where the stake is measured in millions of dollars and the profit and loss are calculated by reference to Libor rate if you fix it [...] It would be like going into the roulette wheel in a casino, placing all your money on red and instead of there being a spin of the wheel, just let the croupier put the ball where it suits him.' Really? Was that what it was like?

It was no defence, Hines said, to say that there wasn't a rule that said you couldn't influence a Libor estimate for commercial reasons. 'Imagine,' said Hines, 'being one of those counterparties if Barclays came to you and said, "Well, I think you ought to check the rules. There's nothing in there that says I can't try and cheat, I can't try and manipulate my Libor submitter to defraud you. It doesn't say so in the rules". You would think that a poor excuse, would you not?' He reassured the jury there was no need to get too deep into the details. 'The dishonest agreement the defendants entered into was a simple one. One: the plan was to trade in deals which used the US dollar Libor benchmark interest rate to work out their profit and loss.

Two: to cheat. In order to maximise profit from those trades, the defendants agreed between themselves to manipulate or rig the US dollar Libor rate their way to advantage their trades and, thus, to disadvantage the people with whom they were doing the deals, those counterparties with whom they traded.'

'Cheat' was a good word for the prosecution. It had no real legal meaning. The jury would get the idea, though. It implied the traders were deliberately breaking a clear set of rules. That was what the indictment said too, that the traders 'deliberately disregarded the proper basis for the submission of those rates'. It had already been decided as a matter of law by a judge that there was an unwritten rule they were breaking when they made a Libor request. The jury members should have been told that before arriving at a verdict, they first had to be sure, as a matter of fact, that the traders had broken the rules deliberately.[1] But just as in the Hayes trial, they weren't.

The Serious Fraud Office had set the indictment period to start in January 2005 and finish on 1 September 2007, which conveniently excluded most of the evidence of lowballing pointing to Bank of England intervention. Just like in the Hayes trial, Saul Haydon Rowe was paid well as an expert witness to say that swaps traders like Jay, Ryan, Alex and Stelios would be well aware why Libor was set 'independently' (meaning without any commercial influence). But he seemed to be struggling to explain some of the basics of what the traders did.

John Ewan, too, looked uncomfortable, as he had at Tom's trial. He was on record in a sworn statement about traders' requests, saying 'At no point during the Relevant Period did I or the BBA have *any suspicion* that this type of behaviour was taking place.'[2] His sworn witness statement for the Court of Appeal said that if any members of the Foreign Exchange and Money Markets Committee that regulated Libor had known about trader requests, 'they would have acted upon it immediately because they would have considered it wrong'. Yet under cross-examination, defence lawyers produced a British Bankers' Association report of a meeting on 8 June 2005 with Jon Wood and others from HSBC saying, 'they suspect that certain nameless contributors might be setting their rates with an eye on their derivatives book'. HSBC were on the FXMMC. Clearly, Wood and colleagues had a suspicion that this 'type of behaviour' was happening. Yet no one seemed to have acted. Then there was the report the BBA had written up after his annual visits to all the banks for their views on Libor. In the third paragraph of its summary, it said: 'There is consensus amongst banks that Sterling LIBOR and US Dollar are being set 3–4 basis points above the true cash rate [...] Those banks whose main business is in derivatives or loans are perfectly happy with this, as it is to their advantage.' That looked very much like Ewan knew about commercial influence on Libor submissions. If it was 3–4 basis points higher than the 'true cash rate', then that meant it was false, for commercial reasons, every day. But Ewan didn't seem to have seen it as an emergency. In fact, he'd attended a meeting at the Bank of England on 18 August 2005, where he'd told Paul Tucker all about it. There they'd discussed a report by Ewan written up after his annual review of Libor in 2005 where he'd said: 'There was a market consensus that the sterling and Dollar LIBOR was some 3 to 4 base points above the actual market rate. This was essentially a construct of the market as it is in the interests of the bank to have a higher Libor.' They were discussing what would later be called interest rate-rigging, happening every day as a matter of routine. Defence barristers pointed out that if the prosecution was right to say, with the Court of Appeal, that any commercial influence on Libor was unlawful, then this appeared to show every Libor submission, every day was unlawful! Yet the Bank of England at the time didn't seem to see it that way. Neither Tucker nor anyone else at the Bank appeared shocked. Given the enormity of what Ewan was telling Tucker, it should have been a matter of great surprise that no one called the police. But somehow it wasn't a surprise at all.

The story the SFO told the jury was that the conspiracy to manipulate Libor had begun with Jay Merchant, who'd urged the other traders in New York to make requests of the cash desk in London. A whizz at maths from a young age, Jay had been raised by a dad who owned a plastics company and a mum who took care of the children and coached him to play tennis. He'd spent the early part of his life outside school devoted to the game, stringing rackets as a teenager at his local tennis club for 50 rupees (65p) a racket and starting down the road to become a professional player. He'd won a tennis scholarship to Southern Illinois University and paid his way through university by coaching tennis before joining the Rick Macci Tennis Academy in Florida where, for a few months, he was a hitting partner for two upcoming young sisters called Venus and Serena Williams. After deciding life as a professional tennis player wasn't for him, he went to the Stern School of Business in New York and later clinched his first job as a trader at Barclays

Capital in London. On the panel that hired him was senior Barclays banker Eric Bommensath. Jay's immediate boss for much of his time at the bank was Mike Bagguley, whose boss in turn was Harry Harrison, reporting to Bommensath. Jay brought his competitive streak and his energy to trading and his life looked up. Bagguley (pronounced 'Bag-lee') had trained him up in how to trade swaps and Jay told the court Bagguley would regularly make requests to the cash desk to put in Libor high or low, depending on 'which way round' the bank was, as a way of reducing the risk on the bank's positions. 'He would sit down with Mr Pabon and myself at least a couple of times a week and discuss how we were reducing risk in the book and every single time we would tell him that one of the things we were doing was suggesting to PJ a rate or high or low.' They'd socialise every weekend and once or twice a week, according to Jay, becoming good friends. After rising to become a senior trader, Jay played a role helping Barclays trade its way through the financial crisis. But since 2012, when Barclays' legal department had lined him up to be prosecuted, he'd struggled like everyone else. His wife, Elena, and his eldest son were in the USA and she was heavily pregnant when Jay's trial began. He'd spent a lot of time before the trial helping his father-in-law, who'd been diagnosed with cancer about four years before and had been battling it ever since. Now, Elena was facing the prospect of losing her father to cancer and her husband to jail as she prepared to give birth to her second son.

This time it was Jay who was being lined up as the 'ringmaster'. It was he, the SFO said, who'd instructed Alex, Ryan and Stelios to communicate with the cash desk in London about Libor. Jay listened, his fury growing, as a story was told to try to jail him that as far as he was concerned was all lies. He had never managed anyone in New York. He was no one's boss! The SFO was telling a story completely at odds with reality.

Jay had told the SFO in interview that the real bosses who outranked him knew all about the practice of making requests for tweaks in Libor, including his immediate boss Mike Bagguley, the boss above him, Harry Harrison, as well as Harrison's boss, Eric Bommensath. All three, Jay alleged, had known about, approved and even instructed him to make requests of the submitters in London. To combat his allegations, the SFO had, with the help of Barclays' legal department, lined up the three bosses Jay named: Mike Bagguley, Harry Harrison and Eric Bommensath. All three denied in their witness statements that they condoned or approved of traders' requests in any way. All three were lined up by the SFO to tell the jury that they didn't know it was going on; and if they had seen it, they would have stopped it because it was clearly wrong.[3]

In his opening speech, Jay's barrister Hugh Davies commented: 'What Mr Merchant says, is that to different degrees, depending how closely he worked with them [...] the general principle of putting in a request was known to each of them, in particular Messrs Bagguley and Harrison who were closer to Mr Merchant. Each of course denies it. In the words of Mandy Rice-Davies, "They would say that, wouldn't they now?", because if they don't, they will be sitting behind those glass panels? They had other reasons to deny it, several million reasons a year each to deny it, if you think about it, because their employment has continued, highly lucrative senior figures in the bank. They're bound to deny it.'

There was a personal twist in this for Jay. Bagguley, a former swaps trader, had been his line manager first in London and then in New York and they'd become close as friends as well as colleagues. Bagguley had even invited Jay to his wedding, long after they'd stopped working together. But now Mike Bagguley was on the witness stand trying to help the SFO lock Jay up, saying they'd never been friends – and he never would have engaged in Libor requests.

'As far as you're aware, the practice that we see here of sending requests to a Libor or benchmark submitter, did you ever know of that practice at Barclays prior to the internal investigation?' Bagguley was asked.

'I did not.'

Later, Bagguley was even more definitive. 'Have you ever regarded a practice such as that as being proper or appropriate?' he was asked.

'No.'

But then the defence produced an email Bagguley had received from 22 March 2006 where one of his staff, Adil Kassam, had written the following: 'PJ submits our settings each day. We influence our settings based on the fixings we all have.'

Bagguley replied to the email chain five days later: 'Adil, as all dealers should have the setting same way, why do they not input low set that day? Hence why do we not see it set down, or does it? E.g. we ask to set lower.'

From that email chain, it looked like Mike Bagguley was not only aware of the practice of making requests of Libor submitters to put in low Libor submissions – but was also advocating it.

'Why did you type the words, "E.g. we ask to set lower",' asked Ryan Reich's barrister Adrian Darbishire in cross-examination. 'Can you tell us? You asked who to set lower?'

'Barclays to submit lower Libor,' said Bagguley.

'So, you're asking the question, "Do we ask our cash desk to submit lower Libor?"'

'No, I am not.'

'Do you have any answer to this jury as to what you were talking about when you wrote, "E.g. we ask to set lower?" if not the swaps desk asking the cash desk?'

'I believe I meant Barclays in its submission.'

'Barclays' submission from the cash desk asks Libor to be set lower?'

'Yes.'

On the witness stand, Bagguley's boss Harry Harrison gave a simpler answer, saying that from Kassam's email: 'It would appear the swaps desk is influencing the Libor fixing.'

'Does it not suggest that the manager knew or was in some way complicit in the Libor manipulation that we've seen?' Harrison was asked.

'It's a very difficult email for Mike to explain. If his purpose was to double-check and push Adil to see what was actually going on, it might be appropriate.'

But it wasn't Mike Bagguley on trial: it was Jay, Alex, Stelios, Ryan and Jon.

Jay's lawyer had advised him to be controlled – giving one-word answers where possible. Combined with his suppressed anger at what he regarded as a judicial stitch-up, it didn't make for a friendly presence whom the members of the jury could relate to. His legal team produced a PowerPoint presentation showing evidence throughout Barclays of knowledge of or involvement in Libor 'rigging' (seeking to influence the rates submitted by the cash desk); in the material disclosed to the defence, there was documented evidence of twenty-two of Harrison and Bommensath's subordinates knowing about it; but somehow no documents to suggest the two of them knew. The defence lawyers claimed evidence showed eighty traders were involved in what the SFO called 'manipulation'. But it was in vain. What really caught the jury's attention, what no one could get out of their heads, were the bankers' pay and bonuses.

All the prosecution really had to say to make the jury dislike Jay Merchant enough to send him down was the following: 'In 2005 he received a salary of £82,500, with a bonus totalling £617,500, making a total of £700,000. In 2006 he received a salary a little higher of £86,600, but a bonus totalling £1,213,400, making a total of £1.3 million. In 2007, a salary just again a tiny bit higher at £87,210, with a bonus of over £2 million, £2,122,621, making his income that year of £2,209,831.'

Reading those numbers, who wouldn't feel an emotion? It might be a sense of alienation from this distant world of banking where money flows so freely; and it might be straightforward envy. But it's also justified outrage. However talented a trader Jay might have been, the jury could hear him on audio tapes swearing, being human, getting upset – just like them. They could hear what he was saying at work. It was nothing so magical or special that it seemed to warrant such exorbitant rewards. The myth that bankers were paid so much because of their extremely rare talents was laid bare. The average wage in the UK in 2016 was £28,200 – little more than an eightieth of what Jay had made in one year. Before the noughties, bankers didn't used to think themselves entitled to such outrageous sums. Going back to the 1980s, bankers were still thought of as slightly dull but morally upstanding members of the community. They'd only gradually acquired that sense of entitlement in the US-led 'bonus culture' that had begun after the deregulation of the City of London in 1986. That culture of entitlement had grown out of control in the 1990s and now lay at the heart of the growing inequality across the UK economy. The amounts bankers had come to pay themselves had become more and more out of step with the rest of the population. The crisis had just made it all the more outrageous – because it turned out that all taxpayers, no matter how modestly paid, had been underwriting the bankers – effectively insuring them against the risk that they screwed up the entire economy. And when they had done so, royally, and taxpayers had spent huge sums rescuing the banks, they'd continued to insist on their right to pay themselves enormous bonuses. Never mind what had been said in the trial, what modestly paid juror wouldn't want to punish the injustice in Jay Merchant's pay? Jay would later bitterly protest that the jury had been turned against him by information about his bonuses – without any knowledge of the much more startling sums paid to the Barclays witnesses who'd been lined up by the prosecution. In the seven years from 2005, when the conspiracy started, to 2011, the year before Barclays was fined, Mike Bagguley had collected £20,239,564 in salary and bonus. In the same period, Harry Harrison had taken home £46,997,380. Eric Bommensath had been paid no less than £92,096,597. Jay's legal team had applied to be able to put that evidence before the jury and were denied. Of course, that wasn't actually what the rate-rigging trials were supposed to be about. Officially at least, being overpaid wasn't the offence on the indictment.

It took nearly two weeks for the juries to arrive at their verdicts. As they were deliberating, a majority of British voters shocked politicians and the media by defying the polls and unexpectedly voting, narrowly but decisively, in favour of exiting the EU. Anything was now possible.

On Wednesday, 29 June 2016, a sweltering hot day, the defendants were called to the court. Everyone knew this was the moment.

'Mr Foreman, have the jury reached a verdict in relation to Jonathan Mathew on the indictment upon which at least ten of you are agreed?'

'Yes, we have,' said the young New Zealander.

'Do you find the defendant Jonathan Mathew guilty or not guilty of conspiracy to defraud?'

'Guilty,' said the foreman, a half-smile on his face. He seemed to be enjoying this.

Jon Mathew gasped in the dock, bent forward and held his head in his hands. Only one juror had disagreed.

'Have you reached a verdict in relation to Jay Merchant on the indictment upon which at least ten of you are agreed?' asked the clerk.

'Yes, we have.'

'Do you find the defendant Jay Merchant guilty or not guilty of conspiracy to defraud?' asked the clerk.

'Guilty,' said the foreman, again with a half-smile. This time it was unanimous.

'Have the jury reached a verdict in relation to Alex Pabon on the indictment upon which at least ten of you are agreed?'

'Yes.'

'Do you find the defendant Alex Pabon guilty or not guilty of conspiracy to defraud?'

'Guilty.'

'How many of you agreed to the verdict?'

'Ten to two.'

They hadn't reached a verdict on either Ryan Reich or Stelios Contogoulas. The media were ordered not to report the verdicts for now. The judge was giving the jury longer to reach a verdict on Ryan and Stelios. By the following

Monday, 4 July, the jury sent a note saying they didn't think any more time to deliberate would make any difference. They'd been out for two weeks. Clearly, at least three jurors were refusing to convict either Stelios or Ryan.

On 7 July, all four convicted defendants (including PJ) were due to be sentenced. The BBC's *Panorama* documentary series had already commissioned a film on the Libor scandal, and I was the reporter. I'd been trying for months now to get any of the defendants to give me an interview. They'd all had advice that they shouldn't. But then, at last, I got a call from Julie Pabon, Alex Pabon's wife. Like Sarah Hayes, she was a lawyer. To her and Alex, who'd been staying in London with their young son while the trial was on, the SFO case had never made any sense. They'd hoped that would come out in the courts before the trial; then when that failed, they'd rested their hopes on the jury. But now Alex was convicted. He and Julie were furious – furious enough to take the risk of giving me a TV interview just two hours before Alex was due to go to jail. We scrambled to get a camera crew to the flat where they were staying.

'We never thought that anything we were doing was wrong,' said Alex. 'I mean, we've been saying the same story for years.'

'They never thought anything they were doing was wrong,' said Julie, dissolving into tears. 'I mean, they didn't do anything wrong. And I don't know what's going to happen from here. And it's just very scary and I feel like it could happen to anyone – you know?' She'd now have to return home with her 3-year-old son, thousands of miles away from her jailed husband.

By now I knew for sure that PJ had been ordered to 'rig' rates against his wishes on instructions from above – including the Bank of England. I'd seen a transcript of his call with Dearlove on 29 October 2008 – something that had never come out in public. He'd not been at the trial because of his decision in 2014 to plead guilty. The sentencing hearing was my one chance to try to throw a question to him. Who knows, he might say something. We stood lurking in front of Southwark Crown Court when I suddenly noticed PJ and his lawyer walking towards us down the pedestrian street at the side of the court building. 'That's them, let's go!' I ran towards the two of them with a radio-controlled mike and then backpedalled as I asked the question I'd been rehearsing in my head for the past hour. 'Peter Johnson. Were you ordered by your bosses to post false Libor rates – under pressure from the Bank of England? Yes or no?'

PJ wasn't stopping. 'No comment,' he said as he moved past us towards the entrance to the court. It was exactly what he'd told Dearlove he'd say eight years before.

Inside the courtroom, Judge Leonard proved far less zealous in his sentencing than his predecessor Jeremy Cooke. Nonetheless, as I reported the sentences on the BBC News channel, I had to disguise how I was feeling. By now it was becoming obvious: this looked like a whole series of miscarriages of justice. It looked to me like requests for 'high' or 'low' Libor submissions, choosing from a range of offers on the market, were clearly normal commercial practice and there was little contemporary evidence that anyone thought it remotely 'reprehensible' until the Commodity Futures Trading Commission and later the US Department of Justice decided, without fully understanding what they were looking at, that trader requests must all be corrupt.

'Four ex-employees of Barclays Bank have been sentenced to jail for rigging Libor, the benchmark for how much it costs banks to borrow from each other,' I reported to the news channel live camera. 'Jay Merchant, who's 45 – he was sentenced to six and a half years. Peter Johnson, who's 61, was sentenced to four years. Jonathan Mathew, 35, was sentenced to four years and Alex Pabon, aged, 38, was sentenced to two years, nine months.'

Our *Panorama* documentary was edited and ready to be broadcast immediately after the trial came to an end. After reporting the sentences, I mentioned on air that it was coming up soon. But days later, we learned the SFO had ordered a retrial for Ryan and Stelios. The BBC's team of media lawyers advised us that if we went ahead with the broadcast we could be held in contempt of court. After all the energy we had put into the film, everyone on the documentary team was gutted. We'd now have to wait months, until after the retrial, before we could broadcast our film.

A few days later, though, there was a consolation. Someone got in touch who'd seen me on the news mentioning the upcoming *Panorama* film – someone who knew things. Much later, I was leaked audio recordings that the authorities had never wanted to come out in public: they included confidential tapes of PJ's recorded line – and John Ewan's.

I'd reached out to Jay by email asking if he'd call me from jail. It could have jeopardised everything for him as he waited for his appeal hearing. But I'd promised him I wouldn't use anything without his permission and not until after the appeal. He was furious and wanted to speak out. In January 2017, he called me from HMP Highpoint North.

'We told the clients all about it; it was a completely open thing,' Jay told me. 'Nobody thought anything was wrong with it. I talked to clients all the time and I told him that we're going to set it higher, or we're going to set it low or "I've told him we want it higher". It was a totally normal conversation. And for them to now pick out these five or six random people out of thousands who have done this, and who all thought it was normal, is just ludicrous. It's like someone going to a foreign country where everyone's driving at 30 miles an hour. If he wants to go 30 miles an hour, that's fine. Five years later the speed limit is changed to 20 miles an hour. Then ten years later they pick out five or six drivers out of the tens of thousands who were doing 30 miles an hour in the past. They say, "You six, you should have known the speed limit was going to be changed to 20 miles an hour five years later. You're going to be charged for it." That's what's happened here.

'By any metric I made zero income from any requests. Zero! The judge is going to look like a fool giving a man six and a half years for a fraud that made zero money. So, what's my motive to be a crook? I mean – there is no motive. Why would I be a crook? I'm already doing well, making a seven-figure income before the indictment period. I take a pay cut of 46 per cent, to move to New York to do something different. So, where's the greed, where's the criminal motivation? My bonus, and compensation over the indictment period is half of what I made before and after. There is no motivation! I'm just following a procedure that I think and was told was the right procedure. And I'm just obeying what my boss says, that's all I'm trying to do. It was a clerical duty we had to do every day. And we did it in front of everybody.'

Later that month, Jay called me again from prison. I asked him how the appeal was going: 'It's getting worse by the day,' he said. 'So, we've been frantically searching for somebody to replace my QC because he said he couldn't do it the first fifteen days of February. They chose a date of February the 7th. So, we had been scrambling around to find a QC and we'd just got somebody on board. Then two days ago, the Lord Chief Justice says, "You know what? I want to be in on this. The only date I have is February 1st. That's the date of the appeal." Now we have seven days less now to do any work. It's a joke. It's doomed to failure. And let's just call it that.'

Resting his elbows on the table, John Thomas put his hands together as if in prayer, touched his fingers to his lips and looked down, deep in thought. There were things the Lord Chief Justice couldn't say. In charge of the judiciary when Jeremy Cooke was appointed to the Hayes trial, John Thomas was at an event held at the Bank of England titled 'Worthy of Trust? Law, Culture and Ethics in Banking', broadcast on the internet. He'd just been asked an awkward question by Alex Brummer, a columnist at the *Daily Mail*. Senior bankers must have had access to the communications that jailed the Libor traders, said Brummer. Why were no senior bankers punished?

The panel at the Bank of England event was such that you wondered how well these people knew each other – the top judges and the central bankers. Hosted by the governor of the Bank of England, Mark Carney, the guests included not only Thomas but the president of the Federal Reserve Bank of New York and at least two Dames. If this wasn't the Establishment, nothing was. When you have spent a lifetime acquiring an impressive-sounding title like 'The Lord Chief Justice of England and Wales', few people question your judgement. But maybe more should.

Seven weeks earlier, Thomas had sat with Lord Justice Nigel Davis and another colleague in long wigs and robes behind the high benches of the Royal Courts of Justice in London, hearing some powerful points. Appealing against Jay Merchant's conviction, and also Jon Mathew's, Jonathan Crow QC demanded logic. The law as it stood made no sense, he said. It couldn't be right that an accurate rate became false just because someone asked for it – or that a trader could go to jail for putting in an accurate rate. 'It is *absurd*,' said Crow. 'The courts are retrospectively criminalising normal commercial practice!'

Hearing journalists tapping away on their laptops, Thomas looked up and suddenly ordered reporting restrictions. Sitting high above the court in a vertiginous press gallery, we – the members of the press – looked at each other, a little shocked. Normally if there were reporting restrictions, there'd be a written notice on the door of the court as you came in so that you wouldn't waste your time. It wasn't supposed to be announced halfway through the hearing, when you'd already spent two hours taking notes and promising your editor that you'd file a story. As the court broke for lunch, I asked the court clerk why it had happened this way and told him we needed to report the hearing for a documentary we were making. When I returned from the sandwich shop, I got a shock. The court clerk tapped me on the shoulder. 'You can make an application,' he said. I had no idea what he meant. 'You can ask to lift the reporting restrictions,' he said.

'So what do I do?' I said, a little panicked.

'You can stand up in court and give your reasons.'

'Okay!' I said, trying to collect myself. 'How do I address the judges?'

'My Lord.'

The three top judges re-entered the court. The Lord Chief Justice sat down and said, 'Right. Mr Verity?'

'Erm – thank you,' I said, standing up and steadying myself by clutching on to the top of the high-backed pew where the press sat. 'My Lord,' I said, feeling ridiculous, 'we were a bit taken aback to be told in the middle of the hearing that reporting restrictions were suddenly imposed when normally you can expect a notice on the door of the court.' I said that it meant that the journalists' time had been wasted. But more than that, this hearing was about matters of serious public interest. The BBC was making a documentary about them and this wasn't how it was normally done – for reporting restrictions to be suddenly imposed as they just had been.

'Thank you,' said Thomas. 'Please don't feel under any obligation, but are you able to tell us what your documentary is about?'

Now he was putting me on the spot. 'Well – I'm not sure my employer would be happy if I said too much.'

'Which is why I said: don't feel obliged,' said John Thomas in his wig and robes.

'I can give you an outline.' The concern, I said, was that most of the real frauds – like banks ruining thousands of small businesses – don't get investigated or prosecuted. Instead, the SFO goes after traders for something that, arguably, wasn't a fraud at all. It looked like the understanding of City practices was light – and that what was being prosecuted was actually just normal practice that no one thought of as illegal at the time. And more importantly, there was concern we were seeing 'a series of miscarriages of justice – and that this whole process of hearings and trials is politicised'. I could hardly believe I was saying it out loud in court.

John Thomas very politely thanked me and later in the hearing announced that the ruling would be returned within two days. But then there was a long delay, and it took three weeks before the ruling was handed down. The court shortened Jay Merchant's sentence from six and a half to five and a half years but refused to overturn the convictions. To

Crow's exasperation, the three judges refused to certify there was a point of law of public importance, effectively blocking the path to the Supreme Court – the third time either Thomas or Davis had done so. The key points about Cooke's rulings being illogical were side-stepped but the ruling did offer one key concession. Cooke, it said, should have directed the jury first to establish as a matter of fact whether the defendants had *deliberately disregarded* the proper basis for the submission of Libor. It was only then that they should ask themselves if they regarded it as dishonest. Thomas's appeal panel decided that it wouldn't have made any difference to the outcome, so Jay's conviction was safe. But in future, juries would have to be directed to find that defendants had deliberately disregarded the rules.

Now, under question at the Bank of England's public event, Thomas had to be careful responding to Brummer's question. 'The deterrent must be to go to those who have been dishonest, and at the highest level you can find that dishonesty [...] The SFO has been doing a *good job*,' he said – hastily adding, 'That is not a comment in relation to Libor.'

Next to Thomas was Bill Dudley, president of the Federal Reserve Bank of New York. In 2008, Bill Dudley was the counterpart of Paul Tucker at the New York Fed, in charge of difficult market issues – like lowballing. The New York Fed had been warned about it repeatedly by PJ, starting in August 2007 (it did nothing) and by Colin Bermingham in April 2008. PJ and Bermingham had both told them it was dishonest. But neither central bank reported it as a crime. Far from it. In October 2008 they had joined in, arranging artificially low Libor rates themselves, nowhere near the real cost of borrowing cash.

'How do you change a culture where silence leads to misconduct?' said Dudley. 'First, it's really important that managers lead by example [...] Employees who speak up should be recognised, positively [...] I think there's a significant value in being able to sleep well at night.'

As the 'Law, Culture and Ethics in Banking' event[4] drew to a close, neither PJ nor Jonathan Mathew nor Tom Hayes nor Jay Merchant could watch it before they returned to their prison bunks and struggled to get off to sleep. For prisoners in jail, there's no internet.

On 9 March 2017, at the retrial at Southwark Crown Court of Ryan Reich and Stelios Contogoulas, Ryan's energetic barrister Adrian Darbishire was carefully setting up his cross-examination of John Ewan. Darbishire had made a name as a 'firebrand' and he was now putting all his brains and experience into getting his client acquitted. There was a key piece of evidence, the significance of which the SFO was keen to play down and, if possible, to keep out of court. It was a letter from July 2008 to John Ewan – when the BBA was reviewing Libor after the *Wall Street Journal* splash of April 2008 – from the Chicago Mercantile Exchange, where most of the world's derivatives contracts were traded. It contradicted everything the SFO had said, and everything the British courts had ruled. It said a cash trader putting in their Libor submission who can borrow 'at any one of a wide range of offered rates *commits no falsehood* if she bases her response to the daily Libor survey upon the lowest of these (or the highest, or any other arbitrary selection from among them)'. The words were unambiguous: 'commits *no falsehood*'. The banks and other investors on the CME traded swaps contracts linked to Libor to the value of trillions of dollars. If anyone cared about Libor being set correctly, it was the CME. Here it was saying that a Libor submitter wasn't saying anything false if they picked a high or low number within the range of offered rates available. It was just what Tom Hayes and every defendant had been trying to say from the start.

Judge Leonard ruled the letter inadmissible on the grounds that it fell outside the indictment period and was talking about lowballing, not trader requests. That meant it couldn't be seen by the jury. But Darbishire argued it had been put to Ewan before and was relevant to Ewan's understanding of the BBA definition – something all the courts had relied on. Even if it couldn't be seen by the jury, there was no good legal reason why it couldn't be used in cross-examination. Leonard couldn't think of a good reason to oppose Darbishire's request. Two days later, on 9 March, with John Ewan on the witness stand, Darbishire handed him the CME letter and asked him to read it, adding, 'Just a reminder, Mr Ewan that you are on oath.' Then Darbishire showed a transcript of a phone call between Miles Storey and Peter Johnson. PJ was telling Storey that the range of interest rates at which the bank might borrow was between 5.10% and 5.25%. Storey was saying that if PJ put in a higher rate, he feared the bank might 'get slaughtered in the press'. Darbishire asked Ewan if PJ would have been entitled to put in a rate at the lower end of the range to reduce the risk of bad press coverage, if it were still within the range where the bank might borrow cash. Would the rate still be accurate if he then asked for the submitter to put in a rate at the lower end of the range, 5.10%?

'It is in line with the definition at the time, yes,' said Ewan.

Storey, in other words, was entitled to ask for a low Libor rate for a commercial reason – avoiding getting slaughtered in the press. Ewan was saying it was OK to pick a rate from within a range on offer for commercial reasons. He had just contradicted the Court of Appeal ruling that drew on his evidence of the rights and wrongs of Libor.

Darbishire followed up, closely echoing the wording of the CME letter that Ewan had just read: 'If [a bank] can borrow in reasonable market size at any one of a wide range of offered rates, then it is not false or inconsistent with the definition for the bank to base its response, in other words its submission, on the lowest of those rates?' asked Darbishire.

'No,' said Mr Ewan.

'Or the highest one or any other arbitrary selection from among them?'

'That's right.'

Forced into a corner by Darbishire, Ewan had just undermined the core of the prosecution case: asking for Libor to be put in 'high' or 'low' could be in line with the BBA definition if it was within the range of rates where cash was trading. Libor requests need not break any rules. There was a range. And Libor could be set high or low within the range – even if it were for commercial reasons.

Ryan Reich's team had come up with something more. Everyone from the DOJ to the SFO to the judges had called the traders' requests 'manipulation'. But there was a problem with that word. If it meant anything in this context, it was 'to control or influence unscrupulously' or 'to alter or present so as to mislead'. The traders were hoping that by making a Libor request for a submission to be put in high or low, it *might* help to nudge the Libor average in the right direction. But they didn't have any level of *control*. They couldn't *alter* the Libor average by themselves. The DOJ had worked out that requests from swaps traders like Alex Pabon were in line with what submitters like PJ put in about 70 per cent of the time. But that didn't mean their requests had had any effect on the average. That was a whole different calculation: one neither the DOJ nor the SFO had ever done. As Jon Mathew had suggested to the DOJ long ago, all the data about what submissions he and PJ had made were still there. You could take Barclays Libor submissions, move them by one basis point in the opposite direction of the traders' requests on that day, then recalculate the average. If it didn't move, the request couldn't possibly have had an effect. Ryan's team had now done that exercise. The startling finding: of 297 requests from Barclays traders, the number of occasions when it was mathematically possible that they could have shifted the Libor average added up to a grand total of ... three. The SFO didn't argue with the maths. The most Ryan or Stelios could have made out of the requests, even if they had worked as hoped on those three occasions, was a matter of a few dollars. In Ryan's case, he couldn't have made more than $30. The idea, made so much of in 2012, that the swaps traders had committed 'atrocious acts' out of greed was falling apart.

Then Ryan Reich's team discovered something unexpected. The expert witness whom the SFO had tasked with explaining all the financial terminology to the jury was Saul Haydon Rowe, who'd been a trader in the 1990s. It was Rowe who'd testified at the trials that all traders would have known that Libor must be set 'independently' – meaning, without any commercial influence such as from traders' requests. He'd also testified that he didn't recognise the term 'permissible range', undermining the traders' defence. His evidence had been used to help convince jurors that traders including Tom, Jay, Alex and Jon Mathew had behaved dishonestly. But it turned out that Rowe himself had been less than perfectly honest.

Rowe had been instructed by the SFO in 2014, giving evidence at the Hayes trial, at the brokers' trial and at both Barclays trials, collecting fees of more than £400,000 for his firm Turing Experts Ltd. In March 2017, for the first time, the defendants were granted disclosure of emails and texts that Rowe had sent. It turned out that he'd been so insecure about his expertise that he'd been breaking the strict rules on criminal trials, texting people for help, illegally, in the middle of his evidence. In the first trial in 2016, he'd texted a trader he knew: 'I don't know the usual trades [short-term swaps traders] put on but I'm learning.'

The trader replied: 'Trouble is, out of context it's actually quite hard to interpret. You get used to the methodology of the people around.'

Rowe had replied: 'Yes I agree. That's what I see on all my cases but it doesn't help when I have to explain a few emails and look knowledgeable.'

Another email he sent was even more blunt: 'We'll get a specialist on any future work as this mission has crept well beyond me.'

It emerged that Rowe had been offering to pay some of the traders he'd been illegally texting to help him. Under the Criminal Procedure Rules 2015, expert witnesses are obliged to disclose all the sources of information they have consulted and to draw the court's attention to questions outside their area of expertise. Asked under cross-examination by Darbishire if he had read those rules, Mr Rowe said he didn't know. But then he acknowledged signing a truth statement saying he had. He'd also sworn that a report he had given as an expert witness was his own work. However, much of the report, used in all four UK trials of traders for manipulating Libor, titled 'Libor and Interest Rate Markets, Products, Concept and Terminology', was in fact written by a colleague of his.

To the traders jailed for 'dishonest' behaviour, this was far worse.

Alex Pabon tried to appeal against his conviction based on what the courts accepted was Rowe's 'disastrous' testimony. His lawyers complained Rowe had 'failed to report with any detail or accuracy as to how he reached his opinions; he secretly consulted with a number of undisclosed advisors; he blatantly disregarded the directions of a trial judge during the course of a criminal trial; and he knowingly gave evidence about matters outside his area of competence. These are deeply troubling failings that bring the system of justice into disrepute.'[5] The SFO was supposed to be proving the defendant's dishonesty. But in order to do so, Alex's lawyers argued, the SFO had called 'a dishonest expert as an essential building block of their case.' The SFO prosecutor James Hines told the court the SFO had itself had 'no inkling' of Rowe's lack of expertise.[6]

Sarah Tighe made a complaint to the Metropolitan Police on Tom Hayes's behalf, alleging Rowe had misrepresented his expertise to make money for his firm and should be investigated. After months of delay, the Met came back to say he hadn't misrepresented his expertise. Emails showed he'd made it very clear to the SFO that he was going to need help with his evidence from others – and Mukul Chawla advised there was nothing problematic in that. It wasn't Rowe, it seemed, who had misrepresented his expertise to the SFO. The SFO knew all about it but were happy to keep him as a witness because he would say what they wanted him to say.

The retrial of Ryan Reich and Stelios Contogoulas was shorter than the 2016 trial and the jury looked like they were paying close attention and understanding the defence teams' points. Since Jay's appeal, the jury had to be directed to find the defendants had deliberately broken the rules before they decided whether or not they had behaved dishonestly. On 5 April 2017, the jury unanimously acquitted Ryan and, a day later, Stelios. On the courtroom steps we caught Stelios for a few words. 'I'm very happy. It's obviously a relief – this has been five and a half years of my life. I just want to go back to my family now,' he said. But before he could get away the jurors, now outside the court, greeted him warmly. Under the rules, you can speak to jurors for their individual opinions; you just have to avoid asking them about what was said in the jury room.

'It shouldn't be the ground level staff that were blamed because instructions must have come from the top. When you look at these people, they cannot have been doing their job without directives,' said one. 'I don't see how you can have something supposed to be as important as Libor and don't train your staff. How are they to know they're doing something wrong?'

On 11 April 2017, the BBC broadcast the *Panorama* documentary I'd been reporting for. 'The Big Bank Fix' showcased the incendiary tape I'd got hold of, never played to Parliament or any of the juries in the rate-rigging trials: the Dearlove–PJ tape from 29 October 2008. An article accompanied it, headlined: 'Libor: Bank of England implicated in secret recording.' Everyone could now hear the tape that had prompted the DOJ to launch its criminal investigation, that called into question evidence given to Parliament in 2012 by the Bank of England governor and deputy governor and the chief of Barclays that they knew nothing about lowballing in 2008. The opposition Labour Party called for an immediate public inquiry as did Treasury committee MP Chris Philp: 'That is shocking,' he told us. 'This tape suggests that in fact, the Bank of England knew about it and indeed were encouraging or even instructing it. We need an immediate inquiry to find out exactly what was going on given what we've just heard on this tape [...] It sounds to me like those people giving evidence [to the Treasury committee in 2012], particularly Bob Diamond and Paul Tucker, were misleading Parliament. That is a contempt of Parliament, it's a very serious matter and I think we need to urgently summon those individuals back before Parliament to explain why it is they appear to have misled MPs. It's extremely serious.'

The article was the top story on the BBC's website and was followed up all around the world. I hoped something might change.

But the SFO weren't backing down. They were now preparing for the climax of their rate-rigging prosecutions: the trial of twelve traders for 'rigging' Euribor. The DOJ had already started its own prosecutions for interest rate 'rigging', trying British and American traders for behaviour that, for now at least, was regarded by the US courts as dishonest and illegal.

15

THE PRICE OF HONESTY

One of the great ironies about the investigations and trials of interest rate 'rigging' is that they were meant to be all about punishing dishonesty. But because of the US system of plea bargaining, they were littered with confessions of dishonesty which were themselves dishonest.

The huge carrot of no jail time if you pleaded guilty and 'cooperated', combined with the giant stick of up to thirty years in an American jail if you went to trial, led many defendants to go along with the US Department of Justice narrative, which now appeared to be set in stone. That narrative said any attempt to influence Libor for commercial reasons was 'manipulation'. To secure the DOJ's recommendation to the court of 'no jail', you had to declare that it was wrong to make or accept a trader request and that you knew it at the time. Forget about whether that was true or not. Making a confession and reinforcing the DOJ view in a sworn statement was the only way out of it. By pleading guilty, you would have a stain on your record, a criminal conviction in the USA. But what did that matter compared to keeping your freedom, keeping your house, keeping your family together?

To most traders who found themselves in the DOJ's sights, so alarming was the US justice system, where more than 90 per cent of prosecutions resulted in a conviction, that to reject the carrot and ignore the stick for the sake of telling the truth was too frightening a prospect. To take a stand and say, 'I'm not going to lie. I didn't think I was doing anything wrong', you had to have guts enough to tell the DOJ prosecutors something they didn't want to hear, disregarding all the risks that went with it. It meant that the traders who rejected the plea-bargain offer were the ones who cared most about not lying, almost to the point of recklessness. The twisted result was that those who ended up on trial for fraud were not the most dishonest, but the polar opposite.

It was around seven in the morning when he was on his normal commuter train from Leigh-on-Sea, Essex to London that former Rabobank trader Tony Conti's phone started buzzing with calls and texts from friends in Singapore, where he'd worked years before. On 16 October 2014, they were at their desks watching the front page of the websites of newswires such as Reuters and Bloomberg. 'Tony, you're all over the newswires. You've been indicted,' said his friend as he read the Reuters article. 'You've been charged with fraud by the US Department of Justice. The article says, "Two Rabobank traders have been charged with manipulating Libor [...] Anthony Allen and Anthony Conti".'

In that moment on the train, Tony knew that his life had changed forever. Feeling sick to his stomach, he googled to find out more with a growing sense of bewilderment. He kept finding articles with his name in them, sitting there, weirdly, near words like 'fraud' and 'Libor rigging'. 'I went in to work to close my positions down as a good person should do. I called a meeting with the compliance manager there and explained to him that I didn't think I'd done anything wrong, but I had now been charged by the DOJ. So he advised that I should leave and go home.'

But Tony couldn't go home. He spent the next five hours wandering around central London, not stopping, not calling anyone, just struggling to comprehend it. 'I mean this is weird shit. It's the magnitude of it that you can't get your head round. I've never worked in America, but I've literally just been charged by the American government! I was just saying to myself, "Why? Why me? I don't get this." I was saying it to myself again and again, on repeat, "I don't understand this, I don't understand this." And you're thinking that you're involved in something that's way, way above your pay grade. I was like, "I'm a nobody! I'm just a normal trader, from fucking Essex, going into work on the train. And now I'm on the world stage because the US Department of Justice is charging me with fraud? It doesn't make sense!"'

Tony couldn't bring himself to pick up the phone to his wife Lisa, who was at home looking after their two young daughters and 5-month-old baby son. As soon as he did, it would make the whole thing real; and it would enter her life as well as his. He wanted to give her just a few hours more of something like normality before the shit hit the fan for both of them. He walked and walked, along the Thames embankment and round again across the City's bridges. Stopping for a while on London Bridge he looked out, then looked down. He didn't feel tempted to jump but for the first time he could understand why some people did. It was the sense of being helpless, not in charge of your life. Why was this happening to him? He kept coming back to the same thing. He hadn't put any wrong Libor rates in. 'You're looking for a life jacket to hang on to while you're in the situation and the life jacket was: "I haven't done anything wrong here." So you're hanging on to that, looking desperately for things that are just going to try and keep you afloat and not sink to the bottom of the ocean.' That day, Tony resisted the temptation to escape what was going on through excess alcohol and just kept wandering, aimlessly, trying to adjust to something that was almost impossible to adjust to. Eventually, he steeled himself to call Lisa and break the shattering news and return home. Lisa already knew; she'd worked in banking and her brother still worked in the industry. He'd seen the story on his Bloomberg screen and called her to see if she and Tony were OK.

In the next eight years, Tony would lose his job, his home, his self-confidence and his mental health. He'd be hauled over to the USA to face trial. He'd be forced to sell the family home to pay the legal fees to defend himself. He'd be found guilty, sentenced, then acquitted eighteen months later on a technicality, so he couldn't tell everyone the US courts had found that he'd done nothing wrong. With his family struggling financially, they'd have to move five times from rented home to rented home. He'd try and fail to find work, suffering severe anxiety and depression from the continual stress. He'd spend years fighting for compensation. He'd never go to prison, but it was still an eight-year sentence.

Every morning as he woke up, every night as he went to bed, he couldn't get it out of his head. Barely a waking hour went by when his thoughts weren't dominated by it. 'It's the injustice of it that I just can't cope with. It's always there. That's where I am really. I can't just get over that hump of what's happened. You just feel like a complete scapegoat: that you are being blamed for everything. It's a really lonely feeling. No one gets it; no one gets you. A lot of people thought, "But you've got the not guilty decision. You should just now be able to flip back." But it's too late; the damage is done. I don't know if it'll ever get better.

'I've changed as a person, really, since this happened,' he told me.[1] 'Everything changes inside. I'm a much more hardened, less trusting individual now after what's happened, compared to what I was before. I was pretty happy-go-lucky. I was a very sociable person. I wasn't necessarily the life and soul of the party every time, but I was always a fun person to be around, constantly joking and having a laugh. Now there's still an effect unfortunately, that I don't really like going out on big social events. I feel uncomfortable, I get a bit anxious, because I have been decimated inside. Like – obliterated. My nerves are shot to pieces. From a life-living perspective, you're just tolerating life. You're not actually enjoying it. I know that's a terrible thing to say. I mean, life should be, you know, highs and lows and I get that; you should garner enjoyment out of things. But inside I'm just kind of ... black. I'm just dark. I wasn't like that before; it wasn't like that. You're just constantly shaking your head going, "I actually can't believe what happened."'

Tony Conti was put on trial by the United States Department of Justice because he refused to lie. To him, it was an easy decision because it just wasn't how he'd been brought up. Born in Islington, north London, to an English mum and a dad from the second generation of a family of Italian immigrants, Tony grew up in a council flat and went to a Catholic school in Holland Park. Tall and slim with dark hair, high cheek bones and a habitually humorous attitude, he left school in the mid-1980s aged 16, starting work soon after at Lloyds Bank in Kentish Town. At 18, he moved on to international banks in the City and later got his first job as a cash trader at Bank of Ireland aged 21. Discovering he was good at spotting money-making opportunities, he started to win a reputation and by the age of 30 was taken on by the Dutch giant, Rabobank. There he met Lisa, who worked in the back office sorting out the paperwork that went with the trades. 'He was very confident, very good at what he did but always very down to earth,' she said. 'Never flash cars – nothing showy-offy. Very humble – just a normal guy – but very kind. I think most people would say he's a really nice guy. Very honest. He's the sort of guy who would never even dream of parking on a double-yellow line. I'm the complete opposite. If I want something at the shop, I'll just park up and nip in – he would never do something like that, he's such a stickler for rules.'

In the early noughties he was assigned to work in the bank's office in Singapore and Lisa joined him. Almost as soon as they arrived there, Tony had a cancer scare. Lisa supported him as he went through the operation and post-op recovery. 'She was amazing. It's not why I proposed, but I did propose soon afterwards,' he said.

Tony got on well with the close-knit team of traders on the cash desk at Rabobank who'd become very close friends. 'I loved working there. We'd go out together and we'd spend so much time together, we got to know each other's lives. We'd be humorous about the work and joke all the time. I mean, I considered these people to be kind of like, you know, not brothers, but the next level down. I trusted them implicitly.' When Lisa and Tony got married in 2004, they invited many of the team of friends and colleagues to their wedding to celebrate. In among their photos are images of some of their friends back then at Rabobank, including one, Paul Robson, who'd play an unexpected role in their family's future.

Tony thrived in his job. Before the credit crunch had turned into a full-blown banking crisis, he set up trades that would benefit from a deeper downturn – and made big money when the crisis came. In 2009, when Rabobank decided to move its cash trading to the Netherlands, Tony had to find other work in order to stay in England and was hired to do a similar job at the London branch of a German bank, Landesbank Baden-Württemberg.

It wasn't until 2012 that the Libor scandal started to intrude on his life. Rabobank was being investigated by the DOJ. Because, like PJ or Jon Mathew, he was the cash trader who submitted the bank's Libor rates, the bank and its lawyers wanted his help understanding how it all worked. Tony wasn't a target of the investigation, he was assured, but just a witness of fact. 'I tried to explain: this is the way it was done. There was a range of rates. So, you know, when someone says high or low, they're not asking me to do anything wrong. They're asking me to just to go up and down in the range.'

It wasn't obvious the message was getting through.

Eighteen months later, he was contacted by the law firm Baker McKenzie, working for Rabobank. The Department of Justice and Financial Conduct Authority[2] were investigating Libor. Could he help, not as a target, but as a witness? Tony agreed to help and then spent three months going through a vast quantity of Libor-related documents, painstakingly explaining them to the lawyers ahead of a voluntary interview he'd give to the DOJ and the FCA in January 2014. When it came time for the interview, though, it felt more like an interrogation. Again, Tony tried to tell the FBI, the DOJ and the FCA: there was a range of rates on offer for cash that were all correct answers to the Libor question, 'At what interest rate could you borrow?' So, if swaps traders were asking for a high or low number, it was within that range of accurate rates. That didn't mean it was corrupt. 'I tried to explain the procedure to them. But they already knew the procedure. They'd already heard it from other people. They just didn't want to accept it.' By now the DOJ, the FBI and the FCA were heavily invested in the story that making or accepting any trader requests was wrong and they weren't about to be deflected.

Then in the summer of 2014, Tony heard from one of the lawyers at Baker McKenzie who, at Rabobank's expense, was representing him. The DOJ were desperate to charge his former boss, Tony Allen, who'd been the head of the desk. They wanted Tony Conti to become a prosecution witness against him. The story they were looking to prove was that his former boss was the one who was in charge, pulling the strings in the fraud conspiracy they wanted to prosecute. It would require him to plead guilty. But if he cooperated, the DOJ dangled the prospect that Tony would avoid prison and instead wear a tag at home for six months.

It was the same no-win situation all the traders prosecuted by the DOJ were put in. If he pleaded guilty and wore a tag, he'd still have a conviction and lose his job. But they'd be able to stay in their family home. He'd probably have his flights and hotel paid for if he went to New York to testify against his old boss. Three of his former colleagues – Paul Robson and Lee Stewart from the London office, and Takayuki Yagami from Tokyo – had already decided to plead guilty. But for Tony, there was an issue with that. The DOJ wanted him to say two things. One: that making or accepting a trader request for high or low Libor rates was wrong and that he knew it at the time. Two: that his former boss was orchestrating a criminal fraud conspiracy. The problem for Tony was that both of those statements were simply untrue. To him it was clear that the DOJ was asking him to lie – to give false witness and dump on his former boss to save his own skin.

'This is the bizarre bit. We're supposed to be talking about the honesty of people. I can't be any more honest than telling them that I'm not going to lie!' Tony laughs. It would have been easier for him to follow the DOJ's narrative and take the 'no prison if you cooperate' option. 'But it wasn't the truthful option, so I wasn't prepared to do it. And that's the insane bit, when you're on a fraud charge and you're actually more honest than the other guys. What the DOJ said – their narrative – is not how it happened. Yet they got people to do it, because those people weighed up: "Well, if I fight, I'm gonna lose my house, I'm probably going to go to jail if I lose" – that sort of thing. People weigh it up, and I kind of understand why they do it. But I don't really understand how they look at themselves in the mirror.

'For my honesty "beacon", I couldn't plead guilty and become a prosecuting witness, because you had to say under oath that back in the day – 2006, 2007, 2008 – you knew it was wrong. And that was just all bullshit. All those people that said they knew it was wrong at the time are lying. The "honest"and "dishonest" bit was all round the wrong way.'

Tony and Lisa talked about it, but it wasn't a long discussion. Telling a lie in court to get out of something – so someone else could go to jail? That wasn't the sort of person he was. 'It was pretty much that easy. It wasn't true! I mean, I'm talking to the Department of Justice, the FBI – the guardians of the free world, the moral compass of the United States of America – and they're asking me to just make shit up? It wasn't … it just wasn't right.'

A year later, in October 2015, Tony and Lisa left their three children Mia, Lilly and Sam with Lisa's parents and flew to New York, where they'd rented a flat on Airbnb ahead of the trial at the Federal District Court in lower Manhattan. They'd already had to sell their one asset, their family home, and move into rented accommodation to afford the large and mounting legal bills for Tony's defence. The DOJ made it clear, the offer to Tony to plead guilty in exchange for no prison would be there right up until the trial began. 'Their number one option was for Tony to plead guilty and say that Tony Allen told him to do what he'd done. And then he would have six months on a tag in the UK,' Lisa said. 'They were bargaining with us, saying, "What would it take, for you to plead guilty? And to admit that Tony Allen told you to do it?" They said to us, "If you plea bargain with us, you'll get nothing." Every one of our friends was saying to us, "You're crazy. Why are you not taking this? Why are you not plea bargaining?" In our eyes, it was never an option. I just wouldn't do that to somebody. Tony Allen has young children, same as us. It wasn't anything to do with friendship – that wasn't the number one factor. It was the fact that he hadn't done any of that. And it was all a lie.'

When Tony joined his former boss Tony Allen in the dock in a New York courtroom in lower Manhattan, they'd both been warned by their lawyers they didn't have much chance at trial. US juries rarely acquit. The accusation against them was that they'd committed 'wire fraud'[13] by obtaining or making false statements, meaning their Libor estimates of the cost of borrowing cash. Their lawyers argued that the rates were accurate because they were 'high' or 'low' within the range of rates being offered on the market that day. The DOJ offered no evidence that the rates Tony had put in were inaccurate. Instead, they said it didn't *matter* if they were accurate or not. The judge at their trial, Jed Rakoff,[4] supported that, telling jurors the relevant issue was not the accuracy of Tony's interest rate estimates of what it would cost to borrow cash, but the intent. Like the British courts, the US courts were relieving the prosecution of any need to prove the fundamental wrongdoing in a fraud case – the making of a false statement. Like the British courts, they were creating a whole new theory of what a fraud was. Once again, a cash trader who'd put in accurate Libor rates could go to jail, and an accurate rate could become fraudulent – just because a swaps trader had asked for it.

'The judge directed the jury that it didn't matter if the rates were accurate, it's the conspiracy – meaning if you say "yes" on an email, it didn't matter if the rates were right. That blew my mind. At that moment I thought, "I'm going to be found guilty now!"' Tony said, laughing. 'My simple view of fraud is that you have to make a false statement or say something misleading. But the judge was actually saying to the jury it doesn't matter about the number, you don't have to think about that! Just: did they conspire? Well – yes, of course, if there's an email and someone says, "yes" then in your world, that's us conspiring. That's why we could never win the trial. It was impossible to win the trial.'

Tony and Lisa's one-time friends and colleagues Paul Robson and Lee Stewart each stepped up to the witness stand and testified that they had known it was wrong at the time to make or accept a request for high or low Libor rates.[5] Robson implicated Tony Allen, as required by the DOJ as a condition of his plea deal. 'Paul Robson walked past us in court and he couldn't even look at us,' Lisa said. DOJ prosecutor Carol Sipperly tore into Tony. He was accused of cheating counterparties in the market, though the DOJ could not demonstrate how or when those counterparties lost money, or who they were, or how much they'd lost, or how much Tony had supposedly gained, or whether any of his submissions after a request had shifted the Libor average, even by a thousandth of a percentage point.

I spoke to Tony first in 2016 after his conviction and again in the summer of 2021. Since Tony had been charged in October 2014 and lost his job as a result, he'd seen a lot more of Lilly and Mia, and especially Sam, who was now 17 months old. The silver lining of the forbidding dark cloud that was his predicament was that he'd been able to grow close to his baby son and spend a lot more time with the girls. But now Tony feared he might be forced to be away from them for a decade or more. From the Airbnb, he made a video call to his parents-in-law where his children were staying. 'And I remember seeing Sam in the lap of my father-in-law. And that just broke me,' said Tony quietly, pausing to try and compose himself as his voice faltered. 'Because I didn't know if I was coming home or not.'

In three weeks, the trial was over. On 5 November, the jury pronounced Tony Conti and Tony Allen guilty. Lisa, who'd flown out for the end of the trial with her best friend for support, felt the shock physically. 'I remember getting into the lift and I couldn't hear anything. My eyes were fuzzy. It was obviously like a sort of a panic attack. My legs were like jelly. I was saying to my friend in the lift, "I can't hear anything." I just had ringing in my ears. That was horrible.'

The DOJ pressed the court to sentence Tony to ten to fifteen years in a US prison. Judge Rakoff gave a much lighter sentence – one year for Tony Conti and two for Tony Allen – and suspended the sentences for Tony and his former boss while they took the case to appeal. That meant he could return home while they waited the months it would take for that to happen. But his career was over with no chance of getting it back. No one was going to hire him to do any job with a conviction for fraud. His daughter Lilly, then 9 years old, burst into tears at school when a classmate said, 'Your dad's going to prison.' Lisa had to see the headmaster to try to explain what was going on. Tony did the school run and helped in the house. At night, when the kids were safely in bed, he'd anaesthetise himself with a bottle of whisky.

In July 2017, a US appeal court overturned the convictions of Tony Conti and Tony Allen. He would no longer face the threat of a US jail. But what should have been a sweet relief left a bitter aftertaste. The one thing both Conti and Allen had really needed was for the court to say they'd done nothing wrong. But that was never addressed. Instead, the case was dismissed on technical grounds. Under the Fifth Amendment of the US constitution, which protects a defendant's right to remain silent, it's a breach of a defendant's rights if evidence which has been compelled is used in criminal proceedings. In a precedent-setting case called *Kastigar v. United States*, the courts had ruled that if any compelled evidence found its way into a criminal trial, it had to be called off. That created problems for cases that had been investigated on both sides of the Atlantic. In the UK, the financial regulator, the Financial Conduct Authority, frequently compelled people to give evidence to its investigations on pain of going to jail. If a witness had read any document based on that compelled evidence, it could 'taint' the witness's evidence and explode the DOJ's efforts to prosecute. Tony Allen's lawyers had discovered that Paul Robson had read compelled testimony. It was only one of a number of complaints they had about the trial, such as the denial of existence of a range, and whether a Libor rate could be fraudulent even if it were accurate. But the US appeal court – in this case, called the 'Second Circuit' – acquitted Tony Conti and Tony Allen on Kastigar grounds. There would be no ruling on the other issues. For the DOJ, it was a big set-back, but it still allowed its next case to go ahead.

For Tony Conti, though, it meant further torment. No one in the courts had said the simple thing he'd been dying for anyone in authority to say: that he'd *done nothing wrong*. That would make it much harder to win compensation and convince anyone he knew that he wasn't a criminal. 'I've met ex-work colleagues who've come up to me and said, like, "Got out of that one, didn't you?" And I'm like – really?'

Without a settled home, Lisa, Tony, Mia, Lilly and Sam kept having to move from one rented home to another. With Tony unable to get work, Lisa had to work full time as he looked after the kids in the daytime. Poor-quality properties and unscrupulous landlords who bumped up their rent meant they couldn't settle down. In four years, they moved home five times, creating a sense of continual upheaval that the kids struggled to adjust to. Tony's hope of being exonerated had disappeared. Anxiety and depression had squashed any sense of hope for the future or enjoyment of the present. As Lisa put it, 'He's really been broken by it. They've just ruined his life.' His attempts to find some mental relief in whisky from the constant thoughts about his case weren't doing him much good. There was something about the Christmas holidays that made it worse. At a party on New Year's Eve, 2018, Tony suffered a full-blown nervous breakdown.

But it wouldn't be until 2022 that Tony would get the biggest kick in the teeth, when the US courts would unexpectedly change their minds about the very thing that had turned his life upside down.

THE PRICE OF DISHONESTY

'You hypocrite, first take the mote out of your own eye, then you will see clearly to remove the speck from your brother's eye.'

(Matthew 7:5)

In the United States District Court for the Southern District of New York, lower Manhattan, Chief Judge Colleen McMahon was furious. A prosecution witness for the US government had just admitted he'd committed perjury, twice, at the direction of a lawyer for Deutsche Bank and a prosecutor for the US Department of Justice. They'd instructed him to make two sworn declarations about the authenticity of documents being used to try and prove the charges against former bankers Matt Connolly and Gavin Black, saying they were original business records from Deutsche Bank. The witness had made it clear to both Deutsche and the DOJ before the trial that they weren't. But they'd nevertheless instructed him to sign the two declarations (also called affidavits). Now, on the witness stand, he'd just acknowledged they were false and that he'd told them so. He'd also pointed to the DOJ lawyer on the front bench of the court who'd given him the instruction.

In her mid-sixties with red hair and a razor-sharp tongue, McMahon, the chief judge in the Southern District of New York, asked the jury to leave, then rounded on the DOJ prosecutors: 'The first one [affidavit] was an outright lie, and you should all be ashamed of yourself for having given it to that man because I know damn well he didn't write it.'

The prosecutor tried to stop her: 'Your Honor—'

'You should be ashamed of yourselves.'

'Your Honor, it was not a lie because there was no intent to deceive—'

McMahon laughed, then cast her eyes heavenwards. 'Oy vey.'

Lead prosecutor Carol Sipperly got up: 'It had the word "copies" in there.'

'Ms. Sipperly, sit down.'

'It had the word "copies".'

'Forgive me if I'm underwhelmed by the government's bona fideness,' said McMahon, now shifting from astonishment to anger. 'I've got to tell you, I am so upset about this affidavit thing. I find it appalling. I find it appalling.'

Matt Connolly, a former supervisor at Deutsche Bank New York from New Jersey, aged 53, and Gavin Black, a 48-year-old former trader at the bank from Twickenham, south-west London, looked on in bewilderment. Surely now, they had to dismiss the case?

Enraged by the prosecutors' behaviour, Black's defence lawyer Seth Levine spent a night without sleep and returned to court the next morning. 'Your Honor, I have an application that in light of what happened yesterday, which I will respectfully say is somewhat beyond my experience, that a government witness claims that he was induced to submit false statements with the assistance of the government, which is what the man said, I—'

'Believe me, I heard what he said,' Judge McMahon interrupted. 'I don't accept any excuses from the front.[1] I don't accept any excuses from him either. He shouldn't have signed it. But it was a lack of intent – I had to laugh when the government said it couldn't be a lie. "Lack of intent." I had to laugh.'

'I move to dismiss this case for prosecutorial misconduct,' said Levine. 'I am not making any judgment about the witness, but the witness said he made false statements. They're sworn statements. Your Honor, this is a case about alleged false statements, although there are really none that have been proven in the case. What has happened here is something that is beyond my experience, and I believe it strikes at the heart of the truth-finding function of our system, and I think, respectfully, and I— This is not an application that I have any interest normally in making. I can't believe this, quite frankly.'

'I'm fairly stupefied by everything that's happened here myself,' said McMahon.[2]

'But, your Honor, I say to you with the enormous respect with which I hold you, this is just wrong … And while I understand what I'm asking for is a dramatic remedy, we've had a lot – we've walked a long road together in this case. This is not the first time we've had this conversation. We've had it about—'

'Twenty times,' interjected Judge McMahon.

It wasn't the first time in the trial that evidence presented by the DOJ had turned out to be false. But McMahon stepped back from doing what you might have thought a judge would do after accusing prosecutors of bringing false evidence to the court. She refused to dismiss the trial.

The incident laid something bare. In an earlier hearing, the DOJ had claimed in court 'the government did not direct Deutsche Bank to conduct an internal investigation'. But months later, evidence emerged showing that in these trials, the US government and the lawyers for the banks were collaborating, hand in glove, and had been doing so for years. In April 2010, Steve Obie[3] at the Commodity Futures Trading Commission had got in touch with Joseph Polizzotto, Deutsche Bank's top lawyer in the USA, requesting that the bank carry out a review of Libor during 2007 to 2008. Polizzotto called a friend, Walter Ricciardi, at the New York law firm Paul Weiss, about conducting a review of Libor for the bank. Over the next five years, Deutsche Bank paid Paul Weiss in the USA and Slaughter & May in the UK to trawl through 158 million electronic documents and conduct nearly 200 interviews of more than fifty bank employees, the transcripts of which it sent straight on to the government. Paul Weiss alone received more than $100 million.[4] The investigation expanded to take in the years 2005 to 2012. Paul Weiss lawyers spoke on the phone to the government 230 times and held thirty meetings in person with DOJ officials. In the last fourteen months of the bank's internal investigation, Paul Weiss held joint 'weekly update calls' to provide the DOJ, CFTC and FBI with the latest developments and afford them an opportunity to 'make new requests'.

It was becoming so obvious that Chief Judge McMahon would rebuke the DOJ for misleading the court when it said it hadn't directed the bank's investigation.[5] Later, months after the jury returned guilty verdicts (and therefore too late for the defendants), she would find that the DOJ had in fact *outsourced* its investigation of interest rate-rigging to Deutsche Bank and Paul Weiss – a firm where McMahon had spent nineteen years of her working life. The DOJ hadn't conducted any interviews of its own, she wrote, unless they had 'first passed through the maw of Paul Weiss's five-year […]

investigative machine and been fully digested for the Government by the target of the investigation. It is hard not to conclude that the Government did not conduct a single interview of its own without first using a road map that Paul Weiss provided – illuminating just how the Government should "investigate" the case against certain Deutsche Bank employees, including Black.'

This pattern wasn't unique to Deutsche Bank. It had happened throughout the Libor investigations and trials. The regulators and prosecutors on both side of the Atlantic – the DOJ, CFTC, SEC, FCA and SFO – all relied almost entirely on the banks' lawyers, funded by the banks, to do their investigation for them. Just as with Barclays, what the bank stood to win in exchange for its 'cooperation' was a non-prosecution agreement that ensured its future survival, and a discount on the inevitable fine. That was known as 'cooperation credit'. But the DOJ's idea of cooperation also came with the expectation that the bank and its lawyers would 'offer up' some real live individuals to be prosecuted.

Evidence emerged in court showing how this outsourcing[6] of a criminal investigation to the target of the prosecution – meaning the bank – could allow the target (or its lawyers) to influence what evidence the prosecution looked at. On 21 January 2015, Paul Weiss was bidding for the maximum discount for Deutsche Bank's 'cooperation', sending a document[7] to the DOJ reviewing its five-year investigation and playing up all the helpful things the bank and its lawyers had done. It was the largest, longest and most expensive internal investigation in the bank's history. Paul Weiss had interacted with the DOJ on 'hundreds of if not thousands of occasions', in writing, by phone and in person. 'Indeed,' said the document, 'we expect that much (if not most) of the information that will ultimately be used in making charging decisions — and that will ultimately form the basis for the DOJ's allegations against the Bank itself — will have come from the Bank's identification of notable communications and its having brought those communications to the DOJ's attention.'

The United States Department of Justice was trusting the target of its investigation to sift and select the information on its behalf – and to direct its attention, fully expecting that the information it supplied would be used to decide whom to prosecute. It revealed a shocking double standard that violated the basic democratic principle of equality before the law. Being a bank wasn't meant to confer any special treatment. Yet if lawyers for Matt

Connolly or Gavin Black had offered to sift the information for the DOJ pros-ecutors, pointing them to what was notable, they'd have got short shrift.

'There are profound implications,' wrote McMahon, 'if the Government, as has been suggested elsewhere, is routinely outsourcing its investigations into complex financial matters to the targets of those investigations, who are in a uniquely coercive position vis-à-vis potential targets of criminal activity.'[8] But again, she wouldn't vacate Matt and Gavin's convictions.

It was coercive because when the traders in all the banks' investiga-tions were interviewed in the early stages by their employer's (or former employer's) lawyers, it looked like a regulatory matter, where the bank was the target, and they were merely witnesses helping the investigation. Where they were employees, they couldn't have refused a request from their bank to be interviewed without jeopardising their jobs. But unbeknownst to them, the lawyers interviewing them might actually be carrying out a criminal investigation for the government which might put them in the dock, robbing them of the protections the US constitution (or the UK crimi-nal law) was supposed to afford. No lawyer present. No caution. No right to remain silent.

In this strange crime scene, Deutsche Bank was the burglar, declaring itself guilty of manipulating Libor. Yet the burglar had been allowed by the US government not only to dust for his own fingerprints, but to supply all the evidence of the crime, name the 'culprits' who were to be thrown under the bus, and line up the witnesses to condemn them.

Naturally, the bank was happier for some people to be in the frame than others. It was undisputed at the trial[9] that Deutsche Bank senior manag-ers, including its global chief executive and co-chairman Anshu Jain,[10] global head of rates Alan Cloete and global head of finance David Nicholls, encouraged derivatives traders and Libor submitters to share information about trading positions, restructuring the bank and its floor plan so the derivatives desk and the cash desk could sit together and share information more easily.

Yet somehow the DOJ hadn't referred to that three years earlier in its offi-cial notice handing Deutsche Bank a record fine.

Had someone senior at Deutsche Bank made it a condition of its deal agree-ing the settlement with the DOJ that it didn't point the finger at the bank's top bosses? Initially, it hadn't planned to let them off lightly. On 31 March

2015, the DOJ's lead prosecutor on the Deutsche Bank Libor case, Jennifer Saulino, had told her colleagues and collaborators at the Financial Conduct Authority, including the lead Deutsche Bank enforcement officer there, Patrick Meaney, that the DOJ was planning to demand a guilty plea from the bank and a $1 billion fine. It had also written a 'relatively strong' piece on senior management. Two weeks later, she shared a draft of it with colleagues at the FCA. In a section titled, 'DB Management Awareness of the Conduct, Tolerance of the Conflicts of Interest and Promotion of Culpable Individuals', it said 'certain DB managers and senior managers' knew about the traders' requests and that they 'recklessly disregarded significant conflicts of interest [such as] encouraging open communications between traders and submitters and seating many of them together in London and in Frankfurt'.

But Deutsche Bank was still negotiating with the DOJ. In the Final Notice, issued on 23 April, the section's title had been toned right down to a bland 'DB Management', losing the damning words that had followed in the section's title in the draft. The reference to 'senior managers', plural, had been taken out. Only one was now identified, David Nicholls, and there was nothing to indicate the top bosses, Anshu Jain and Alan Cloete, were involved. And the damaging phrase saying senior managers 'recklessly disregarded' conflicts of interest had been removed.

Deutsche Bank's shareholders were informed they had to absorb total fines for Libor rigging of $2.5 billion, the highest that had ever been levied. There was a 30 per cent discount for Deutsche Bank for carrying out the DOJ's investigation into itself. Sorry, I meant to say, 'for its cooperation'. The fine, in any case, would be paid by shareholders. No member of senior management would be fined, deregistered or prosecuted. That would only happen to two traders, one of whom had stopped working at Deutsche Bank more than a decade before the trial.

When I first spoke to Matt Connolly in 2019, he'd been found guilty by a New York jury and had just a few months to go before his sentencing hearing. Talking to me, a journalist, was risky at any point but especially at that stage; the judge could retaliate and give him a longer jail sentence. But there was something in Matt that relished the fight. Physically fit for his 53 years, normally seen wearing a short, greying beard and shaven headed with a large forehead he liked to joke about, Matt was already planning to publish a book about his extraordinary experiences. Calling it *Target: A Scapegoat's*

Guide to the Federal Justice System,[11] he didn't mince words. He'd grown up in Warren, New Jersey, in a chaotic Irish Catholic family, where a huge and frightening elder brother had terrorised not only Matt and his six other brothers and sisters but also their parents. 'I was the target of the bullying in the house because I was the fattest, the ugliest and the most docile,' he told me. The young Matt withstood ongoing fat-shaming from his older brother, who'd steal his food. With so many kids in the house, his parents wouldn't always cook meals for them together but would typically leave food out for the kids to help themselves. Cereal, doughnuts, cookies – all Matt's favourite things – would disappear and be hidden away from him. When he came into the TV room, the channel would get changed to snow. When his brother felt like it, he'd pummel him. No one in the family seemed to stand up for him. 'So I've grown up the opposite way of that. Which is, somebody needs to either stand up to the bully or stand up for the people getting bullied, or else it just keeps going on and on and on.' This time, Big Brother was the DOJ. The opportunity to throw a few punches in public by talking to the BBC was one he couldn't resist. 'If I have to face more jail time for getting the truth out there, so be it. Because right now no one realises what's gone on and how bad it is. I can't stay silent.'

That pugnacious attitude, augmented (as he'd tell you straight away) by running every day, playing golf and imbibing 'brown courage' (also known as bourbon), had somehow carried Matt Connolly through the nightmare of being targeted for prosecution by the DOJ. When I asked him about the evidence against him, he started laughing.

'How many emails did they have?' I asked.

'I'll have to check for you. I think it's about a half dozen.'

A few hours later, he called me again. 'Actually, I forgot about this. I don't know why,' he said, laughing again with genuine mirth. 'But I just went back and checked. It's four.'

'Really! They put you on trial for only four emails requesting high or low Libors?'

'Well, no, actually, let me count them.' (Matt liked to tell everyone he was slow-witted.) 'One of them I'm only copied in on.'

'So only three. Only three emails making Libor requests?'

'Well yeah. I know. Fucking hilarious! And also, I didn't actually trade anything linked to Libor. I stayed away from it. I wasn't a trader. I was a supervisor. So these emails were just me passing on requests from other people.'

He sent me the emails, the transcripts of his trial, and all the public documents. I started going through them. It was true. Matt Connolly was being prosecuted as a fraudster over three emails, the most recent of which was no less than twelve years old. Here's what the first of these criminal communications said. Matt Connolly to Mike Curtler and James King, 23 November 2005: *'OTC*[12] *request 3-month LIBOR as high as possible Thursday and Friday if you see the market higher. Thanks.'*

Here's the second damning email chain, from five days later. Mike Curtler to Matt Connolly: *'1 mth over the turn is looking like 26–32 hahaha – anything either way from you guys? We are still short.'*

Matt Connolly, 28 November 2005: *'Hahahah never fails. We would prefer it higher. We have about 15 BB 1 mo receives.*[13] *Thanks. Just asking is very much appreciated ...'*

Mike Curtler: *'will do like James then – ask, and do the opposite ... let us know the days you rec, first fix tom will set the tone.'*

And here's the third email. Matt Connolly to Mike Curtler and James King, 12 August 2007: *'If possible, we need in NY 1 mo libor as low as possible next few days ... tons of pays coming up overall ... thanks!'*

The DOJ was especially keen on the second email chain. You could tell from the way the criminals laughed that they were up to no good. True, it did look like the Libor submitter in London was joking about how his colleague habitually did the opposite of what the New York guys wanted, which didn't really support the idea that they were conspiring in a fraud to make money for the swaps traders. But the DOJ weren't going to let that put them off.

If you looked further down the first email chain, you saw the reason why he was joking about that. On the morning of 24 November 2005 at 6.18 a.m. London time, James King on the London cash desk replied: *'Matt, we've gone in relatively neutral as a high 3s doesn't suit London at the moment. Hope that's ok. James.'*

Bummer. He'd asked for 'as high as possible' and they'd gone neutral because it didn't suit London to go high. In this criminal conspiracy, that must have made Matt Connolly feel thwarted. In which case, his reply was remarkably sanguine. *'Doesn't matter to me,'* he wrote back at 13.01, London time, 8.01 a.m. in New York. *'May matter to OTC/rates NY ... we will all find out I guess.'*

OTC stands for 'over the counter'. Because there was no regulated exchange for trading swaps and other derivatives, they were bought and sold direct between banks – transactions known as 'over the counter' trades. That was the main desk for trading swaps in Deutsche Bank New York. But there was a problem for the theory that Matt was acting out of greed. The OTC desk was nothing to do with the desk he supervised, so even if the request had been accommodated, there was no way he could have made money from any hoped-for shift in the Libor average.

Adding it up, that made one email where the Libor submitter had rejected Matt's request; and another where he couldn't possibly have made money. In the case of the third, when you looked back at the published Libor submission on that day, Deutsche Bank had been an outlier. Its submission would have been excluded and therefore couldn't possibly have affected the Libor average.

Keep in mind all that evidence against him as you read these words from the opening speech to his trial by the DOJ's lead trial prosecutor, Alison Anderson: 'Good morning, ladies and gentlemen. Ker-ching. You know what that sound is, right? The sound of making money. Ker-ching. In the words of the defendant Gavin Black, he tells you what his and the defendant Matt Connolly's crime was all about, and it was all about making every extra dollar that they could. And in their quest to make every extra dollar that they could to push their profits to the max, you're going to learn that they cheated. They cheated by rigging the Libor interest rate, which you're going to learn is a very important interest rate for the global economy. They were bankers in New York and in London that you will see were so greedy that they abused their bank's inside role in determining that interest rate; so greedy that they did this despite the fact that they knew that interest rate served as a basis for millions of financial products and trades throughout the entire world; and so greedy that they did it just to make more money – more money for their bank and in turn more money for themselves. And you will see that in doing this, they cheated businesses and defrauded businesses around the world, right here in the United States and right here in New York.'

As with all the other cases, the DOJ couldn't name the businesses that had been 'defrauded'. And they couldn't identify any gains for the 'cheats'.

They couldn't show any instances where their requests had succeeded in shifting the Libor average. Nor did they have any data to link any of either Gavin or Matt's Libor requests to the trades that were supposed to be motivating them to do evil. These were unnecessary details, because the DOJ had cooperators. 'You're also going to hear from three of the defendants' accomplices, three bankers who worked at Deutsche Bank and sat right next to the defendants day in and day out, working at Deutsche Bank. And they are going to give you an inside view, as only insiders can, as to what the defendants and their co-conspirators were thinking and doing at the time of the fraud.'

The others on these supposedly damning email chains had all decided to cooperate and become prosecution witnesses. James King, a Libor submitter on the Deutsche Bank cash desk in London, was not charged with any crime and was offered a non-prosecution agreement in exchange for his cooperation. James King's immediate boss in London, Mike Curtler, and Tim Parietti, formerly of Deutsche Bank New York, both pleaded guilty[14] and neither received any jail time. The odd thing was that there was much more evidence against the prosecution witnesses, who'd decided to plead guilty and cooperate with the DOJ, than there was against Matt. The more evidence against you there was (emails requesting high or low Libors or accepting those requests), the less chance you'd have at trial, meaning it was all the more appealing to avoid a trial and strike a plea bargain. The incentives were so strong that defendants against whom the evidence seemed most damning were keener than anyone to cooperate. In the scramble to plead guilty, the only ones left in the dock in the rate-rigging trials had two criminal attributes in common. One: they refused to be bullied. Two: they didn't like lying.

For any banks' lawyers doing the Department of Justice's or Serious Fraud Office's investigation for them, the ideal banker to be 'offered up' was one who no longer worked for their bank, and who preferably also knew nothing that might implicate senior management. Matt Connolly fitted the bill. He'd left Deutsche Bank way back in March 2008. Having been director of the pool trading desk, he had a supervisor role. That made it look like they were getting someone senior, rather than allowing the buck to stop at the bottom. But the demands of the plea-bargaining process had left the DOJ with a strange sort of case. The guys in the dock had never met before.

Like some of the Barclays defendants, the international fraud conspirators Gavin Black and Matt Connolly met for the first time at court in the run-up to the trial. But with them, the weirdness was even deeper. They'd never spoken on the phone. They hadn't even exchanged a single email person to person. The international fraud conspirators simply didn't know each other.

James King, Mike Curtler and Tim Parietti each took the witness stand. They'd all initially said they didn't think what they were doing by making or accepting trader requests was wrong. But faced with the DOJ's sink-or-swim dilemma, they'd all changed their minds. It was wrong, apparently, and they knew it at the time. They just hadn't told the truth before the DOJ came along to help them refresh their memories. Following the DOJ incentives, though, had its downsides. The DOJ got its pound of flesh for its recommendation of no jail time, which entailed the defendants spending hundreds of hours working with the DOJ and learning exactly what was required of them. And for all your hard work 'cooperating', you might be embarrassed on the witness stand by a defence lawyer with a gift for satire who was trying to show the jury what was really going on:

'Mr Curtler,' said Levine. 'Life is fleeting, and I'm going to give you an opportunity now. Would you like to tell this jury that you have been lying throughout your direct testimony so we can move on with this matter?'

'Objection. Argumentative,' said Alison Anderson for the DOJ.

'The objection is sustained,' said Judge McMahon.

'So, Mr Curtler,' resumed Levine, 'you are a criminal. Is that right?'

'I am, yes.'

'You are in fact the leader of an international conspiracy that spanned the continents for many, many years. Is that right?'

'No.'

'No?'

'No.'

'I see. Well, I noticed in your testimony you used the word "we" when you talked about Libor submissions. Do you remember that?'

'Yes.'

'Did you supervise the US dollar Libor submissions?'

'Yes.'

'And you did it as part of your leadership, your supervision of this vast criminal conspiracy, right?'

'No.'

'There was no criminal conspiracy?'

'Yes, there was.'

'It wasn't vast?'

'It was vast, yes.'

Levine then wanted to know[15] not how big the conspiracy was, but how long it lasted. 'Now, when is it exactly that you say your criminal conspiracy came to an end? What's the date?'

'Objection,' interjected Alison Anderson. 'Calls for a legal conclusion.'

'Overruled. Overruled,' said Judge McMahon.

'When the investigation started,' answered Curtler.

'OK,' said Levine. 'Now, we saw an email from— The government put up something about the SEC [Securities and Exchange Commission] started investigating in 2008. So it stopped in 2008?'

'No.'

'I thought you said when the investigation started.'

'At Deutsche Bank.'

'Oh, so that's what, 2010?'

'Yes.'

'That's when it stops?'

'Yes.'

'A hundred per cent?'

'Yeah, I believe so. Yes.'

'You "believe so" or— I mean, have you been involved in other criminal conspiracies?'

'No.'

'So, your first criminal conspiracy is always the most memorable, isn't it?'

'I don't know. Yes.'

'So you probably know when it started and when it ended, huh?'

'No.'

'"No." So you were just sort of walking down the street one day, and you just realised, hey, I'm in a criminal conspiracy. Is that how it went?'

'No.'

Occasionally, when there was a lively exchange, members of the jury would look up. But one juror spent a lot of time picking at his shoes. They weren't all picking up the irony in Seth Levine's tone, which should have led them straight to a conclusion. This criminal fraud conspiracy the prosecution witnesses were confessing to was, to put it politely, made up.

There was one more email chain used to condemn Matt. This time it was a request from someone working for him, a trader called Tim Parietti, who'd got in touch with the junior Libor submitter on the London cash desk, James King, copying in Matt: *'Regarding Mondays 3m Libor, MMD NY [the money markets desk in New York] is receiving 3mL on USD 6.5 billion so hoping for a higher 3mL.'*

Parietti would testify that Matt Connolly had instructed him to make Libor requests, saying 'Start sending requests to London. Tell them what your positions are. They're going to do what they're going to do.' Or again, 'I'm tired of all this Libor BS. Here is what we're going to do. You have a big fix position in Libor. Send an email to the cash guys in London. Let them know which way around, how much you have, and then just let them do whatever they do, that's it.'

Matt had been friendly with Tim Parietti, a trader a few years younger than Matt whom he'd supervised. For years they'd car-shared to commute into Manhattan from Basking Ridge, New Jersey. Since Matt had left Deutsche Bank in March 2008, every year or so he'd get together with Parietti and a few other former colleagues for, as Matt put it, 'a beer or ten'. In early 2013, they'd met up one-on-one for the first time in The Station pub in Bernardsville, New Jersey, not far from where they both lived. Matt had heard about the Libor investigation and that Deutsche Bank had let Parietti go and asked him out for a drink. He didn't feel worried about it on his own account. At Deutsche Bank, Matt had sensed early on there was something wrong with Libor and he'd done his best to ensure his team had as little as possible to do with it. He felt some responsibility for Parietti, though, and wanted to make sure he was OK and that the bank had let him go on good terms so he could keep his career. As they drank, Parietti told Matt a lot about the emails he'd sent requesting moves in Libor that Matt had suggested he'd send. Matt tried to reassure him, saying he was sorry he had to deal with it, but he shouldn't worry about the emails because it was Deutsche Bank's policy. The top bosses had repeatedly said they wanted swaps traders to communicate their trading positions to the cash desk in London. If he was asked about the Libor requests, Matt said, he could simply be honest about what they did – since the emails were no issue. Not once did Matt imagine that Parietti might be looking for him to say something to incriminate himself. Nor did he dream that he himself could be lined up for prosecution, or that Parietti would testify against him. Yet five years later, that's what happened.

Tim Parietti had an even stronger incentive to cooperate with the DOJ than most. The DOJ initially planned to charge him with participating in a fraud conspiracy that ran from 2005 to 2011. The problem for him was that he'd collected a bonus of $9 million in 2009. If he pleaded guilty to a conspiracy lasting until 2011, he might lose some or all of it in 'forfeiture' proceedings. Later, in cross-examination of Parietti at the trial, Matt's lawyer Ken Breen exposed how far the DOJ was prepared to go to ensure it had his cooperation.

On 26 May 2016, Parietti went to the New York court to plead guilty before District Judge Paul Engelmayer. There, in front of his own team of lawyers and the team of prosecutors from the DOJ he read an 'allocution' – the confession document that goes with a guilty plea in the USA – where the duration of his professed criminal activity was much shorter. It confessed to asking Libor submitters to take his trading positions into account from 'early 2006 through approximately 2008'. The moment he read that phrase, there was a commotion in court. The DOJ needed to talk, immediately, about the time range he'd confessed to. Lead prosecutor Carol Sipperly and the rest of the DOJ team had a hasty discussion with Parietti's lawyers.[16] He'd need to make a clarification. When the lawyers had settled down and everyone was back in their seats, Parietti stood up. 'Your Honor, I would like to clarify. Earlier I had said that the practice I engaged in occurred from early 2006 through *approximately* 2008, and I should have said *at least* 2008.'

As he'd later accept on the witness stand,[17] Parietti wanted the shorter time frame so he could keep his $9 million. But the prosecutors needed the conspiracy they were seeking to prove to last longer than that. They had in mind that at the trial, he'd testify to a conspiracy through to 2010. By saying 'at least' 2008, he could still give evidence of a time frame beyond what he'd confessed to. The incident showed something that Matt and his lawyers found deeply disturbing. The DOJ had done a 'side deal' that wasn't mentioned in the cooperation agreement being examined by the judge.[18] At the plea hearing, Judge Engelmayer was given no idea about it. The DOJ had agreed a deal giving a confessed criminal a $9 million benefit for cooperating[19] and had kept it from the judge who sentenced him. But there were no consequences for the DOJ prosecutors.

In these criminal proceedings that were supposed to be all about the dishonesty of the defendants, it was not the alleged 'fraudsters' who kept getting accused by the judge of making false or misleading statements to the court. It was the US Department of Justice. Months before the trial, in July 2017, Gavin Black's defence team had sought a Kastigar hearing to dismiss the whole prosecution on the grounds that compelled testimony had been used. Gavin had given a compelled interview to the FCA ahead of its regulatory notice. If the DOJ prosecutors or any of its witnesses had seen that interview transcript, or any other compelled evidence, it would taint the trial. Knowing what had just happened in the appeal of Tony Conti and Tony Allen, the DOJ prosecutors were desperate to prevent the same thing happening twice. By now, the DOJ had spent eight years investigating Libor and failed to lock up a single banker. For an organisation that judged its success on how many convictions it secured, it wasn't looking good. As Levine pressed for a Kastigar hearing, they pulled out all the stops to prevent it. The court had to be assured that no compelled testimony had tainted the DOJ's investigation and prosecution of Gavin Black.

The lawyer who led the DOJ team investigating Deutsche Bank's Libor submissions, Jennifer Saulino, had been in regular contact for years with the senior official at the FCA in the UK who was leading its investigation into Deutsche Bank's Libor 'rigging', Patrick Meaney. In his forties, a little overweight, bald and habitually wearing a trimmed dark beard on his chin and upper lip but not his cheeks, Meaney was a career regulator who'd been pursuing the 'rigging' of Libor since he joined the FCA's predecessor, the Financial Services Authority, in 2011. He'd been there at the interviews Tom Hayes gave to the SFO in 2013. He'd overseen the process as cash traders from RBS tried to resist being ousted from the industry for making or accepting a Libor request. Now he was pitching in to help the DOJ keep the show on the road in the USA.

At the DOJ's request, on 30 August 2017, Patrick Meaney wrote a letter to the DOJ in his capacity as a senior enforcement official at the FCA, avowing that there had been no instance where testimony compelled by the FCA had been shared with the DOJ. In paragraph 6 of the letter, Mr Meaney wrote: 'The FCA did not share any information obtained or derived from any compelled interview, including Mr Black, with the DoJ.' The letter also said: 'The FCA did not provide copies of its draft or actual Warning, Decision or Final Notices in respect of Deutsche Bank to the DoJ or the Commodity Futures Trading Commission ("CFTC").'

Neither statement was true. But no one on the defence teams knew that yet. At that point, the evidence that would show those statements to be false or misleading was available to both Meaney and the DOJ on their email records but not to the defence, or the judge. The next day, 31 August, the DOJ used Patrick Meaney's letter to push back, saying a Kastigar hearing was unnecessary. In November 2017, after Colleen McMahon set a date of 13 December for a Kastigar hearing, more stops were pulled out.

On 15 November, in an interview with the FBI, Meaney repeated the key point that 'the FCA did not share any information related to compelled testimony during the Libor investigation with any individual organisation other than DB's defense council'. But he also told the FBI about an email he'd sent to Jennifer Saulino on 21 April 2015 at 10.13 a.m. discussing compelled testimony. The DOJ didn't disclose it to the defence ahead of the December hearing.

On 6 December, Saulino filed a sworn declaration. It said neither she nor anyone else on her team had attended Gavin Black's compelled interview. But it didn't disclose that she'd asked the FCA if she could attend other compelled interviews (which might have contradicted what Patrick Meaney had said), or that she had been a recipient of sections of the FCA draft notice accompanying its fine, which was based largely on compelled testimony.

It wasn't until the morning of a second Kastigar hearing on 24 April 2018, over four months later, that crucial exhibits were handed to the defence after they'd spotted some emails were missing from the evidence disclosed to them (apparently, the DOJ told them, due to a 'technical error'). They flatly contradicted the statement the FCA had given to the DOJ seven months before – that it hadn't shared any information from any compelled interview with the DOJ.

The newly disclosed evidence included an email chain Mr Meaney was copied into in February to March 2015, showing the FCA had indeed shared a portion of its Final Notice fining Deutsche Bank for Libor rigging with the CFTC. The email chain showed that sections to be forwarded to the DOJ contained compelled testimony. They were then forwarded to Jennifer Saulino.

It also included the email from Meaney to Saulino sent on 21 April 2015 at 10.13 a.m. It revealed that Meaney had told Saulino by email that the FCA's entire Final Notice was riddled with compelled testimony. 'It would be very difficult to identify parts that weren't influenced by compelled testimony and even if we could, it would be such a small part that it would make the Notice meaningless.'

Shown the emails in court, an FCA official on the Deutsche Bank Libor investigation accepted the statements in Mr Meaney's August 2017 letter were false.

Judge McMahon had been angry about it too. She didn't throw the case out then, either.

The emails that contradicted the claims in Meaney's letter were available to both the FCA and the DOJ on their email records at the time the statements were put into court. No one at either agency, it seemed, had checked their email records before giving false written assurances to be used in criminal proceedings.

When the BBC published an article reporting this, we asked Patrick Meaney if he'd checked his emails before sending the 30 August letter to the DOJ. He said through his lawyers that he hadn't, saying it was a mistake that had been corrected in a declaration to the court in December 2017. The FCA nevertheless felt compelled to write to the DOJ to correct the record in May 2018.

'This was supposed to be a trial all about dishonesty,' said Matt. 'The allegation was that we'd made false statements, even though they couldn't prove we made any. But the prosecutors kept using false evidence. The judge would get mad and say stuff but, in the end, it was just words. By the end of the trial, we had pages and pages of prosecutor misconduct. But there were no consequences for them. Fucking zero. They have blanket immunity.'

Matt's lawyer Ken Breen and Gavin Black's lawyer Seth Levine fought as hard as they could to get the trial thrown out. The government's theory of the 'crime' didn't make sense, said Levine. The cash traders who submitted the Libor rates, Mike Curtler and James King, also traded derivatives linked to Libor themselves.

'The government has charged Mr Black with a crime. And the crime is that because he's a derivatives trader, he shouldn't be influencing the Libor submission; he shouldn't be saying his trading positions, because the setters can't hear that, right?' said Levine. 'Well, wait a second. The government's theory is that you need to separate the derivatives traders from the setters, right? That's why this is bad. Mr Curtler and Mr King trade derivatives, the same products Gavin Black trades. So what are we talking about here? As the government said, every day you put down your coffee and you sit at your desk and you think, what should I set Libor at? Okay. But I can't hear about these derivatives trades, because that's going to do something bad, right? Well, wait a second. Those derivatives trades are in my head too. Because I trade them with Mr Curtler, just like Mr Black. So I've got my Libor submission job and I've got my derivatives traders' trading positions in the same head at the same time. What are these guys supposed to do, cut their head in half? Divide their mind? Of course not. That's ridiculous.'

But that was what the crime of 'Libor manipulation' was. To avoid committing it, a cash trader had to banish any thought of their bank's trading positions when estimating the cost to their bank of borrowing cash. Otherwise, they'd be guilty of a thought crime called 'rigging' Libor.

Matt Connolly and Gavin Black's legal teams had exposed prosecutor misconduct, presented evidence of violations of the US constitution, proved to the judge that the DOJ was doing a side deal so a prosecution witness could keep $9 million. But Colleen McMahon still wasn't ready to dismiss the trial. On 17 October 2018, the members of the jury, who hadn't seemed too interested in all their efforts (perhaps not fully understanding what was being said), did what most juries in the USA do. They took the government's word for it that these bankers were criminals and found them guilty.

Matt and Gavin were allowed bail, pending the judge's decision on Seth Levine's motion to throw out the case on grounds of prosecutorial misconduct. Sentencing wouldn't come until months later. On 2 May 2019, Chief Judge Colleen McMahon delivered her decision. In Matt's household, it was his daughter's birthday. The number two lawyer on his team, Phara Guberman, got in touch to say they'd just have to fight on to the US appeals court covering New York state, the Second Circuit. McMahon had dismissed their attempt to get the trial thrown out.

It was, in Matt's words, 'a kick in the nuts'.

'That was an ugly night. I was seriously shocked. I really thought we had a pretty good chance of getting our convictions overturned or a new trial and instead it was the exact opposite. Then this decision came out and it was like it was written by a different human being from the judge who was at my trial. All of a sudden, it was saying totally opposite things from what she'd said all trial long. She was now saying, "plenty of evidence to convict these men".'

McMahon's ruling accepted much of the obvious evidence of prosecutorial misconduct. She also ruled that the government had outsourced its investigation to the bank's lawyers. Yet in spite of all her earlier outrage at the DOJ's conduct, McMahon now ruled that it didn't matter because the defendants were still guilty of multiple illegal counts of conspiracy to commit wire fraud.

Crucial to that conclusion was a ruling that the defence had failed to establish that there was a range of rates to choose from when setting Libor. To conclude that, she'd relied on evidence from Deutsche Bank's main Libor submitter Mike Curtler. Before he'd pleaded guilty, Curtler had defended his conduct in accommodating trader requests, saying submitters had 'leeway' to adjust their Libor submissions up or down. But at the trial, when the government asked its cooperator, 'Have you ever heard of anything called the range?' Curtler's response was, 'No.' He'd never heard of 'the range' until 2015. Therefore, Judge McMahon said, the defence had not proved there was a range of rates.

'It was wordplay,' said Matt. 'I wrote a big thing on my blog, "The little movements up and down." In Libor you can say "the range", you can say "leeway" you can say "fine tuning". I found five different names people used to use – "skewing" was another. They all meant the same thing, right? So, whether you call it a range or leeway, who fucking gives a shit? It's the fucking same thing! She used wordplay. That stupid little comment, about not knowing what the range was, was being used to throw me in jail. So I went ballistic.'

The sentencing hearing, where he'd be sent to prison for his sinful emails from twelve years ago, was set for October 2019. For the three emails he'd sent and the one he'd been copied in on, the DOJ prosecutors were asking for a sentence of nine years. But Matt wasn't to be intimidated. In a mood of defiance, he went for what he called 'the nuclear option'. He published his book, launched a website with a blog and got as loud and accusatory as he possibly could on Twitter. When I heard about the judgment, I phoned the law firm listed as representing him on the public court documents to see if I could speak to Matt, fully expecting to get no result. But then I got a call back from Ken Breen. 'I wouldn't advise him to,' he said. 'But I think he's going to want to do it.' I started speaking to Matt, reading documents he sent me and arranging it all in that simple yet powerful investigative tool: a timeline. The picture started to become clearer. In September 2019, Matt travelled in by train to a place he hated to travel to because of the memories – Manhattan – to give an interview at the BBC's New York offices. In his interview, he summed up everything that was wrong with the Libor trials. 'It's not about the truth. Instead, it's "win at all costs" for the DOJ. That saddens me because I want the truth. The only thing our trial and our case proved was that the Department of Justice can take anyone they want and make them a criminal,' said Matt. 'It wasn't interest rates that were rigged. It was our investigation and prosecutions.'

On 7 October 2019, the BBC broadcast the interview all around the world and published two lengthy articles[20] exposing some of what had gone wrong in the trial of Matt Connolly and Gavin Black. They contained a link to the article from 11 April 2017 headlined 'Libor: Bank of England implicated in secret recording'.

Three weeks later, Matt Connolly packed a bag of clothes and once again made his way to the court in Lower Manhattan for the sentencing hearing, accompanied by his wife, Beth, and son, Adam. The DOJ had been pressing for a sentence of thirteen to fifteen years. They wanted the judge to use Connolly and Black's sentences to 'send a message' to the world of banking that fraudulent behaviour would not be tolerated. Neither Matt nor his lawyers knew what to expect from Chief Judge McMahon – or how long he'd be jailed for. But then neither did the DOJ.

'Defendants didn't put anything over on Deutsche Bank,' said the Chief Judge, after hearing submissions from all parties at the trial. 'What was going on was no secret, and was – from all the evidence I have seen and heard – encouraged, if not orchestrated, by senior officials at the bank for the benefit of the bank. As government acknowledged, this practice was widespread. Indeed, at certain times, such as during the height of the 2008 financial crisis, submissions were actually being manipulated at the request of the Bank of England.'

In the dock, Matt was starting to hope it might not be so bad. She'd clearly been reading about it. Maybe she'd even read the articles from his interview. And then it got better. The judge acknowledged that while the jury had found him guilty on some of the eight counts, they'd acquitted him on the allegations made by Tim Parietti. The judge said that in her opinion, Parietti was guilty of 'quibbling' – meaning lying by evasion – 'and quite possibly outright lying at several points during his testimony'.[21] On her reading of the verdict sheet the jury did not believe him. 'The evidence from Mr Parietti, I believe, was to the effect that senior management at the bank directed this activity. This part of his testimony I believe. I don't believe he did what he did because Matt Connolly told him to – and neither did the jury – but I do believe his testimony that senior management at the bank directed this activity. And Matt Connolly was not part of the senior management at Deutsche Bank.'

McMahon turned to Gavin Black, asking him if he wanted to say anything.

'Yes, please, your Honor,' said Gavin, his first words in the whole trial process. 'As I believe you are aware, this process has completely shattered me. I have come to this country voluntarily because I believe in the process and the law. I am devastated by the fact I ended up here before you. I feel incredible remorse for my involvement in these events and so profoundly for my wife and children and those that rely on me and believe in me. My life will never be the same. I am committed to my family and all those who supported me over these past many years. I ask for leniency, your Honor, because I want to be able to spend the rest of my days making it up to them. And most importantly, I want to thank my wife and children whose love and support is my entire world.'

'Okay,' said McMahon. 'I have to turn to the elephant in the room because it is raised without being named by anyone's presentation. Mr Connolly – who was lucky that I don't bear him a grudge for the silly thing he did last summer – stole my thunder on this one. He called his self-published screed "Scapegoat."' Colleen McMahon held up a copy of Matt's book and showed it to the court. ('Oh God,' thought Matt to himself, 'what's going to happen now?')

'It is a word that I have thought of often over the past three years,' the judge went on.[22] 'The Levitical scapegoat was a real goat. Mr Connolly believes that he and Mr Black are being made scapegoats here, to which I say: yes and no [...] It's not quite fair, gentlemen, to say that you're being blamed for the wrongdoing of others. The scapegoat was sinless; you are not. You haven't done nothing wrong. You were found guilty by a jury of twelve, and there is evidence to support their verdict, and you should be sentenced for what you did. But I do think it is fair to say that the government has used Mr Connolly and Mr Black, as well as a few other people – none of whom was at the highest levels – as proxy wrongdoers, to make them an example for the wrongdoings of those two institutions, Deutsche Bank and Rabobank in this court, and for similar wrongdoing of other unindicted institutions as well [...] I yet cannot make Mr Connolly and Mr Black scapegoats for the sins of the entire industry.

'I can't bring myself to impose a sentence of incarceration in the United States for Mr Black. And since I can't impose a sentence of incarceration to be served in the United Kingdom on Mr Black – which, as I said, I wouldn't do – I am remitted to sentencing him to some form of home confinement to be served in his native country, and I do that because – while, Mr Black, I don't like the way you played the game – you were really a bit player in this. Mr Connolly was barely a player at all. And certainly, if I'm not going to sentence Mr Black to one, I can't mete out a sentence of imprisonment on Mr Connolly, who truly – I have been through this evidence – is the least culpable person I have heard about.'

Colleen McMahon then referred to all the senior people who were absent from the dock. 'And given what has happened to everybody else in this case, and what has not happened to a lot of people who aren't in this case – and aren't in other cases – it would be a travesty to sentence Matt Connolly to a term of incarceration. I'm always uncomfortable when I'm asked in any context – it usually happens in the drug context – to sentence the low man on the totem pole while the big guy goes free.'

Chief Judge McMahon seemed to Matt to have flipped back to being the person she seemed to be throughout the criminal proceedings of 2016 to 2018.

'Mr Connolly, will you please rise. I hereby sentence you to time served, plus a term of two years' supervised release, to include a term of six months' home confinement [...] Mr Black, I hereby sentence you to a term of time served, plus three years of supervision, to include a term of nine months' home confinement to be served in the United Kingdom.'

'I should say,' Colleen McMahon added, 'and this applies to both of you: during the period of home confinement you must remain in your residence, and you may not leave – in your case for six months; in your case for nine months – for any purpose except the following: to attend medical appointments, to attend religious services, to attend any further court appearances that may be necessary. I rather imagine there will be an appeal in this case. The idea is you're a prisoner in your own home. And I assure you that after six months in your case, Mr Connolly, or nine months in your case Mr Black – and I've heard this from people – you will hate the sight of your own home, and you will be very, very happy to get out.'

'I can't wait to get the fuck out of *here*,' thought Matt.[23] A minute later, as the proceedings were brought to a close, he turned to Ken Breen. 'I'm relieved. I'm a happy man. So don't get the wrong impression when I grab my wife and son and get the fuck out of here immediately.' Matt found Adam and Beth, who was crying tears of relief.

They spent much of the train ride home to Basking Ridge, glancing at each other, open-mouthed, hardly daring to believe it was real. There was still a fight on for Matt to appeal his conviction and the government could appeal his light sentence of home confinement. But after more than three years of being railroaded, Matt, his wife and son could barely take in the fact that something had gone their way. As they thought back to the hearing, they each kept repeating one thought: 'That was fucking crazy.'

But then again: the whole thing was.

Later Matt cracked a joke about his sentence on Twitter. 'My wife stood up and said – so he'll be home for six months? What the hell did I do?!'

That day, 24 October 2019, Matt and Beth could have no way of knowing that billions of people were about to be sentenced to exactly the same punishment: four months later, the pandemic struck.

17

RUN!

October 2019. In HM Prison Wandsworth, Carlo Palombo, convicted of conspiracy to defraud for 'manipulating' Euribor, was getting alarmed about the state his cellmate was in. A Romanian in his thirties, jailed for stealing cars, he was a sweet-natured guy who could have been a friend if he'd stayed off drugs. But he'd spend all day, every day, high on spice. Because he had no money, in the morning when Carlo went to work in the prison library, he'd steal the food Carlo had bought from the shelf and trade it with other prisoners for more spice. Unlike other drugs, where you had to pay the prison guards a full mark-up, spice was cheap; the synthetic cannabinoids, designed to mimic the effects of the active ingredient in cannabis but much more concentrated, could be dissolved and sprayed on to paper and sent to prisoners in the mail. The drug-rinsed paper would then be broken up into little bits and bought and sold. The health hazards of spice were well known – breathing difficulties, heart palpitations, seizures – but were ignored by inmates seeking oblivion to escape the sheer boredom of being stuck for twenty-three and a half hours a day in a room measuring 3m x 2m.

Carlo's cellmate would create a makeshift pipe using the single-portion milk cartons that came with the meagre prison breakfast, smoke the fumes from the bits of paper and spend the rest of the day off his face. The first day he'd arrived, Carlo could see it was going to be a problem. On a high, his cellmate lost his balance and grabbed at a makeshift curtain, made from a bedsheet, that was awkwardly strung up to afford some measure of privacy between the open toilet and the bunks twelve inches away, bringing the whole structure crashing down. During the day, he was too high to eat the prison food. Once, he was so high he couldn't figure out how to chew, so he spat out his mouthful and collapsed on the floor. When the evening came, and he was coming down from the drugs, he'd get hungry and steal more of Carlo's food to eat. After a few days of that, Carlo had caught him at it and tried to stop him. But he'd quickly become violent, and they'd wrestled until Carlo stopped, seeing how serious he was about the food, and just let him have it. Each time Carlo returned to the cell from the library, he'd find him passed out on the floor or slumped on the toilet, his body, arms and legs at bizarre angles.

This time he'd passed out on Carlo's bed on the lower bunk. Carlo tried to talk to him. No response. Eyes open, staring, no movement. This was worse than usual. Carlo didn't want him to die there in the cell. He walked quickly down the long, narrow walkway outside his cell to find a prison guard to help. But when he got there, they didn't want to listen to a word.

'We're having a chat. Go away.'

'But this is serious–'

'Go away!'

'But—'

'Have you heard me?!' The guard was angry now. 'GO! AWAY!' He slammed the door of the office shut in front of Carlo.

Carlo slowly walked back. As he approached the door to his cell, he could see something was happening. Half a dozen people were crammed into the tiny Victorian cell. 'Stay out!' said one. Carlo looked on, aghast. Someone had passed by the cell, seen his cellmate having a seizure and fetched the nurses. As they worked to bring him back from the brink, someone had called for the prison guards, the same ones who'd just slammed the door in Carlo's face. Now here they were at his cell.

'You see,' said Carlo, furious with them. 'You're not doing your job! Do you understand what's happened here? Do you understand this? He was nearly dying! Do you understand what you're doing? Or – you just don't? Can you please apologise to me and start to do your job seriously, and take me seriously!'

The guard turned to him slowly, his face a picture of contempt. 'Who the fuck do you think you're talking to? Don't you dare talk to me like that,' he said, his lip curling. 'We'll be finding you a cell in the drug wing.'

The nurses gradually succeeded in resuscitating Carlo's cellmate from his seizure. But then they just left him there on the bunk, with no further medical attention. It was going to be hard for Carlo to sleep. His cellmate had just nearly died. And he'd been told he was going to be moved to the one place worse than where he already was. In Wandsworth's wing for drug addicts, the chances of having a violent, unmanageable cellmate were much higher. He'd have to somehow get some help to avoid that. The next day the librarian he worked with intervened, speaking to the officer in charge of the wing to promise that Carlo would never again complain about anything again – ever – if he could only stay where he was.

It kept happening. He'd tried, when he first arrived, to normalise the situation by making conversation with the guards, asking questions so he could understand how things worked, unaware that he was breaking an unwritten rule. 'When you ask questions, even if you ask very politely and nicely, what you get back is horrible. Because you're not a human being, you're a pest. You'll just get, "just leave me alone" or "fuck off". When you come from the normal world into that world, it's something that's really hard to get used to,' says Carlo. 'In normal life, nice people try to respect each other. And there are also rules people follow – about how you talk to each other, how you behave to each other. Once you go to prison, you've lost your humanity. And the way prisoners get treated by prison guards, it's not like human beings anymore. It's like – you're just a piece of shit. You have no right to be treated respectfully. You're a number. No, not just a number – you're a nasty number: someone who is probably dangerous. All the rules about how to treat each other, they just go out the window. They don't apply anymore. And there is nobody checking how prison guards treat prisoners. The prison guards have power and zero accountability, meaning complete freedom to do whatever they want. So especially at the beginning, when you come in as a normal, middle-class person who's never had any problem with the law, it's a complete shock. You never knew that world existed.'

Wandsworth was far worse than anything he'd ever known before. But it wasn't Carlo's first experience of a culture of ritual humiliation. Seventeen years earlier, he'd arrived in London as a 23-year-old graduate to work as a trainee at Barclays Capital. Slim and fit with spectacles, little hair on top and a short, dark beard, Carlo was raised in Milan and was blessed with a great head for maths. After school he'd studied economics at the University of Milan and gone on a placement in the USA where he'd had the time of his life. When he'd finished his degree, his sole aim was to get away from his home town and live in another country. He almost got a job with the engineering giant, Philips, in the Netherlands. But foreign graduates could also apply to Barclays Bank in London. It was the opportunity to be in London, as opposed to banking, that attracted him. He was invited to the recruitment weekend where Barclays put bright graduates through their paces with maths problems, IQ-style intelligence tests and role play. He was one of the few selected to join and began work in 2002 on the huge, noisy trading floor in Barclays Capital's Canary Wharf headquarters.

Under Bob Diamond, who'd convinced Barclays in the late 1990s to revive its investment bank activity and fund Barclays Capital, a hard-charging atmosphere had developed that Carlo struggled to fit in with. Like every other graduate trainee on the trading floor, he started as the coffee boy. Carlo would get in at 6 a.m., print out all the overnight research for the twenty people on the team, then collect all their orders for breakfast and coffee – a lot of breakfast and a lot of coffee. He'd spend the morning on a training programme then come back and collect their orders for lunch. The trading floor was almost completely male, and he hated the atmosphere.

'People had been watching way too many Wall Street movies. It's that kind of environment where you humiliate people. And then once you rise up the ranks, then you have the power to humiliate somebody else. And you do it because that's part of what the game is. It's incredibly unpleasant. One day, I made a mistake and one of the traders just above me [in rank] threw a full Starbucks cup of coffee at me. And I had to get up and walk across the trading floor, completely drenched in coffee, to go to the bathroom and clean myself up. It was in front of everybody else and nobody said anything about it. It was done openly. That was just one example of many. People would punch their computer screens if something hadn't worked out for them and often break them. That was completely normal. They'd throw telephones. Men wouldn't hire women for anything else than to look at them, or because they thought they might get something out of them. If a woman walked past, they'd message each other giving her a grade out of ten.'

And that was before the alcohol started to flow. Soon after he joined, Carlo made the mistake of inviting his girlfriend who was visiting from Italy to a dinner he'd been invited to by some of Carlo's senior bosses at Barclays.

'We were very sweet, but naïve 23-year-olds. They were all talking about parties with prostitutes and people taking cocaine up their bums. And they'd invited sex workers to the dinner party. These were senior bosses at the bank.' Carlo's nice, young Italian girlfriend was traumatised. 'When the traders would go out with the brokers, they were always talking about orgies with prostitutes. And that was just the norm, talking about parties with all sorts of drug-taking in the most incredible settings. Parties where one boss steals the drugs from another boss. That was normal conversation at the pub.'

Carlo recoiled from the toxic masculinity. At work he adjusted to his surroundings by sealing himself off in a bubble with another trader he'd befriended who was as reserved and modest as he was. He ducked out of the decadent dinners with bosses. It was when he was still a trainee, trying to do exactly as he was told, that he learned about the practice they had of trying to help the bank quote its Euribor rate in line with the trading positions. The managers would look at the overall position of their trading team, and whether they would prefer the rate to be higher or lower. And then, based on the position of the team, they would ask people trading euros on the cash desk (Colin Bermingham and Sisse Bohart) for a high or low Euribor submission.

'Hi, Sisse,' wrote the young trainee on his bosses' instructions. 'Today, if possible, we would prefer to have a high rate.' It took about ten seconds to write and send. It was one of about a dozen similar emails he'd send over the next four years, all in all taking a maximum of ten minutes of his working life. Fourteen years later, those same emails would be used by a judge to sentence Carlo to four years in prison. The bosses who gave him the instructions would keep their freedom.

I first saw Carlo Palombo when he was sitting beside Philippe Moryoussef, Colin Bermingham, Christian Bittar, Achim Kraemer and Sisse Bohart on 11 January 2016 at Westminster Magistrates Court on Marylebone Road, central London. They were in the dock inside a courtroom behind bullet-proof glass next to two police officers, hearing a magistrate read the charges against them for the first time in unusually aggressive tones. Right from the start there was something that didn't add up. Eleven defendants were named on the Serious Fraud Office indictment, but only six were in the dock. Four other defendants from Germany and one from France had simply stayed away.[1] The SFO was trying to bring them to the UK by obtaining

European Arrest Warrants. But in Germany the courts had refused to execute them. France, too, was proving tricky.

'If we came to London in 2016 to listen to our charges, it was just because we were convinced of our innocence,' said Philippe Moryoussef. 'And we were convinced that we would win a trial. Actually, we were not even thinking it would go that far or last so long. We thought the case would be dismissed: because we didn't make anything out of those requests. It was like – how can you be guilty of a market practice with no victim, with no complaints, with no profit? We thought it was impossible for us to be convicted.'

The defendants who turned up that day were the ones who believed in the British justice system. They had faith that the courts were rational and independent enough to recognise and reject an SFO case that, to them, was obviously misconceived. They'd worked on the trading floor; they knew how Euribor worked. Just like Libor, it involved banks submitting estimates of the interest rates they'd have to pay to borrow cash, but with forty-six rather than sixteen banks contributing their submissions. Just like Libor, the highest and the lowest estimates would be removed, making it very hard for any one bank to shift the average deliberately. Just like Libor, there'd always be a narrow range of interest rates from other banks or money market funds offering to lend euros (2.13%, 2.15%, 2.14%). Just like Libor, it had long been the case that banks had adjusted their Euribor estimates within that range of rates according to which way their bank was 'facing', also known as 'which way round' it was – meaning whether it was in the bank's interest to have a higher Euribor average or a lower one. At any point the swaps desk would have thousands of trades on linked to Euribor, some of which would benefit from a higher rate, some from a lower. They'd add up the money at stake in the former, then they'd do the same for the latter to calculate the net position for the desk. If it would benefit the bank's swaps trades to have a higher Euribor average (known to traders as the 'fix'), they'd ask the cash desk to submit a high Euribor estimate. If the trades would benefit from a lower fix, they'd ask for a lower rate. It might – or might not – shift the fix by a thousandth of a basis point; but it took so little time and effort it was worth doing just on the hope. As with Libor, putting in a request to the cash desk was always an afterthought – a tidying-up exercise. Setting up or closing trades and managing how much money you might make or lose – your risk – was the main focus of what traders did for most of the day.

To the SFO, this case was 'the big one'. All of its previous efforts were meant as no more than a prelude to catching the biggest fish, Christian Bittar, once Deutsche Bank's star trader. To investigators who'd convinced themselves that asking for a high or low interest rate submission was wicked and wrong, he was the Lucifer of interest rate-rigging. A dark-haired maths whizz from Senegal with a short, dark beard and olive skin, he'd become famous in the City of London for having made huge sums in the financial crisis for the bank and for himself.

Christian would message his former colleague and close friend Philippe Moryoussef at Barclays, also a native French speaker but from Morocco, and they'd try to help each other. If either of them had a big trading position, they'd not only ask their own submitters to tweak their rates. They'd also message each other by Bloomberg's messaging system, asking each other to ask their cash desks for a favourable rate to be submitted. Even that probably wouldn't make much difference to the fix. But when Bittar had a very large trade on, as he often did, it might conceivably make a tiny difference to the average. Because there were billions of euros at stake, it was worth a try. Christian and Philippe were almost constantly messaging each other about anything and everything. There were long periods of boredom, where they'd wind each other up just to keep each other amused. One day, 7 September 2006, Christian had a big position which would lose money if Euribor was too high. Deutsche Bank's cash desk traders were the other way round, wanting the Euribor average high. So they were ignoring his requests for a low submission – putting it as high as they could, within the range of rates on offer to borrow euros. He was hoping Philippe might ask his own cash desk at Barclays to put in a low submission to offset it when the submissions were averaged.

'I'm begging u, don't forget me ... pleasssssssssssssssssssssseeeeeeeeeeeee ... I'm on my knees ...' said Christian's message to Philippe.

'I told them 1M up, is that right?' replied Philippe, teasing Christian that he'd do the opposite of what was requested.

'Please, pal insist as much as you can ... my treasury is taking it to the sky ... I'm begging u ... can you beg the cash guy as well?'

'Ok I'm telling them,' said Philippe, relenting a little.

That exchange was cited as damning evidence of misconduct by the New York Department of Financial Services to justify its portion of Deutsche Bank's $2.5 billion penalties – one among dozens of similar messages. But just as with Libor, the authorities couldn't show any false statements were being procured; they never bothered to check if the exchange had resulted in Euribor submissions outside the range of interest rates where cash was on offer.

At the onset of the credit crunch in the summer of 2007, Christian had picked up from colleagues that something felt very wrong in the credit markets. He took the view that if banks lost huge sums on subprime US mortgages gone bad, they'd become reluctant to lend to each other until they knew how much they'd lost. At the same time, to deal with the crisis, central banks would have to cut short-term interest rates by much more than the market was expecting. Christian lined up his trades to benefit – and was soon proved spectacularly right. But then came the most lucrative judgement. Rather than take profits on a successful trade, he kept doubling down on the pessimistic view that the credit crunch would keep getting worse. And whether it was by luck or judgement, over 2008 that was exactly what transpired. As the credit crunch intensified over 2008 and early 2009 into a full-blown banking crisis and recession, central banks including the Fed, the European Central Bank and the Bank of England slashed interest rates from around 5% to 0.5% or less. The money market desk where Christian worked made profits of an astonishing €1.9 billion in 2008.[2] Christian had an unusual contract that entitled him to 11 per cent of the profits from his own book. That meant he was due a bonus of some €70 million.

Embarrassed to be awarded so much when the banking world was in crisis and many were losing their jobs, Christian offered to let some of that huge sum go. His bosses explored if he might be awarded less but Deutsche Bank's HR department said it was a contractual entitlement. However, he would never see around half of that deferred bonus after the bank, its lawyers and senior managers arranged to throw him under the bus, have him sacked for alleged misconduct and prosecuted by the SFO.

Once again, the SFO had decided, following the reasoning in the fines for Deutsche Bank by the DOJ, SEC, CFTC and FCA, that any attempt to influence Euribor submissions to suit the bank's commercial interests such as its trades was corrupt. Once again, the evidence against the eleven accused of conspiracy to defraud consisted of messages sent by traders like Philippe, Christian and Carlo to cash traders like Sisse Bohart and Colin Bermingham who put in the bank's Euribor submissions.

'People just make those numbers up [...] pretty much like Libors tho!' said one email from 21 August 2008.

'There is a philosophical saying: One Greek says, "all Greeks are lying". Who do u trust?' said another from 16 July 2009. As with Libor, the only really damning emails or messages referring to false Euribor submissions came from the credit crunch and its aftermath, when lowballing was going on. There was no talk of made-up numbers or false rates from before the credit crunch. Once again, the regulators were conflating two very different things: lowballing and trader requests. And once again, it was the thing that mattered, that really involved false numbers and that really caused losses – lowballing – that didn't get prosecuted.

Christian and Philippe had spent months working together in Paris to prepare their defence, hoping to use clear evidence and rational argument to show the British courts why the SFO's case against them was misconceived. Their argument, and that of all the others who turned up for the criminal proceedings in January 2016, was similar to that of Tom Hayes, Matt Connolly, Gavin Black, Jon Mathew, Jay Merchant and all the other traders. They may have sworn and behaved in an immature way in their twenties and thirties in the heated atmosphere of the trading floor; but they were playing well within what they understood to be the rules of the rate-setting game.

But they were to learn the hard way that the British justice system is not, unlike the French one, focused on seeking the truth. In the adversarial system of the UK and the USA, it's as much about winning or losing. The SFO was determined to score a success and, judging by the Court of Appeal rulings, the judiciary seemed to be sympathetic.

The SFO sought to apply the same template to the Euribor trial that had been used to jail Tom Hayes, Jay Merchant, Jon Mathew, Alex Pabon and Peter Johnson. Because the offence was 'conspiracy to defraud', they wouldn't have to produce any victims of the fraud. Nor would they have to show how much had been gained or lost. They didn't have to show money changing hands or identify a fraudulent transaction. All they'd have to show was that there was an agreement to do something unlawful when a trader asked a submitter to put in their Euribors high, low or unchanged.

At that point, though, the SFO lawyers on the Euribor case faced the same problem their colleagues had faced ahead of the Tom Hayes trial. Where was the unlawful act the traders were meant to be conspiring to commit? In the Hayes trial, the SFO had had the help of Lord Justice Nigel Davis, who'd ruled in the Court of Appeal that it was 'self-evident' that a submitter couldn't put in an interest rate to the Libor process influenced by what would help the bank's trades. While there were no written rules, all the Libor convicts had been locked up on the basis that there was an unwritten rule banning banks from taking account of their commercial interests when setting Libor. With Euribor it was different. There *was* a set of written rules that the founders of Euribor had written down when they launched the benchmark in 1998. The only problem for the SFO was that it didn't help their case.

Like the Libor allegations, the SFO indictment said that between 1 January 2005 and 31 December 2009, the traders had 'dishonestly agreed to procure or make submissions of rates into the Euribor setting process which were false or misleading in that they:

a. were intended to create an advantage to trading the positions of employees of one or more of the above-mentioned banks and

b. deliberately disregarded the proper basis for the submission of those rates, thereby intending that the economic interests of others may be prejudiced.'

It 'disregarded the proper basis', the SFO wanted to say, because it contravened the code of conduct which set out the proper basis for making Euribor submissions.

But there was nothing in the Euribor code of conduct prohibiting traders from making requests for Euribor rates to be submitted high or low. The SFO claimed that although it was not explicitly in the code, it was an *implied* term of the contract which the banks contributing their Euribor estimates had signed. In Article 6 of the code, it said: 'Panel banks must quote the required euro rates: to the best of their knowledge, these rates being defined as the rates at which euro interbank term deposits are being offered within the EMU zone by one prime bank to another at 11.00 am. Brussels time ("the best price between the best banks").'

The judge appointed to the case, Michael Gledhill, was no specialist in financial markets. But it was being left to him to decide the English law on Euribor, a benchmark that fell under a Belgian civil law contract drawn up in Brussels.

Christian Bittar and Philippe Moryoussef came up with what they thought should be a devastating blow to the prosecution case. If the SFO wouldn't consult any independent market practitioners, then *they* would. They tracked down the three top European bankers who founded Euribor in 1998: Helmut Konrad, Nikolaus Bömcke and Jean-Pierre Ravise. Nikolaus Bömcke was the same lawyer who had written the very code of conduct that the SFO was relying on. They also gathered witness statements from three leading market practitioners who'd overseen the setting of Euribor since its inception.

'They were ready and willing to be witnesses because they all said that what the English government was doing to us was absolutely wrong, and an incredible injustice,' said Carlo. 'And it was a complete misunderstanding of financial markets and financial markets regulation. So they were very, very willing to come and try to tell the judge that he was wrong, and try to explain how financial markets regulation actually worked in Europe twenty years ago.'

The Euribor founders drew up witness statements and offered to attend in order to explain more to the court. 'Commercial interest was welcome when quoting for [Euribor],' said Bömcke's statement. 'Therefore a panel bank might also consider its position in the derivatives market when quoting, as long as that bank could justify it as being a rate at which one prime bank could lend to another prime bank.' It couldn't be clearer. The traders' requests were allowed. 'Furthermore, the consideration of commercial interest by a panel bank did not necessarily render the submitted Euribor rate false, as long as the submission could be justified by that bank as a rate at which one prime bank could lend to another prime bank.'

It flatly contradicted every element of the SFO case. The other Euribor founders made similar points, as did three further witness statements from the senior market practitioners. Taking account of commercial influence was how the system was expected to operate. That's why there was a trimming process to strike out the outliers, to set limits on the extent to which commercial influence could change the rate through one or two banks going too high or too low. It was how the system was supposed to work. Christian and Philippe were convinced now: the case would get thrown out.

At a pre-trial hearing in June 2017, the defendants' lawyers told Judge Gledhill that the founders of Euribor were willing to testify. They had signed statements that said, among other thing, that there were no implied terms. The Code of Conduct didn't prohibit commercial interest. On the contrary, it was expected and welcomed. The SFO had had three months to prepare for the hearing; but the SFO's team now told the judge they were not ready. It was obvious to the defendants that if the court took account of the evidence of the Euribor founders before deciding the English law on Euribor, the SFO couldn't claim traders' requests were prohibited in the code of conduct – so there would be no case against them.

A hearing to decide the English common law view of Euribor was postponed to September 2017. At the hearing, the SFO argued that as long as Gledhill was sure about his interpretation of the Belgian law that governed Euribor, then he didn't need to take any evidence from anyone else. Gledhill agreed, deciding he didn't need or want to hear from the founders of Euribor before he decided the English law about it. He was sure that when Article 6 said banks must quote the required euro rates 'to the best of their knowledge', it meant that they could not take account of their trading positions, even when selecting from within a range of justifiable rates. By law, the interpretation of the Euribor code of conduct was a matter for him. He didn't need to hear the views of the man who wrote it. On 22 September 2017, he ruled that it was prohibited in England for banks to make Euribor submissions influenced by their trading positions.

The defendants appealed, hoping the Court of Appeal would do its job and correct what they regarded as an arrogant, wilfully ignorant ruling. On 31 January 2018, the Court of Appeal decided Gledhill was right and again didn't certify there was a point of law of public importance that might allow defendants to appeal to the Supreme Court. The senior judge sitting on the appeal panel was a familiar face: Lord Justice Davis.

That threw all the Euribor defendants into crisis. They had tried everything they could to show the SFO and the courts why the case was misconceived. They couldn't have done anything more powerful than to get the founders of Euribor to testify that the requests they had made for Euribor to be set with the banks' trades in mind – the practice that had been called interest rate 'rigging' – were in fact not only allowed but expected. But this judge, it appeared, didn't want to hear it. Nor, based on its ruling, did the judges at the Court of Appeal. What more could they do? To them, it now seemed painfully obvious. This trial process wasn't a conscientious attempt to get to the truth and offer them a fair chance to defend themselves. It wasn't just the SFO. It was the British judiciary who seemed determined to lock them up, no matter what evidence or witnesses they offered.

'I don't want to criticise British justice as a whole. But in this story, it has been frightening. You know, I believed in the justice system, I went through all the process. I spent a lot of money on lawyers, believing in my innocence. But I was trapped at every stage of the process,' Philippe Moryoussef said. 'We were accused of breaching the Code of Conduct. Who is in a better position than the Euribor founders to say if we breached the code that they had written? They all read all our conversations. And they all testified that giving a commercial interest was part of Euribor's construction, and that we were allowed to do it. They were even saying that the aggregation of all the commercial interests was part of the construction and was giving a fair rate.'

Christian Bittar could show mathematically that he personally made zero from Euribor trader requests. The big money he made for Deutsche didn't come from nudging Euribor. But now it was obvious to him that the courts weren't interested in seeking the truth from the sources best placed to reveal it. He'd spent years pleading with the SFO and the English judges to behave in a rational, logical way, looking at the law and the evidence. But there was only one sort of pleading they seemed to be interested in – the sort that included the word 'guilty'. In this case, it was now perfectly clear to him that the British courts weren't that interested in being logical or rational. This was political. It wasn't the higher goal of justice, but making an example of the traders, that was the goal.

A deep depression had been weighing on Christian ever since the September hearing. Now it was followed by a cold-light-of-day calculation. If he confessed and got five years in jail, the SFO would recommend a light confiscation order. For Christian and his family, a guilty plea and a shorter spell in jail might be easier. In March 2018, he went to court, pleaded guilty and went to prison.

In 2019, I visited him at HMP Maidstone. He looked relieved. 'You know, ever since this started seven years ago, I don't think I had one waking minute where I didn't think about Libor and Euribor. It was constantly, constantly there. The minute I came here, I thought – "I don't have to think about it any more". The relief was unbelievable! After that, I just had to get used to being here and do the time.'

Christian had pleaded guilty (when he felt guilty of nothing) and had lost his freedom. But inside, he felt liberated: free at last from the constant strain of trying to use reason and evidence to bring sanity to a misconceived, politicised prosecution. Compared to that ordeal, serving time in HMP Maidstone was positively bearable.

Ever since Tom Hayes was convicted and sentenced to fourteen years on 3 August 2015, Philippe Moryoussef had been worried about his chances of a fair trial. When the sentence was reported he was in his home country, Morocco, with his wife Karinne, who'd met Philippe years before on the trading floor of RBS. 'I was actually in shock. I was mentally destroyed after this conviction. At that point, I started to think that I was in danger, because the system was just wrong. And if it was driven by politics, then I could be scapegoated. But I decided to follow the process, to go to all the hearings. Then when they decided not to listen to the founders of Euribor, that's when I really thought that my trial couldn't be fair.'

Philippe was also profoundly shocked, two years later, by Christian's decision to plead guilty. He'd given his old friend and colleague no warning. They'd worked together for months preparing their defence but now, with Christian's plea, it was over. Most of the messages and emails used against Christian also had Philippe's name on them. There'd be next to no chance of winning in court.

After years of fighting, Philippe was yearning for an end to it and almost did the same. He spent ten hours with his lawyers in London who wanted him to strike a deal – plead guilty, spend some time behind bars and keep more of his money. His French lawyer, François de Castro, couldn't believe what he was hearing. Without telling him, Philippe started exploring it with his London lawyers. 'At some stage it's not about right and wrong any more. It's a business decision. I was being told, "if you go to prison and spend two and a half years behind bars, at least you know what's coming. And it will soon be out of the way." So my barrister called me, and I assumed that she was online with James Waddington [the prosecutor]. And we struck a deal for confiscation of £200,000 and at a discount of 30 per cent on the sentence. And then we fixed the date. And she told me, "The judge is very happy." Okay. Then I started to think I'd call my lawyer François. And he told me, "Philippe, I respect your decision. But you shouldn't. Here are the reasons. You didn't do anything wrong. You shouldn't go behind bars." I called my English barrister. I told her, "Listen. I won't come to that hearing in April. I won't be there."' She was put out, concerned she would be professionally embarrassed by his change of mind. 'She said, "The judge will be quite upset." I replied, "Am I not allowed to change my mind for a decision as important as going to jail?"'

Philippe had hoped the British justice system would recognise his innocence if he got the right lawyers and used reason to show why the SFO case was flawed. But to him it was now so obvious he wouldn't have a chance at a fair trial that it was better for him to flee from British justice than to face it. He'd rather go 'on the run' and become, in the eyes of the British state, a fugitive.

'I felt so free in my mind when I decided that. It was like, the best decision in my life. Actually, at that moment, for the first time in seven years, I realised I was in control – not them. You understand that feeling? You are in control? Because everything had felt so out of control for so long. They were driving the bus. We hadn't been in control. Now, I thought, "You're not controlling me anymore!"'

Philippe's lawyer François de Castro wrote to the SFO to say he wouldn't be attending trial. The refusal to allow key defence witnesses to be heard was a violation of his rights as a defendant, his letter said. Michael Gledhill was incensed. It was, he declared, 'an affront to justice'. The SFO wanted Philippe still to be tried, even though he wouldn't be in court. Gledhill agreed.

In the public gallery of Southwark Crown Court in April 2018, Amy Wilson was finding it very stressful and upsetting to watch the man she loved, Carlo Palombo, on trial. From the disturbing moment three and a half years earlier, when he'd first been informed that the SFO wanted to interview him as a criminal suspect, it had been obvious to them both that irrational political forces were threatening to turn their lives upside down. She'd spent much of her adult life helping young people in special schools and refugee centres; she knew how to support vulnerable people through times of great need. But here, with her own husband, there was nothing she could do.

'I've always felt like I've got the tools and resources to deal with pretty much any situation that has arisen in my life,' said Amy. 'And this was one where I was very much out of my depth. Like – a criminal investigation? I don't think I've known anyone that's ever been under criminal investigation. I had no idea how to help. But I knew that it was coming from a place of power that I had no access to. And that was petrifying.'

When, four and a half years before the trial, Amy Wilson had ventured onto Tinder, Carlo was her first date. Warm, intelligent and outgoing with dark hair and an uproarious laugh, Amy, like Carlo, had just finished her master's at Birkbeck College. They discovered they'd just missed sharing a class together. Both of them loved philosophy and they soon got lost in each other's company.

'She was amazing,' says Carlo. 'I just thought I'd met this really cool and nice and interesting person. And for me, it was such a major shift to leave all the horrible people and just bad vibes of the banking world.'

Carlo won a scholarship to study for a PhD at the University of California, where he'd also have a job teaching philosophy. He invited Amy to join him out west. Less than a year after they met, they got married in Las Vegas in a 1950s-style diner, with Elvis marrying them. 'I thought: new life, new place!' said Carlo. But only three months into his new role studying for a PhD and teaching undergraduates about ethics, he got a call from his lawyers saying the SFO had opened a criminal investigation and wanted to interview him. 'I was like, "They want to interview me? As what? As a person to inform them of the facts?" And then they said, "No, no, no. If they want to interview you, it means that most likely they want to charge you."' What Carlo calls his 'Kafka nightmare' had begun.

'If someone is coming after you for a criminal investigation of some sort, if you've done something, then you might see it coming, or you at least know what the problem is – what you might have done wrong. But I was in a situation where I had people coming after me for something that I didn't even understand – without even knowing what the crime is – without having ever thought that I had done anything even vaguely wrong. So I didn't even know how to *relate* to this whole thing that was happening to me. And the mind just cannot make sense of things like that. The whole thing was so absurd, there were moments of extreme weirdness. But most of the time, I think the whole thing was just so nonsensical, that the mind would just push it away.'

Amy's Jewish grandparents on her mum's side of the family had fled Nazi-occupied Europe. When the judge, Michael Gledhill, decided he should not listen to the founders of Euribor before he decided what the English law on Euribor was, it set off something inside her. She wanted to leave the country, fast. 'It was just like: this has been decided in advance. My mom says we've got a refugee mentality. That mentality is: "Quick, get all the valuables and go! They're persecuting you. They're after you. Run!" It was as if an innate, genetic thing had kicked in.' But Carlo was not interested. 'He was like, "We're going to do this properly and face things. The system will support us. I haven't done anything wrong. We'll get the right lawyers and we can do this.'"

It was already clear to both Amy and Carlo that the trial wasn't going to be fair. The judge had already decided the main issue – that seeking to influence Euribor for commercial reasons was unlawful. Carlo's twelve emails, all of them between nine and thirteen years old, clearly showed he was seeking to influence Euribor for commercial reasons. The jury would be asked to decide if it was dishonest or not. But if the judge had already told them it was unlawful, how could they conclude it was done honestly? The only way he'd win was if his lawyers could convince the jury that the prosecution's story made no sense. His lawyers felt strongly that the prosecution case was ridiculous.

At the trial, Carlo listened in the dock behind bullet-proof glass alongside Achim Kramer, Colin Bermingham and Sisse Bohart as the SFO prosecutor James Waddington kept repeating that the jury didn't need to worry about whether the alleged conspiracy was a crime. Christian Bittar had pleaded guilty. That proved that a criminal conspiracy existed. No need to fuss too much about the details. They only had to decide if the other defendants took part. The traders had 'cheated', he said, just like cricketers in a ball-tampering scandal.

'It's just really, really frustrating because they say all these things about you, about me being a cheat, a crook, dishonest, having left my moral compass at home, and the most horrible things. And none of this is real. None of it makes any sense,' said Carlo. 'But you can't say that. You've got to be in the dock with a police officer next to you to make sure that you behave. And it's really hard to get your head around the fact that this is actually an adversarial system, where the prosecution's job is to do whatever is permitted to convict you. And they'll play whatever dirty tricks they're allowed to.'

Among the prosecution witnesses at the trial was former Deutsche Bank head of global trading Alan Cloete.[3] He said Euribor submissions should be 'professionally neutral' and shouldn't take into account the position of an individual trader or the benefit to a bank, which amounted to market manipulation. It was, he said, 'unacceptable [...] to ask to have a high submission – and it's unacceptable for the submitters to accede to his request'.[4]

On 29 June 2018, the jury convicted Philippe Moryoussef and Gledhill sentenced him, in absentia, to eight years in prison. A confiscation hearing later ordered him to pay €53,000 – the supposed proceeds of a crime that merited an eight-year sentence – although, like Christian Bittar, Philippe could prove mathematically that he made nothing at all from the 'fraud'. A few weeks later, Christian was sentenced to five years and four months in jail, a sentence he'd already begun in March after his guilty plea. Achim Kraemer was acquitted. But the jury couldn't reach a verdict on Carlo, Colin Bermingham or Sisse Bohart.

Knowing there'd be a retrial and confident they would win an acquittal the second time round, Amy and Carlo made a decision not to put life on hold any longer. When the retrial began on 14 January 2019, Amy was entering the second trimester of her pregnancy. 'My hormones were telling me, "everything's wonderful" and I felt positive throughout. Because my system would not have been able to cope with even the idea that Carlo was going to be convicted at the end of this, I was so much more optimistic. I 100 per cent believed that everything was going to be fine.'

But then it wasn't.

As previously, Harry Harrison and Eric Bommensath took the witness stand to claim it wasn't permitted to move a Libor submission high or low based on the bank's commercial interests. As previously, the prosecution was allowed to use the defendants' high pay and bonuses to turn the jury against them, but the jury didn't hear about the much higher pay of Harrison and Bommensath. Carlo's legal team had done some calculations to show by how much it might have boosted his bonus had all his twelve requests nudged the Euribor average by the maximum hoped for amount – at most by a thousandth of a percentage point. The answer was £80. Considering he was earning over £200,000, it wasn't obvious why he'd become a criminal for that sum. But the prosecution argued the calculations were too complicated for the jury to understand and shouldn't be allowed into evidence. Judge Gledhill agreed.

The jury retired on 14 March 2019. Carlo and Amy, now six months pregnant, had to be there at Southwark Crown Court for every day of the deliberations. They'd hoped it would be quick, convinced that the jury would see that the case didn't make sense. They'd been so sure he'd be acquitted that they'd just put in an offer on a house.

'We were out at lunch near the court and my friends and my mum were with me – luckily. And we came back in, and we knew. I could feel it.' Amy's speaking quietly now, with a shake in her voice. 'And I was incredibly tense, and I knew something was coming.'

From the dock, Carlo watched the jurors coming back into court and sitting down. 'I remember the faces of some of the jurors as they came in. This self-righteous and cocky face. It was a very young jury, mostly white and male. They came in and they looked very self-assured. It felt to me like they weren't understanding the seriousness of what they were doing. It was frightening to look at their faces. The feeling of having my life being entrusted to a bunch of kids who are doing what authority is telling them to do, in a very murky setting ... Scary.'

In the gallery, Amy was filled with anxiety and tension. 'My friends and my mum were saying, "Oh, it will be fine." But I was thinking, "No it won't." And then they said, "We have a verdict on Carlo Palombo".' Amy pauses, collecting the strength to continue. 'And then – yeah – total shock [...] I think I shouted. I can't remember. But I remember my friends and mum holding me and my understanding was that Carlo was just going to be taken away right then and there.' A BBC article from that day reported that on hearing the verdict, 'the defendant's heavily pregnant wife burst into tears'.

Judge Michael Gledhill had steered the jury to acquit Sisse Bohart and they did so. But Colin Bermingham, one of the original whistleblowers of the real rate 'rigging', lowballing, was also convicted. Sentencing him, Michael Gledhill was struggling to identify his motive for his crimes. 'The answer as to why you became involved in the conspiracy is more difficult to answer than in the case of the other defendants. You were well remunerated by Barclays for your work but you received nothing more for accommodating traders' requests. So there was no personal gain for you.'

So much for the 'greedy trader' thing. So why did he take part in a criminal conspiracy? 'Part of the answer lies in a desire to help Barclays prosper and perhaps it had something to do with a desire to be respected by others,' said Gledhill.

These were interesting motives to become a criminal. Trying to help your employer prosper and wanting to be respected by others? Now just imagine if we all behaved like that.

The police officer who'd been sitting next to Carlo for the whole trial handcuffed him and led him out of the courtroom. They took a lift to the lowest floor. His voice drops and his speech is slow as he recalls it. 'They put me in a little cell in the basement of the court building – a concrete, tiny, horrible hole, 1½m by 2m, for the next four hours or so. At that point, the absurdity of this whole situation almost made it bearable, because I couldn't really believe that any of this was real. I felt like I was in some kind of mediaeval film where people get thrown into some stony room in the basement of a castle and they slam the door behind them.'

Carlo's next destination, HMP Wandsworth, didn't let inmates out on day release to attend a birth. Unlike some prisons, though, Carlo's cell did have a phone. He was determined to support her, spending the first weeks in prison accumulating phone credits so that when Amy went into labour, he could be on the line. He stayed glued to it for five days in his 3m-long cell, his cellmate on the bunk a yard away, until Amy gave birth to their daughter, Luna. Amy has a picture from just after the birth of her closest friend holding the phone to their newborn daughter's ear as she lay in her arms, so that Carlo could whisper his first words to her.

On 19 October 2019, the SFO announced it was dropping its inquiry into lowballing.[5] I wrote a report for the BBC website: 'An investigation into the rigging of Libor, the benchmark interest rate that tracks the cost of borrowing cash, has been unexpectedly closed. The decision comes despite evidence that implicates the Bank of England. It means no one will now be prosecuted in the UK for so-called "low-balling", where banks understate the interest rates they pay to borrow cash.'

On Twitter, a wag asked if I meant to say '*despite* evidence that implicates the Bank of England'. Shouldn't that be '*because of*'?

To Philippe Moryoussef, now a fugitive, hearing that news was more serious. 'I was really upset. Because that is the real manipulation. We didn't manipulate anything. Manipulation was done by central banks, and it had a big effect on rates. Our requests had zero effect on rates, and we can prove it. We did the maths a while ago. At the most, my requests might have made €5,000 or €10,000 of profit for the bank. But those actions from central banks had a huge impact. With our requests, they might possibly have moved the fix by a thousandth of a basis point. With central bank manipulation, we're talking about hundreds of basis points.'

The SFO had tried to bring Philippe back to trial by applying for a European Arrest Warrant in 2018. For the warrant to be executed by the French police, a French judge first had to approve it. For more than a year, nothing happened. But then in 2020, after a push by the SFO, Philippe found himself attending court in Paris to oppose the execution of the arrest warrant. If the hearing went the wrong way, Philippe would soon be on his way to a British prison to begin the eight-year sentence. On 4 June, he was waiting for his lawyer in a Paris café near the courtroom where the decision would be made, trying not to stare too hard at the abyss that might lie ahead. The French government lawyer – the Avocat Général – was about to make the case for arresting Philippe and sending him to the UK, where he would go straight to jail. This would be the most important hearing of his life.

In came François de Castro looking strangely cheerful.

'Philippe, do you believe in God?'

With only thirty minutes to go until the hearing, the SFO had just announced it was dropping the charges against all the remaining 'conspirators': Joerg Vogt, Ardalan Gharagozlou and Kai-Uwe Kappauf in Germany,[6] and Stephane Esper in France, were all discharged. Yet they'd been charged for exactly the same conduct for which the French court was now being asked to send Philippe to the UK. The SFO had just shot itself in the foot.

In court, a few minutes later, François de Castro saw the Avocat Général and asked if he was aware of the latest events.

He wasn't. 'Has there been a coup de théâtre?'[7] he asked, looking shocked.

'I'm really surprised you didn't know,' responded François with some irony. 'Where is the cooperation between you and the SFO?'

The judges weren't amused. 'Are you telling me that those just discharged were meant to be charged for the same conspiracy – the same facts?' said one, clearly surprised by the news. 'And because they communicated with Moryoussef?' She postponed the hearing and ordered the Avocat Général to seek some explanations from the SFO.

Philippe couldn't help dwelling on a bitter irony. If, like Stephane Esper and the German defendants, he had simply refused the summons to turn up at Westminster Magistrates Court on 11 January 2016, he would have been completely in the clear. If he'd gone 'on the run' from the start, he'd be free of any stain of criminality. His great mistake, and that of his old friend and colleague Christian Bittar, was that they'd put their faith in the British justice system.

In correspondence with the court, the SFO said Philippe's case was different. Unlike the others, he had been convicted. By the time it came to the postponed hearing on 4 November 2020, he was again very worried he might be sent to the UK to serve an eight-year prison sentence. 'I hesitated to enter the court room. Then I decided to go in and one Bloomberg journalist told me, "You know it's like a penalty in soccer. You jump to the side and you have a chance." I hid in the court room, seated behind my lawyer so that the judges couldn't see my face. The judge said with a big smile, "Monsieur Moryoussef, don't hide!" I stood up and I had my eyes closed, looking down; I didn't know what was going to happen. And then she announced with a big smile that they had refused the arrest warrant.' An intense feeling of relief surged through him as his friends and family let out a cheer. A smile crept onto his face. The court clerk approached him with a document he had to sign before leaving. His hand was shaking so much that he couldn't put pen to paper.

'That's the emotion,' the clerk told him with a smile.

Philippe Moryoussef is free in France but less free than the rest of us. If he crosses a border, he could be still arrested and taken to a British prison over a conviction at a trial where he wasn't present to defend himself, for a 'crime' that wasn't regarded by anyone as a crime when it happened. 'But you know what?' he says, 'When I look in the mirror every morning, I see an innocent person. And my inner freedom is much more important. But I will never give up fighting this.'

In January 2021, Sarah Tighe called her contacts in the media to a location near Ford open prison in Sussex, where her now ex-husband Tom Hayes had spent the last two years. Cameras captured the scene as he got out of the van that had just picked him up, on the day he completed his full prison tariff of half his sentence. He'd served five and a half years inside. Josh, now 9 years old, ran towards his dad who picked him up and gave him a joyful hug. For the first time since his trial, Tom stood once again in front of a scrum of a dozen photographers from the newswires and a TV camera. This time, though, he had a voice. No lawyer was there to tell him not to speak out.

'Today I've been released from prison after being sentenced for eleven years for following bank practice and doing my job the way I was trained to do it. After a traumatic sentence, I begin the process of rebuilding my life.' I interviewed him later, at a social distance, on a bandstand in Regent's Park, central London, and asked him why, even after being released, he was still fighting the jury's verdict.

'I don't blame the jury for it, but they were presented with a false narrative and they reached a conclusion based on those facts. I believe had they seen the full evidence, full disclosure, they would have reached a very different conclusion. At the time, it was expedient that, for political reasons, a banker went to prison. And I was that banker. And I was given an egregious sentence and – my life destroyed.'

Now, at last, Tom could say it. He and the other thirty-six traders and brokers had been prosecuted for a made-up crime. The real fraud was lowballing and that was ordered from the top – 'the top' meaning banks' boards, central banks and governments. But lowballing was never prosecuted. 'No one had any desire to follow the evidence. Senior managers were looking for somebody to throw under the bus. And the prosecutors were looking for someone to put in prison. The establishment were looking for people who could disguise their own complicity in the real scandal of the case, which was the actual submission of false rates. And so I had this confluence of extremely powerful interests set against me. I had banks with a market capitalisation of a quarter of a trillion dollars. I had a central bank, and a treasury, all geared to find an expedient prosecution: a prosecution that would satisfy this public desire to see a banker prosecuted and put in prison; a prosecution that would allow the behaviour of the Treasury and the Bank of England to go unseen and uninvestigated; a prosecution that would allow ambitious prosecutors on both sides of the Atlantic to burnish their credentials by putting a banker in prison. That was what this prosecution was about. This prosecution wasn't about the truth. No one wanted to investigate what was going on higher up. No one wanted to investigate high level senior managers within banks. This prosecution was a stitch-up.'

In March 2021, Carlo Palombo emerged from jail having served his full tariff. Colin Bermingham was released six months later.[8] Now at last Carlo could be with the daughter to whom he'd whispered the first words she'd ever heard, down the line on the phone from his Wandsworth cell. But his Kafka nightmare wasn't over. There were daily reminders that he'd been branded a criminal. While he was still on licence, he couldn't travel to see his family in Italy. He had to get approval from the probation officer just to spend a night away from his north London flat; and getting that approval could take months. He couldn't drive because no one would grant him car insurance. It was apparently for the sake of protecting public security that he also wasn't allowed to meet friends if they'd ever worked at Barclays.

For the twenty-four bankers wrongfully prosecuted in the UK, there is still, as at the date of writing this book, no justice. But on 27 January 2022, something unexpected happened in the USA. An appeal court fully acquitted Matt Connolly and Gavin Black, overturning their convictions.[9] Even more importantly, it flatly contradicted the whole basis for bringing the prosecutions. After thoroughly examining the evidence and the law, three senior US judges ruled that the conduct for which they'd been prosecuted, making requests for high or low Libor submissions, was not a crime.

The US court ruling also directly contradicted the UK appeal court rulings in Libor and Euribor that were used to prosecute twenty-four traders between 2015 and 2019. The United Kingdom was now the only country in the world where a trader request for a high or low Libor was treated as a criminal act.

Elated for himself and his co-defendant Gavin Black, Matt Connolly was still well aware that, for others, justice had not been served. 'My family and I are very thankful this ordeal is finally ending, and that the courts have finally recognised once and for all my innocence,' he said. 'I am hoping the rest of the story emerges, so others that have been denied justice can get their peace as well. The nine trials on both sides of the Atlantic have been a whole series of miscarriages of justice, where innocent people were jailed who had done nothing wrong. The only Libor "rigging" that was really bad was the lowballing. That was ordered from the top – by banks' senior management, central banks and governments. And neither the Department of Justice nor the Serious Fraud Office has ever brought that to trial.'

Among those still denied justice in the USA were two British former traders, Tony Allen and Tony Conti. There was a bitter irony. When they'd appealed against their convictions in 2015, they'd made all the arguments that Matt's lawyers had just made. But because the appeal judges chose to focus on the Kastigar issue, they hadn't ruled on whether making or accepting trader requests for high or low Libors within a range of offered rates was illegal. This was the first time any court in the USA had ruled on the very thing that had turned their lives upside down.

The outcome of the whole story for Tony Conti was so twisted it bordered on the insane. Over eight years, he'd lost his job, his career, his home and his mental health. His family had had to move from one rented house to another, five times. He'd been charged by a country he'd never worked in and hauled over to the USA for a trial that was unwinnable. He'd been convicted, sentenced, acquitted, then spent four years of further torment trying to win a settlement from his former employer to get his family out of poverty. Then, eight years after it had started, the US legal system had decided he didn't do anything wrong in the first place.

Had the US legal system made that decision earlier, there would have been no trial of Matt Connolly and Gavin Black; and it would have been much easier for them to win compensation that came close to making up for what they and their families had suffered.

Looking back over the history of interest rate 'rigging' and its prosecution, the implications were mind-blowing. After a decade of the US Department of Justice calling trader requests 'corrupt', 'fraudulent' and 'criminal', the US courts had just ruled that they weren't even against any rules. The SFO's prosecutions would never have happened but for a statement in the DOJ's 2012 press release announcing the fine for Barclays, where, without referring to any laws, it declared that the trader requests were 'illegal'. That word 'illegal' was crucial. Without it, without a doubt, there would have been no media outrage, no public outcry, and no political pressure on the SFO to reverse its earlier decision not to prosecute. Seven trials of traders in the UK for Libor and Euribor 'manipulation' would not have gone ahead. The UK and US regulators had extracted almost $9 billion in fines from banks' shareholders that would have been much harder to extract without the criminal prosecutions. The criminal authorities had let the banks investigate themselves through their lawyers, who'd supplied to prosecutors the victims to be thrown under the bus and drawn their attention to the 'evidence' with which to do so. But now the US courts had decided that that statement by the US government a decade before, that traders' requests were illegal, had been wrong all along. Ten years of suffering for the traders and their families – and ten years of cover-up by the Bank of England, the Fed, the regulators, the UK government and the DOJ – need never have happened.

In February 2022, the BBC broadcast a five-part podcast series, *The Lowball Tapes*, laying out evidence of a cover-up, at the highest levels of the US and British financial establishments, of a fraud ordered from the top that had never been prosecuted: lowballing. Any listener could now hear the audio recordings that authorities on both sides of the Atlantic never wanted the public to hear from the phone lines of PJ, John Ewan and their bosses. They could also read the evidence[10] that the interest rate-rigging trials were a whole series of miscarriages of justice in which the original whistleblowers of the whole scandal, Peter Johnson and Colin Bermingham, had been thanked by the authorities for their honesty by being prosecuted and sent to jail.

The regulatory and criminal pursuit of Libor and Euribor 'manipulation' was sunk in irony. It wasn't the traders' requests that were 'rigged': it was the investigations, the trials – the whole system. The collusion between prosecutors and their supposed targets allowed banks' lawyers to manipulate justice to pass the buck downwards and ensure the banks' top directors got away, scot-free, with no personal accountability to match their exorbitant rewards. Far from punishing dishonesty, the pursuit of traders and brokers for 'rigging' interest rates was in itself dishonest and self-interested. First, regulators rode a wave of justified public anger towards the banks. Then bank lawyers, prosecutors and judges combined to deflect that anger – away from the truly greedy, truly reckless culprits of the financial crisis at the top, and down to the traders and brokers below.

The traders who were jailed are now out of prison, but they aren't free. They are yet to be released from the injustice that is almost constantly at the forefront of their minds. The lives of the scapegoats and their families have been devastated. Unless and until their convictions are overturned, they'll still be wrongly branded 'fraudsters' and treated in their daily lives like criminals.

'It's just the injustice of the whole system,' says Carlo. 'It's just haunting me every day. The senselessness of it – and feeling … persecuted. Every night I go to bed and I can't sleep thinking of the injustice of the whole thing. I keep replaying the words of the prosecutor and the judge, in my mind, every day, every night. The whole experience has just completely traumatised and shocked me to the point that yes, now I'm back in the world, I can see my daughter and be with my wife. But I'm disengaged, I don't trust society. I don't trust my fellow human beings after seeing what a jury could do to me. I'm just afraid of the world around me, knowing how violent people can be, and especially how violent people can be when they feel they're in the right and feeling that they're punishing someone who needs to be punished. The experience has just destroyed me. Destroyed my trust in the world, society, people. All of it.'

EPILOGUE:
THE PRICE OF SILENCE

When the BBC broadcast *Panorama*'s 'The Big Bank Fix' on 10 April 2017, we asked Sir Paul Tucker, Baron Mervyn King and Bob Diamond for an interview. They declined or didn't reply, as did Sir Jeremy Heywood, Sir Tom Scholar, Angela Knight, Steve Obie, Gary Gensler, Greg Mocek and John Ewan. In February 2022 when the BBC broadcast the investigative podcast, *The Lowball Tapes*, there was a similar lack of openness. Two judges, Jeremy Cooke and Michael Gledhill, declined to comment on the basis of the convention that judges do not comment on the cases they have presided over. For this book,[1] the former Lord Chief Justice of England and Wales, John Thomas, has similarly declined to comment – as did former Lord Justice Nigel Davis, Lanny Breuer, Eric Holder and Sir David Green.

At first, most of the defendants at the rate-rigging trials also had no wish to speak to us. When you are in trouble you understandably cleave to your lawyer's advice, which is typically: 'Don't talk to the media; and especially not until the trial's over.' This has the unfortunate consequence that if anyone thinks they have been the victim of a miscarriage of justice, their lawyers advise them against making a noise about it, especially if they have not yet been sentenced. Each defendant at first fully expected us to do exactly what most other members of the media had done: copy the prosecutor's story, dump the blame on them for something that really wasn't their fault and fail to listen when they tried to explain why they were innocent.

After all, as people in the audience at executions all around the world have known for centuries, satisfying a sense of collective anger by hanging a miscreant is more fun than trying to understand the evidence (or wrestling with the logical absurdity of the law). It took months of persuasion and a *Panorama* documentary to convince most of the defendants that someone in the media was indeed listening.

Freedom of Information requests on matters as contentious as this are well defended. The Bank of England, in particular, has consistently refused requests to release documents relating to its own knowledge of Libor 'manipulation' in general and lowballing in particular – in spite of a public pledge in 2017 to do so when the trials were over. Given the evidence we now have of Bank of England involvement in manipulating Libor on a much larger scale than any of the jailed traders, and of government involvement in the same, is it tolerable that this information should remain secret?

There is a cure for the non-disclosure agreements and gagging clauses that have been signed by many of those who were involved. It's called a parliamentary inquiry. Because of parliamentary privilege, debate in the House of Commons or its committees is protected from legal interference; lawyers for the banks or the wealthy individuals at the top could not seek to silence key witnesses by threatening to sue them for breach of contract or libel. If parliamentary privilege is designed for anything, it is to get to the bottom of scandals like this one and demand answers – such as who at the Bank of England knew that it spent the crisis of 2007/08 pressuring Barclays and other banks to lower (or raise) their Libors? Why have they watched the trials unfold, seen traders jailed and never said anything about what they knew about the extent of their own involvement? Why did neither the US Department of Justice nor the Fed tell Congress about the evidence they had of the Fed's knowledge of and involvement in lowballing? Did Gordon Brown press for Libors to be lowered in October 2008 to show his emergency crisis measures were working and try to restore confidence? Did anyone tell the then prime minister that, according to the definition of Libor, it had to reflect the real cost on the money markets of borrowing cash; that forcing it down was against the rules? Did Brown urge other countries and central banks, already cooperating in tackling the global financial crisis, to co-ordinate their instructions to banks to get Libor and Euribor down? He declined offers of an interview for *The Lowball Tapes*. But he did give an interview to a friendly journalist, a few weeks after our series was broadcast, saying he regretted not jailing bankers after the crisis. Of course, strictly speaking, it's not for a prime minister, former or current, to initiate a criminal investigation, for good reasons to do with the independence from politics of the courts (so little in evidence in the rate-rigging trials). After our 2017 film, MPs called for an immediate inquiry and the Labour Party leadership did the same. But then they got distracted by other matters – terrorism, elections, Brexit, Trump, etc. – and forgot. In 2022, there were similar calls, somewhat drowned out on the news bulletins by the horrors emerging from the conflict in Ukraine. MPs who truly care about getting to the truth of this mess have in this book all the evidence they need to renew their demands for an inquiry – evidence that points to dishonesty, not at the bottom but at the top of the financial establishment. And it needs to be rigorous this time, with no interference from, and the full cooperation of, top officials from governments and central banks.

One obvious reform could improve matters. Advocates of banking reform say the law must be changed, as it has been in health and safety, to ensure responsibility rests at the top by making chief executives liable if they fail to prevent any criminal misconduct anywhere in their bank under their watch. In the case of health and safety, just the threat of prosecution of senior directors transformed the industry, cutting the number of accidents due to criminally negligent safety standards and improving the industry's reputation. Not a soul had to go to jail to achieve that. A similar law came into effect in the Bribery Act; if chief executives fail to prevent bribery by the companies they lead, then they can be prosecuted. It could also be the case that if chief executives preside over the crime of fraud carried out by their companies, then they, as individuals, are criminally liable. That would be a far more effective method of stopping real wrongdoing than the mass of red tape that has descended on banks' trading floors since the various rigging scandals. And that way the top bankers' extravagant rewards, far out of line with the banking salaries of the past, would be a little less indefensible on one ground at least: it would be the responsibility of bank chief executives to prevent criminal activity.

Ultimately, the truth is that neither the traders nor the Financial Services Authority nor the Bank of England should have been prosecuted. Libel lawyers: relax. It's important to say clearly, for the record, that any evidence that Paul Tucker, Angela Knight, Miles Storey, Mark Dearlove or John Ewan condoned or engaged in 'rigging' Libor does not, in fact, suggest they were acting with any criminal intent. As their defenders are keen to say, they were simply trying to do their jobs. Very difficult jobs, in the middle of the worst financial crisis in eighty years.

But here's the thing. So too were the traders. Their conduct, like that of the bank bosses and central bankers, was caught by the sweeping judge-made law retrospectively criminalising any commercial influence on the setting of Libor and Euribor – a highly questionable law the Supreme Court has never had the chance to examine. If there's anything here to judge 'harshly', it is the way regulators and prosecutors, without any sanction from Congress or Parliament, effectively privatised their investigations, relying on banks' lawyers to do their jobs for them. That opened the way for justice to be manipulated and for innocent scapegoats to be targeted and 'thrown under the bus' – a cynical practice that's now all too familiar in Wall Street and the City of London. What made it worse was the comprehensive failure of those in the establishment who knew what had really gone on to have the guts to stand up and speak about it in public. The Commodity Futures Trading Commission and later the DOJ needed to be told they had got it wrong by someone who knew. What they should have been saying is that the criminalisation of traders' requests is nonsensical and that there are good reasons why we don't criminalise commercial practices in ret-rospect. You end up locking up people who were merely doing what their bosses had told them to do. Yet instead of bringing sanity to proceedings, everyone in prominent positions ran scared of the US authorities.

In his classic 1890 work on the anthropology of beliefs, *The Golden Bough*, Sir James Fraser described how in pre-Old Testament Jewish culture and in countless other religious and pre-religious traditions, the belief was that if evil struck, it could be expelled if an animal were magically loaded up with the evil and sent out of the village. Everyone could then rest easy. In our own eyes, we think we're more civilised than we were then, when punish-ments were savage and based on mythical beliefs and stories. But myths were created in the Libor trials too, such as the prosecution story of the fine upstanding Libor submitter who would always set a 'true cash rate'. Prices are not true or false, they just *are*.

We have the same brains as the people of the past who believed their scapegoat would rid them of the evil come among them. The same hard wiring, the same emotional responses, the same capacity for anger and indignation. We may no longer be literally lobbing stones. But if we secretly enjoy seeing someone condemned to jail, we need to be careful. Similar brain circuitry is firing. And someone may have had an ulterior motive for accusing their neighbour of a stoning offence.

It is ironic that as an audience, our own judgement of the Libor scandal is twisted by self-interest. We believe what we wish to believe and what is within the comfort zone of our normal experience. Our sentiments are unimaginatively confined to: 'They jailed some corrupt traders – good.' It's far easier to go along with the prosecutor's story and parrot it in news reports than it is to listen to and check out the extraordinary claims of miscarriages of justice and a cover-up by the authorities. Especially when the evidence supporting the true facts – known to a select few who don't wish the truth to come out – is carefully withheld from official announcements or, worse, withheld from juries. Instead of digging deeper to see the reality of it, we all too easily go along with the story that those in the financial and legal establishment would prefer us to believe. A bunch of crims down the ranks of the banks went rogue and did some dodgy stuff. But the truth is more shocking, more revealing and, above all, stranger.

NOTES

Chapter 1: Lowball

1 This email, together with other communications from Barclays about Libor and Euribor, was published by the Federal Reserve Bank of New York on 13 July 2012, in response to a congressional request. Barclays redacted PJ and Dearlove's names from the email chain. I have confirmed PJ as the author from internal Barclays documents shared with regulators in the UK, USA and Europe: Federal Reserve Bank of New York, 'New York Fed Responds to Congressional Request for Information on Barclays – LIBOR Matter', 13 July 2012 (www.newyorkfed.org/newsevents/news/markets/2012/Barclays_ LIBOR_Matter.html). I have prepared a free interactive timeline to accompany the book that allows readers to view documentary evidence and hear audio recordings. To view the timeline, search 'Andy Verity Rigged Interactive Timeline'.

2 Barclays Capital is now named Barclays Corporate and Investment Bank.

3 Jerry del Missier would take home £47.3 million in 2010. Similar sums were extracted from Barclays over the years by Rich Ricci and Bob Diamond. Harry Wilson, 'Jerry del Missier is highest paid employee of Barclays', *The Telegraph*, 8 March 2011 (www.telegraph.co.uk/finance/newsbysector/banksandfinance/8367108/Jerry-del-Missier-is-highest-paid-employee-of-Barclays.html).

4 The account given here is based on testimony given to the DOJ by Jerry del Missier in February 2011 (also mentioned in Chapter 8). It was disclosed in US proceedings in the 2016 trial in New York of Tony Conti and Tony Allen, two British former Rabobank traders.

5 For the sake of verbal economy, traders typically mention only the first two figures after the decimal point and leave out the figure that precedes it, e.g. '5.30%' becomes '30'; and '5.50%' becomes '50'.

Chapter 2: Instructions to Lie

1 In April 2017, following a BBC *Panorama* film on the rate-rigging scandal titled 'The Big Bank Fix', the Bank of England said in a statement: 'The Bank is committed

to publishing materials relating to the SFO's investigations into benchmark manipulation when it is appropriate to do so. Until the SFO's ongoing prosecutorial activity relating to Libor and other benchmarks has concluded, the Bank is not in a position to publish these materials.' The SFO's investigation and prosecution of Libor formally ended in 2019 and its investigation of Euribor closed soon after that date. Since then, all requests to the Bank of England for such material under the Freedom of Information Act have been refused. However, suppressed Bank of England material has been leaked, cross-referenced and authenticated.

2 I co-presented *Wake Up to Money* from 2005 to 2013 alongside Mickey Clark. Mickey read out this text at the very end of the programme.

3 The G7 group of advanced industrial nations includes the USA, Canada, the UK, France, Germany, Italy and Japan.

4 A transcript of this conversation was released by the Federal Reserve Bank of New York in anonymised form on 13 July 2012. The official is named only as 'Mark'. Federal Reserve Bank of New York, 'New York Fed Responds to Congressional Request for Information on Barclays – LIBOR Matter', 13 July 2012 (www.newyorkfed. org/newsevents/news/markets/2012/Barclays_LIBOR_Matter.html). This is one of several records published at the same time.

5 Dearlove gave this information to senior executives at Barclays in 2012 and also revealed it to the DOJ in 2011 (see pages 149 and 172).

6 These and other email exchanges between Tucker, Heywood and Scholar were extracted through a Freedom of Information request from John Mann, a member of the Treasury committee of MPs, in July 2012. They were published by *The Guardian* ahead of Tucker's first appearance before the Treasury committee's inquiry into Libor on 9 July 2012. Staff, 'Libor rate-fixing scandal: Paul Tucker and Jeremy Heywood emails', *The Guardian*, 9 July 2012 (www.theguardian.com/business/ interactive/2012/jul/09/libor-jeremy-heywood-paul-tucker-emails).

7 Tucker twice raised the calls he'd received from senior Whitehall figures about Barclays' Libor submissions, according to Diamond's file note of 29 October 2008. The full text is as follows:

> Further to our last call, Mr Tucker reiterated that he had received calls from a number of senior figures within Whitehall to question why Barclays was always toward the top end of the Libor pricing. His response was "you have to pay what you have to pay". I asked if he could relay the reality, that not all banks were providing quotes at the levels that represented real transactions, his response "oh that would be worse".
>
> I explained again our market rate driven policy and that it had recently meant that we appeared in the top quartile and on occasion the top decile of the pricing. Equally I noted that we continued to see others in the market posting rates at levels that were not representative of where they would actually undertake business. This latter point has on occasion pushed us higher than would otherwise appear to be the case. In fact, we are not having to pay up for money at all. Mr Tucker stated the levels of calls he was receiving from Whitehall were 'senior' and that while he was certain we did not need advice, that it did not always need to be the case that we appeared as high as we have recently. – RED.

This can be found at the following link: https://publications.parliament.uk/pa/cm201213/cmselect/cmtreasy/481/48106.htm.

8 The 'ratios' set by Group Treasury, the Bank of England and the FSA were the amount of cash or other liquid assets (i.e. assets that could be quickly sold, such as government bonds) that Barclays was required to hold against the loans it had lent out.

9 Setting Libor rates at one level and paying another in the markets amounted to lowballing, which according to the US regulators was one form of Libor 'manipulation'. This email chain is one of a number of pieces of evidence that calls into question Bob Diamond's evidence to Parliament that he didn't know about lowballing until July 2012.

10 The official is identified, without a surname, as 'Peggy' in documents released in July 2012 by the New York Fed: Federal Reserve Bank of New York, 'Unofficial transcript of telephone call on 27 October 2008 at 12: 17 GMT between and an individual named Peggy at the Federal Reserve Bank of New York', 27 October 2008 (www.newyorkfed.org/medialibrary/media/newsevents/news/markets/2012/libor/October_27_2008_transcript.pdf).

11 Whitehall is the street in Westminster, central London, on or near which the headquarters of central government departments are located, including the Treasury. As some government departments have been relocated elsewhere, 'Whitehall' has come to be used to refer more broadly to all UK central government departments, wherever they are located.

12 This account draws on Bob Diamond's testimony to the Treasury committee of 4 July 2012. See Question 82, at: https://www.parliament.uk/globalassets/documents/commons-committees/treasury/Treasury-Committee-04-July-12-Bob-Diamond.pdf.

13 This paragraph draws on the account of Jerry del Missier to the Treasury committee on 16 July 2012 Question 825. His oral evidence is here: https://publications.parliament.uk/pa/cm201213/cmselect/cmtreasy/481/48102.htm

14 Halifax Bank of Scotland was formed from the 2001 merger of Bank of Scotland (distinct from RBS – Royal Bank of Scotland) and the UK's biggest building society, Halifax.

15 The US investigation was into dollar Libors set by PJ and others. Neither the US agencies nor the Financial Services Authority set out the evidence acquired by investigators about the Bank of England's interventions in the setting of sterling Libor, in both August 2007 (see page 52) and October 2008. This made it harder for UK small business customers to sue Barclays for manipulating the sterling Libor rate used to set interest rates on their bank loans.

16 CPFF: the Commercial Paper Funding Facility was one of a number of schemes brought in by the Federal Reserve Bank of New York to inject liquidity into frozen interbank cash markets. The New York Fed created a special purpose vehicle offering to buy commercial paper (short-term IOU notes issued by banks).

17 The data can be cross-checked here: Simon Rogers, 'The Libor rate submissions by each bank, 2005 to 2008', The Guardian, 3 July 2012 (www.theguardian.com/news/datablog/2012/jul/03/libor-rates-set-banks).

NOTES

Chapter 3: The Secret Orchestra

1 Angela Knight was contacted for her comments on the passages referring to her. She said she was not able to comment in detail due to ongoing legal proceedings but said 'there was nothing untoward whatsoever in the BBA's handling of Libor matters in the financial crisis and it is completely wrong to say or imply that the BBA or I "knew" of anything inappropriate'.

2 Carrick Mollenkamp, 'Bankers Cast Doubt On Key Rate Amid Crisis', *The Wall Street Journal*, 16 April 2008 (www.wsj.com/articles/SB120831164167818299).

3 Knight's concern is underlined in an email chain, sent as a follow-up to her memo on 9 April (set out on page 46). It is dated 2 May 2008 and was exhibited in the trial of Tom Hayes on 9 June 2015.

4 In 2013, when the FSA's internal audit team reported the results of a trawl of the FSA's records to see what it knew about Libor manipulation, it found a record of this meeting being arranged, but no record of the meeting itself. See the bottom of page 80, Communication 65, at the following link: www.fca.org.uk/publication/corporate/fsa-ia-libor.pdf.

5 Ewan originally sent a memo to Knight setting out the proposals on 27 March 2008, outlining a 'carrot and stick' approach to fixing lowballing. Recommendation 1 – orchestrating coordinated movement – was the 'carrot' because no one bank need be out of line with competitors. Recommendation 2 – spot checks on the veracity of Libor submissions accompanied by the threat of being removed from the panel – was the stick. Most of the wording of Knight's memo of 9 April 2008 was lifted from Ewan's original memo of 27 March, which was exhibited at the trial of Tom Hayes, 9 June 2015 (transcript page 9).

6 In 2017, banks formed a new trade association together with the Council of Mortgage Lenders and Payments UK to be called UK Finance. While this has been reported as a merger, UK Finance has confirmed that the BBA remains a separate legal entity and said 'the BBA does not form part of UK Finance. The BBA was never merged with UK Finance nor is UK Finance a "successor" organisation to the BBA.'

7 The role of the FXMMC and the BBA in Libor was taken over by the Incontintental Exchange (ICE); BBA Libor became ICE Libor on 1 February 2014. This followed an official review of Libor by incoming FCA regulator Martin Wheatley, who recommended that Libor should be retained but reformed. His recommendations included stripping the BBA of its responsibility and bringing it under FCA regulation. However, in July 2017, his successor as FCA chief executive, former Bank of England chief cashier Andrew Bailey, announced the FCA would no longer require banks to submit estimates to Libor after 2021, signalling the beginning of a transition away from Libor for use on regulated markets. ICE Libor has now been discontinued for some currencies and will be discontinued (no longer be representative) after June 2023.

8 See Chapter 6 for an explanation of why traders wanted estimates of the cost of borrowing cash (Libor submissions) adjusted to take account of their trading positions. The information in this paragraph is taken from comments given to Ewan in annual reviews he conducted of the Libor setting process. The BBA would invite banks to comment and they'd send their views to him. The reviews were exhibited

at the later trials of traders that took place between 2015 and 2019 for 'rigging' Libor or Euribor. These were exhibited in both the Hayes trial (trial transcript 05/06/15) and the two Barclays trials (e.g. 15 June 2016).

9 The defaulting mortgages that caused the credit crunch were largely 'subprime', meaning they were lent to homebuyers with poor credit records or on modest incomes that would normally be ruled out for mortgages, as opposed to 'prime' borrowers with higher incomes and stronger credit records.

10 The BBA definition states: 'A BBA Libor contributor panel bank will contribute the rate at which it could borrow funds were it to do so by asking for and then accepting interbank offers in reasonable market size just prior to 1100.'

11 I have deliberately postponed the more detailed explanation of what caused the losses on investments linked to US mortgages and therefore have avoided using the term 'subprime' until there's the necessary space to explain what it means. It was of course, largely 'subprime' mortgages, meaning loans lent to people with poor credit records ('subprime') that caused the crisis. They were lent without properly assessing how affordable or not the loans would be after introductory offers of cheap initial interest rates expired and loans reset at much higher rates. The resets often doubled or trebled the borrowers' repayments. Many borrowers responded by simply sending their keys back to the mortgage companies (a phenomenon known as 'jingle mail'), crystallising losses for the investment vehicles that had bought the right to collect the mortgage repayments.

12 A transcript of this call, and other calls, was adduced and exhibited in the trial of Tom Hayes in June 2015.

Chapter 4: Collusion

1 Ewan's original draft, which took the form of a memo from him to Angela Knight dated 27 March 2008, contained the following: 'The CEOs or the chairman of the banks on the FX committee make up the majority of the BBA board and I believe it's these individuals alone who have the authority and strategic outlook necessary to effect this change.'

2 Ewan's draft memo was exhibited at the trial of Tom Hayes on 9 June 2015.

3 This is recorded in leaked minutes of the Money Markets Liaison Group, cross-referenced and authenticated by the author.

4 The dialogue contains extracts from the full transcript, published by the New York Fed following a congressional request in July 2012. Barclays supplied the transcript, originally collated by Barclays' external lawyers Sullivan & Cromwell in response to a CFTC request. Barclays Legal redacted the transcript to remove Colin Bermingham's name. The redacted version is here: Federal Reserve Bank of New York, 'Unofficial Transcript: ID09274211', 11 April 2008 (www.newyorkfed.org/medialibrary/media/newsevents/news/markets/2012/libor/April_11_2008_transcript.pdf).

5 The quotes in this chapter, like almost all the conversations in this book, are either verbatim or very close to verbatim, with small edits to tidy up the text or for clarity, selected from transcripts of contemporaneous audio recordings.

6 John Ewan tells Miles Storey in this phone call that RBS wasn't at the meeting but he appears to have made an error. The presence of RBS is confirmed in the minutes.

7 This email was exhibited and discussed in detail, as were the Storey–Ewan phone calls in this chapter on 16 April and 10 October, at the Tom Hayes trial on 9 June 2015.

Chapter 5: A Point to Prove

1 Banks had failed to warn investors of the extent to which the value of those investments depended on the repayments of millions of mortgage borrowers known as 'subprime' because they had low incomes or patchy credit records. Mortgage brokers had sold the borrowers home loans with cheap discounted interest rates for the first two years but failed to warn them that when those discounts came to an end, their repayments might double or treble. When that happened, millions simply left their homes and sent their keys back through the mail – a phenomenon known as 'jingle mail'. With house prices slumping, the loans couldn't be recouped by selling the house.

2 This account of events at the CFTC draws on published articles and also material from interviews with Steve Obie and Gary Gensler published in the 2016 book *The Fix*, by Bloomberg journalists Liam Vaughan and Gavin Finch.

3 Ken Silverstein, 'Senator Sanders Blocking Key Obama Nomination', *Harper's*, 23 March 2009 (https://harpers.org/2009/03/senator-sanders-blocking-key-obama-nomination/).

4 The term 'lowballing' was used by *The Wall Street Journal* in 2008 but was not widely adopted in London until after 2012. The FSA classified these communications as referring to 'lowballing' the phenomenon (as opposed to 'lowballing' the term), meaning banks posting Libor rates that were false because they were too low to reflect the real interest rates they would have to pay to borrow cash.

5 Financial Services Authority, *Internal Audit Report*, p.23, Communication 10 (www.fca. org.uk/publication/corporate/fsa-ia-libor.pdf). This evidence is one of a number of contemporaneous documents that call into question evidence given by Paul Tucker to Parliament on 9 July 2012, claiming he wasn't aware of lowballing until 2012.

6 Financial Services Authority, *Internal Audit Report*, p.31, Communication 19 (www. fca.org.uk/publication/corporate/fsa-ia-libor.pdf).

7 'Misleading statements in relation to bench marks' were outlawed for the first time in Section 91 of the Financial Services Act 2012 (www.legislation.gov.uk/ukpga/2012/21/section/91).

8 Hector Sants stepped down as chief executive of the FSA in June 2012, before the publication on 27 June 2012 of the first fine for Libor manipulation, against Barclays Bank plc.

9 Federal Reserve Bank of New York, 'New York Fed Responds to Congressional Request for Information on Barclays - LIBOR Matter', 13 July 2012 (www.newyorkfed. org/newsevents/news/markets/2012/Barclays_LIBOR_Matter.html). The evidence of the New York Fed's knowledge of lowballing was disclosed in July 2012, including a number of transcripts of recorded calls and emails, supplied to the Fed by Barclays with names redacted. I have discovered the names by matching with transcripts from the Barclays internal investigation that have been leaked.

10 Margaret Cole left the FSA on garden leave in March 2012, three months before the FSA published its regulatory notices fining Barclays. When asked to respond to

references to her in this book before publication, Ms Cole stressed in a statement through her lawyers that she had not had a leading role in relation to concerns which arose in relation to Libor and, to the extent she was involved, she worked diligently and professionally. As director of enforcement of the FSA, she had always pursued the investigation into possible improper conduct properly and without hesitation or deviation, resulting in adverse regulatory findings against Barclays and the imposition of a very substantial financial penalty. There had been no failings on her part.

11 This information comes from a leaked Bank of England roundup of market intelligence, written by Christian Hawkesby, of Paul Tucker's markets division, titled 'Bilateral meetings with bank treasurers and fund managers – 29 Oct to 7 Nov 2008'.

12 Financial Services Authority, *Internal Audit Report*, 80, Communication 65 (www.fca. org.uk/publication/corporate/fsa-ia-libor.pdf). Names have been matched from an organogram on page 6 of the FSA Annual Report 2008/09.

Chapter 6: Lip Service

1 PJ's nickname at work for Jonathan was 'JJ'.

2 Much of the information on Jonathan Mathew in this and the following chapters is taken from his testimony at his trial in May 2016, supplemented by summaries and transcripts of interviews given to Barclays' compliance officials and external lawyers, the DOJ and the SFO.

3 The money brokers were even more male-dominated than the trading floors, with very few women dealing with the cash traders, who were also overwhelmingly male.

4 The lenders weren't just banks but also specialised money market funds – whose whole purpose was to take deposits from retail customers and lend cash to the market – along with central banks and large corporations with spare cash to lend.

5 Itsu is a chain of sushi restaurants in the UK.

6 Sisse, a Danish female name, is pronounced 'See-suh'.

Chapter 7: Confirmation Bias

1 Bob Diamond was known to prefer to give instructions verbally, keeping his emails to a minimum.

2 This definition is from Oxford Languages, via Google.

3 The account here draws on material published in the 2016 book *The Fix*, whose authors Liam Vaughan and Gavin Finch interviewed Steve Obie. I approached Obie to comment but without success.

Chapter 8: A Tangled Web

1 Jonathan Mathew evidence-in-chief, 13 May 2016, trial transcript p.2.

2 Barclays announced on 14 August 2013 that Chris Lucas was stepping down as finance director due to ill health. I offered him via email the opportunity to comment on the evidence of directions he gave about Libor while on the board of Barclays. A representative of his responded on his behalf to say Mr Lucas's health situation was such that he could not take up the invitation.

3 An extract from Jerry del Missier's February 2011 interview at the DOJ in Washington was disclosed in the 2016 New York trial of two British bankers, Tony Allen and Tony Conti of Rabobank. They were initially convicted but were acquitted on appeal to the Second Circuit of the US criminal courts. Tony Conti's story is set out in Chapter 15.

4 Jonathan Mathew evidence-in-chief, 13 May 2016 p.106.

5 On 24 August 2017 the DOJ formally indicted two French Société Générale employees, Danielle Sindzingre and Muriel Bescond, with manipulating Libor – in this instance lowballing (www.justice.gov/opa/pr/two-international-bank-managers-charged-libor-interest-rate-manipulation-scheme). This did not concern the lowballing in the financial crisis – which has never been prosecuted – but instead allegations of lowballing between May 2010 and October 2011. However, in the five years since then, Sindzingre and Bescond have never travelled to the USA to face criminal proceedings (the alleged offences aren't regarded in France as criminal and previous requests to execute arrest warrants from France have been refused). Bescond has for years been applying to the US courts, from France, to have the US indictment dismissed. While a lower US court in May 2019 decided Muriel Bescond was a fugitive, refusing her application, in August 2021 a higher US court overturned that ruling (www.reuters.com/article/us-societe-generale-decision-bescond-idUSKBN2F6239). On 29 March 2023 the DOJ submitted a motion to a US court in Long Island, New York, to dismiss Bescond's indictment.

Chapter 9: Diamond Geezer

1 James Burton, 'Fred the Shred in line for a £17m pension: Bumper retirement pot for man who took RBS to brink of collapse', *This is Money*, 14 September 2018 (www.thisismoney.co.uk/money/markets/article-6169589/Fred-Shred-line-17m-pension.html).

2 John Paul Ford Rojas, 'London riots: Lidl water thief jailed for six months', *The Telegraph*, 11 August 2011 (www.telegraph.co.uk/news/uknews/crime/8695988/London-riots-Lidl-water-thief-jailed-for-six-months.html).

3 BBC News, 27 June 2012.

4 Becky Barrow, James Salmon and Rob Preece, 'Ed Miliband demands CRIMINAL probe into Barclays interest rate rigging scandal as £3.2bn is wiped off bank in share plunge', *Daily Mail*, 27 June 2012 (www.dailymail.co.uk/news/article-2165468/Ed-Miliband-demands-CRIMINAL-probe-Barclays-scandal-3-2bn-wiped-bank-share-plunge.html).

5 Jill Treanor, 'Bob Diamond stands firm against MPs' calls he forgo his bonus', *The Guardian*, 11 January 2011 (www.theguardian.com/business/2011/jan/11/bob-diamond-stands-firm-mp-bonus).

6 Bob Diamond, 'Today business lecture 2011', BBC Radio 4 (http://news.bbc.co.uk/today/hi/today/newsid_9630000/9630673.stm).

7 Because civil servants, bankers and lawyers worked around the clock at government offices on Whitehall, central London on the weekend of 11–12 October, they ordered takeaway Indian meals – mostly baltis – to sustain them.

8 BBC News, 28 June 2012.

9 HC Deb, 28 June 2012, col 465 (https://publications.parliament.uk/pa/cm201213/cmhansrd/cm120628/debtext/120628-0002.htm).

10 BBC News, 28 June 2012.

11 *Question Time*, BBC One, 28 June 2012.

12 One of Smith's own employees, Noel Cryan, would later be thrown under the bus and prosecuted together with other money brokers as part of an alleged conspiracy to defraud. The jury would find all of the brokers not guilty.

13 In the UK, there were seven rate-rigging trials in the UK brought by the SFO between 2015 and 2019. In none of them did the SFO produce a victim of the alleged fraud conspiracies to testify.

14 The DOJ announcement is here: US Department of Justice, Office of Public Affairs, 'Barclays Bank PLC Admits Misconduct Related to Submissions for the London Interbank Offered Rate and the Euro Interbank Offered Rate and Agrees to Pay $160 Million Penalty', 27 June 2012 (www.justice.gov/opa/pr/barclays-bank-plc-admits-misconduct-related-submissions-london-interbank-offered-rate-and). The CFTC announcement, with links to false statements, is here: Commodity Futures Trading Commission, 'Release Number 6289-12', 27 June 2012 (www.cftc.gov/PressRoom/PressReleases/6289-12). The FSA press release is here: Financial Services Authority, 'Barclays fined £59.5 million for significant failings in relation to LIBOR and EURIBOR', 27 June 2012 (www.fca.org.uk/news/press-releases/barclays-fined-%C2%A3595-million-significant-failings-relation-libor-and-euribor).

15 Bob Diamond, oral evidence to the Treasury committee, 4 July 2012. Q 237: 'The amount of money we have spent on this investigation is about £100m.' (https://publications.parliament.uk/pa/cm201213/cmselect/cmtreasy/481/120704.htm).

16 The Libor trials took place within the jurisdiction of England and Wales and of the United States of America. No trials have been held in either Scotland or Northern Ireland. Where the term 'British courts' is used, it is to distinguish the cases heard in London from those heard in New York.

17 See Chapters 1, 2, 3 and 8.

18 The full Final Notice is here: Financial Services Authority, 'Final Notice: 122702', 27 June 2012 (www.fca.org.uk/publication/final-notices/barclays-jun12.pdf).

19 On paragraph 47 of the DOJ Statement of Facts it said: 'On October 29, 2008, a senior Bank of England official contacted a senior Barclays manager. The Bank of England official discussed the external perceptions of Barclays's Libor submissions and questioned why Barclays's submissions were high compared to other contributor Panel banks. As the substance of the conversation was passed to other Barclays employees, certain Barclays managers formed the understanding that they had been instructed by the Bank of England to lower Barclays's LIBOR submissions, and instructed the Barclays Dollar and Sterling LIBOR submitters to do so – even though that was not the understanding of the senior Barclays individual who had the call with the Bank of England official' (www.justice.gov/iso/opa/resources/9312012710173426365941.pdf).

20 Please see page 86 and accompanying note.

21 The central banks involved in the coordinated official cut on 8 October were the Fed, the Bank of England, the ECB, the Bank of Canada, the Swiss National Bank and the Swedish central bank, Sveriges Riksbank. The Bank of Japan was also involved in discussions between central banks. However, the central banks had also seen how

previous coordinated cuts, earlier in the crisis, had not been transmitted – meaning that the official rate cut had not been passed on in lower lending rates in the real economy. The real cost of money was measured by Libor and Euribor. The failure of Libor to fall fast enough to show emergency measures were working led to serious concern in Downing Street, as evidenced by emails disclosed to the Treasury committee from Jeremy Heywood, Tom Scholar and Paul Tucker.

22 The publisher sent the FCA (formerly FSA) a detailed sixteen-point right of reply letter in December 2022. The regulator replied in March 2023 saying it was 'wrong that the FSA took no action concerning the taped telephone call between Mark Dearlove and Peter Johnson on 29 October 2008. This matter was thoroughly investigated as part of the Barclays Libor investigation and the FSA's conclusions are set out in paragraph 176 and following in the Barclays Final Notice of 27 June 2012.'

Paragraph 176 is the paragraph quoted earlier in this chapter, pages 147–148, which claims that Barclays' Libor submitters (PJ and Pete Spence) lowered the bank's Libor submissions because they mistakenly believed they were operating under a Bank of England instruction owing to a 'misunderstanding or miscommunication' as the Tucker-Diamond call was relayed down the chain of command. Neither this paragraph nor any following it mentions the UK government.

The regulator did not deny most of the detailed points citing evidence of its knowledge of both lowballing and central bank/government involvement.

23 See the evidence set out in Chapters 1, 2, 3 and 5.

24 See the evidence set out in Chapters 1, 2, 5 and 8.

25 It was undisputed at the Barclays trial that the maximum shift in Libor a request could have obtained was one eighth of a basis point. The lowballing instructed from the top was 20–30 basis points (from Barclays' senior management) and up to 50 basis points in the crisis (from the Bank of England and UK government). Taking 20 basis points, $20 \div 0.125 = 160$.

26 Channel Four published the full statement here: Bob Diamond, 'Barclays' Bob Diamond: response in full', Channel Four, 28 June 2012 (www.channel4.com/news/barclays-bob-diamond-response-in-full).

27 Dominic Lawson is the son of Nigel Lawson, Chancellor of the Exchequer in Margaret Thatcher's government, 1983–89. The column is here: Dominic Lawson, 'An eyebrow raised and Diamond's done for', *The Times*, 1 July 2012 (www.thetimes.co.uk/article/an-eyebrow-raised-and-diamonds-done-for-hdml6vd8mwl).

28 BBC News, 'Profile: Barclays chairman Marcus Agius', BBC, 2 July 2012 (www.bbc.co.uk/news/uk-18668643).

29 BBC News, 'Ministers to order Libor bank rate review', BBC, 30 June 2012 (www.bbc.co.uk/news/uk-politics-18640916).

30 Lord Turner, evidence to the Treasury committee, 17 July 2012. Question 1 (https://publications.parliament.uk/pa/cm201213/cmselect/cmtreasy/535/120717.htm).

31 Jill Treanor, 'Barclays chief executive Bob Diamond resigns', *The Guardian*, 3 July 2012 (www.theguardian.com/business/2012/jul/03/bob-diamond-resigns-barclays).

32 Barclays, 'Supplementary information regarding Barclays settlement with the Authorities in respect of their investigations into the submission of various interbank offered rates (AMENDED)', 3 July 2012 (https://home.barclays/content/dam/home-barclays/documents/investor-relations/IRNewsPresentations/2012News/03-july-supplementary-information-on-libor.pdf).

33 Jill Treanor, '£9m leaving deal for Barclays deputy Jerry del Missier', *The Guardian*, 26 July 2012 (www.theguardian.com/business/2012/jul/26/9m-payoff-barclays-jerry-del-missier).

34 Becky Barrow, James Salmon and Rob Preece, 'Ed Miliband demands CRIMINAL probe into Barclays interest rate rigging scandal as £3.2bn is wiped off bank in share plunge', *Daily Mail*, 27 June 2012 (www.dailymail.co.uk/news/article-2165468/Ed-Miliband-demands-CRIMINAL-probe-Barclays-scandal-3-2bn-wiped-bank-share-plunge.html).

35 Bob Diamond's oral evidence to the committee is available here: House of Commons Treasury Committee, 'Uncorrected transcript of oral evidence: House of Commons oral evidence taken before the Treasury Committee, evidence from Bob Diamond', HC 481-I, 4 July 2012 (https://www.parliament.uk/globalassets/documents/commons-committees/treasury/Treasury-Committee-04-July-12-Bob-Diamond.pdf).

36 Financial Services Authority, 'Final Notice 122702', paragraph 177, 27 June 2012 (www.fca.org.uk/publication/final-notices/barclays-jun12.pdf). Leaked transcripts show the submitter sending the email was the sterling Libor submitter, Pete Spence.

37 US Commodity Futures Trading Commission, 'Order instituting proceedings pursuant to sections 6(c) and 6(d) of the Commodity Exchange Act, as amended, making findings and imposing remedial sanction', 27 June 2012 (www.cftc.gov/sites/default/files/idc/groups/public/@lrenforcementactions/documents/legalpleading/enfbarclaysorder062712.pdf). On page 24, the third paragraph refers to Jerry del Missier's reiteration of his instruction a few days later. It's also referred to in the last sentence of paragraph 179 of the FSA's 'Final Notice 122702' (www.fca.org.uk/publication/final-notices/barclays-jun12.pdf).

Chapter 10: The Seriously Flawed Office

1 Lady Brenda Hale, 'Equality and Human Rights Oxford Equality Lecture 2018', Law Faculty at the University of Oxford, 29 October 2018 (www.supremecourt.uk/docs/speech-181029.pdf). She was succeeded as president by Baron Robert Reed in 2020.

2 David Green gave this anecdote in a 2018 address. It refers without naming him to Peter Henry Goldsmith, Baron Goldsmith PC KC, best known for his advice to Tony Blair on the legality or otherwise of the 2003 Iraq War. David Green, 'E. Lawrence Barcella Memorial Keynote Address', ABA Criminal Justice Section, 13 March 2018, YouTube video, 27:36 (www.youtube.com/watch?v=ZGa9KztXWiM).

3 The allusion is to 'The Only Way is Up', a song written by George Jackson and Johnny Henderson, originally released by soul singer Otis Clay, which became a number one hit in 1988 for Yazz and the Plastic Population.

4 See Chapter 5, page 89.

5 George Osborne would later say the FSA wasn't able to pursue derivatives traders under its powers to pursue insider trading. However, the FSA did have powers to pursue criminal investigations beyond insider trading including a wider offence of market abuse.

6 House of Commons Treasury Committee, 'Treasury Committee – Minutes of Evidence', HC 481-II, 9 July 2012, Q334–335 (www.parliamentlive.tv/Event/Index/5b3a1065-a3ee-4f0d-ab97-ae51c2b3e2e8). Tucker testimony to Treasury committee.

7 Treasury Committee, 'Minutes', Q422–423. The event can still be seen on the internet archive of Parliament TV, 'Treasury Committee', 9 July 2012 (www.parliamentlive.tv/Event/Index/5b3a1065-a3ee-4f0d-ab97-ae51c2b3e2e8). The relevant passage begins just before 5.52 p.m.

8 House of Commons Treasury Committee, 'Treasury Committee - Minutes of Evidence', HC 481-II, 16 July 2012, Q 825, (https://publications.parliament.uk/pa/cm201213/cmselect/cmtreasy/481/120716.htm).

9 The representatives del Missier spoke to, according to contemporary records, were Spence, Bermingham and Dearlove. Jerry del Missier mentioned the money markets desk but was not asked who the key players on it were.

10 House of Commons Treasury Committee, 'Treasury Committee – Bank of England June 2012 Financial Stability Report – Minutes of Evidence', HC 535, 17 July 2012, Q55 (https://publications.parliament.uk/pa/cm201213/cmselect/cmtreasy/535/120717.htm).

11 Evidence exhibited in trial of Tom Hayes, 8 June 2015. The Bank of England employee was Tarkus Frost. SONIA, the 'Sterling Overnight Index Average', is an alternative benchmark, based not on estimates but on transactions of cash between banks, now administered by the Bank of England.

12 Call log dated 22/08/2007 – between Ben Wensley of the Bank of England and Rupert Labrum of Deutsche Bank – cited in trial of Tom Hayes, 8 June 2015.

13 See Chapter 5, pages 84 and 103.

14 The initial inquiry into Libor was the forerunner of a long-running Parliamentary Commission on Banking Standards, chaired by Andrew Tyrie and involving MPs from both the Commons and the Lords. However, the inquiry into Libor itself and lowballing was taken no further.

15 Many small business customers of the bank would seek to use the Libor scandal in litigation against the banks where they had been ruined by interest rate hedging products, also known as 'swaps'. Because they had been linked to Libor, the argument was that lowballing had damaged the business customers. However, the greatest damage was done by official movements in interest rates which put the swaps 'out of the money'. The FCA found that in more than 90 per cent of cases, business customers had not been warned when they were sold the swaps that they might expose them to large outflows of cash and jeopardise their solvency.

16 Section 2 of the Fraud Act 2006 outlaws fraud by false representation, saying: 'A person is in breach of this section if he a) dishonestly makes a false representation and b) intends, by making the representation to i) make a gain for himself or another, or ii) to cause loss to another or to expose another to a risk of loss.'

17 The SFO didn't seek to interview Stone, Storey or Dearlove until late 2016, after receiving Right of Reply letters from BBC *Panorama* questioning its failure to investigate the Libor 'rigging' ordered from the top.

18 When the SFO was asked during the trial of Tom Hayes why it hadn't investigated the Bank of England, the answer came back that it hadn't needed to – because the Treasury committee had investigated it.

19 Simon Bowers, 'Judge Serious Fraud Office on its Libor probe, David Green tells MPs', *The Guardian*, 13 November 2012 (www.theguardian.com/business/2012/nov/13/sfo-director-says-libor-probe-crucial).

Chapter 11: The Man Who Couldn't Lie

1　The SFO announced its first arrests in the Libor investigation that afternoon. The text is as follows: 'Today the Serious Fraud Office, with the assistance of the City of London Police, executed search warrants at three residential premises in Surrey (1) and Essex (2). Three men, aged 33, 41 and 47, have been arrested and taken to a London police station for interview in connection with the investigation into the manipulation of LIBOR. The men are all British nationals currently living in the United Kingdom.' Serious Fraud Office, 'LIBOR: three arrested', 11 December 2012 (www.sfo.gov.uk/2012/12/11/libor-three-arrested/).

2　As Nick Hayes is keen to point out, the editor of *World in Action* at the time of the first documentary and several follow-ups, the man to whom the Birmingham Six said they owed 'a great debt of gratitude', was his predecessor, Ray Fitzwalter.

3　See Chapter 5, pages 80–2 for a fuller explanation of derivatives.

4　Later, Chris Salmon would take on Paul Tucker's former role as executive director, markets, giving speeches including one in 2017, while Tom was in jail, on the need to move away from benchmarks such as Libor towards 'risk-free alternatives'. The speech made no mention of his nephew (www.bankofengland.co.uk/-/media/boe/files/speech/2017/the-bank-and-benchmark-reform-speech-by-chris-salmon.pdf?la=en&hash=597E3C1B41FBFFAFB6A05DFFE148F1E0B53BEB3F).

5　This is a verbatim quote from exhibit PMC 086, the SFO's scoping interview of 31 January 2013, a long extract of which was read to the jury at the Hayes trial on 2 June 2015, transcript 2/06/2015, p.113.

6　Interview with Tom Hayes. The story of how Citigroup let Tom Hayes keep his signing-on bonus was first reported during his 2015 trial: Simon Goodley, 'Trader in Libor trial was allowed to keep £2.2m bonus after he was sacked', *The Guardian*, 2 June 2015 (www.theguardian.com/business/2015/jun/02/trader-tom-hayes-libor-rigging-trial-2m-bonus-after-sacked). It's confirmed in a termination notice read out at trial (transcript 02/06/2015, p.93), which relates how Citigroup would not exercise its right to keep special cash awards of 292 million yen or £2.219 million (equivalent at prevailing exchange rates to approximately $3 million).

　　In 2011, Citigroup removed McCappin from his role in Japan (www.ft.com/content/645da6a2-27d6-11e1-a4c4-00144feabdc0). This notice from the Japanese Financial Services Authority refers to the president and CEO of Citigroup Global Markets Japan: Financial Services Authority, 'Administrative Action on Citigroup Global Markets Japan Inc', 16 December 2011 (www.fsa.go.jp/en/news/2011/20111216-2.html).

7　Financial Services Authority, 'Final Notice: 186958', 19 December 2012, paragraph 99 (www.fca.org.uk/publication/final-notices/ubs.pdf).

8　The press conference can still be viewed here: www.c-span.org/video/?310034-1/international-banking#.

9　Scot J. Paltrow, 'Insight: Top Justice officials connected to mortgage banks', Reuters, 20 January 2012 (www.reuters.com/article/us-usa-holder-mortgage-idUSTRE80J0PH20120120).

10　Collateralised debt obligations, also known as CDOs. The investments were sold by the billion to hedge funds and other investors around the world on the basis that they offered a safe, higher return than other investments at a time of ultra-low interest rates. They gave investors the right to collect the repayments of mortgage borrowers including many who had poor credit ratings or modest incomes, known as 'subprime' borrowers. When the cheap, discounted two-year interest rate reset at much higher rates, often two or three times the original level, borrowers couldn't afford to repay, quit their homes and sent their keys back to the mortgage companies – a phenomenon known as 'jingle mail'. As the scale of the problem became apparent, the banks, unaware of the scale of their own exposures and those of other banks to the defaulting mortgages, started to hoard cash and avoid lending to each other – meaning no bank was willing to lend cash in the interbank market. The journalistic shorthand for it was the 'credit crunch'.

11 US Department of Justice, Office of Public Affairs, 'Federal Government and State Attorneys General Reach $25 Billion Agreement with Five Largest Mortgage Servicers to Address Mortgage Loan Servicing and Foreclosure Abuses', 9 February 2012 (www.justice.gov/opa/pr/federal-government-and-state-attorneys-general-reach-25-billion-agreement-five-largest). Also see the excellent book by David Dayen, *Chain of Title* (https://thenewpress.com/books/chain-of-title).

12 David Green admitted later in 2013 that the SFO's handling of the Libor cases had caused a 'rift' with the US authorities: Harry Wilson, 'SFO plots charges over Libor scandal', *The Telegraph*, 28 December 2013 (www.telegraph.co.uk/finance/financial-crime/10540896/SFO-plots-charges-over-Libor-scandal.html). A former SFO prosecutor told me that the DOJ would refuse to return calls from the SFO for years afterwards because of the Hayes case. The US charges against Tom Hayes and Roger Darin were finally dismissed ten years later, on 31 October 2022: Andy Verity, 'US throws out charges against interest rate "rigger"', BBC News, 31 October 2022 (www.bbc.co.uk/news/business-63446174).

13 Prior to publication, the Serious Fraud Office was shown passages in the book relating to twenty-one detailed points and invited to comment. In response, the SFO defended its approach to the Libor and Euribor trials by reference to the decisions of judges in the criminal court and the Court of Appeal. Where its responses advanced my understanding of the story, they have been incorporated into the text. I'd like to make it crystal clear that of course there are many diligent and conscientious people at the Serious Fraud Office who work hard in a difficult job pursuing highly complex fraud cases. I'd also like to defend the SFO from those who would seek to abolish it altogether because it remains one of the few serious challenges to the many genuine white-collar criminals who are all too rarely arrested, investigated and punished. When an organisation – public or private – gets something profoundly wrong, the responsibility must rest not with the staff who work there but with the people at the top who run it.

Chapter 12: The Ringmaster

1 Between June 2012 and this pre-trial hearing in October 2014, banks and City brokers paid fines totalling $5 billion to the CFTC, DOJ, FSA/FCA, the Swiss financial supervisory authority and the European Commission. Subsequent to that date, more than $3.8 billion in fines were levied, bringing the total to $8.8 billion. I've used prevailing exchange rates at the time fines were levied to arrive at this figure. Those paying the fines include Barclays, UBS, RBS, ICAP, Rabobank, Lloyds, Deutsche Bank, Societe Generale and Citigroup.

2 While Roger Darin was named as a co-conspirator, first by Lanny Breuer then later by the SFO, Switzerland refused to extradite him to face trial in the UK.

3 The BBA definition of Libor is: 'The rate at which an individual Contributor Panel bank could borrow funds, were it to do so by asking for and then accepting inter-bank offers in reasonable market size, just prior to 11.00 London time.'

4 The body that ran Libor was the Foreign Exchange and Money Markets Committee of the BBA. Ewan was the secretary to the FXMMC.

5 Witness statement of John McInnes Ewan, paragraph 60. The Relevant Period was 1 January 2005 to 31 December 2010. See also Chapter 14, page 243.

6 John Ewan has repeatedly been invited to comment on these issues but has never responded to correspondence.

7 This is known as the Ghosh test after a precedent-setting case. To decide if a defendant has done something dishonest, jurors are supposed to answer two questions in turn: first, an objective question about everyone's standards of what was honest or dishonest; and second, a subjective one about the defendant's state of mind. The two questions are: 1) Was what was done dishonest according to the standards of reasonable honest people? (Objective) 2) Did the Defendant realise that reasonable and honest people regard what he did as dishonest? (Subjective). If the answer to the first is no, the second doesn't get asked. If the answer to the second is no, it's not dishonest.

8 Much of this evidence is set out in Chapters 1–5 of this book.

9 Manslaughter sentencing guidelines specify a starting point of twelve years for high culpability manslaughter (www.sentencingcouncil.org.uk/offences/crown-court/item/unlawful-act-manslaughter/).

Chapter 13: The Sushi Conspiracy

1 I've asked Paul Tucker on at least four occasions to talk about the Libor scandal and have pointed out more than once that there were serious concerns that innocent people may be in jail. Each time he has refused to comment publicly and also to speak informally.

2 Like other Greek men of the same first name, Stylianos Contogoulas mostly shortens his name to Stelios.

3 Stelios's fantasy book would later become a real one in which PJ did feature: Stelios Contogoulas, *Truth & Li(e)bor* (London: Austin Macauley, 2021).

Chapter 14: Better Not Call Saul

1 At Jay Merchant's appeal in early 2017, Lord Chief Justice Thomas and others decided the jury should have been directed to decide whether he *deliberately* broke the rules ('disregarded the proper basis') as a matter of fact before deciding whether what he did was dishonest. That became part of the instructions to the jury in the retrial of Ryan Reich and Stelios Contogoulas, which began soon after the appeal. The jury acquitted the two defendants within a matter of hours. However, Thomas et al. decided Jay Merchant's conviction was nevertheless 'safe'. The ruling can be found here: 'R v. Merchant' (2017), England and Wales Court of Appeal (Criminal Division), CaseMine (www.casemine.com/judgement/uk/5b46f20c2c94e0775e7f1537).

2 My italics. The 'Relevant Period' was 1 January 2005 to 31 December 2010. See note 5.
3 Barclays trial transcript, Thursday, 7 April 2016, p.64.
4 This is available to view online: Mark Carney, 'Banking Standards Board: Worthy of Trust? Law, ethics and culture in banking – opening remarks by Mark Carney', Bank of England, 21 March 2017, YouTube video, 1:44:30 (www.bankofengland.co.uk/speech/2017/banking-standards-board-worthy-of-trust-law-ethics-and-culture-in-banking).
5 Alex Julian Pabon appeal: 'R v. Pabon' (2018), England and Wales Court of Appeal (Criminal Division) (www.judiciary.uk/wp-content/uploads/2018/03/r-v-pabon-march18.pdf).
6 'R v. Pabon' (2018).

Chapter 15: The Price of Honesty

1 I first met Tony Conti in 2016 and interviewed him by phone in the summer of 2021. I asked him for an interview more recently and he declined.
2 The Financial Services Authority was renamed the Financial Conduct Authority in 2013 and given new powers.
3 In the USA, 'wire fraud' is when an individual uses a phone or information technology such as email or other internet communications to commit financial fraud.
4 Before his appointment to the case, Judge Rakoff had publicly criticised the DOJ for doing too little to prosecute Wall Street executives. Randall Smith, 'Two Former Traders Found Guilty in Libor Manipulation Case', *The New York Times*, 5 November 2015 (www.nytimes.com/2015/11/06/business/dealbook/two-former-traders-found-guilty-in-libor-manipulation-case.html).
5 Lee Stewart later said under cross-examination that he didn't know it was wrong.

Chapter 16: The Price of Dishonesty

1 'The front' refers to the team of DOJ prosecutors, sitting on the front bench of the court.
2 The quotes and information in this section are from the trial of Connolly and Black, 25–26 September 2018, Master Trial Transcript, pp.809–831.
3 See Chapter 5, pages 83, 106 and 109 for Steve Obie's role in the Libor investigation.
4 Evidence of Walter Ricciardi, Master Trial Transcript, p.1518.
5 Connolly and Black, 'Memorandum decision and order denying defendants' motion to vacate convictions and dismiss the indictment on the basis of prosecutorial misconduct', p.47, line 5.
6 As an alternative to 'outsourcing', it could also be called a privatisation of a criminal investigation.
7 The document is titled, 'Submissions in aid of resolution of Ibor investigation', marked 'Defence Exhibit 0862', Paul Weiss 21 January 2015.
8 The decision can be found here: 'USA v. Connolly and Black' (2019), US District Court, Southern District of New York, case 1:16-cr-00370-CM (wallstreetonparade.com/wp-content/uploads/2019/05/US-v-Connolly-Memorandum-Decision-and-Order-Denying-Defendant-Gavin-Blacks-Motion-.pdf). See especially pp.2 and 23.

9 Prosecution witnesses accepted on cross-examination that the traders and submitters were carrying out a Deutsche Bank policy instructed by Anshu Jain, Alan Cloete and others.

10 During the indictment period, Anshu Jain was head of Deutsche Bank's corporate and investment bank. He became global chief executive officer in 2012.

11 Published by Unpolished Press, 2019.

12 OTC stands for 'over the counter'. Swaps weren't traded on a regulated exchange like shares but were instead bought and sold direct between banks and termed 'over the counter'. The OTC desk, unrelated to the division Matt supervised, was the main New York division of Deutsche Bank that traded swaps.

13 When swaps traders say 'receives' they mean derivatives trades where they are receiving a variable rate at Libor and paying a fixed rate, in swaps contracts which will go up in value if Libor is higher.

14 After Matt Connolly and Gavin Black were acquitted in January 2022 by a higher court, which ruled that they had not broken any rules, both Tim Parietti and Mike Curtler applied successfully to have their guilty pleas thrown out. Parietti's was overturned by Judge Engelmayer on 5 August 2022 and a $1 million fine he had paid was ordered to be returned to him. Jonathan Stempel, 'Deutsche Bank ex-trader's conviction thrown out in U.S. Libor-rigging probe', Reuters, 5 August 2022 (www.reuters.com/business/finance/deutsche-bank-ex-traders-conviction-thrown-out-us-libor-rigging-case-2022-08-05/). Mike Curtler then applied and his guilty plea was overturned by Chief Judge Colleen McMahon on 24 August 2022. Andy Verity, 'Interest rate "rigger" guilty conviction thrown out', BBC News, 6 September 2022 (www.bbc.co.uk/news/business-62801918).

15 Connolly and Black, Master Trial Transcript, pp.1789–1812.

16 Connolly and Black, Master Trial Transcript, p.1268.

17 Cross-examination of Tim Parietti, Master Trial Transcript, pp.1269–1270.

18 Connolly and Black, 'Memorandum decision and order denying defendants' motion to vacate convictions and dismiss the indictment on the basis of prosecutorial misconduct', May 2019, p.57, first paragraph.

19 Connolly and Black, Master Trial Transcript, p.1270.

20 The first is: Andy Verity, 'I'm being jailed – but the court was misled' BBC News, 7 October 2019 (www.bbc.co.uk/news/business-49841360). The second is: 'I'm being jailed for four emails from 12 years ago', BBC News, 7 October 2019 (www.bbc.co.uk/news/business-49841361).

21 Connolly and Black, Sentencing Hearing Transcript, 24 October 2019, p.41.

22 Connolly and Black, Sentencing Hearing Transcript, 24 October 2019, p.84.

23 Matthew Connolly, Target: A Scapegoat's Guide to the Federal Justice System (Unpolished Press, 2019), p.336.

Chapter 17: Run!

1 The five who chose not to attend were Joerg Vogt, Ardalan Gharagozlou, Kai-Uwe Kappauf, Stephane Esper and Andreas Hauschild.

2 Report by German regulator Bafin, 11 May 2015, p.7.

3 See Chapter 16, pages 275–6.

4   Barney Thompson, 'Euribor messages amounted to market manipulation', *Financial Times*, 3 May 2018 (www.ft.com/content/2693a4a2-4eee-11e8-9471-a083af05aea7).

5   In July 2018, the SFO had also closed its investigation into more than a dozen employees of Lloyds Banking Group, citing insufficient evidence. Reuters Staff, 'Britain's anti-fraud body closes investigation into rate rigging at Lloyds', Reuters, 4 July 2018 (www.reuters.com/article/lloyds-libor-idINKBN1JU1HB).

In May 2019, Bloomberg reported that the SFO was still investigating lowballing. However, no arrests were made: Andy Verity, 'Libor rigging inquiry shut down by Serious Fraud Office', BBC News, 19 October 2019 (www.bbc.co.uk/news/business-50107320).

6   Andreas Hauschild was arrested at Rome airport in August 2018. He was extradited to the UK and granted conditional bail on 24 October, standing trial the following year. On 4 July 2019, he was acquitted.

7   A *coup de théâtre* translates roughly to 'a spectacular turn of events'.

8   On 22 October 2021, a few weeks after Bermingham's release and seven months and after Carlo Palombo was released, the CFTC paid an anonymous whistleblower a record-breaking award of nearly $200 million in connection with its fine of Deutsche Bank for Libor manipulation after the whistleblower litigated. The reasons given were that the whistleblower's 'specific, credible, and timely original information significantly contributed to an already open investigation and led to a successful enforcement action, as well as to the success of two related actions, by a U.S. federal regulator and a foreign regulator [...] the whistleblower's information led the CFTC to important, direct evidence of wrongdoing.' Three months later, the court ruled the alleged misconduct hadn't broken any laws or rules and acquitted Matt Connolly and Gavin Black.

9   Following the successful appeal of Gavin Black and Matt Connolly, those who had pleaded guilty in his trial, Tim Parietti and Mike Curtler, applied successfully to have their US guilty pleas overturned. Parietti's was overturned in August 2022: Jonathan Stempel, 'Deutsche Bank ex-trader's conviction thrown out in U.S. Libor-rigging probe', Reuters, 5 August 2022 (www.reuters.com/business/finance/deutsche-bank-ex-traders-conviction-thrown-out-us-libor-rigging-case-2022-08-05/). Curtler's was overturned in September 2022: Andy Verity, 'Interest rate "rigger" guilty conviction thrown out', BBC News, 6 September 2022 (www.bbc.co.uk/news/business-62801918). On 31 October 2022, a US court approved an application by the DOJ to dismiss all charges against Tom Hayes to 'serve the interests of justice'. As this book went to print, he still awaited a decision from the Criminal Cases Review Commission.

10 Andy Verity, 'The whistleblowing bankers who were sent to jail', BBC News, 1 March 2022 (www.bbc.co.uk/news/business-60561679).

Epilogue: The Price of Silence

1   Months in advance of publication, right of reply letters were sent to individuals and organisations mentioned in these pages in what might (or might not) be regarded as a critical context. Most did not reply. Where the replies that did arrive advanced my understanding of the story, the information contained in them has been incorporated.

INDEX